Green Internet of Things and Machine Learning

Scrivener Publishing
100 Cummings Center, Suite 541J
Beverly, MA 01915-6106

Publishers at Scrivener
Martin Scrivener (martin@scrivenerpublishing.com)
Phillip Carmical (pcarmical@scrivenerpublishing.com)

Green Internet of Things and Machine Learning

Towards a Smart Sustainable World

Edited by
Roshani Raut, Sandeep Kautish,
Zdzislaw Polkowski, Anil Kumar
and
Chuan-Ming Liu

Scrivener
Publishing

WILEY

This edition first published 2022 by John Wiley & Sons, Inc., 111 River Street, Hoboken, NJ 07030, USA and Scrivener Publishing LLC, 100 Cummings Center, Suite 541J, Beverly, MA 01915, USA
© 2022 Scrivener Publishing LLC
For more information about Scrivener publications please visit www.scrivenerpublishing.com.

Wiley Global Headquarters
111 River Street, Hoboken, NJ 07030, USA

For details of our global editorial offices, customer services, and more information about Wiley products visit us at www.wiley.com.

Limit of Liability/Disclaimer of Warranty

Library of Congress Cataloging-in-Publication Data

ISBN 978-1-119-79203-1

Cover image: Pixabay.Com
Cover design by Russell Richardson

Set in size of 11pt and Minion Pro by Manila Typesetting Company, Makati, Philippines

10 9 8 7 6 5 4 3 2 1

Contents

Preface

The Internet of Things (IoT) is an evolving idea which is responsible for connecting billions of devices that acquire, perceive, and communicate data from their surroundings. Because this transmission of data uses significant energy, improving energy efficiency in IOT devices is a significant topic for research. The green internet of things (G-IoT) makes it possible for IoT devices to use less energy since intelligent processing and analysis are fundamental to constructing smart IOT applications with large data sets. Machine learning (ML) algorithms that can predict sustainable energy consumption can be used to prepare guidelines to make IoT device implementation easier.

The G-IoT, an updated version of the IoT, is applied for different applications to improve energy efficiency. Therefore, the material collected in this book has been edited to enhance the reader's knowledge about the current research achievements and challenges in the area of G-IoT and ML applications. The book targets senior and junior engineers, undergraduate and postgraduate students, researchers, and anyone else interested in the trends, developments, and opportunities afforded by the G-IoT and ML concepts.

Although it was impossible to include all current aspects of the research in the targeted area in the twelve chapters of this book, it will be a useful tool in terms of the various possible methodologies that can provide G-IoT applications through the use of ML. A brief description of the various application fields and methodologies covered in each chapter follows:

- Chapter 1 provides a brief introduction to various artificial intelligence (AI), ML, and IoT-based approaches with their real-life applications. It encompasses the many aspects of the G-IoT based on IoT device use and presents an outline of how each web search engine, such as Bing or Google, is used to search the internet, as they employ strategies such as learning algorithms to rank the websites. For example, every time Facebook is used to identify the photo of friends, online fraud detection, online customer assistance, video surveillance, face recognition, email spam, and malware are based on various learning algorithms.

- Chapter 2 presents an AI equipment design that focuses on IoT applications. The design is established on the standard of learning automata, characterized by utilizing propositional logic. The reasoning-based support empowers low-vitality impressions just as high learning accuracy throughout is used for preparing and surmising, which are vital criteria for competent AI with a long working life. Methodical encoding of the input information into optimally equal reasoning blocks is essential to this circuit. The distribution of these squares is improved through a plan investigation and robotization stream utilizing field programmable entryway exhibit-based quick models and programming recreations. The plan stream considers an assisted hyperparameter search for matching the clashing demands of economy and high accuracy. Broad approvals of the equipment execution of the new engineering employing single- and multiclass AI datasets reveal potential for fundamentally reduced vitality compared to the current AI equipment structures.

- Chapter 3 focuses on the IoT as a technology that connects everything to the smart world. To develop a practical smart scenario, this chapter explores numerous technologies along with the difficulties involved in fulfilling the goal of a G-IoT. Since energy-efficient communication in large-scale IoT devices has become a key concern in recent years, there is a fundamental need in such networks to minimize overall battery-powered device power consumption to reduce data transmission costs and lengthen network life. This study requires a scalable and energy-efficient approach for G-IoT heterogeneous nodes. These nodes need to create energy-efficient power conservation mechanisms to provide a long-lived network.

- Chapter 4 discusses the role of ML and the G-IoT in agriculture. Machine learning and its various application domains are explained and extensively covered in the first part of the chapter. In agricultural and farming applications, there are pros and cons to using the IoT to preserve biodiversity and reduce greenhouse gas emissions. To minimize the drawbacks, the smart food and agricultural enterprises built using G-IoT and green nanotechnology are discussed. Furthermore, how the IoT and G-IoT empower agriculture with accurate and sustainable farming approaches is also discussed.

– Chapter 5 demonstrates the use of analytics and machine learning to improve crop data. For optimal crop growth, pH, water content, and humidity are key. Inadequate inputs might lead to a growth imbalance in crops. Machine learning approaches can profit from prediction and classification challenges. To monitor the health of crops in the field, CIoT (Crop Internet of Things) was mostly required to assist in humidity, soil pH, soil wetness, soil type, and crop quality monitoring. Various sensors, like humidity sensors, pH sensors, soil quality sensors, and temperature sensors, can be utilized to detect crop yield and ML algorithms to calculate yields alongside descriptive analytics. Decisions on types of pesticides to use and the nutritional requirements of individual crops can be made with ML algorithms. Farmers would benefit from the early use of ML for soil mapping to produce a better environment for future crops.

– Chapter 6 explores smart farming using deep learning (DL) techniques. In the modern world, trending automation techniques are mixed with traditional farming approaches. A variety of crops are cultivated in various seasons from farmland. Farmers face several obstacles such as climatic calamities, pests, seed quality, soil quality, etc. Therefore, DL technologies are being used to turn traditional farming into smart farming.

– Chapter 7 presents the use of G-IoT and ML for agriculture applications. The IoT is a network of diverse sensors, software, and other technologies embedded in a system that retains flexibility. This design combines many sensors and software to perform multiple functions simultaneously. Artificial neural networks, C-means, K-means, Bayesian model and so on are used to make cost-effective, low-power IoT devices. Approaches like green computing, green wireless sensor networks, etc., create a difference in criteria for energy consumption.

– Chapter 8 presents an IoT-enabled AI-based model to assess land suitability for crop production. It briefly covers the IoT sensors used in horticulture and presents a summary of ML,

AI, and DL techniques for farmers. Current challenges in the field of agribusiness are shown with the evaluation of the study. The review reveals that explicit model assessment is supported by a wholly automated approach.

- Chapter 9 introduces green cloud computing (GCC) and G-IoT applications for agriculture and healthcare systems. In this chapter, the technology and issues relating to GCC and G-IoT, as well as the ability to minimize energy usage through the combination of these two approaches, are discussed. The green information and communication technologies (GICTs) that facilitate the G-IoT are extensively discussed. Additionally, the possibilities of a healthcare and G-IoT application system using a digital wireless sensor cloud with discrete integration or digital summation modeling are presented.

- Chapter 10 discusses how the G-IoT can be used for smart transportation. This is a global technical necessity since building an energy-efficient IoT ecosystem reduces CO_2 emissions from sensors, devices, and services that are implemented in IoT applications. The IoT is used in smart transportation (cars, trains, buses, etc.) to provide an effective way to avoid more energy use. This chapter looks at the G-IoT, along with its various challenges and issues, and the various technologies utilized in it.

- Chapter 11 discusses the use of the G-IoT and ML in the banking industry. It provides an overview as to how banking institutions are making use of the G-IoT and its life cycle. Also, it focuses on the use of AI and ML in the banking industry, along with scrutinizing their important role in the banking sector, and identifies the latest technologies which can be adopted for reducing carbon footprints with the IoT.

- Chapter 12 presents the G-IoT technologies and the future challenges they face. The IoT appends everything in the smart world. Consequently, the utilization of IoT advancements in applications has become an energized area of research. Enlivened by achieving low power consumption using the IoT, a green IoT is proposed. This chapter fundamentally discusses the existing procedure of the G-IoT, which contains green development, green reprocessing, green execution, and green improvement. A study is presented that analyzes the principles of the G-IoT, and plots the pivotal energy of the G-IoT and its structure.

Machine learning and deep learning, along with the developments in the IoT, are accelerating the value of different applications, thereby increasing the prospects for boosting operational effectiveness and productivity. However, security and scalability still need to be achieved for many processes, goods, and services since many of the devices remain susceptible to malicious acts due to a lack of end-to-end security solutions. Nonetheless, ML-enabled IoT devices have faster, flexible, high-performance networks that connect a wide variety of devices that provide numerous functions and applications to the end user.

The Editors
November 2021

G-IoT and ML for Smart Computing

Karunendra Verma[1]*, Vineet Raj Singh Kushwah[2] and Nilesh[3]

*[1]Chitkara University School of Engineering & Technology, Chitkara University,
Himachal Pradesh, India*
*[2]Department of Computer Science & Engineering, IPSCTM,
Gwalior, M.P., India*
*[3]Department of Computer Science & Engineering, Rama University,
Kanpur, U.P., India*

Abstract

Today's life is going to be easy with the use of various devices. Mostly, devices are based on various Machine Learning (ML) techniques, which is one of the most thrilling technologies of Artificial Intelligence (AI). If such devices are operated by internet, then this will increase the efficiency and effectiveness of the working and such type of technology is based on Internet of Thing (IoT). Every web search like Bing or Google is used to search on the internet using these techniques and retrieved results, efficient and accurate in short span of time as they used such learning algorithms to rank the web pages. Like every time, Facebook is used to identify the friends' photo that is also ML. Product recommendation, online fraud detection, online customer support, videos surveillance, healthcare industries, face recognition, email spam, and malware are also based on various learning algorithms. The objective of this article is to give the brief introduction of various AI, ML, and IoT-based techniques with their applications in real life. Article also included the various aspect of Green IoT (G-IoT) which is based on utilization of IoT with environment friendly.

Keywords: Artificial intelligence, IoT, G-IoT, machine learning, deep learning, supervised learning, unsupervised learning

*Corresponding author: k.verma2006@gmail.com

Roshani Raut, Sandeep Kautish, Zdzislaw Polkowski, Anil Kumar and Chuan-Ming Liu (eds.) Green Internet of Things and Machine Learning: Towards a Smart Sustainable World, (1–26) © 2022 Scrivener Publishing LLC

1.1   Introduction

Artificial Intelligence (AI) refers to the system where machines are given AI and such machines are called intelligent agents. These days AI is growing to be popular due to their features. It is simulating the natural intelligence in machines that are performing the mimic and learn actions of humans. These agents are able to learn with knowledge and carry out human-like work. As AI is continued to grow, they are having a big impact on our worth of life [1].

AI is also defined as follows:

- An intelligent agent shaped by humans.
- Capable to perform tasks intelligently without human interventions.
- Able to think and act sensibly as human.

1.2   Machine Learning

When a machine gains the capability to learn from practices and experience rather than just by preset instructions is called Machine Learning (ML). It is the subset of AI. ML algorithms produce results and improve their own results on the basis of past experiences. It produces the desired output by modifying its own produced output according to available datasets and implicitly comparing the current outcome to the final output [2].

1.2.1   Difference Between Artificial Intelligence and Machine Learning

In a general sense, AI and ML are much the same, but the fact is ML is the subset of AI as depicted in Table 1.1 [3].

1.2.2   Types of Machine Learning

- Supervised learning
- Unsupervised learning
- Semi-supervised learning
- Reinforcement learning

Figure 1.1 depicts the various types of machine learning techniques.

Table 1.1 Difference between AI and machine learning.

Artificial Intelligence	Machine learning
AI enables the machines to behave or simulate like humans.	ML permits a machine to learn from available past data without giving instructions to it explicitly.
AI is used to make such systems which can solve complex problems like humans.	ML goal is to make a machine to be trained itself from historical data without any human intervention.
AI has ML and DL as subset.	ML has DL as subset.
Following three types of AI: general AI, strong AI, and weak AI.	Following four types of ML: semi-supervised, unsupervised, reinforcement, and Supervised learning.
AI focuses to maximize the chance of success.	Machine learning focuses on accuracy and patterns.
AI uses structured, unstructured data, and semi-structured.	ML uses structured and semi-structured data only.

1.2.2.1   *Supervised Learning*

In the supervised ML, a machine learns from past data and then produces the desired output [4]. A machine gets its training from already available dataset using appropriate algorithms and inferred function. This inferred function predicts the output and gives an approximate desired result. The used labeled data set helps the algorithm to understand the data and produce the labeled output for more accurate results [5]. Figure 1.2 shows the complete process of supervised learning.

The following are some algorithms which are based on supervised learning:

- Linear Regression
- Naive Bayes
- Nearest Neighbor
- Neural Networks
- Decision Trees
- Support Vector Machines (SVM)

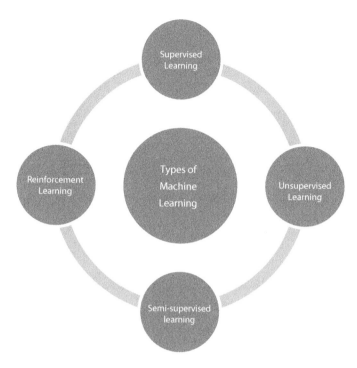

Figure 1.1 Classification of machine learning.

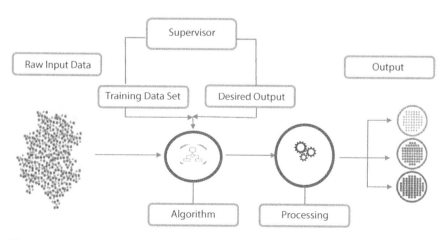

Figure 1.2 Process of supervised learning.

1.2.2.2 Unsupervised Learning

When a machine learns from unlabeled data or it discovers the input pattern itself, it is known as unsupervised learning. It divides the learning data into diverse clusters. Therefore, this learning is known as clustering algorithm. In this learning, the training data will not be labeled and inferences functions create its own inferences by exploring the unlabeled dataset in order to find suitable patterns [6]. Figure 1.3 shows the complete process of unsupervised learning.

Name of common unsupervised algorithms:

- Anomaly detection
- K-means clustering
- Neural networks
- Hierarchal clustering
- Independent component analysis
- Principle component analysis

1.2.2.3 Semi-Supervised Learning

When the machine learns from both labeled and unlabeled data, it is known as semi-supervised learning. When it is not feasible to label the data due to lack of resource to label it or due to the large size of the data, semi-supervised learning is used [7]. It lies among the supervised and unsupervised learning. For the model building, semi-supervised learning is best. Semi-supervised learning makes use of small amount of labeled data but large amount of unlabeled data [8].

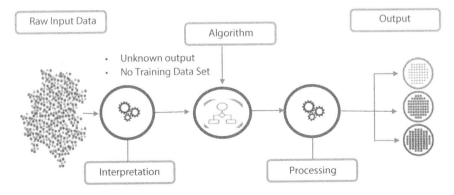

Figure 1.3 Process of unsupervised learning.

Figure 1.4 Process of reinforcement learning.

1.2.2.4   Reinforcement Learning

Reinforcement learning does not need training examples. In the reinforcement learning, models are given an environment, group of some actions, a goal and a reward. This algorithm learns by rewards and penalties. For every correct output, a reward is given and a penalty for every wrong output. To produce the desired output, the algorithm has to maximize these rewards. It is named reinforcement learning because for every reward the model gets a reinforcement that it is on right path. The reward feedback system helps the model to predict future behavior [9]. Figure 1.4 shows the complete process of reinforcement learning.

The following are algorithms which are based reinforcement learning:

- State Action Reward State action (SARSA)
- Q-Learning
- Deep Q Neural Network (DQN)

1.3   Deep Learning

Deep Learning (DL) is the concept AI that acts like the human brain to process and creating the patterns which helps to take the decisions. It is a subset of ML in AI that has ability to learning from unsupervised, unlabeled or unstructured. DL is becoming more popular as it achieves high accuracy and helps us in making decisions, translating languages, detecting objects, and recognizing speech [10].

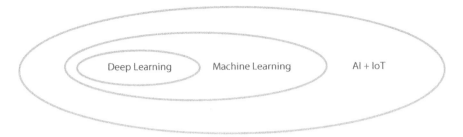

Figure 1.5 Correlation between AI, ML, and DL.

1.4   Correlation Between AI, ML, and DL

Figure 1.5 [9] depicts the correlation among ML, DL, and AI. Here, as we can see that DL is the subset of ML, and ML is the subset of AI. Hence, initially, AI came into the existence first, and later, ML erupted from it. To be more specific and denser, DL is derived from ML further.

1.5   Machine Learning–Based Smart Applications

1.5.1   Supervised Learning–Based Applications

1.5.1.1   Email Spam Filtering

It helps in filtering junk e-mail or unwanted commercial e-mail and bulk e-mail from the true e-mails. With the usage of these learning algorithms, spam filter helps the user not to be flooded with the bulk or junk e-mails. The spam filter learns by watching the pattern of genuine e-mails and junk e-mails [11].

1.5.1.2   Face Recognition

Human face is not unique. Various factors cause to vary the face. With the help of these learning algorithms, face recognition has become easier. Face recognition is used in various situations such as security measure at an ATM, criminal justice system, image tagging in social networking sites like Facebook, an image database investigation, and areas of surveillance [11].

1.5.1.3   Speech Recognition

To recognize the speech, the ML methods can be used. It involves two different learning phases: The first phase is speaker dependent where, after purchasing, the software user has to train the model by his/her voice to achieve accuracy, and in the second phase, before the software is shipped, the model is trained by default. It is speaker independent fashion [12].

1.5.1.4   Handwriting Recognition

Automated handwriting recognition through supervised ML really solves a complex problem of humans and cut down a large amount of time. Therefore, it is being utilized in various applications [12].

1.5.1.5   Intrusion Detection

Intrusion is the biggest problem of today's era. When a person or a process wants to enter unauthorizedly into another network, it is known as Intrusion. Therefore, this intrusion detection is important to scrutinize and to identify the threats or violations to the computer security. Learning algorithms helps in finding the intrusion.

1.5.1.6   Data Center Optimization

Huge energy requirement and environmental responsibility are rising a pressure day by day to Data Center (DC) companies to keep a DC operating efficiently. The ML algorithms help the DC to monitor the energy consumptions and pollution levels relentlessly to improve the operating efficiency [13].

1.5.2   Unsupervised Learning–Based Applications

1.5.2.1   Social Network Analysis

Identification of a person with in a large or small circle on social media platforms such as Facebook and Instagram has become easier with the help of unsupervised learning. It assists in maintain the similar posts in the proper way [14].

1.5.2.2   Medical Records

Automation helped the medical industry to manage the records in better way. Now, e-medical records have turn out to be ubiquitous [15]. Therefore, medical data is getting shape of medical facts and surprisingly helping to understand the disease in better way.

1.5.2.3 Speech Activity Detection

Speech activity detection (SAD) helps to detect the presence or absence of human speech for speech processing. ML assists to reduce the unwanted noisy and long non-speech intervals from the speech. SAD helps in making human-computer interfaces. It helps the hearing-impaired people to use the machine or computer using the voice commands [16]. It is language independent program. SAD is having two types: supervised SAD and unsupervised SAD. Supervised SAD uses the available training data and models a system accordingly, while unsupervised SAD is a feature-based technique.

1.5.2.4 Analysis of Cancer Diagnosis

Nowadays, human life is being saved with the help of medical science and technology. Therefore, the contribution of technology to fight against the cancer is not surprising anymore. It is first step to find the type of cancer in order to cure it. Now, it is possible with the help of classification process by collecting patient samples. Some ML techniques like radial basis function (RBF), Bayesian networks, and neural networks trees are used to detect the cancer and its type [17].

1.5.3 Semi-Supervised Learning–Based Applications

1.5.3.1 Mobile Learning Environments

Mobile learning means with the help of mobile device and internet facility, we can learn anywhere any time. To learn from mobile, various mobile apps are available which are based on various ML algorithms. Such type of learning is similar to where network bandwidth is consumed to operate [17].

1.5.3.2 Computational Advertisement

Online computational advertisement is the new concept in this scientific era. It is different from classical or traditional advertisement process. Computational advertisement is based on best match of the users. It is reached to the relevant user in digital format or online mode by using various ML techniques, and those are based on recommendation system, text analysis, information retrieval, classification, modeling, and optimization techniques. Within short span and in cost-effective way, it targets the number of relevant person [18].

1.5.3.3   Sentiment Analysis

Sentiment analysis is different from the text analysis. Text analysis is focused to retrieve the facts and information but not be able to find the customer's sentiments which lead to misunderstand the customers need. This misunderstanding may be loss of the valuable information. Hence, sentiment analysis is important to find the product's review either a positive or negative. Sentiment categorization used in movie reviews, recommendation systems, and business intelligence applications [18].

1.5.4   Reinforcement Learning–Based Applications

1.5.4.1   Traffic Forecasting Service

Traffic forecasting system is the real-time prediction of the traffic on the road. Day by day, numbers of vehicles are increasing on the road, which leads to increase the road accident. So, it is very necessary for traffic management. Using ML method, we can predict the real-time traffic and easily solve this problem. Such types of the systems find the digital traffic flow using satellite map and routing-based information [19].

1.5.4.2   Computer Games

The gaming industry has grown-up extremely in the recent time. AI-driven applications are widely used to create interactive gaming experience for the users. Such agents can take a multiple roles such as teammates, player's opponents, or other non-player characters [19]. Different fields of ML help the programmers to develop games that are well suited to the present market demands.

1.5.4.3   Machinery Applications

Current era is the digital and robotic era. There will be requirement of such machine which can be work without human intervention. This is leading the automation of machine. Some works are very difficult and lives threaten, like to learn to fly the helicopter or any vehicles. Such types of situation can be handling by implementing such types of simulators, which gives the similar types of environment for training purpose. Such simulators are implemented by using AI algorithms.

1.5.4.4   Stock Market Analysis

To make profit in financial market, it is necessary to analyze and predict the stock market trends. For this proper understanding and prediction, skills are required. This is possible by using ML algorithms. Reinforcement learning and SVM [19] are used to predict such types of market trends, which help us to maximize the stock profit with low risk.

1.6   IoT

Due to cheap and high speed internet connection, the internet is growing very rapidly with various internet devices, and these internet devices are connected with the help of IoT (Internet of Things). IoT includes some physical devices with internet connection to provide smart or intelligence applications in real world. Such types of physical devices are capable to analyze, process, and store the sensor data. These devices are some types of embedded machines which can be controlled from around the world using some processing elements and software.

"Internet of Things" is a combination of various software and hardware that support connectivity among the globe. IoT devices can sense the situation, processed data, and interact with others. It becomes a great and prominent technology which reduces the irregularities present in the real world. As it provided many solutions using advanced technology like radio-frequency identification (RFID) [20], QR codes, biometrics, sensor networks, and nanotechnologies will be the main pillar of the upcoming IoT, which helps in communication, embedding, real problem addressing like smart grid computing, e-health, manage e-transportation, etc. IoT maintains the required privacy during communication within the devices. In a simple way, we can say that IoT is everything that is around us and we can sense, connect, and communicate on the internet, e.g., smart rooms with fully equipped with sensors and embedded systems [20]. Table 1.2 gives various works in RFID field time to time.

In IoT, all devices having their own unique IP address and sensors are the brains of this. These sensors can be microelectromechanical systems (MEMS) which respond results in the form of weight, temperature, time, sound, light, humidity, motion, pressure, etc., and take further action which is decided through programming [28]. The Internet is everything which is

Table 1.2 Time line of investigation in RFID.

Year	Summary of the research	Reference
2008	Discussed decomposable RFID devices for healthcare	[21]
2010	Discussed various protocols to increase energy savings at the reader by decreasing collisions between tag responses	[22]
2011	Discussed RFID inventory technique called automatic power stepping (APS) based on tag response and variable slot sizes	[23]
2012	Discussed energy-efficient probabilistic estimation techniques to minimize the energy disbursed by active devices	[24]
2013	Discussed a cost-effective RFID devices with printing facilities in order to attain eco-friendly tag antennas	[25]
2014	Discussed Reservation Aloha for No Overhearing (RANO) for effective communication intervals to removing problem in active RFID	[26]
2017	Discussed RFID size reduction of non-decomposable substantial in their industrial	[27]

connected to all living thing and nonliving thing to exchange the information. Nonliving things like any machines or objects could be received and send information to each other, without human intervention.

1.7   Green IoT

Environmental problems are obtaining more consideration as the broad public develops more alert of the terrible significances of the environmental ruin causes. Current technological lead to spreads and increases in the carbon imprint. The development in this arena is concrete on green IoT (G-IoT). Latest few years there will be green support for managing various tasks. The G-IoT is projected to introduce substantial changes in daily life and would help to grasp the visualization of green ambient which joins our real world through these green systems (grid). G-IoT helps to decrease discharges and smog to make it environmentally convenient and surveillance and reduces the power consumption and functioning costs [28]. The aim of G-IoT is to become energy efficient in terms of the design and development of IoT. To become the energy-efficient procedures, IoT focused on decreasing the green house conclusion of current applications and amenities or to decrease the effect of greenhouse influence of IoT them self. G-IoT life cycle consists of G-design, G-production, G-utilization, and, finally, G-disposal/recycling to have no or very small effect on the atmosphere. As per global consultants Gartner, Inc. (GCG), ICT currently produces carbon discharges of approximately 0.86 MGT annually (about 2% of universal carbon discharges) and, if ICT including IoT, its decreasing effect of carbon dioxide (CO_2) emissions [29].

G-IoT not only designates green atmosphere but also protects energy and time. It provides an efficient resolution that permits green and ecological development of the culture. It includes revolutions and applications for addressing community challenges like smart ecological city, smart transport, and proficient depletion of energy, to create a G-IoT atmosphere. IoT results can be examined online, and user can trace those data online.

1.8   Green IoT–Based Technologies

IoT comprises of six components that are identification, communication technologies, sensing, services, computation, and semantic.

1.8.1   Identification

Identification is the process which comprises of labeling, coding, identifying, resolution, transmission, and application of the objects or things in IoT. For orderly management, things identification is a primary requirement. This may be information given by a wearable device, an appliance, or a group of devices.

1.8.2   Sensing

Sensing is the name of activity where data is collected from various objects and it is sent to a data center, database, data warehouse, etc. According to the required services, this stored data is analyzed further and specific operations are performed. There can be various sensors such as temperature sensors, humidity sensors, mobile phones, and wearable sensing devices.

Specific sensors are used as per the required service. Hence, sensing is categorized into environmental, biometric, biological, audible or visual, or all the above.

1.8.3   Communication Technologies

Communication technologies are used to connect various components to provide specific services. It uses either wide area network (WAN) communications or Wi-Fi (wireless LAN-based communications), Bluetooth, Z-wave, Near Field Communication (NFC), LTE Advanced, Wi-Fi, ultra wide bandwidth (UWB), IEEE 802.15.4, etc., which are the protocols used by IoT for communication [29].

1.8.4   Computation

Computation is the stage which is performed by the various hardware processing units such as microprocessors, microcontrollers, field programmable gate arrays (FPGAs), system on chips (SoCs), and software applications. To perform the computation, various hardware platforms such as Raspberry PI, Arduino, Intel Galileo, UDOO, Friendly ARM, and Gadgeteer are available, and many software platforms like LiteOS, TinyOS, and Riot OS are used. The important computational component of IoT is the Cloud platform. Since cloud platform has the high capability of computation in order to extract the valuable information from the stored data. Now, the transmission of this stored data takes place to a cloud-based service where other information that arrives from the IoT device is collected along with the cloud-based data in order to yield vital information to the end-user [30]. The data is gathered from the internet and other similar devices connected to the IoT. A process called "Data Processing" is required to extract vital information from the data.

1.8.5   Services

Services of IoT are broadly divided into below classes:

- Identity-related services
- Information aggregation services
- Collaborative-aware services
- Global services

Identity-related services are the foundation for all other services because identification of the object is the primary step for translating the real-world objects to the virtual world.

As the name describes, information aggregation service is used to accumulate the data from various sources. This data is then summarized and processed in order to gain fruitful results. This analyzed information is nowadays helping in making decisions and predictions. Global services denote the services provided to anyone on the demand, anywhere and anytime.

1.8.6   Semantic

Semantic is the name of task where knowledge is extracted intelligently from the mass of data to yield the demanded services. This is done by discovering resources, utilization of resources, modeling information, recognition, and analyzing data. Web ontology language (OWL), efficient XML interchange (EXI), resource description framework (RDF), etc., are the most common semantic technologies.

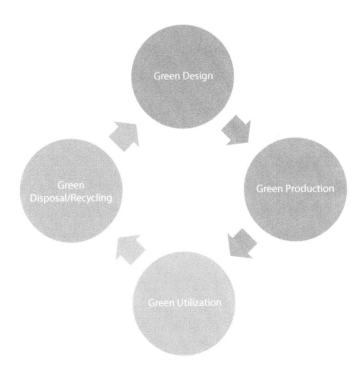

Figure 1.6 Life cycle of Green IoT.

1.9   Life Cycle of Green IoT

There is huge growth in IoT and its components in upcoming time. Therefore, it is needed to mitigate the number of resources to implement the logic and the reduction of energy as well to keep the things working for longer time. G-IoT relies on the optimum energy consumption.

For the smooth functioning of smart world, IoT should consume less energy and should reduce the green house effects at the same time. It has to focus on to mitigate the emission of CO_2 from the devices and sensors [31].

Figure 1.6 represents the life cycle of G-IoT. It has four phases; they are green design, green production, green utilization, and green disposal/recycle. Here, green disposal means the disposal should be in such a way that there should be no adverse effect on environment. Figure 1.6 depicts the life cycle of G-IoT.

1.10   Applications

In this section, we will discuss the various application based on G-IoT. Figure 1.7 depicts some applications, those that are based on G-IoT.

1.10.1   Industrial Automation

1.10.1.1   Machine to Machine Communications

Automation can be achieved through RFID tags. Without any sort of human intervention, direct communication is made by RFID to the robot [32].

1.10.1.2   Plant Monitoring

IoT helped to the industry for monitoring the various parameters of any plant like temperature, machine faults, and air pollution.

1.10.2   Healthcare

1.10.2.1   Real-Time Tracking

It helps in the monitoring of the patients and tracking of medical equipment.

It also helps in the tracking of the medical instruments in order not to be left in the body of the patient during surgery.

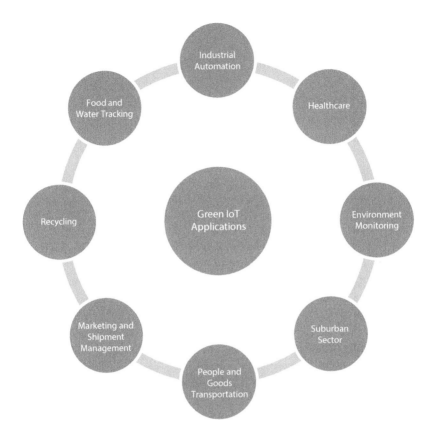

Figure 1.7 Green IoT–based applications.

1.10.2.2 Identification

IoT helps is the identification by coherent tracking methods. RFID-based identification is the easiest way to do it. It provides quick retrieval of patient information and finding the current location of the patient in the hospital. This also helps to reduce the blunder rate of patient incidents like overdose, wrong drug, infant identification (to prevent mismatching), etc., to a great extent by the constant monitoring of the patient information [33].

1.10.2.3 Smart Data Collection

It aids to reduce the processing time in every section either it is related to auditing, searching, or analysis. It also helps in reducing the cost. It provides automated care.

1.10.2.4   *Smart Sensing*

Various sensors can be used to access the real-time health of patient within seconds.

1.10.3   Environment Monitoring

It helps in monitoring the various changes happening in the environment whether it is temporal, organism, physical, or spatial made by human or nature itself.

1.10.3.1   *Agriculture*

It measures the water level, this way it helps in suggesting the suitable crop to be grown. It helps in saving of the water by sensing the humidity of the soil. Only required amount of water is supplied then. It prevents forest fires also.

1.10.3.2   *Smog Control*

IoT Academy (IoTA) worked to improve the air quality in UK. It is employing sensors and other gadgets for improving the air quality in London. IoTA proposed a solution named "BuggyAir project". According to this, to measure the street level smog various sensors are to be installed in strollers (buggies) and the data will be recorded for analysis. The exact location of the pollution will be given the GPS installed in the stroller. This way, with the usage of IoT it will be easier to understand the complexity of the pollution and to control the air quality also to the great extent [34].

1.10.3.3   *Waste Management*

It has become a serious problem due to the rapid rise in the volume of solid and hazardous waste. It causes a serious impact on the environment. It is challenging because the costs for waste disposal are significant especially in densely populated countries. There are many types of waste such as biomedical waste, municipal waste, electronic waste, industrial waste, and biomedical waste. Various corporate and municipal bodies are working day and night to lessen the impact of waste dumping. RFID technology can be helpful in the handling of waste management. RFID-enabled trash is thrown into the bin, as it receives the trash the antenna and reader communicate through RFID tags, and automatic bin identifies the junk and helps in reprocessing accordingly. This leads to better health management [34].

1.10.3.4   Smart Water

Various sensors can be used to monitor the emissions of factories, the quality of tap water, toxic gages generated by cars, etc.

1.10.4   Suburban Sector

1.10.4.1   Smart Buildings

A homeowner can monitor all their instruments and devices easily and can track which device is wasting unnecessary energy in order to save energy. Solar panels are one of them to save energy and to promote green energy. Various IoT solutions suggest how to allocate energy properly without wasting money. The better the analysis of data provided by IoT; the more energy can be saved. It is directly proportional. Now, we have heat and motion sensors, with this energy can be saved. When a person comes into the room, the light automatically turns on and when he/she goes out, the light automatically turns off [35].

1.10.4.2   Garbage Collection

These days, some cities are using smart dust bins that tell automatically once they get full. This saves a large amount of time for dust bin collectors and helps in keeping the environment clean.

1.10.4.3   Water Sensors

These sensors help in finding where the taps are open unnecessarily and which restaurant and hotels are blocking the sewers.

1.10.4.4   Smart Metering

Smart meter provide the reading of consume electricity to the electricity board which helps for better billing and monitoring purposes. Traditional meters only provide information such as total consumption only while Smart meters provides information about how the energy is being disbursed. By using smart meters, a householder can manage their energy consumption in proper way, can save his/her money by cutting the bills, and can help to mitigate the carbon emissions [36].

1.10.5   People and Goods Transportation

With the passage of time, the world population has been grown also. Therefore, to manage the traffic in a sustainable way these days, trains, cars, bicycles, buses, and roads are equipped with tags, actuators, and sensors to provide accurate and real-time information to traffic controllers. This advanced transportation system is the backbone of on-time delivery and keeping the information up to date for better services. It provides the tourists with appropriate information on the go.

1.10.5.1   Smart Parking

IoT helps to ascertain the vacant space for packing in densely populated cities.

1.10.5.2   Smart Traffic Congestion Detection

Now, the world's population has become the biggest problem and it is rising by leaps and bounds. Therefore, in this scenario, managing the traffic is a tough job. Here, vehicular ad hoc network (VANET) provides a way to escape traffic jamming. This enables the vehicles to connect nearer one for gaining traffic information in a better way. It helps to build a green environment by cutting carbon emissions to a larger level [37].

1.10.6   Marketing and Shipment Management

1.10.6.1   Smart Logistics/Shipment

Supply chain management provides real-time monitoring information by RFID, NFC, and sensors. With the help of these technologies, companies are now able to handle responses to the demands of the market within a short span. Enterprises such as Metro and Walmart are using the technology to meet the demands of customer within days.

1.10.6.2   Managing Quality

Product quality and quantity can be monitored by using such technology which helps to the customer to getting quality product from company.

Many products like meat and fruits dairy products need to be monitored regularly to ensure quality standards. It is possible due to IoT to maintain the transparency in marketing. IoT also helps in limiting the carbon footprint [38].

1.10.7   Recycling

Public is now more aware and serious about the new paradigm of energy resources. Now, all are focusing on several renewable resources rather than traditional nuclear energy or fossil resources. IoT is emphasizing the more flexible design of the electrical grids which can handle power fluctuations efficiently according to the consumption behaviors of the consumers. IoT has changed our lives dramatically [39]. Day by day, all the IoT-based companies are making our life easier and greener. Moreover, IoT is leading us to a better and greener environment and making this planet safer for future generations.

1.11   Challenges and Opportunities for Green IoT

There is an important role of Green technologies in empowering the energy competent IoT [40]. Various constraints are to be measured. Some issues for further consideration are as follows.

1.11.1   Architecture of Green IoT

For any type of network communication has to follow either TCP/IP model or ISO OSI model. In the network, when IoT devices will be used, they must be compatible according to the network. It is also important that used IoT devices can be energy efficient, environment friendly, and compatible according to network architecture [41].

1.11.2   Green Infrastructure

Using the redesign approach, energy-efficient infrastructure for IoT can be attained.

1.11.3   Green Spectrum Management

Green mobile services are the current restriction of RF system which can be eliminated through the cognitive radio approach [42].

1.11.4   Green Communication

Constant energy supply to the component is really a big challenge in the way of energy-efficient communication. It supports energy-efficient communication protocols to communicate reliably with peers. IoT seems promising in the efficient implementation of new sources like solar, thermal, and wind.

1.11.5   Green Security and Servicing Provisioning

Privacy and security is the crucial factor of IoT deployment. Really, a significant amount of processing is required from devices to implement the security algorithms [43].

1.12   Future of G-IoT

IoT has changed our lives in a big manner. We can feel it everywhere. It has brought a digital revolution around the globe. It collects the real-time data with the help of smart sensors then this data is analyzed to extract valuable information from it which indeed helps in the decision making. In this way, it has improved transparency and reduced the processing time. It has created a wide and new market for sensors, and day by day, it is booming. IoT is improving our lives every day whether it is home, workplace, or playground. Soon, we will see automated door locks, intelligent street lights, industrial robots, smart cars, artificial hearts, etc. The upcoming generation is the world of IoT.

1.13   Conclusion

Ecological issues are obtaining more devotion as the universal public come to be more aware of the significances that atmosphere deprivation causes. We need to focus on the field of authority, safety, and standardization for the smooth operation of IoT which can help the people entirely. This research highlights several related tools, technologies, and worries about G-IoT for a smarter sphere. IoT characterizes an important pattern change in ICT which gives smooth growth of smart cities around the globe. The G-IoT is likely to take in remarkable revolutions in daily routine and would assist the dream of a green ambient world. This research also focused on ML and its various applications which give the ability to the machines to think logically, using training data. A remarkable contribution to the various areas has been made by the AI techniques from the last some decades. This article is focused on various applications based on AI and ML with IoT, that lead to providing various facilities to human lives. Some areas where AI algorithm used to detect intrusion in the network to defend our private network from invaders, AI also focused on the field of medicine, where medical image classification helps to predict disease in advance. AI algorithms are also involved to design the various level of computer gaming where people enjoyed a IoT. It is also used to control the traffic with smart devices and dropped misshaping on the road, etc. Such latest technologies are offered more easiness, reliability, effectiveness, and efficiency in human life.

References

1. Tzanis, G. *et al.*, Modern Applications of Machine Learning. *Proceedings of the 1st Annual SEERC Doctoral Student Conference–DSC*, 2006.
2. Horvitz, E., Machine learning, reasoning, and intelligence in daily life: Directions and challenges. *IEEE Proceedings*, vol. 360, 2006.
3. Mitchell, T.M., *The discipline of machine learning*, Carnegie Mellon University, School of Computer Science, Machine Learning Department, Pittsburgh, July 2006.
4. Ball, G.R. and Srihari, S.N., Semi-supervised learning for handwriting recognition. *Document Analysis and Recognition, ICDAR'09. 10th International Conference on IEEE*, 2009.
5. Valenti, R. *et al.*, Machine learning techniques for face analysis. *Mach. Learn. Techniques Int. J. Comput. Appl.* (0975 – 8887), 115, 9, Springer Berlin Heidelberg, 159–187, 2008.
6. Al-Hmouz, A., An adaptive framework to provide personalisation for mobile learners, Doctor of Philosophy thesis, School of Information Systems & Technology, University of Wollongong, Australia.
7. Al-Hmouz, A., Shen, J., Yan, J., A machine learning based framework for adaptive mobile learning. *Advances in Web Based Learning-ICWL 2009*, Springer Berlin Heidelberg, pp. 34–43, 2009.
8. Graepel, T., Machine Learning Applications in Computer Games. *ICML 2008 Tutorial*, Helsinki, Finland, 5 July 2008.
9. Gabrilovich, E., Josifovski, V., Pang, B., *Introduction to Computational Advertising*. Association for Computational Linguistics Columbus, Ohio, USA, June 2008.
10. Cunningham, S.J., Littin, J., Witten, I.H., *Applications of machine learning in information retrieval*. University of Waikato, Department of Computer Science, Hamilton, New Zealand, 1997.

11. Bratko, A. *et al.*, Spam filtering using statistical data compression models. *J. Mach. Learn. Res.*, 7, 2673–2698, 2006.

12. Kaur, H., Singh, G., Minhas, J., A Review of Machine Learning based Anomaly Detection Techniques., Int. J. Comput. App. Technol. Res., 2, 2, 2(2), 185–187, 2013.

13. Gao, J. and Jamidar, R., Machine Learning Applications for Data Center Optimization, Google, 2014. Retrieve: https://docs.google.com/a/google.com/viewer?rl=www.google.com/about/datacenters/efficiency/internal/assets/machine-learning-applicationsfor-datacenter-optimization-finalv2.pdf

14. Haider, P., Chiarandini, L., Brefeld, U., Discriminative clustering for market segmentation. *Proceedings of the 18th ACM SIGKDD international conference on Knowledge discovery and data mining*, ACM, 2012.

15. Kononenko, I., Machine learning for medical diagnosis: history, state of the art and perspective. *Artif. Intell. Med.*, 23, 1, 23(1), 89–109, 2001.

16. Sadjadi, S.O. and Hansen, J.H.L., Unsupervised Speech Activity Detection Using Voicing Measures and Perceptual Spectral Flux. *IEEE Signal Proc. Let.*, 20, 3, March 2013.

17. Hwang, K.E., Cho, D. Y., Park, S.W., Kim, S.D., Zhan, B. T., Applying machine learning techniques to analysis of gene expression data: cancer diagnosis, Methods of Microarray Data Analysis, Kluwer Academic Publishers, Springer US, pp. 167–182, 2002.

18. Pang, B., Lee, L., Vaithyanathan, S., Thumbs up?: sentiment classification using machine learning techniques. *Proceedings of the ACL-02 conference on Empirical methods in natural language processing*, vol. 10, Association for Computational Linguistics, 2002.

19. Horvitz, E.J., Apacible, J., Sarin, R., Liao, L., Prediction, Expectation, and Surprise: Methods, Designs, and Study of a Deployed Traffic Forecasting Service. *Microsoft Research*, 2012. Retrieve: https://www.microsoft.com/en-us/research/wp-content/uploads/2014/06/horvitz_traffic_uai2005.pdf

20. Clarke, B., Fokoue, E., Zhang, H.H., Principles and theory for data mining and machine learning, Springer Series in Statistics, Springer Verlag New York, 2009.

21. Mowry, M., A Survey of RFID in the medical industry with emphasis on applications to surgery and surgical devices. MAE188, Introduction to RFID, Dr. Rajit Gadh, UCLA, p. 22, Jun. 9, 2008. Retrieve: https://silo.tips/download/a-survey-of-rfid-in-the-medical-industry-contents#

22. Namboodiri, V. and Gao, L., Energy-aware tag anti-collision protocols for RFID systems. *IEEE Trans. Mob. Comput.*, 9, 1, 44–59, 2010.

23. Xu, X., Gu, L., Wang, J., Xing, G., Cheung, S., Read more with less: An adaptive approach to energy-efficient RFID systems. *IEEE J. Sel. Areas Commun.*, 29, 8, 1684–1697, 2011.

24. Li, T., Wu, S., Chen, S., Yang, M., Generalized energy-efficient algorithms for the RFID estimation problem. *IEEE ACM Trans. Netw.*, 20, 6, 1978–1990, 2012.

25. Amin, Y., *Printable green RFID antennas for embedded sensors*. PhD dissertation, KTH School of Information and Communication Technology, Kista, Sweden, 2013.

26. Lee, C., Kim, D., Kim, J., An energy efficient active RFID protocol to avoid over heading problem. *IEEE Sens. J.*, 14, 1, 15–24, 2014.

27. Shaikh, F., Zeadally, S., Exposito, E., Enabling Technologies for GreenInternet of Things. *IEEE Syst. J.*, 11, 2, 983–994, 2017.

28. Minerva, R., Biru, A., Rotondi, D., *Towards a definitionof the Internet of Things (IoT)*, IEEE Internet initiative, Telecom Italia S.P.A., May 2015.

29. Atzori, L., Iera, A., Morabito, G., The Internet of Things: A survey. *Comput. Network*, Elsevier, 54, 15, 2787–2805, Oct. 2010.

30. López, T.S. *et al.*, Adding sense to the IOT-An architecture framework for smart object systems. *Pers. Ubiquit. Comput.*, 16, 3, 291–308, Mar. 2012.

31. Gershenfeld, N., Krikorian, R., Cohen, D., The Internet of Things. *Sci. Am.*, 291, 4, 76–81, 2004.

32. Murugesan, S., Harnessing green IT: Principles and practices. *IEEE IT Prof.*, 10, 1, 24–33, Jan.-Feb. 2008.

33. Xu, L.D., He, W., Li, S., Internet of Things in industries: A survey. *IEEE Trans. Ind. Inf.*, 10, 4, 2233–2243, Nov. 2014.

34. Perera, C., Liu, C.H., Jayawardena, S., The Emerging Internet of Things Marketplace From an Industrial Perspective: A Survey. *IEEE Trans. Emerg. Topics Comput.*, 3, 4, 2015.

35. Zhu, C., Leung, V.C.M., Shu, L., Ngai, E.C.-H., Green Internet of Things for Smart World. *IEEE Access*, 3, 2151–2162, 2015.

36. Rose, K., Eldridge, S., Chapin, L., *The Internet of Things (IoT): An Overview, Understanding the issues of more connected world*, Karen Rose, Scott Eldridge, Lyman Chapin, Internet Society, 2015.

37. Gershenfeld, N., Krikorian, R., Cohen, D., The Internet of Things. *Sci. Am.*, 291, 4, 76–81, 2004.

38. Rawashdeh, S., Eyadat, W., Magableh, A., Mardini, W., Yasin, M.B., Sustainable Smart World. *10th International Conference on Information and Communication Systems (ICICS)*, 2019.

39. Albreem, M.A.M., El-Saleh, A.A., Isa, M., Salah, W., Jusoh, M., Azizan, M.M., Ali, A., Green internet of things (IoT): An overview. *IEEE 4th International Conference on Smart Instrumentation, Measurement and Application (ICSIMA)*, 2017.

40. Poongodi, T., Ramya, S.R., Suresh, P., Balusamy, B., *Application of IoT in Green Computing, Advances in Greener Energy Technologies*, Springer Singapore, 2020.

41. Lohan, V. and Singh, R.P., Research challenges for Internet of Things: A review. *International Conference on Computing and Communication Technologies for Smart Nation (IC3TSN)*, 2017.

42. Haldorai, A., Ramu, A., Murugan, S., *Computing and Communication Systems in Urban Development*, Urban Computing, Springer Nature Switzerland AG, 2019.

43. Mohana Sundaram, K., Hussain, A., Sanjeevikumar, P., Holm-Nielsen, J.B., Kaliappan, V.K., Kavya Santhoshi, B., Deep Learning for Fault Diagnostics in Bearings, Insulators, PV Panels, Power Lines, and Electric Vehicle Applications—The State-of-the-Art Approaches. *IEEE Access*, 9, 41246-41260, 2021.

Machine Learning–Enabled Techniques for Reducing Energy Consumption of IoT Devices

Yogini Dilip Borole[1*], Jaya Dofe[2†] and C. G. Dethe[3‡]

[1]Department of E&TC, Assistant Professor, SPPU Pune University, Pune, India
[2]Faculty at California State University, Fullerton, California, USA
[3]UGC-Academic Staff College, Director, Nagpur, India

Abstract

Vitality effectiveness keeps on being the center plan challenge for man-made brainpower artificial intelligence equipment architects. In this paper, we propose another artificial intelligence equipment design focusing on Internet of Things (IoT) applications. The design is established on the standard of learning automata and characterized in utilizing propositional rationale. The rationale-based supporting empowers low-vitality impressions just as high learning precision during preparing and surmising, which are vital prerequisites for proficient artificial intelligence with long working life. We present the primary experiences into this new engineering as a custom designed incorporated circuit for unavoidable applications. Essential to this circuit is methodical encoding of binaries input information took care of into maximally equal rationale blocks. The distribution of these squares is advanced through a plan investigation and robotization stream utilizing field programmable entryway exhibit–based quick models and programming recreations. The plan stream considers an assisted hyperparameter search for meeting the clashing prerequisites of vitality cheapness and high exactness. Broad approvals on the equipment execution of the new engineering utilizing single- and multiclass artificial intelligence datasets show potential for fundamentally lower vitality than the current AI equipment structures. Furthermore, we exhibit test precision

Corresponding author: yoginiborole@gmail.com
†*Corresponding author*: jayadofe@gmail.com
‡*Corresponding author*: cgdethe@gmail.com

Roshani Raut, Sandeep Kautish, Zdzislaw Polkowski, Anil Kumar and Chuan-Ming Liu (eds.) Green Internet of Things and Machine Learning: Towards a Smart Sustainable World, (27–86) © 2022 Scrivener Publishing LLC

strengthening the coordination of the product execution and beating other best in class artificial calculations.

Keywords: Internet of Things, artificial intelligence hardware devices, energy consumption, machine learning

2.1 Introduction

The significance of energy proficiency of structures is underlined in orders of European Parliament and Council (especially in the mandates 2012/27/EU and 2010/31/EU) which express that 40% of all energy utilization in the European Union (EU) has a place with the structure area which is itself extending. Hence, the order defines the objective of lessening energy utilization by 20% and expanding the common in the EU by 2020 and requires activities that will empower cost-effective energy investment funds. Thus, various public activity plans for expanding energy productivity have been established. Croatia is among the most noteworthy 10 energy force nations in EU. The legislature of Croatia has set up the focal data framework for overseeing energy—Croatian energy the executive's data framework (EMIS). The framework assembles information about open area structures—their constructional and fiery attributes, just as their energy utilization information and CO_2 emanation in a unified data set with a web application available by all the directors of all public structures, neighborhood, and public government. The circumstance is comparable in other European nations, albeit a large portion of those frameworks depend on standard measurable approach and need astute models dependent on machine learning just as big data stages that empower handling enormous measures of information. There is a need of such canny frameworks that is destined to be ready to make forecasts and highlight extraction with the plan to help [1–3]. Uncommon papers propose the design of shrewd structure data frameworks. One of the ongoing one is proposed by Marinakis and Doukas [168] who proposed a serious Internet of Things (IoT)–based framework for keen energy of the executives in structures. The examination indicates to craft by Marinakis and Doukas [168] and proposes a adjusted model which centers around prescient investigation that could be coordinated into the savvy building idea. Accordingly, this paper expects to satisfy the hole by recommending a design of the savvy (shrewd) energy the board framework explicitly intended for public part that can uphold speculation choices in the public area on the nearby as well as on the public level. The design of the MERIDA framework recommended in this paper depends on our past examination wherein machine learning models have been created to anticipate the energy proficiency level of public structures, just as energy utilization of flammable gas and power. It likewise consolidates the capacities of IoT to encourage information assembling just as Big Information innovation to store and cycle information [2]. The Artificial Intelligence techniques used to make prescient models were counterfeit neural organizations, uphold vector machines and recursive apportioning, for example, characterization and relapse trees [7, 8], restrictive surmising trees, irregular woodland, and angle supported trees. The models were tried on genuine information from Educational Management Information System framework, and the best ones were remembered for the plan of the machine learning–based data framework engineering that could be utilized in public area. The article gives a diagram of related writing in the following area, after which the portrayal of information and techniques is given with the emphasis on preprocessing strategies and Artificial Intelligence techniques used to make prescient models. Section 2.4 presents the outcomes, for example, the proposed design of the canny framework, and talks about its conceivable execution, trailed by the end.

2.1.2   Motivation

A wide series of present day improvements, for example, correspondence frameworks (e.g., 5G), smart robots, and the IoT, are required to enable the fourth modern upset [4–6]. IoT interconnects various devices, individuals, information, and procedures, by permitting them to impart The worldwide energy request rose by 2.3% in 2018 contrasted with 2017, which is the most noteworthy increment since 2010 [9]. Subsequently, CO_2 outflows from the vitality area hit another record in 2018. Thought about to the pre-modern temperature level, an Earth-wide temperature boost is moving toward 1.5°C, no doubt before the center of the 21st century [10]. On the off chance that this pattern wins, an unnatural weather change will surpass the 2°C target, which will severely affect the planet and human life. The ecological concerns, such as a worldwide temperature alteration and nearby air contamination, shortage of water assets for warm force age, and, what is more, the constraint of draining fossil vitality assets, raise a critical requirement for progressively effective utilization of energy, and the utilization of sustainable power sources (RESs). Various examinations have demonstrated that a non-fossil energy framework [10] is practically unthinkable without productive utilization of energy or potentially decrease of energy request, furthermore, a significant level coordination of RESs, both at a nation level [11], territorial [12], or wide-ranging [13].

In bright of the United Nations Sustainable Development Goals plan [14], energy proficiency is one of the key drivers of manageable advancement. Besides, energy effectiveness offers financial advantages in long haul by lessening the expense of fuel imports/supply, energy stage, and decreasing productions from the energy division. For improving energy productivity and an increasingly ideal energy of the executives, a successful investigation of the continuous information in the energy inventory network assumes a key job [15]. The energy production network, from asset extraction to conveying it in a valuable structure to the end clients, incorporates three significant parts: (i) energy supply including upstream treatment facility forms; (ii) energy change forms including transmission and circulation (T&D) of energy bearers; and (iii) energy request side, which remembers the utilization of energy for structures, transportation division, and the business [16]. Figure 2.1 shows these three sections with their applicable segments. Under the extent of this paper, we talk about the job of IoT in every single diverse section of the energy production network.

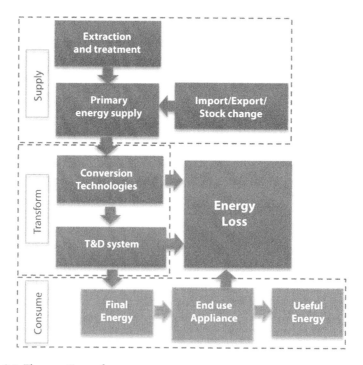

Figure 2.1 Three sections of energy segment.

Our point is to show the potential commitment of IoT to skillful utilization of energy, decrease of energy request, and expanding the portion of RESs.

IoT utilizes sensors and correspondence innovations for detecting and transmitting ongoing information, which empowers quick calculations and ideal dynamic [17]. In addition, IoT can support the energy division to change from a brought together to a conveyed, smart, and incorporated energy framework. This is a key prerequisite in sending area, spread RESs, for example, wind- and sun-oriented energy [18], also as transforming some little scope end clients of vitality into prosumers by accumulating their age and enhancing their interest at whatever point helpful for the framework. IoT-based frameworks mechanize, incorporate, and control forms through sensors and correspondence advances. Huge information collection and utilization of acute calculations for continuous information investigation can assist with checking energy utilization examples of various clients and devices in various time scales and control that utilization all the more productively [19]. Figure 2.2 indicates the benefits of IoT in renewable energy sources.

Also, the utilizations of IoT in sustainable power source creation include sensors that are joined to age, transmission, and dissemination gear. These gadgets help organizations to screen and control the working of the gear remotely progressively. This prompts diminished operational expenses and brings down our reliance on the effectively constrained petroleum

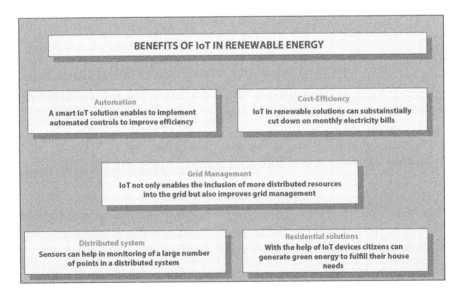

Figure 2.2 Benefits of IoT in renewable energy sources.

derivatives. The utilization of sustainable power source assets as of now gives an assortment of advantages over regular ones. The usage of IoT will assist us with using these spotless vitality sources to a further degree.

2.1.3   Methodology

The use of IoT in various areas and enterprises has been broadly talked about and checked on in the writing (for instance, [20–22]). In addition, difficulties and openings regarding the organization of one or a gathering of IoT advancements have gotten an elevated level of specialized evaluation, e.g., sensors [23] or 5G arrange [24]. As for the vitality area, a large portion of study examines have concentrated on one explicit subsector, e.g., structures or the specialized capability of a certain IoT innovation in the vitality area. For instance, Stojkoska *et al.* [25] audit keen home utilizations of IoT and the prospect of coordinating those applications into an IoT empowered condition. In an examination by Hui *et al.* [26], the strategies, late advances, and execution of 5G are concentrated uniquely with concentrating on the vitality request side. The job of IoT in improving vitality effectiveness in structures and open vehicle has been talked about in [27, 28]; individually, Khatua *et al.* [29] survey the key difficulties in the appropriateness of IoT information change and correspondence conventions for arrangement in smart grids. Be that as it may, not at all like the inspected writing where the spotlight is generally either on a particular subsector in the energy area or certain IoT advances, this paper surveys the utilization of IoT in the energy area, from energy stage to transmission and dispersion (T&D) and request side. In that capacity, the fundamental commitment of this paper is to broaden the current group of writing by giving energy strategy producers, financial specialists, energy specialists and superiors with a general diagram of the chances, and, what is more, difficulties of applying IoT in various pieces of the whole energy area. Right now, quickly present are the IoT structure and its empowering advancements to frame a reason for examining their job in the energy section.

To lead this overview, a precise pursuit was completed to gather and survey the ongoing collection of writing on the job of IoT in the energy segment. Initially, we looked through the expressions "Web of Things" and "Energy", case indefinite, in the title, theoretical, and sayings of distributions put away in SCOPUS, IEEE, Hindawi, and Google Scholar databases. At that point, we restricted the extent of search results to designing, financial aspects, and the board branches where conceivable. Next, papers distributed before 2012 and the greater part of meeting papers with no data on the friend audit process were rejected. At last, we grouped the significant papers in sub-classifications of energy age (counting power plants, auxiliary administrations, and unified sustainable power source), T&D frameworks (counting power, gas and region warming systems, and keen networks), and the interest side (counting vitality use in structures, transportation, and the business segment). We center around the IoT applications that can be for the most part material to the greater part of vitality frameworks without examining explicit cases and their limit conditions. For instance, we talk about the job of IoT in knowledge structures, without falling into the subtleties of building typology, building material, inhabitants' energy utilization example, type and number of home apparatuses, and so forth.

The rest of this paper is organized as follows. Sections 2.2 and 2.3 present IoT and empowering advances, including sensors and correspondence innovations, distributed computing, and information scientific stages. Section 2.4 surveys the job of IoT in the vitality area. Section 2.5 talks about the chances and, furthermore, difficulties of sending IoT, while Section 2.6 depicts future patterns. The paper closes in Section 2.7.

2.2   Internet of Things (IoT)

IoT is a rising innovation that utilizes the internet and means to give availability between physical devices or "things" [30]. Instances of physical devices incorporate home apparatuses and modern equipment. Utilizing fitting sensors and correspondence organizes, these devices can give important information and allow offering various organizations for individuals. For example, controlling energy utilization of structures in an extreme manner empowers diminishing the energy costs [31]. IoT has a wide scope of uses, for example, in assembling, coordination's and development industry [32]. IoT is too broadly applied in ecological testing, medicinal services frameworks and administrations, effective administration of energy in arrangements, and automaton-based organizations [33–36]. When arranging an IoT application which is the initial phase in constructing IoT frameworks, the determination of sections of IoT, for example, sensor device, correspondence convention, information storing, and calculation, should be fitting for the expected application. For instance, an IoT stage, planned to control warming, cooling, and cooling (HVAC) in a structure, requires using significant ecological sensors and utilizing reasonable communication innovation [37]. Figure 2.3 shows the various parts of an IoT stage [38]. IoT devices, which are the second parts of the IoT stages, could be as sensors, actuators, IoT entryways, or any device that joins the pattern of information combination, transmission, and preparing. For instance, an

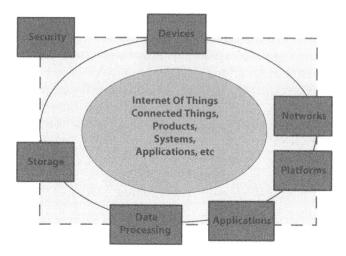

Figure 2.3 Chart representing the parts of an IoT stage.

IoT entry device allows routing the information into the IoT framework and setting up bi-directional interchanges between the gadget-to-entryway and entry-to-cloud.

The correspondence conventions that are the third part of the IoT stage empower the various devices to impart and impart their information to the controllers or the dynamic focuses. IoT stages offer the flexibility to choose the sort of the correspondence advancements (each having explicit highlights), as indicated by the necessities of the application. The instances of these advances incorporate Wi-Fi, Bluetooth, ZigBee [39], and cell innovation, for example, LTE-4G and 5G systems [40]. The information stockpiling is the fourth part of the IoT stage which empowers the board of gathered information from the sensors.

On a fundamental level, the information gathered from the devices is huge. This requires arranging a proficient information stockpiling that can be in cloud servers or at the edge of an IoT arrange. The put away information, which is utilized for diagnostic purposes, frames the fifth segment of the IoT stages. The information examination can be performed disconnected in the wake of putting away the information or it very well may be in type of ongoing investigation. The information diagnostic is performed for dynamic about the activity of the application. In light of the need, the information examination can be performed disconnected or ongoing. In disconnected examination, the put away information is first gathered and afterward pictured on premises utilizing representation apparatuses. If there should arise an occurrence of constant investigation, the cloud or edge servers are utilized to give perception, for example, stream investigation [41].

2.3 Empowering Tools

IoT is a worldview in which articles and components of a framework that are furnished with sensors, actuators, and processors can speak with one another to offer important types of assistance. In IoT frameworks, sensors are utilized to detect and gather information, and through passages course the gathered information to control focuses or the cloud for additional capacity, handling, investigation, and dynamic. After the choice is made, a relating order is then sent back to the actuator introduced on the framework because of the detected information. As there are variety of sensor and actuator gadgets, correspondence advances, and information registering drew nearer, right now, clarify the current innovations which empower IoT. At that point, we give models from the writing how these advances are utilized in the energy division.

2.3.1 Sensor Devices

Sensors are the key drivers of IoT [42]. They are utilized to gather and transmit information progressively. The utilization of sensors upgrades feasibility, usefulness, and assumes a basic job in achievement of IoT [43]. Various kinds of sensors exist that are produced for different application purposes. The models of these applications incorporate farming industry, natural observing, social insurance frameworks, and, what is more, administrations and open well-being [44]. By and by, in the vitality segment including vitality creation, transmission and conveyance, and creation, numerous these sensors are utilized. In the vitality part, sensors are utilized to make reserve funds in both expense and vitality. Sensors empower brilliant energy of the executives' framework and give ongoing vitality streamlining and encourage new methodologies for energy load the board. The examination and future patterns of the sensor gadgets additionally focus on improvement of sensor applications to improve load forming and customers' mindfulness just as advancement of explicit offices to upgrade creation of sustainable power sources [45]. In nutshell, the utilization of sensor devices inside IoT, in the vitality area to a great extent improves diagnostics, dynamic, investigation, streamlining forms, and incorporated execution measurements. Because of the enormous number of sensors utilized in the vitality area, in the accompanying, we clarify scarcely any instances of usually applied sensor devices in energy creation and utilization.

Temperature sensors are utilized to distinguish the changes in warming and cooling a framework [46]. Temperature is a significant and normal natural parameter. In the energy division, the essential standard of intensity age is the way toward changing mechanical energy into electrical energy, though mechanical energy is accomplished from heat energy, e.g., warm force plants, wind, water stream, and, what is more, sun-oriented force plants. These energy changes are acquired utilizing warm, i.e., temperature. In the energy utilization side, the temperature sensors are utilized to amplify the presentation of a framework at the point when temperature changes during ordinary activities. For instance, in local locations, the best time for killing on or the ventilation and cooling [47, 57–61] frameworks is perceived by temperature sensors; in this way, the vitality can be overseen accurately so as to spare energy [42].

Light sensors are utilized to gauge luminance (encompassing light level) or the splendor of a light. In energy utilization, light sensors have a few uses in mechanical and ordinary shopper applications. As a primary wellspring of energy utilization in structures identifies with lighting, which, individually, represent about 15% of all out power utilization [48]. On worldwide scale, around 20% of power is devoured for lighting [49]. In this manner, light sensors can be used to naturally control lighting levels inside and outside by turning on-and-off or darkening the light levels, such that the electric light levels consequently can be balanced because of changes in encompassing light. Right now, vitality required for the lighting for the indoor conditions can be diminished [19]. Passive Infrared (PIR) sensors, otherwise called movement sensors, are utilized for estimating the infrared light radiation produced from objects in their environment. In energy utilization, these sensors are used to lessen the energy utilization in structures. For instance, by utilizing PIR sensors, the nearness of people inside spaces can be identified. In the event that there is no development recognized in the space, at that point the light control of the space kills the light, i.e., keen control of lighting. Right now, power utilization of the structures is diminished [50]. Additionally, this can be applied for cooling frameworks which expend almost 40% of the energy in structures [48]. Closeness sensors are used to recognize the nearness of close by objects with no physical contact [51]. The model utilization of vicinity sensors is in wind vitality creation. These sensors give life span and dependable position detecting execution in wind turbines. In wind turbines, the utilizations of nearness sensors incorporate edge pitch control, yaw position, rotor, and yaw brake position; brake wear observing; and rotor speed checking [52].

A) Proximity Sensors

A Proximity Sensor is a non-contact type sensor that recognizes the nearness of an article. Proximity Sensors can be actualized utilizing various procedures like Optical (like Infrared or Laser), Ultrasonic, Hall Effect, Capacitive, and so on.

B) Ultrasonic Sensor

An Ultrasonic Sensor is a non-contact type gadget that can be utilized to gauge separation just as speed of an article. An Ultrasonic Sensor works dependent on the properties of the sound waves with recurrence more noteworthy than that of the human perceptible range. Using the hour of trip of the sound wave, a Ultrasonic Sensor can quantify the separation of the article (like SONAR). The Doppler Shift property of the sound wave is utilized to gauge the speed of an article.

You can discover various kinds of Sensors in our homes, workplaces, vehicles, and so on, attempting to make our lives simpler by turning on the lights by recognizing our essence, modifying the room temperature, identifying smoke or fire, making us scrumptious espresso, opening carport entryways when our vehicle is close to the entryway, and numerous different errands.

Figure 2.4 shows different types of sensors which can be used in different applications.

2.3.2   Actuators

Actuators are devices that change a specific type of energy into movement. They take electrical contribution from the mechanization frameworks, change the contribution to activity, and follow up on the devices and machines inside the IoT frameworks [53]. Actuators produce distinctive movement examples, for example, direct, oscillatory, or pivoting movements. In view of the energy sources, actuators sorted as the accompanying types [54].

Pneumatic actuators utilize compacted air for producing movement. Pneumatic actuators are created of a cylinder or a stomach so as to produce the thought process power. These actuators are utilized to control forms which require fast and exact reaction, as these procedures need not bother with a lot of thought process power.

Hydraulic actuators use the fluid for creating movement. Pressure-driven actuators comprise of chamber or, on the other hand, liquid engine that utilizes water-driven capacity to give mechanical activity. The mechanical movement gives a yield as far as straight, rotary, or oscillatory movement.

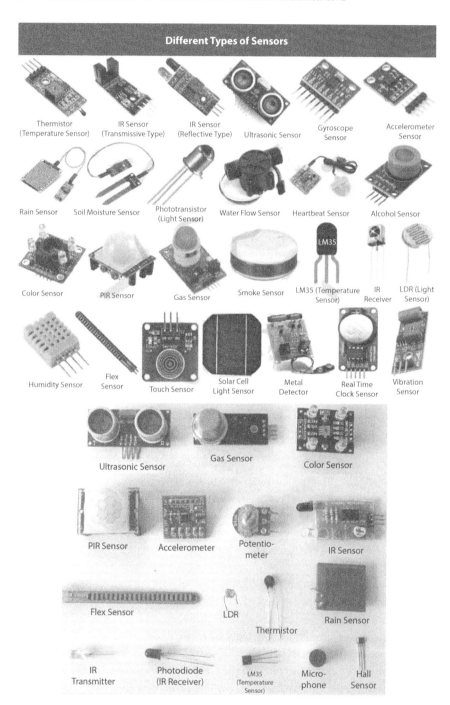

Figure 2.4 Different types of sensors for different applications.   (*Continued*)

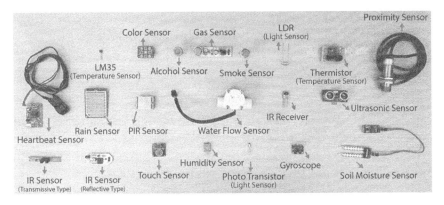

Figure 2.4 (Continued) Different types of sensors for different applications.

These actuators are utilized in modern process control where rapid and huge powers are required.

Thermal actuators utilize a warmth hotspot for producing the physical activity. Thermal actuators convert heat energy into kinetic energy or movement. By and large, thermostatic actuators are made out of a temperature-detecting material fixed by a stomach which pushes against an attachment for moving a cylinder. The temperature-detecting material can be any kind of fluid, gas, wax-like substance, or any material that changes volume dependent on temperature.

Electric actuators apply outer energy sources, e.g., batteries to produce movement. Electric actuators are mechanical devices equipped for changing over power into active energy in either a solitary straight or revolving movement. The plans of these actuators depend on the planned assignments inside the procedures.

In the energy area, for instance, in power plants, pneumatic actuators are generally applied to control valves. Electric control-valve actuator innovation empowers accomplishing vitality proficiency. They are additionally frequently utilized as the last control component in the activity of a force plant [55]. Likewise, there are assortment of actuators created for energy industry, e.g., LINAK electric actuator (https://www.linak. com/business-area/energy/) that offer answers, for instance, for limiting the energy squander when opening trapdoors and securing brakes wind turbines and making movement in sun powered following boards. In the writing, there are likewise numerous investigations meant to delineate the uses of the actuators inside IoT. For example, the examination in [56] proposes a remote sensor and also actuator system to give an IoT-based programmed insightful framework. While, by advancing the activity of gadgets and machines in the IoT, the proposed framework accomplishes decrease in their in general energy utilization at a given time.

2.3.3   Communication Technologies

With the ascent of the IoT, implanted originators are, like never before, concentrating and endeavors on framework vitality utilization. A prime model is a remote sensor hub—a moderately basic gadget from an utilitarian perspective that is required to carry out its responsibility for an all-encompassing period (at times, years) while fueled by a battery.

Plan contemplations incorporate significant framework components, for example, the microcontroller (MCU), remote interface, sensor, and framework power of the board. Figure 2.5 shows example of wireless sensor node architecture.

The MCU should be amazingly vitality proficient. Computational necessities will probably direct the determination of a 32-piece or 8-piece MCU, yet low vitality prerequisites stay paying little mind to the MCU decision. Vitality utilization in low-force and dynamic modes, just as the need to rapidly wake up from low-power modes to max throttle activity, will have a noteworthy effect in monitoring battery power.

"Scheme reflections include key system elements such as the microcontroller (MCU), wireless communication, sensor devices and power system management."

Consider how much the picked MCU can manage without really utilizing the CPU center itself. For instance, huge force reserve funds can be accomplished through independent treatment of sensor interfaces and

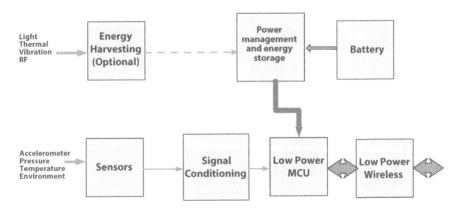

Figure 2.5 Classic wireless sensor node design.

other fringe capacities. Having the option to create the improvement sign, or force supply, for the sensor from the MCU and read back and decipher the outcomes without waking the MCU until "helpful" information is gotten can go far toward boosting the framework's battery life.

How about we think about the remote availability. The system topology and the selection of conventions will both affect the force spending plan required to keep up the remote connection. At times, a straightforward point-to-point interface utilizing an exclusive sub-GHz convention may appear to be a suitable decision to yield the most reduced interest on power from the battery. Be that as it may, this design can restrain the extent of where and how the sensor can be conveyed. A star design based on either 2.4 GHz or sub-GHz advances builds the adaptability for different sensor organization, yet this would almost certainly expand the intricacy of the convention, along these lines expanding the measure of RF traffic and framework power.

A third choice to consider is a work setup dependent on a convention, for example, ZigBee. While a work organize forces the greatest channel on the sensor hub battery, it additionally gives the best degree of adaptability. Contingent on the remote stack, a work system can likewise furnish the most dependable organization choice with a self-mending network. In a sensor hub, the measure of information to be sent over the remote connection ought to be moderately little. All things considered, ZigBee gives an ideal work organizing arrangement; Bluetooth Smart is a fantastic decision for norms based, power-touchy point-to-point designs, and exclusive sub-GHz arrangements give greatest adaptability to organize size, transmission capacity, and information payloads in star or point-to-point setups.

For wide regions, long-extend advances and stages, for example, LoRa and Sigfox, empower high hub check systems coming to up to many kilometers and with low-power frameworks. Information security is getting increasingly significant. On the off chance that the MCU used to run the stack does not have encryption equipment, it should consume various cycles to run the calculation in programming affecting the general force utilization. Various sensor decisions are accessible and can extend from discrete to completely coordinated arrangements. Discrete arrangements might be power proficient, yet place extra handling prerequisites on the MCU.

Building signal molding into the sensor gives some noteworthy points of interest. The information that is sent to the MCU will be significant information that can be rapidly and effectively deciphered by the application, which implies the MCU can stay unconscious as far as might be feasible. Having preconditioned information sent over a computerized interface, for example, SPI or I2C, likewise implies the MCU can accumulate the information more proficiently than if it were utilizing its ADC. A last structure thought for low-vitality applications is controlling the framework itself. Contingent on the kind of battery utilized in the application, there is regularly a necessity for help converters or lift exchanging controllers. A cautious decision can bigly affect the framework's general force utilization as arrangements extend from 1- to 7-µA utilization.

For progressively complex frameworks, a force of the executives' incorporated circuit (PMIC) gives increasingly exact power over the entire framework. From a solitary force source, you can create various voltage rails to drive various components of the installed framework, tuning every voltage rail to give simply enough capacity to the application. A PMIC may likewise offer extra usefulness for general framework control, for example, guard dog clocks and reset capacity.

At last, there are a wide range of framework structure viewpoints associated with planning low-vitality, battery-fueled applications. Not with standing low-power semiconductor segments, the way to deal with programming, including remote stacks, encryption and information preparing, are significant contemplations. Every one of these plan components can significantly affect the framework's general force spending plan, while empowering designers to make low-vitality IoT gadgets that augment valuable battery life.

So, wireless communication frameworks assume the significant job in initiating IoT. Wireless frameworks interface the sensor gadgets to IoT passages and perform start to finish information interchanges between these components of IoT. Wireless frameworks are created dependent on various remote benchmarks and the utilization of every one relies upon the prerequisite of the application, for example, correspondence go, data transfer capacity, and, what is more, power utilization prerequisites. For instance, regularly infinite sources of energy, including wind and sunlight-based force plants are generally situated in extremely remote zones [63, 123].

In this way, guaranteeing a dependable IoT correspondences in remote spots is testing. Utilizing IoT frameworks on these locales requires determination of reasonable correspondence innovation that can ensure a proceeds with association interface and support current information move in an energy productive way. Because of the significance of correspondence advances in IoT, right now survey a portion of these innovations. We additionally show to not many guides to show their job in the vitality division. At that point, we give a correlation in Table 2.1 to appear the distinction of every one of the advancements when applied with IoT.

Table 2.1 Evaluation chart of different wireless technologies [62, 93–98].

Technology	Range	Data rate	Battery usage	Security	System cost	Applications
LoRA	≤50 km	0.3–38.4 kbps	Very low (8–10 years)	High	Low	Smart buildings
NB-IoT	≤50 km	≤100 kbps	High (1–2 years)	High	Low	Smart grid communication
LTE-M	≤200 km	0.2–1 Mbps	Low (7–8 years)	High	Moderate	Smart meter
Sigfox	≤50 km	100 bps	Low (7–8 years)	High	Moderate	Electric plugs
Weightless	<5 km	100 kbps	Low (very long)	High	Low	Smart meter
Bluetooth	≤50m	1 Mbps	Low (few months)	High	Low	Smart home appliances
Zigbee	≤100m	250 Kbps	Very low (5–10 years)	Low	Low	Smart metering in renewable energies
Satellite	≥1,500 km	100 kbps	High	High	Costly	Solar and wind power plants

Bluetooth Low Energy (BLE) is a short-range remote correspondence innovation for IoT that empowers trading information utilizing short radio frequencies (https://www.bluetooth.com/). BLE is less expensive to send, with a common scope of 0 to 30 m, which empowers making a moment individual territory organize [64]. BLE targets little scope IoT applications that expect gadgets to convey little volumes of information devouring insignificant force. Businesses in the energy segment with an all-around planned IoT procedure can make new types of machine-to-machine (M2M) and machine-to-human correspondence utilizing this innovation.

In the energy segment, BLE is broadly utilized on the energy utilization in private and business structures. For example, the creators of [65] portray a brilliant office energy the board framework that decreases the energy utilization of PCs, screens, and lights utilizing BLE. Another investigation proposes an energy of the board framework for savvy homes that uses BLE for correspondence among home machines targeting diminishing the vitality at homes [66]. So also, utilizing BLE the examination in [67] presents a fluffy-based answer for brilliant energy the board in a home computerization, pointing improving home energy the board conspires.

ZigBee is a correspondence innovation, which is intended to make individual zone arrange and targets little scope applications (https://zigbee. org/). ZigBee is anything but difficult to execute and intended to give minimal effort, low-information rate, and exceptionally dependable systems for low-power applications [68, 69].

ZigBee likewise uses a work arrange detail where devices are associated with numerous interconnections. Utilizing the work organizing highlight of ZigBee, the most extreme correspondence extend, which is up to 100 m, is broadened fundamentally. In the vitality area, the model IoT utilizations of ZigBee incorporate lighting frameworks (structures and road lighting), keen networks, e.g., savvy electric meters, home robotization frameworks, and modern computerization. These applications mean to give draws near for expending vitality in a productive manner. In writing, expecting to limit the vitality costs of the buyers, the exploration in [70] assesses the exhibition of home vitality of the executive's application through building up a remote sensor organize utilizing ZigBee.

The inventors of [71] additionally present smart home interfaces to permit interoperability among ZigBee devices, electrical hardware, and sharp meters to use the energy all the more productively. The work in [72] presents a ZigBee-based checking framework which is utilized to gauge and move the vitality of home apparatuses at the outlets and the lights, targeting to lessen the vitality utilization. Another examination [73] presents field tests utilizing ZigBee advances for observing photovoltaic and wind vitality frameworks. The consequences of the investigation show the capability of ZigBee devices applied in conveyed infinite stage and brilliant metering structures.

Long Range (LoRa) is a remote correspondence innovation intended for IoT (https://loraalliance.org/). LoRA is a financially savvy correspondence innovation for huge organization of IoT, and it can add numerous years to battery life. LoRa is likewise used to build up significant distance communicates (more than 10 km in country territories) with low force utilization [74]. The highlights of this innovation make it a reasonable correspondence innovation to be utilized in the vitality segment for the most part in keen urban communities, for example, keen networks and building computerization frameworks, e.g., savvy metering.

In writing, the work in [75] targets enhancing energy utilization by sending building energy of the executives' framework utilizing LoRa. The work proposes a stage by incorporating numerous frameworks, for example, cooling, lighting, and vitality observing to perform building energy improvement. The result of stage brought about a 20% energy sparing. In [76], the creators created an AI-based brilliant controller for a business structures HVAC using LoRa. The brilliant controller recognizes when a room is not vacant and kills the HVAC, decreasing its energy utilization up to 19.8%. Utilizing LoRa innovation, another examination [77] presents execution of an electronic stage for vitality of the executives in open structures. Through a test, the created stage permits sparing the vitality for a lighting framework by 40%.

Sigfox is a wide territory arrange innovation which utilizes a ultra-tight band (https://www.sigfox.com/). Sigfox permits gadgets to speak with low force for empowering IoT applications [78]. For the fittingness of this innovation in the vitality area for instance, the examination in [79] audits the innovative advances and presents Sigfox as extraordinary compared to other low force contender for savvy metering for empowering constant vitality administrations for family units. What is more, the investigation in [80] looks at diverse low force wide territory arrange advancements and presumes that Sigfox is a reasonable answer for be utilized with electric fittings sensors alert in shrewd structures [46, 142–146].

Narrowband IoT (NB-IoT) is a LPWAN correspondence innovation that bolsters enormous number of IoT devices and administrations with a high information rate with exceptionally low idleness (https://www.3gpp.org/newsevents/1733-niot/). NB-IoT is a minimal effort arrangement that has long battery life and gives upgraded inclusion. As indicated by the creators of [81], because of the dormancy highlights of NB-IoT, this innovation is a potential answer for shrewd energy dissemination organizes by giving minimal effort interchanges to keen meters. Furthermore, the investigation in [82] exhibits the NB-IoT innovation for shrewd metering. As another use of NB-IoT in the energy division, the work in [83] presents NB-IoT as a potential answer for brilliant framework correspondences by contrasting NB-IoT and other correspondence advancements regarding information rate, idleness, and correspondence go.

Long haul Evolution for Machine-Type Communications (LTE-M) is the 3GPP (the third-age association venture) institutionalization, which is intended to lessen the gadget multifaceted nature for machine-type correspondence (MTC) [84]. LTE-M underpins secure correspondence, gives universal inclusion, and offers high framework limit. LTE-M likewise offers administrations of lower dormancy and higher throughput than NB-IoT [85]. Furthermore, this innovation offers energy proficiency asset assignment for little controlled gadgets, making it to be a potential answer for keen meter [86] and brilliant framework correspondences [87].

Weightless is LPWAN open remote standard that is created to build up correspondence among incredible number of IoT gadgets and machines (http://www.weightless.org/). Weightless is a potential answer for shrewd metering in the vitality segment [88]. In light of the examination in [89], weightless is a reasonable remote innovation can be utilized in keen home IoT applications for smart metering and brilliant structure interchanges.

Satellite is another correspondence innovation that has a wide-region inclusion and can bolster low information rate applications in machine-to-machine (M2M) style [90]. Satellite innovation is reasonable for supporting IoT gadgets and machines in remote spots. The investigation in [91] presents an IoT-based M2M satellite correspondence that is material to the keen network, especially for the T&D area. A comparable report features the significance of utilizing satellite-based IoT interchanges in energy area, for example, sun-based and wind power plants [92].

2.3.4   IoT Data and Computing

Assuming and examining the information produced by IoT permits increasing further understanding, precise reaction to the framework, and helps settling on reasonable choices on vitality utilization of the frameworks [99].

Notwithstanding, registering IoT information is a difficult issue. Since, IoT information known as Big information alludes to enormous measure of organized and unstructured information, produced from different components of IoT frameworks for example, sensors, programming applications, keen or clever gadgets, and correspondence systems.

Because of the attributes of big information, which are huge volume, high speed, and high assortment [100], it should be productively prepared and broke down [101]. Handling the Big information is past the limit of conventional strategies, i.e., putting away it on neighborhood hard drives, registering, and dissecting them a while later. Propelled registering and explanatory techniques are expected to deal with the big information [102, 103]. In the followings, we clarify distributed computing and mist figuring, which are broadly utilized for handling, and, what is more, processing the big information.

2.3.4.1   Distributed Computing

Distributed computing is an information preparing approach that offers administrations, applications, stockpiling, and, what is more, figuring through the web and permits calculation of information gushed from IoT gadgets. In distributed computing, cloud alludes to the "Web" and figuring alludes to calculation and preparing administrations offered by this methodology [104]. Distributed computing comprises of both application benefits that are gotten to by means of the Internet and the equipment frameworks, which are situated in server farms [105]. Utilizing these qualities, distributed computing empowers handling the enormous information, and gives complex calculation capacities [106]. The fundamental advantages of utilizing cloud frameworks depend on [107] (i) essentially diminishing the expense of equipment; (ii) upgrading the figuring force and capacity limit; and (iii) having multi-center structures, which facilitates the information of the executives. Besides, distributed computing is a made sure about framework, which gives assets, processing force, and capacity that is required from a topographical area [108]. These highlights of distributed computing empowers the large information came about because of the developing uses of IoT to be effectively examined, controlled and arranged productively [109]. What is more, distributed computing takes out the costs required for buying equipment and programming and running the calculations for handling the IoT information, coming about in extensively minimization of power required for neighborhood information calculation.

2.3.4.2 Fog Computing

In spite of the fact that distributed computing is a standout among other figuring standards for information handling for IoT applications. Because of the deferral and data transmission confinement of brought together assets that are utilized for information handling, progressively productive ways are required. Mist processing is a circulated worldview and an expansion of the cloud, which moves the registering and explanatory administrations close to the edge of the arrange. Haze processing is a worldview that extends the cloud at a more noteworthy scale and can bolster bigger outstanding task at hand [110]. In haze registering, any gadget with processing, stockpiling, and system association capacity fills in as haze hub. The instances of these gadgets incorporate, however, are not restricted to, individual PCs, modern controllers, switches, switches, and installed servers [111]. Right now worldview, haze gives IoT information preparing and capacity locally at IoT gadgets as opposed to sending them to the cloud. The upsides of this methodology incorporate upgraded secure administrations required for some IoT applications just as decreasing system traffic and dormancy [112]. In this manner, as opposed to the cloud figuring, mist offers preparing and registering administrations with quicker reaction with higher security. This empowers quicker dynamic and taking fitting activities.

2.4   IoT in the Energy Sector

Today, the vitality area is profoundly reliant on non-renewable energy sources, comprising about 80% of last vitality all inclusive. Unreasonable extraction and burning of petroleum products has unfriendly natural, well-being, also, monetary effects because of air contamination and environmental change to give some examples. Energy productivity, i.e., devouring less vitality for conveying a similar help, and the organization of sustainable power source sources are two principle choices to lessen the unfriendly effects of non-renewable energy source use [12, 13].

Right now, talk about the job of IoT in the energy part, from fuel extraction, activity, and, what is more, upkeep (O&M) of vitality producing resources, to T&D and end utilization of vitality IoT can play a significant job in decreasing vitality misfortunes and bringing down CO_2 emanations. An energy executive framework in view of IoT can screen constant energy utilization and increment the degree of mindfulness about the vitality execution at any degree of the inventory network [15, 113]. This segment examines the use of IoT in energy stage organizes first. At that point, we proceed with the idea of keen urban areas, which is an authority term for some IoT-based subsystems, for example, excellent matrices, smart structures, powerful manufacturing plants, and, what is more, understanding transportation. Next, we examine every one of the previously mentioned segments independently. At long last, we abridge the discoveries of this area in Tables 2.2 and 2.3.

2.4.1   IoT and Energy Generation

Programming mechanical processes and supervisory control and information obtaining frameworks became well known in the force part in 1990s [37]. By checking and controlling hardware and procedures, beginning times of IoT began to add to the force part by easing the danger of loss of creation or, on the other hand, power outage. Dependability, productivity, ecological effects, and upkeep issues are the primary difficulties of old force plants. The period of hardware in the force division and poor upkeep issues can prompt elevated level of vitality misfortunes and untrustworthiness. Resources are, in some cases, more than 40 years of age, pricey, and cannot be supplanted without any problem. IoT can add to diminishing some of these difficulties in the administration of intensity plants [37]. By applying IoT sensors, Internet-associated gadgets can recognize any disappointment in the activity or irregular reduction in energy effectiveness, disturbing the requirement for upkeep. This expands dependability and productivity of

Table 2.2 Claims of IoT in the energy region (1): rule, marketplace, and energy quantity side.

	Claim	Region	Explanation	Profits
Rule and Marketplace	Energy democratization	Regulation	Providing access to the grid for many small end users for peer to peer electricity trade and choosing the supplier freely.	Improving the chain of command in the energy supply chain, market power, and regional supply; running the energy market and reducing the prices for consumers; and creating awareness on energy use and efficiency
	Combination of Small manufacture by consumers (practical power plants)	Energy marketplace	Conglomerating load and age of a gathering of end clients to offer to power, adjusting, or save markets.	Activating little loads to take an interest in serious markets; helping the framework by lessening load in top occasions; hedging the danger of high power bills at top hours; also, improving adaptability of the framework and decreasing the requirement for adjusting resources; offering benefit to buyers
	Protective conservation	Upstream oil and gas industry/ service firms	Error, drip, and exhaustion checking by analyzing of big data collected through stationary and portable devices or cameras.	Decreasing the risk of distress, creation misfortune and support personal time; diminishing the expense of O&M; and forestalling mishaps also, expanding well-being.

(Continued)

Table 2.2 Claims of IoT in the energy region (1): rule, marketplace, and energy quantity side. (*Continued*)

	Claim	Region	Explanation	Profits
Energy Source	Fault maintenance	Upstream oil and gas industry/ service organizations	Recognizing disappointments and issues in vitality systems, what is more, potentially fixing them basically.	Improving unwavering quality of an assistance; improving rate in fixing spillage in area warming or disappointments in power frameworks; and decreasing support time and danger of well-being/security.
	Energy storing and analytics	Manufacturing dealers or service companies	Breaking down market information and opportunities for enacting adaptability alternatives, for example, energy storing in the framework	Diminishing the danger of market interest imbalance; expanding benefit in energy exchange by ideal utilization of adaptable and capacity choices; and guaranteeing an ideal system for capacity resources.
	Digitalized control group	Service firms and system operative	Dissecting large information of and controlling numerous age units at various time scales.	Improving security of supply; improving resource utilization and the executives; lessening the cost of arrangement of reinforcement limit; quickening the reaction to the loss of burden; also, diminishing the danger of power outage.

the structure, furthermore to decreasing the expense of upkeep [114]. As per [115], another IoT-based force plant can spare 230 million USD during the lifetime and a current plant with a similar size can spare 50 million USD on the off chance that outfitted with the IoT stage.

For diminishing petroleum derivative use and depending on neighborhood energy assets, numerous nations are advancing RESs. Climate reliant or variable sustainable power source (VRE) sources, for example, wind and sun-based energy, present new difficulties to the energy framework known as "the discontinuity challenge". In an energy framework with a high portion of VRE, coordinating age of energy with request is a major test due to inconstancy of market interest, bringing about confuse in various time scales. IoT frameworks offer the adaptability in offsetting age with request, which thus can decrease the difficulties of sending VRE, bringing about higher coordination portions of clean energy and less GHG discharges [116]. What is more, by utilizing IoT, a progressively proficient utilization of vitality can be accomplished by utilizing AI calculations that help decide an ideal parity of various organic market advancements [37]. For example, the utilization of manmade reasoning calculations can adjust the force yield of a warm force plant with the wellsprings of in-house power age, e.g., collecting some little scope sunlight-based PV boards [117]. Table 2.2 abridges the utilizations of IoT in the energy division, from energy supply guideline furthermore, markets.

2.4.2   Smart Metropolises

These days, the amazing pace of urbanization just as overpopulation has brought numerous worldwide concerns, for example, air and water contamination [118], vitality get to, and natural concerns. In this line, one of the principle challenges is to give the urban communities perfect, reasonable, and dependable energy sources. The ongoing improvements in advanced advances have given a main thrust to apply practicality, IoT-based answers for the current issues in a keen city setting [119]. Bright factories, smart homes, power plants, and homesteads in a city can be associated and the information about their vitality utilization in various hours of the day can be accumulated. On the off chance that it is discovered that a segment, e.g., local locations, expends the most energy toward the evening, at that point, naturally energy given to other sections, e.g., industrial facilities, can be limited to adjust the entire framework at any rate cost and danger of blockage or power outage. In a shrewd city, various procedures, i.e., data transmission and correspondence, keen recognizable proof, area assurance, following, observing, contamination control, and personality the board can be overseen consummately by the guide of IoT innovation [120]. IoT innovations can assist with checking each item in a city. Structures, urban framework, transport, energy systems, and utilities could be associated with sensors. These associations can guarantee a vitality effective shrewd city by steady observing of information accumulated from sensors. For instance, by checking vehicles with IoT, road lights can be controlled for ideal utilization of energy. Likewise, the specialists

Table 2.3 Uses of IoT in the energy area (2): energy grids and request side.

	Application	Sector	Description	Benefits
Communication and Supply	Smart grid-irons	Electric grid organization	A policy for functioning the grid using big data and ICT skills as opposite to old grids.	Improving energy proficiency and joining of disseminated age and burden; improving security of supply; and lessening the requirement for reinforcement supply limit and expenses.
	System administration	Electric grid procedure and controlling	Using large data at different ideas of the grid to achieve the grid more optimally.	Recognizing feeble focuses and strengthening the matrix likewise and decreasing the hazard of power outage.
	Combined control of rechargeable vehicle fleet (EV)	Electric grid procedure and controlling	Evaluating information of charging locations and charge/ discharge cycles of EVs.	Improving the reaction to charging request at top occasions; breaking down and determining the effect of EVs on load; and recognizing regions for putting in new charging stations and support of the appropriation lattice.

(*Continued*)

Table 2.3 Uses of IoT in the energy area (2): energy grids and request side. (*Continued*)

	Application	Sector	Description	Benefits
	Regulator and managing of vehicle to grid (V2G)	Electric grid procedure and controlling	Examining load and charge/discharge design of EVs to for supportive grid when desired.	Improving the adaptability of the framework by actuating EVs in providing the matrix with power; reducing the requirement for reinforcement limit during top hours control and the executives of EV armada to offer ideal collaboration between the lattice and EVS.
	Microgrids	Electricity grid	Stages for handling a grid self-regulating from the significant grid.	Improving security of supply; making interoperability and adaptability between Microgrids and the primary network; and offering stable power costs for the customers associated with the microgrid.

(*Continued*)

Table 2.3 Uses of IoT in the energy area (2): energy grids and request side. (*Continued*)

	Application	Sector	Description	Benefits
Claim Side	Regulation and supervision of the District heating (DH) network	DH network	Examining large information of the temperature and burden in the organize and associated customers.	Improving the effectiveness of the matrix in meeting request; lessening the temperature of hot water supply and sparing vitality when conceivable; and distinguishing network focuses with the requirement.
	Request reaction	Domestic/ marketable and manufacturing	Significant control (i.e., by detaching, shifting, or flattening).	Falling request at peak time, which itself decreases the grid jamming.
	Request reply (request side controlling)	Domestic/ marketable and manufacturing	Focal control (i.e., by shedding, moving, or then again leveling); heap of numerous shoppers by investigating the burden and activity of apparatuses.	Decreasing interest at top time, which itself decreases the network clog; lessening purchaser power bills; and diminishing the requirement for interest in framework reinforcement limit.

(*Continued*)

Table 2.3 Uses of IoT in the energy area (2): energy grids and request side. (*Continued*)

	Application	Sector	Description	Benefits
	Innovative metering organization	End users	With sensors and devices to gather and examine the load and fever data in a consumer of site.	Approaching determined load varieties in distinctive time scale; recognizing zones for improving energy effectiveness (for instance, excessively cooled rooms or additional lights when there is no tenants); and diminishing the cost of energy use.
	Battery-operated energy controlling	End users	Data examination for starting battery at the most appropriate time	Deal technique for charge/release of battery in various time scale; improving energy proficiency and helping the framework at top times; and diminishing the expense of energy use.

(*Continued*)

Table 2.3 Uses of IoT in the energy area (2): energy grids and request side. (*Continued*)

	Application	Sector	Description	Benefits
	Smart structures	End users	Central and remote control of applications and strategies.	Improving comfort by optimal control of appliances and HVAC systems; reducing manual intervention, saving time and energy; increasing knowledge on energy use and environmental impact; improving readiness for joining a smart grid or virtual power plant; and improved integration of distributed generation and storage systems.

can approach the assembled data and can settle on progressively educated choices on transportation decisions and their energy request.

2.4.3   Smart Grid

Smart grid frameworks are current lattices conveying the most secure and trustworthy ICT innovation to control and streamline vitality age, T&D frameworks, and end use. By associating many acute meters, a practicality matrix builds up a multi-directional progression of data, which can be utilized ideally for the executives of the framework and effective vitality circulation [121]. The utilization of savvy framework can be featured in various subsectors of the vitality framework independently, e.g., energy stage, structures, or, on the other hand, transportation, or they can be viewed as inside and out.

In conventional lattices, batteries were energized by connectors through power links and AC/DC inverter [121]. These batteries can be charged remotely in a shrewd lattice, utilizing an inductive charging innovation. What is more, in a keen matrix, the energy request example of end clients can be dissected by gathering information through an IoT stage, for instance, the hour of charging of cell phones or electric vehicles. At that point, the closest remote battery charge station can apportion the ideal schedule opening and that gadget/vehicle can be charged. Another favorable position is that the utilization of IoT will prompt better control and, what is more, will check the battery-prepared gadgets, and in this way, first, the energy appropriation can be balanced, and second, the conveyance of power to these vehicles can be ensured. This will decrease unessential energy utilization impressively. Moreover, IoT can be applied in secluded and microgrids for certain islands or associations, particularly when vitality is required each and every minute with no special case, e.g., in databases. In such frameworks, all the advantages associated with the network can communicate with one another. Additionally, the information on energy request of any advantage is available. This cooperation can guarantee the ideal administration of the energy dispersion at whatever point and wherever required. Regarding community effect of practicality lattices, for what it is worth appeared in Figure 2.6, in a savvy city furnished with IoT-based shrewd frameworks, various areas of the city can be associated together [121].

During the collective correspondence between various areas, the shrewd lattice can caution administrators through brilliant apparatuses before any intense issue happens [113, 122]. For instance, through steady checking, it very well may be distinguished if energy request surpasses the limit of the lattice. In this manner, by securing ongoing information, various methodologies can be embraced by specialists and energy utilization can be

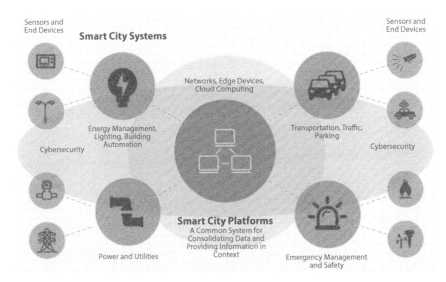

Figure 2.6 An integrated information connectivity in a smart city model.

rescheduled to an alternate time when there is lower anticipated interest. In certain districts, shrewd (or dynamic) valuing duties have been considered at variable energy costs right now. Real time pricing (RTP) duties just as the energy cost will be higher at a specific time when the utilization of vitality is probably going to be higher. Through the information accumulated from the segments of the shrewd framework, energy utilization and age can be splendidly streamlined and overseen by a long shot located systems. Decrease of transmission misfortunes in T&D organizes through dynamic voltage the board or decrease of non-specialized misfortunes utilizing a system of shrewd meters are different instances of applying IoT [37].

2.4.4   Smart Buildings Structures

The energy utilization in urban areas can be isolated into various parts; private structures (local); and business (administrations), including shops, workplaces, and schools, and transport. The local energy utilization in the private segment incorporates lighting, hardware (apparatuses), local high temp water, cooking, refrigerating, warming, ventilation, and cooling (HVAC) (Figure 2.7). Air conditioning energy utilization commonly represents half of energy utilization in structures [124].

In this manner, the administration of HVAC frameworks is significant in decreasing power utilization. With the headway of innovation in the

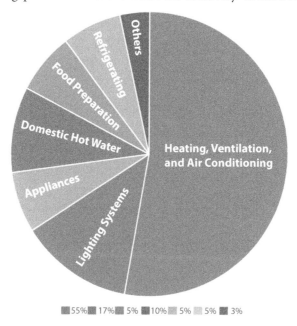

55%■ 17%■ 5%■ 10%■ 5%■ 5%■ 3%

Figure 2.7 Segment of domestic energy intake.

business, IoT gadgets can assume a significant job to control the vitality misfortunes in HVAC frameworks. For instance, by finding some remote indoor regulators dependent on inhabitance, empty spots can be figured it out. When an empty zone is identified, a few activities can be taken to bring down energy utilization. For example, HVAC frameworks can lessen the activity in the empty zone, which will prompt huge decrease in energy utilization and misfortunes. IoT can likewise be applied to deal with the energy misfortunes of lighting frameworks. For instance, through applying IoT-based lighting frameworks, the clients will be cautioned when the energy utilization goes past the standard level. Besides, by a proficient investigation of the ongoing information, load from high-pinnacle will be moved to low-top levels. This makes a noteworthy commitment to ideal utilization of electrical energy [119, 125] and decreasing related ozone depleting substance outflows. Utilizing IoT, the interest reaction will be progressively nimble and adaptable, and the observing and request side administration will become increasingly effective.

2.4.5   Powerful Use of Energy in Industry

IoT can be utilized to structure a completely associated and adaptable framework in the business to decrease energy utilization while streamlining creation. In conventional manufacturing plants, a ton of vitality is spent to deliver the finished result and control the nature of the final result. Additionally, checking each single procedure requires HR to be included. Be that as it may, utilizing a dexterous and adaptable framework in shrewd production lines assists with perceiving disappointments simultaneously instead of remembering them by observing the items toward the finish of creation line. Consequently, an appropriate move can be made immediately to turn away inefficient creation and related waste energy. As far as checking forms during assembling, IoT, and its empowering innovation play a critical job. Door gadgets, IoT center point systems, web servers, and cloud stages, which are available with savvy cell phones (e.g., advanced cells or PCs), can be models of observing hardware [151–167].

Remote correspondences, for example, Wi-Fi, Bluetooth, ZigBee, Z-wave, or, on the other hand, wired interchanges, for example, Local Area Network (LAN), can be utilized to interface all pieces of hardware [126]. In addition, to utilize IoT all the more effectively, by introducing sensors on every part of a mechanical site, the segments that expend more vitality than their ostensible energy level can be recognized. Therefore, each and every segment can be handily dealt with, the issues of segments can be fixed, and what is more, the energy utilization of every segment can be streamlined. This famously brings about lessening the energy misfortunes in savvy plants. In a understanding plant, information handling is the key component in the entire framework, through which information in the cloud stage (goes about as a cerebrum) will be broke down to help administrators settling on progressively proficient choices in time [127]. As far as observing and keeping up resources of assembling, the enormous issue in production lines is the devaluation of machines and mechanical gadgets. With a fitting IoT stage and instruments, the best possible gadget size can be chosen to lessen mileage and the related upkeep costs. IoT-based contingent checking guarantees the mechanical gadget never arrives at its edge limit. This essentially implies the device keeps going longer and endures less disappointments. In addition, the disappointments that cause energy misfortune can be foreseen to be handled. IoT-based light-footed frameworks can give a keen framework to joint effort between clients, produces, and organizations. Along these lines, a particular item will be produced straightforwardly agreeing to clients' structure. Along these lines, energy expended during the way toward putting away extra parts also as the energy squandered in distribution centers to keep the extra parts will be dwindled altogether. Just a certain number of items in different sorts will be produced and put away, which upgrades the executives of energy utilization and creation proficiency [126].

2.4.6   Insightful Transportation

One of the significant reasons for air contamination and vitality misfortunes in large urban communities is abuse of private vehicles rather than open transportation. Instead of a conventional transportation framework where every framework works autonomously, applying IoT advancements in transportation, alleged "smart transportation", offers a worldwide administration framework. Additionally, the constant information handling assumes a noteworthy job in rush hour gridlock the board. All the segments of the transportation framework can be associated together, and their information can be handled together. Blockage control and understanding stopping frameworks utilizing on the web maps are a few utilizations of shrewd transportation. Keen utilization of transportation empowers travelers to select a more cost-sparing choice with shorter separation and the quickest course, which spares a noteworthy measure of time and vitality [120]. Residents will have the option to decide their appearance time and oversee their calendar all the more proficiently [125]. In this manner, time of city excursions will be abbreviated, and the vitality misfortunes will be decreased fundamentally. This can astoundingly lessen CO_2 outflows and other air dirtying gases from transportation [119]. Table 2.3 outlines the

Figure 2.8 Claims of IoT in an incorporated smart energy arrangement.

uses of IoT in the vitality segment, from practicality energy lattices to the end utilization of energy. The IoT-based digitalization changes an energy framework from a unidirectional bearing, i.e., from age through energy networks to customers, to a coordinated energy framework. Various pieces of such an incorporated smart energy framework are portrayed in Figure 2.8.

2.5   Difficulties of Relating IoT

Other than all the advantages of IoT for vitality sparing, sending IoT in the energy area speaks to moves that should be tended to. This area tends to the difficulties and existing answers for applying IoT-based energy frameworks. Moreover, in Table 2.4, we condense the difficulties and current arrangements of utilizing IoT in the energy area.

2.5.1   Energy Consumption

In the vitality frameworks, the significant exertion of IoT stages are sparing the vitality. In vitality frameworks to empower correspondence utilizing IoT, monstrous number of IoT gadgets transmit information. To run the IoT framework and transmit immense measure of information produced from the IoT

Table 2.4 Challenges and current solutions of using IoT in the energy sector.

Task	Problem	Model answer	Advantage
Construction proposal	Providing a consistent end-to-end assembly	Using varied reference constructions	Communicating things and society
	Different tools	Relating open customary	Scalability
Integration of IoT with subsystems	IoT information controlling	Scheming co-simulation simulations	Real-time information among procedures and subsystems
	Combination IoT with in effect structures	Molding integrated energy schemes	Decrease in cost of conservation
Regularization	Substantial arrangement of IoT devices	Significant a scheme of structures	Regularity among various IoT devices
	Changeability among IoT devices	Open information copies and procedures	Covering various technologies
Energy depletion	Communication of high information rate	Arrangement of efficient communication rules	Equivalent energy
	Efficient energy consumption	distributed computing techniques	Equivalent energy
IoT Security	Threats and cyber-attacks	Encryption schemes, distributed control systems	Improved security
User privacy	Maintaining users' personal information	Asking for users' permission	Enables better decision-making

gadgets, extensive measure of vitality is required [128]. Hence, the vitality utilization of IoT frameworks stays as a significant challenge. Nonetheless, different methodologies have attempted to diminish the force utilization of IoT frameworks. For instance, by setting the sensors to rest mode and simply work when essential. Planning effective correspondence conventions which permit circulated registering methods that empowers vitality effective correspondences has been concentrated significantly. Applying radio improvement strategies, for example, balance advancement and helpful correspondence has been considered as an answer. Additionally, vitality effective steering procedures, for example, group models and utilizing multi-way directing methods was comprehended as another arrangement [129–131].

2.5.2 Synchronization of IoT With Subsystems

A principle challenge remembers the joining of an IoT framework for subsystems of the energy framework. Since subsystems of the energy area are one of a kind utilizing different sensor and information correspondence advancements. In this manner, arrangements are required for dealing with the information trade among subsystems of an IoT-empowered energy framework [132–134]. A methodology for discovering answers for the reconciliation challenge, considering the IoT necessities of a subsystem, relates to displaying a coordinated structure for the energy framework [132]. Different arrangements propose structuring co-reenactment models for vitality frameworks to incorporate the framework and limit synchronization defer mistake between the subsystems [135, 136].

2.5.3 Client Privacy

Protection alludes to one side of individual or helpful energy purchasers to keep up privacy of their own data when it is imparted to an association [137, 138]. In this manner, getting to legitimate information, for example, the quantity of energy clients just as the number and kinds of apparatuses which utilize vitality become incomprehensible. In reality, these kinds of information which can be assembled utilizing IoT empowers better dynamic that can impact the energy creation, dispersion and utilization [139]. In any case, to diminish the infringement of clients' protection, it is suggested that the energy suppliers request client authorization to utilize their data [140], ensuring that the clients' data would not be imparted to different gatherings. Another arrangement would likewise be a confided in security the board framework where energy buyers have authority over their data and security is recommended [141].

2.5.4   Security Challenges

Web of Things is one of the advances that is getting very mainstream in vitality segment everywhere throughout the world. Organizations are utilizing this innovation to their focal points and there are certainly numerous preferences to procure from it also. From shrewd inventories to keen homes and even savvy structures IoT gadgets are all over the place and vitality division is beginning to utilize these gadgets to their advantage too. Other than the cost sparing and vitality preservation viewpoint there is another significant thing related with brilliant gadgets and IoT which is the heaps of business-basic information that is gathered from them. This information can help organizations in settling on brilliant choices and permit them to offer better types of assistance to their clients. One of the most presumed organizations all over Europe for information assortment and investigation explicitly identified with the vitality part is Electrigence. With aptitude and involvement with the applicable field, they are known for giving customer driven information arrangements that can assist organizations with developing utilizing IoT and large information.

In any case, the entire procedure of coordinating IoT gadgets in the total vitality framework is not a simple assignment for any organization and they face a few difficulties in the manner. This is one of the principle reasons why in spite of having various points of interest organizations at times stay reluctant in getting a full IoT-based upgrade to improve their framework.

One of the primary issues looked by power organizations in actualizing IoT-based arrangements is the multifaceted nature of the way toward coordinating this framework over the current one. Coordinating IoT innovation on any current stage can be a major test for any organization and the entire circumstance turns out to be considerably increasingly troublesome in the vitality division because of the mind boggling nature of the framework. For an organization lacking legitimate range of abilities, this mix turns out to be practically unthinkable which is the reason the undertaking is dropped before it even starts. In the event that electric organizations need to receive the full reward of IoT bases frameworks they ought to be happy to put resources into it first. Legitimate groups of specialists ought to be enlisted to actualize and direct the entire procedure of usage. Individuals ought to likewise be utilized to supervise the framework after its execution with the goal that the organization can get legitimate profit by these gadgets just as the information gathered from these gadgets.

Another issue that organizations face with respect to IoT gadgets in vitality arrangement is information security. There is a great deal of urgent buyer information engaged with this sort of arrangement which in an inappropriate can end up being awful for the shoppers and totally annihilate the notoriety of the organization. This is a significant motivation behind why organizations should reexamine and update their information security arrangements when they move toward an IoT-based framework. Organizations should do substantial interest right now well to ensure that all the information which they gather from buyers stays safe from cybercriminals. This extra venture is something that has made a great deal of organizations to reevaluate their choice with respect to IoT-based plan of action.

2.5.5   IoT Standardization and Architectural Concept

Extreme items produce enormous volumes of information. This information should be overseen, handled, moved, and put away safely. Institutionalization is vital to accomplishing all around acknowledged details and conventions for genuine interoperability among gadgets and applications.

The utilization of principles:

- Guarantees interoperable and practical arrangements
- Opens up circumstances in new regions
- Permits the market to arrive at its maximum capacity

The more things are associated, the more noteworthy the security chance. Thus, security principles are likewise expected to ensure the people, organizations and governments which will utilize the IoT. IoT utilizes an assortment of advances with various measures to interface from a solitary gadget to an enormous number of gadgets. The irregularity among IoT gadgets that use various principles shapes another challenge [147]. In IoT-empowered frameworks, there are two kinds of benchmarks, including system conventions, correspondence conventions, and information accumulation benchmarks just as administrative principles related to security and protection of information. The difficulties confronting the appropriation of gauges inside IoT incorporate the gauges for taking care of unstructured information, security, and protection issues notwithstanding administrative principles for information markets [148]. A methodology for beating the test of institutionalization of IoT-based vitality framework is to characterize an arrangement of frameworks with a presence of mind of comprehension to permit all on-screen characters to similarly access and use. Another arrangement relates to creating open data models and conventions of the benchmarks by the participating gatherings. This will bring about principles which are uninhibitedly and openly accessible [149].

IoT-empowered frameworks are made out of assortment of advances with expanding number of practicality interconnected gadgets and sensors. IoT is relied upon to empower interchanges at whenever, anyplace for any related administrations, by and large, in an autonomic and specially appointed manner. This implies that the IoT frameworks dependent on their application reasons for existing are planned by perplexing, decentralized, and, what is more, portable attributes [149]. Considering the qualities and necessities of an IoT application, a reference design cannot be a special answer for these applications. In this manner, for IoT frameworks, heterogeneous reference models are required which are open and adhere to measures. The models likewise ought not constrain the clients to utilize fixed and start to finish IoT interchanges [149, 150].

2.6   Future Trends

IoT is all over. Working connected at the hip with advancements like blockchain and AI, it is making a huge difference, from the manner in which we request food supplies, to the manner in which we keep up machines and gear. The utilizations of IoT cuts over all fields and ventures. From utility administration and transportation to instruction and horticulture, helping organizations to convey more an incentive to customers, decrease their uses, and eventually increment their overall revenue, along these lines, it is reasonable that practically all ground breaking firms currently have IoT procedures to develop their business. Notwithstanding, for people who are new to this, and working in areas of the economy that are not legitimately identified with innovation, it could all be a great deal to fold your head over. Along these lines, throughout the following not many articles, I will be sharing about how IoT is changing assorted enterprises, one industry after the other. This will include use cases, current industry patterns and future applications with the point of giving helpful knowledge to all trying to send IoT-based arrangements.

We will commence this arrangement by analyzing the uses of IoT in the energy business. We will take a gander at how IoT is being utilized or can be utilized to change the energy segment from vitality age to transmission, dispersion, and utilization.

In this session, we are presenting block chain technology, AI technology, and Green IoT (G-IoT) technology that can help to solve some problems.

2.6.1   IoT and Blockchain

Blockchain innovation could give a straightforward foundation to two gadgets to legitimately move a bit of property, for example, cash or information between each other with a made sure about and dependable time-stepped legally binding handshake. To empower message trades, IoT gadgets will use brilliant agreements which at that point model the understanding between the two gatherings. This element empowers the independent working of keen gadgets without the requirement for unified power. On the off chance that you, at that point stretch out this shared exchange to human-to-human or human-to-objects/stages, you end up with a completely circulated dependable computerized framework.

Blockchain enables the IoT gadgets to upgrade security and get straightforwardness IoT environments. As indicated by IDC, 20% of all IoT arrangements will empower blockchain-based arrangements by 2019. Blockchain offers an adaptable and decentralized condition to IoT gadgets, stages, and applications. Banks and Financial foundations like ING, Deutsche Bank, and HSBC are doing PoC to approve the blockchain innovation. Aside from money related establishments, a wide scope of organizations have wanted to encounter the capability of the blockchain. Then again, the IoT opens up endless open doors for organizations to run brilliant activities. Each gadget around us is presently furnished with sensors, sending information to the cloud. In this way, joining these two advances can make the frameworks effective as described in Figure 2.9 innovation in energy sector with blockchain and IoT.

Energy division leaders [18] and service organizations [78] have attested that blockchains might offer answers for difficulties in the vitality business. The German Energy Agency [18] claims that blockchain advances can possibly improve the productivity of current vitality practices and procedures, can quicken the advancement of IoT stages and computerized applications and can give development in P2P vitality exchanging and decentralized age. Furthermore, they report that blockchain innovations can possibly fundamentally improve current acts of vitality undertakings and service organizations by improving inside procedures, client administrations, and expenses [18]. Energy frameworks are experiencing a transformational change activated by the headway of disseminated vitality assets and data and correspondence advancements (ICT). One of the principle challenges is the rising decentralization and digitalization of the vitality framework, which requires the thought, investigation and reception of novel ideal models and appropriated innovations. Because of their inborn nature blockchains could give a promising answer for control and oversee progressively decentralized complex vitality frameworks and microgrids [15, 79, 80]. Coordinating little scope renewables, disseminated age, adaptability administrations and buyer cooperation in the vitality advertise is a requesting task. A few creators [79] contend that blockchains could give imaginative exchanging stages where prosumers

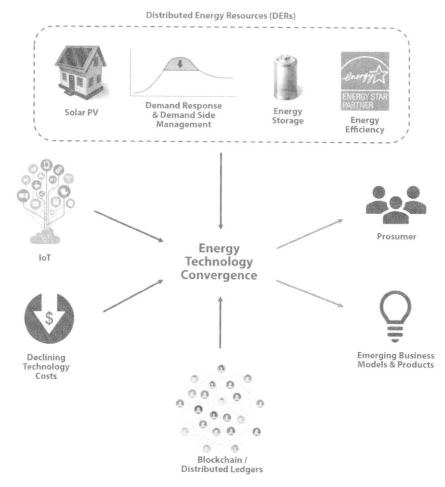

Figure 2.9 Innovation in energy sector with blockchain and IoT.

and shoppers can exchange conversely their vitality surplus or adaptable interest on a P2P premise. Dynamic purchaser cooperation can be made sure about and recorded into permanent, straightforward and carefully designed savvy contracts. Empowering such mechanized exchanging stages could be an effective method for conveying value signs and data on vitality expenses to purchasers [80], at the same time furnishing them with motivators for request reaction and keen administration of their vitality needs. Blockchains can empower neighborhood vitality and customer arranged commercial centers or microgrids that intend to help nearby power age and utilization [29]. One of the significant advantages from this methodology is diminishing transmission misfortunes and conceding costly system redesigns. Then again, vitality is as yet conveyed through the physical lattice, request and supply need to painstakingly be overseen and controlled to agree to genuine specialized imperatives and force framework solidness. As indicated by an as of late distributed report by Eurelectric [43], the physical trade of power has so far hindered bigger selection of blockchains in the vitality segment, instead of utilizations in the money division. Blockchains can safely record possession and causes of the vitality devoured or provided. Thus, blockchain arrangements could be used for brilliant charging courses of action and sharing of assets, for example network stockpiling or microgrids, yet in addition for utilizations of information stockpiling in keen matrices and cybersecurity [81, 82]. A key test as volumes of RES keep on expanding is keeping up the security of supply and improving system strength. By encouraging and quickening IoT applications and empowering increasingly effective adaptability markets, blockchains could improve arrange versatility and security of supply [79]. A report by the Research Institute of the Finnish economy [16] contends that blockchains could guarantee interoperability in practicality framework and IoT applications by offering open and straightforward arrangements. As indicated by Deloitte [20], vitality showcase activities could turn out to be progressively straightforward and proficient. Thus, this could improve rivalry and encourage customer versatility and exchanging of vitality providers. Whenever cost investment funds openings are acknowledged, we could use the innovation to enhance fuel neediness and energy moderateness issues.

By ideals of focal points offered, blockchains might give arrangements over the vitality trilemma: they could diminish costs by enhancing vitality forms, improve energy security regarding cybersecurity, yet in addition go about as a supporting innovation that could improve security of supply, lastly advance manageability by encouraging inexhaustible age and low-carbon arrangements.

2.6.2   Artificial Intelligence and IoT

The sustainable power source division is a developing financial power and a viable system toward improving natural maintainability. Man-made reasoning is being incorporated across significant segments of this industry, expanding the limit of information investigation.

The variable idea of climate presents innate difficulties which may make providers depend on conventional vitality sources to satisfy customer needs. Subsequently, AI-driven vitality estimating stages may hold guarantee for furnishing vitality providers with the information required to react to changes that may adversely influence activities and to design as needs be.

The IoT has become sweeping. It is in telephones, PCs, vehicles, fridges, car ports, windows, lighting installations, traffic lights—anyplace a gadget can be fitted with WiFi which can be remotely controlled, IoT has decent footings. Appropriately, the prevalence of information has extended, giving knowledge. Some portion of sustainable power source proficiency will include turning gadgets on and off when they are or are not required. Take streetlights. There are times where, factually, lights will be required—and times when they would not. Utilizing IoT and AI mechanization to decide such limits can help ration vitality, permitting inexhaustible sources to have more noteworthy adequacy. Artificial intelligence can likewise be utilized to consequently remind individuals relating to specific exercises that could conceivably monitor vitality. In the event that you left a light on in a room where no one is, an AI gadget could check an IoT movement sensor, decide abundance light is not required, naturally turn it off, cut your service bill, and preserve vitality. Utilizing such AI with neighborhood utilities encourages you locate the most practical Texas power plans for homes or organizations.

Figure 2.10 shows virtual power plant with artificial intelligence and IoT.

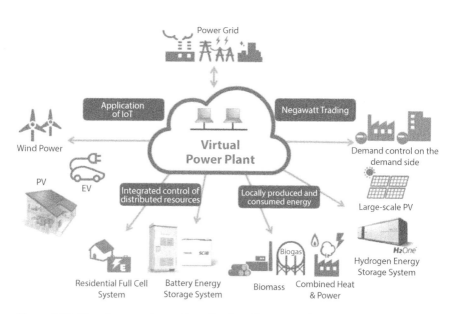

Figure 2.10 Virtual power plant with artificial intelligence and IoT.

2.6.3   Green IoT

The splendid eventual fate of G-IoT will change our tomorrow condition to get more beneficial and green, high QoS, socially and naturally feasible and financially moreover. These days, the most energizing territories center around greening things, for example, green correspondence and systems administration, green structure and executions, G-IoT administrations and applications, vitality sparing techniques, incorporated RFIDs and sensor systems, portability and system the board, the participation of homogeneous and heterogeneous systems, savvy articles, and green confinement. The following examination fields have should have been explored to create ideal and effective answers for greening IoT:

- There is a requirement for UAV to supplant a huge number of IoT gadgets particularly, in an agribusiness, traffic, and checking, which will assist with decreasing force utilization and contamination. UAV is a promising innovation that will prompt G-IoT with minimal effort and also high proficiency.
- Transmission information from the sensor to the portable cloud be progressively valuable. Sensor-cloud is incorporating the remote sensor system and portable cloud. It is a very hot and guaranteed innovation for greening IoT. A green interpersonal organization as an assistance (SNaaS) may explore for vitality productivity of the framework, administration, WSN and cloud of the executives.
- M2M correspondence assumes a basic job to diminish vitality use, dangerous outflows. Keen machines must be more brilliant to empower robotized frameworks. Machine computerization defer must be limited on the off chance that of traffic and making important and quick move.
- Configuration G-IoT might be acquainted from with points of view which are accomplishing amazing execution and high QoS. Finding appropriate methods for upgrading QoS parameters (i.e., data transfer capacity, deferral, and throughput) will contribute successfully and productively to greening IoT.
- While going toward greening IoT, it will be required for less vitality, searching for new assets, limiting IoT negative effect on the soundness of human and upsetting the earth. At that point G-IoT can contribute fundamentally to manageable practicality furthermore, green condition.

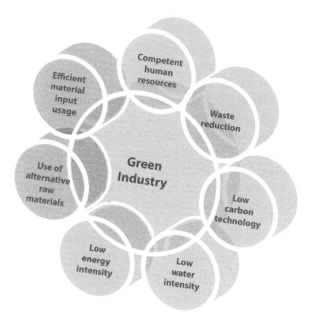

Figure 2.11 Green Internet of Things (G-IoT) as a crucial technology.

- In request to accomplish vitality adjusting for supporting green correspondence between IoT gadgets, the radio recurrence vitality collect ought to be taken into thought.
- More research is expected to build up the structure of IoT gadgets which assists with lessening CO_2 emanation and the vitality utilization. The most basic undertaking for shrewd and green ecological life is sparing vitality and diminishing the CO_2 emanation.
- Figure 2.11 shows the future trends in G-IoT.

2.7   Conclusion

Organizations in the matter of sustainable power source have been encountering generous worldwide development in the course of the most recent few years. Nonetheless, with colossal scaling comes the test of continuing benefits and profitability. Dealing with these continually extending matrices expects organizations to pay special mind to ways and strategies to streamline their abilities across remote areas. One of the manners in which organizations can drive effectiveness is by grasping the universe of IoT. By actualizing keen machines and associated contraptions, organizations can utilize cutting edge sensors to accumulate huge measures of constant vitality information and transmit it to the force lattice—for cutting edge stockpiling and examination. IoT sensors can empower ongoing observing of intensity networks while giving chiefs the chance to assemble information driven streamlining techniques.

They can likewise give better straightforwardness in the manner the energy is being devoured. That permits individuals to comprehend their vitality utilization propensities and modify them as needs be to advance use. IoT has improved the utilization of renewables radically. Energy utilities are currently utilizing the renewables to give predictable power stream to its residents. The IoT has just raised the reception of sun powered and wind vitality. Its applications are to be seen for geothermal, biogas, and hydroelectric force plants. According to a study, the worldwide geothermal asset base is considerably bigger than that of coal, gas, uranium, and oil consolidated. Unmistakably, renewables are the fate of presence. Their acknowledgment will step by step however certainly satisfy our developing power necessities.

IoT has entered the energy business, making changes and giving certain points of interest. It is giving advantages to the vitality supplier just as the vitality shopper, the new advancements, transmission, and utilization improvements are adding to more note worthy's benefit of saving energy. Notwithstanding these advantages, IoT still needs to confront a few difficulties in the energy business as a result of the obsolete existing frameworks and availability issues. IoT can likewise assist us with giving energy at less expense by reusing systems and cost-cutting techniques. Use of IoT with blockchain AI and G-IoT consolidated all together can change the entire energy industry by observing the energy stage equipment and decreasing work.

References

1. Stearns, P.N., Conceptualizing the Industrial Revolution. *J. Interdiscip. Hist.*, 42, 442–, 2011.
2. Mokyr, J., The second mechanical transformation, 1870–1914, in: *Storia dell'Economia Mondiale*, pp. 219–245, Citeseer, 1998, Accessible on the web: http://citeseerx.ist.psu.edu/viewdoc/download?doi=10.1.1.481.2996&rep= rep1&type=pdf (got to on 16 January 2020).

3. Jensen, M., The Modern Industrial Revolution, Exit, and the Failure of Internal Control Systems. *J. Financ.*, 48, 831–880, 1993. [CrossRef].

4. Kagermann, H., Helbig, J., Hellinger, A., Wahlster, W., *Suggestions for Implementing the Strategic Initiative Industrie 4.0: Securing the Future of German Manufacturing Industry*; Final Report of the Industrie 4.0 Working Gathering, Forschungsunion, Frankfurt/Main, Germany, 2013.

5. Witchalls, C. and Chambers, J., *The Internet of Things Business Index: A Quiet Revolution Gathers Pace*, pp. 58–66, The Economist Insight Unit, London, UK, 2013.

6. Datta, S.K. and Bonnet, C., MEC and IoT Based Automatic Agent Reconfiguration in Industry 4.0, in: *Proceedings of the 2018 IEEE International Conference on Advanced Networks and Telecommunications Systems (ANTS)*, Indore, India, 16–19 December 2018, pp. 1–5.

7. Shrouf, F., Ordieres, J., Miragliotta, G., Shrewd production lines in Industry 4.0: A survey of the idea and of vitality the board drew nearer underway dependent on the Internet of Things worldview, in: *Proceedings of the 2014 IEEE International Conference on Industrial Engineering and Engineering Management (IEEM)*, Selangor Darul Ehsan, Malaysia, 9–12 December 2014, pp. 697–701.

8. Bandyopadhyay, D. and Sen, J., Web of Things: Applications and Challenges in Technology and Institutionalization. *Wirel. Pers. Commun.*, 58, 49–69, 2011. [CrossRef].

9. Global Energy Agency (IEA), Worldwide Energy and CO2 Status Report, 2019. Accessible on the web: https://www. iea.org/geco/(got to on 27 September 2019).

10. Intergovernmental Panel for Climate Change (IPCC), Worldwide Warning of 1.5 C: Summary for Policymakers, 2018. Accessible on the web: https://www.ipcc.ch/sr15/section/spm/(got to on 27 September 2019).

11. Zakeri, B., Syri, S., Rinne, S., Higher sustainable power source joining into the current vitality arrangement of Finland–Is there any most extreme cut-off? *Vitality*, 92, 244–259, 2015. [CrossRef].

12. Connolly, D., Lund, H., Mathiesen, B., Keen Energy Europe: The specialized and monetary effect of one potential 100% sustainable power source situation for the European Union. Reestablish. Continue. *Vitality Rev.*, 60, 1634–1653, 2016. [CrossRef].

13. Grubler, A., Wilson, C., Bento, N., Boza-Kiss, B., Krey, V., McCollum, D.L., Rao, N.D., Riahi, K., Rogelj, J., De Stercke, S. *et al.*, A low vitality request situation for meeting the 1.5 C target and reasonable improvement objectives without negative discharge advances. *Nat. Vitality*, 3, 515–527, 2018.

14. UN, *Unique Edition: Progress towards the Sustainable Development Goals*, UN, New York, NY, USA, 2019.

15. Tan, Y.S., Ng, Y.T., Low, J.S.C., Web of-things empowered ongoing checking of vitality proficiency on fabricating shop floors. *Proc. CIRP*, 61, 376–381, 2017. [CrossRef].

16. Bhattacharyya, S.C., *Vitality Economics: Concepts, Issues, Markets and Governance*, Springer, Berlin/Heidelberg, Germany, 2011.
17. Tamilselvan, K. and Thangaraj, P., Units—An epic insightful vitality productive and dynamic recurrence scalings for multi-center inserted models in an IoT domain. *Microprocess. Microsyst.*, 72, 102907, 2020. [CrossRef].
18. Zhou, K., Yang, S., Shao, Z., Vitality Internet: The business point of view. *Appl. Vitality*, 178, 212–222, 2016. [CrossRef].
19. Motlagh, N.H., Khajavi, S.H., Jaribion, A., Holmstrom, J., An IoT-based mechanization framework for more established homes: An utilization case for lighting framework, in: *Proceedings of the 2018 IEEE eleventh Conference on Service-Oriented Registering and Applications (SOCA)*, Paris, France, 19–22 November 2018, pp. 1–6.
20. Da Xu, L., He, W., Li, S., Web of Things in Industries: A Survey. *IEEE Trans. Ind. Advise*, 10, 2233–2243, 2014.
21. Talari, S., Shafie-Khah, M., Siano, P., Loia, V., Tommasetti, A., Catalão, J.A., survey of shrewd urban communities dependent on the web of things idea. *Energies*, 10, 421, 2017. [CrossRef].
22. Ibarra-Esquer, J., González-Navarro, F., Flores-Rios, B., Burtseva, L., Astorga-Vargas, M., Following the advancement of the web of things idea across various application spaces. *Sensors*, 17, 1379, 2017. [CrossRef].
23. Swan, M., Sensor lunacy! the web of things, wearable processing, target measurements, and the evaluated self 2.0. *J. Sens. Actuator Netw.*, 1, 217–253, 2012. [CrossRef].
24. Gupta, A. and Jha, R.K., An overview of 5G arrange: Architecture and rising advances. *IEEE Access*, 3, 1206–1232, 2015. [CrossRef].
25. Stojkoska, B.L.R. and Trivodaliev, K.V., A survey of Internet of Things for keen home: Challenges and arrangements. *J. Clean. Push.*, 140, 1454–1464, 2017. [CrossRef].
26. Hui, H., Ding, Y., Shi, Q., Li, F., Song, Y., Yan, J., 5G organize based Internet of Things for request reaction in brilliant lattice: An overview on application potential. *Appl. Vitality*, 257, 113972, 2020. [CrossRef].
27. Petroşanu, D.M., Căruţaşu, G., Căruţaşu, N.L., Pîrjan, A., A Review of the Recent Developments in Integrating AI Models with Sensor Devices in the Smart Buildings Sector with the end goal of Attaining Improved Sensing, Energy Efficiency, and Optimal Building Management. *Energies*, 12, 4745, 2019. [CrossRef].
28. Luo, X.G., Zhang, H.B., Zhang, Z.L., Yu, Y., Li, K.A., New Framework of Intelligent Public Transportation Framework Based on the Internet of Things. *IEEE Access*, 7, 55290–55304, 2019. [CrossRef].
29. Khatua, P.K., Ramachandaramurthy, V.K., Kasinathan, P., Yong, J.Y., Pasupuleti, J., Rajagopalan, A., Application and Assessment of Internet of Things toward the Sustainability of Energy Systems: Challenges Support. Urban areas Soc., 2, 101957, 2019. [CrossRef].

30. Haseeb, K., Almogren, A., Islam, N., Ud Din, I., Jan, Z., An Energy-Efficient and Secure Routing Protocol for Interruption Avoidance in IoT-Based WSN. *Energies*, 12, 4174, 2019. [CrossRef].

31. Zouinkhi, A., Ayadi, H., Val, T., Boussaid, B., Abdelkrim, M.N., Auto-the board of vitality in IoT systems. *Int. J. Commun. Syst.*, 33, e4168, 2019. [CrossRef].

32. Höller, J., Tsiatsis, V., Mulligan, C., Avesand, S., Karnouskos, S., Boyle, D., *From Machine-to-Machine to the Web of Things: Introduction to a New Age of Intelligence*, Elsevier, Amsterdam, The Netherlands, 2014.

33. Atzori, L., Iera, A., Morabito, G., The Internet of Things: A study. *Comput. Netw.*, 54, 2787–2805, 2010. [CrossRef].

34. Hui, T.K., Sherratt, R.S., Sánchez, D.D., Significant prerequisites for building Smart Homes in Smart Cities based on Internet of Things advancements. *Future Gener. Comput. Syst.*, 76, 358–369, 2017. [CrossRef].

35. Evans, D., *The Internet of Things: How the Next Evolution of the Internet is Changing Everything*, vol. 1, pp. 1–11, CISCO White Pap, 2011.

36. Motlagh, N.H., Bagaa, M., Taleb, T., Vitality and Delay Aware Task Assignment Mechanism for UAV-Based IoT Platform. *IEEE Internet Things J.*, 6, 6523–6536, 2019. [CrossRef].

37. Ramamurthy, A. and Jain, P., *The Internet of Things in the Power Sector: Opportunities in Asia and the Pacific*, Asian Development Bank: Mandaluyong Philippines, 2017.

38. Jia, M., Komeily, A., Wang, Y., Srinivasan, R.S., Receiving Internet of Things for the improvement of savvy structures: An audit of empowering advancements and applications. *Autom. Constr*, 101, 111–126, 2019. [CrossRef].

39. Karunarathne, G.R., Kulawansa, K.T., Firdhous, M.M., Remote Communication Technologies in Internet of Things: A Critical Evaluation, in: *Proceedings of the 2018 International Conference on Intelligent and Imaginative Computing Applications (ICONIC)*, Plaine Magnien, Mauritius, 6–7 December 2018, pp. 1–5.

40. Li, S., Da Xu, L., Zhao, S., 5G Internet of Things: A study. *J. Ind. Inf. Integr.*, 10, 1–9, 2018. [CrossRef].

41. Watson Internet of Things, *Safely Connect with Watson IoT Platform*, 2019, Accessible on the web: https://www.ibm.com/web of-things/arrangements/iot-stage/watson-iot-stage (got to on 15 October 2019).

42. Kelly, S.D.T., Suryadevara, N.K., Mukhopadhyay, S.C., Towards the Implementation of IoT for Environmental Condition Monitoring in Homes. *IEEE Sens. J.*, 13, 3846–3853, 2013. [CrossRef].

43. *Newark Element. Keen Sensor Technology for the IoT*, 2018, Accessible on the web: https://www.techbriefs.com/segment/content/article/tb/highlights/articles/33212 (got to on 25 December 2019).

44. Rault, T., Bouabdallah, A., Challal, Y., Vitality proficiency in remote sensor arranges: A top-down review. *Comput. Networks*, 67, 104–122, 2014. [CrossRef].

45. Di Francia, G., The advancement of sensor applications in the divisions of vitality and condition in Italy,1976–2015. *Sensors*, 17, 793, 2017. [CrossRef].
46. ITFirms Co., *8 Types of Sensors that Coalesce Perfectly with an IoT App*, 2018, Accessible on the web: https://www. itfirms.co/8-sorts of-sensors-that-mix impeccably with-an-iot-application/(got to on 27 September 2019).
47. Morris, A.S. and Langari, R., *Level Measurement. In Measurement and Instrumentation*, second ed., A.S. Morris, and R. Langari, (Eds.), Chapter 17, pp. 531–545, Academic Press, Boston, MA, USA, 2016.
48. Pérez-Lombard, L., Ortiz, J., Pout, C., A survey on structures vitality utilization data. *Vitality Build.*, 40, 394–398, 2008. [CrossRef].
49. Moram, M., Lighting up Lives with Energy Efficient Lighting, 7, 4–9, 2012, Accessible on the web: http://aglobalvillage.organization/diary/issue7/squander/lightinguplives/(got to on 27 December 2019).
50. Riyanto, I., Margatama, L., Hakim, H., Hindarto, D., Movement Sensor Application on Building Lighting Establishment for Energy Saving and Carbon Reduction Joint Crediting Mechanism. *Appl. Syst. Innov.*, 1, 23, 2018. [CrossRef].
51. Kim, W., Mechitov, K., Choi, J., Ham, S., On track following paired closeness sensors, in: *Proceedings of the IPSN 2005—Fourth International Symposium on Information Processing in Sensor Networks*, Los Angeles, CA, USA, 25–27 April 2005, pp. 301–308.
52. Pepperl+Fuchs, *Sensors for Wind Energy Applications*, 2019, Accessible on the web: https://www.pepperl-fuchs. com/worldwide/en/15351.htm (got to on 27 December 2019).
53. Kececi, E.F., Actuators, in: *Mechatronic Components*, E.F. Kececi, (Ed.), Chapter 11, pp. 145–154, Butterworth-Heinemann, Oxford, UK, 2019.
54. Nesbitt, B., *Handbook of Valves and Actuators: Valves Manual International*, Elsevier, Amsterdam, The Netherlands, 2011.
55. Beam, R., Valves and Actuators. *Force Eng.*, 118, 4862, 2014.
56. Blanco, J., García, A., Morenas, J., Plan and Implementation of a Wireless Sensor and Actuator Network to Bolster the Intelligent Control of Efficient Energy Usage. *Sensors*, 18, 1892, 2018. [CrossRef] [PubMed].
57. Martínez-Cruz, and Eugenio, C., Assembling minimal effort wifi-based electric vitality meter, in: *Proceedings of the 2014 IEEE Central America and Panama Convention (CONCAPAN)*, Panama City, Panama, 12–14 November 2014, pp. 1–6.
58. Rodriguez-Diaz, E., Vasquez, J.C., Guerrero, J.M., Canny DC Homes in Future Sustainable Energy Frameworks: When proficiency and knowledge cooperate. *IEEE Consum. Electron. Mag.*, 5, 74–80, 2016. [CrossRef].
59. Karthika, A., Valli, K.R., Srinidhi, R., Vasanth, K., Robotization Of Energy Meter And Building A Network Utilizing Iot, in: *Proceedings of the 2019 fifth International Conference on Advanced Computing Communication Frameworks (ICACCS)*, Coimbatore, India, 15–16 March 2019, pp. 339–341.

60. Lee, T., Jeon, S., Kang, D., Park, L.W., Park, S., Structure and execution of keen HVAC framework in light of IoT and Big information stage, in: *Proceedings of the 2017 IEEE International Conference on Consumer Hardware (ICCE)*, Las Vegas, NV, USA, 8–10 January 2017, pp. 398–399.
61. Lee, Y., Hsiao, W., Huang, C., Chou, S.T., An incorporated cloud-based savvy home administration framework with network chain of command. *IEEE Trans. Consum. Electron.*, 62, 1–9, 2016. [CrossRef].
62. Kabalci, Y., Kabalci, E., Padmanaban, S., Holm-Nielsen, J.B., Blaabjerg, F., Web of Things applications as vitality web in Smart Grids and Smart Environments. *Gadgets*, 8, 972, 2019. [CrossRef].
63. Jain, S., Pradish, M., Paventhan, A., Saravanan, M., Das, A., Savvy Energy Metering Using LPWAN IoT Innovation, in: *ISGW 2017: Compendium of Technical Papers*, pp. 19–28, Springer, Berlin/Heidelberg, Germany, 2018.
64. Lee, J., Su, Y., Shen, C.A., Comparative Study of Wireless Protocols: Bluetooth, UWB, ZigBee, and Wi-Fi, in: *Proceedings of the IECON 2007—33rd Annual Conference of the IEEE Industrial Electronics Society*, Taipei, Taiwan, 5–8 November 2007, pp. 46–51.
65. Choi, M., Park, W., Lee, I., Savvy office vitality the executives framework utilizing bluetooth low vitality based reference points also, a portable application, in: *Proceedings of the 2015 IEEE International Conference on Consumer Electronics (ICCE)*, Las Vegas, NV, USA, 9–12 January 2015, pp. 501–502.
66. Collotta, M. and Pau, G., A Novel Energy Management Approach for Smart Homes Using Bluetooth Low Energy. *IEEE J. Sel. Reg. Commun.*, 33, 2988–2996, 2015. [CrossRef].
67. Collotta, M. and Pau, G., An answer dependent on bluetooth low vitality for shrewd home vitality the board. *Energies*, 8, 11916–11938, 2015. [CrossRef].
68. Craig, W.C., *Zigbee: Wireless Control that SimplyWorks*, Zigbee Alliance ZigBee Alliance, Davis, CA, USA, 2004.
69. Froiz-Míguez, I., Fernández-Caramés, T., Fraga-Lamas, P., Castedo, L., Structure, usage and commonsense assessment of an IoT home mechanization framework for haze processing applications dependent on MQTT and ZigBee-WiFi sensor hubs. *Sensors*, 18, 2660, 2018. [CrossRef].
70. Erol-Kantarci, M. and Mouftah, H.T., Remote Sensor Networks for Cost-Efficient Residential Energy The board in the Smart Grid. *IEEE Trans. Shrewd Grid*, 2, 314–325, 2011. [CrossRef].
71. Han, D. and Lim, J., Brilliant home vitality the board framework utilizing IEEE 802.15.4 and zigbee. *IEEE Trans. Consum. Electron.*, 56, 1403–1410, 2010. [CrossRef].
72. Han, J., Choi, C., Park, W., Lee, I., Kim, S., Brilliant home vitality the board framework including sustainable vitality dependent on ZigBee and PLC, in: *Proceedings of the 2014 IEEE International Conference on Consumer Hardware (ICCE)*, Las Vegas, NV, USA, 4–6 January 2014, pp. 544–545.

73. Batista, N., Melício, R., Matias, J., Catalão, J., Photovoltaic and wind vitality frameworks checking and building/home vitality the board utilizing ZigBee gadgets inside a shrewd network. *Vitality*, 49, 306–315, 2013. [CrossRef].

74. Augustin, A., Yi, J., Clausen, T., Townsley, W., An investigation of LoRa: Long range and low force systems for the web of things. *Sensors*, 16, 1466, 2016.

75. Mataloto, B., Ferreira, J.C., Cruz, N., LoBEMS—IoT for Building and Energy Management Systems. *Hardware*, 8, 763, 2019. [CrossRef].

76. Javed, A., Larijani, H., Wixted, A., Improving Energy Consumption of a Commercial Building with IoT and AI. *IT Prof.*, 20, 30–38, 2018. [CrossRef].

77. Ferreira, J.C., Afonso, J.A., Monteiro, V., Afonso, J.L., An Energy Management Platform for Public Buildings. *Hardware*, 7, 294, 2018. [CrossRef].

78. Gomez, C., Veras, J.C., Vidal, R., Casals, L., Paradells, J.A., Sigfox vitality utilization model. *Sensors*, 19, 681, 2019. [CrossRef].

79. Pitì, A., Verticale, G., Rottondi, C., Capone, A., Lo Schiavo, L., The job of brilliant meters in empowering constant vitality administrations for family units: The Italian case. *Energies*, 10, 199, 2017. [CrossRef].

80. Mekki, K., Bajic, E., Chaxel, F., Meyer, F., Outline of Cellular LPWAN Technologies for IoT Deployment: Sigfox, LoRaWAN, and NB-IoT, in: *Proceedings of the 2018 IEEE International Conference on Pervasive Registering and Communications Workshops (PerCom Workshops)*, Athens, Greece, 19–23 March 2018, pp. 197–202.

81. Nair, V., Litjens, R., Zhang, H., Improvement of NB-IoT organization for shrewd vitality conveyance systems. *Eurasip J. Wirel. Commun. Netw.*, 2019, 186, 2019. [CrossRef].

82. Pennacchioni, M., Di Benedette, M., Pecorella, T., Carlini, C., Obino, P., NB-IoT framework sending for savvy metering: Evaluation of inclusion and limit exhibitions, in: *Proceedings of the 2017 AEIT International Yearly Conference*, Cagliari, Italy, 20–22 September 2017, pp. 1–6.

83. Li, Y., Cheng, X., Cao, Y., Wang, D., Yang, L., Shrewd Choice for the Smart Grid: Narrowband Internet of Things (NB-IoT). *IEEE Internet Things J.*, 5, 1505–1515, 2018. [CrossRef].

84. Shariatmadari, H., Ratasuk, R., Iraji, S., Laya, A., Taleb, T., Jäntti, R., Ghosh, A., Machine-type correspondences: Current status and future points of view toward 5G frameworks. *IEEE Commun. Mag.*, 53, 10–17, 2015. [CrossRef].

85. Lauridsen, M., Kovacs, I.Z., Mogensen, P., Sorensen, M., Holst, S., Inclusion and Capacity Analysis of LTE-M and NB-IoT in a Rural Area, in: *Proceedings of the 2016 IEEE 84th Vehicular Technology Conference (VTC-Fall)*, Montreal, QC, Canada, 18–21 September 2016, pp. 1–5.

86. Deshpande, K.V. and Rajesh, A., Examination on imcp based grouping in lte-m correspondence for savvy metering applications. *Eng. Sci. Technol. Int. J.*, 20, 944–955, 2017. [CrossRef].

87. Emmanuel, M. and Rayudu, R., Correspondence advances for savvy network applications: An overview. *J. Netw. Comput. Appl.*, 74, 133–148, 2016. [CrossRef].

88. Webb, W., Weightless: The innovation to at long last understand the M2M vision. *Int. J. Interdiscip. Telecommun. Netw. (IJITN)*, 4, 30–37, 2012. [CrossRef].

89. Sethi, P. and Sarangi, S.R., Web of things: Architectures, conventions, and applications. *J. Electr. Comput. Eng.*, 2017, Hindawi Publication, 2017. [CrossRef].

90. Wei, J., Han, J., Cao, S., Satellite IoT Edge Intelligent Computing: A Research on Architecture. *Hardware*, 8, 1247, 2019. [CrossRef].

91. Sohraby, K., Minoli, D., Occhiogrosso, B., Wang, W., A survey of remote and satellite-based m2m/iot benefits on the side of keen lattices. *Crowd Syst. Appl.*, 23, 881–895, 2018. [CrossRef].

92. De Sanctis, M., Cianca, E., Araniti, G., Bisio, I., Prasad, R., Satellite Communications Supporting Internet of Remote Things. *IEEE Internet Things J.*, 3, 113–123, 2016. [CrossRef].

93. GSMA, Security Features of LTE-M and NB-IoT Networks; Technical Report, GSMA, London, UK, 2019.

94. Sigfox, Make Things Come Alive in a Secure Way; Technical Report, Sigfox, Labège, France, 2017.

95. Sanchez-Iborra, R. and Cano, M.D., Cutting edge in LP-WAN answers for mechanical IoT administrations. *Sensors*, 16, 708, 2016. [CrossRef].

96. Siekkinen, M., Hiienkari, M., Nurminen, J.K., Nieminen, J., How low vitality is bluetooth low vitality? near estimations with zigbee/802.15. 4, in: *Proceedings of the 2012 IEEEWireless Communications furthermore, Networking Conference workshops (WCNCW)*, Paris, France, 1 April 2012, pp. 232–237.

97. Lee, J.S., Dong, M.F., Sun, Y.H., A primer investigation of low force remote advancements: ZigBee and Bluetooth low vitality, in: *Proceedings of the 2015 IEEE tenth Conference on Industrial Electronics and Applications (ICIEA)*, Auckland, New Zealand, 15–17 June 2015, pp. 135–139.

98. Fraire, J.A., Céspedes, S., Accettura, N., Direct-To-Satellite IoT-A Survey of the State of the Art and Future Research Perspectives, in: *Proceedings of the 2019 International Conference on Ad-Hoc Networks and Remote*, Luxembourg, 1–3 October 2019, pp. 241–258.

99. Jaribion, A., Khajavi, S.H., Hossein Motlagh, N., Holmström, J., [WiP] A Novel Method for Big Data Analytics also, Summarization Based on Fuzzy Similarity Measure, in: *Proceedings of the 2018 IEEE eleventh Conference on Administration Oriented Computing and Applications (SOCA)*, Paris, France, 19–22 November 2018, pp. 221–226, [CrossRef].

100. Stojmenovic, I., Machine-to-Machine Communications With In-Network Data Aggregation, Processing, also, Actuation for Large-Scale Cyber-Physical Systems. *IEEE Internet Things J.*, 1, 122–128, 2014. [CrossRef].

101. Chen, H., Chiang, R.H., Story, V.C., Business insight and examination: From large information to enormous effect. *MIS Quart.*, 36, 4, 1165-1188, December 2012.

102. Intel IT Center, *Huge Data Analytics: Intel's IT Manager Survey on How Organizations Are Using Big Data; Specialized Report*, Intel IT Center, Santa Clara, CA, USA, 2012.

103. Stergiou, C., Psannis, K.E., Kim, B.G., Gupta, B., Secure combination of IoT and Cloud Computing. *Future Gener. Comput. Syst.*, 78, 964–975, 2018. [CrossRef].

104. Josep, A.D., Katz, R., Konwinski, A., Gunho, L., Patterson, D., Rabkin, A., A perspective on distributed computing. *Commun. ACM*, 53, 2010. MDPI Publication. [CrossRef].

105. Ji, C., Li, Y., Qiu, W., Awada, U., Li, K., Huge Data Processing in Cloud Computing Environments, in: *Proceedings of the 2012 twelfth International Symposium on Pervasive Systems, Algorithms and Networks*, San Marcos, TX, USA, 13–15 December 2012, pp. 17–23.

106. Encourage, I., Zhao, Y., Raicu, I., Lu, S., Distributed computing and Grid Computing 360-Degree Compared, in: *Proceedings of the 2008 Grid Computing Environments Workshop*, Austin, TX, USA, 16 November 2008, pp. 1–10.

107. Hamdaqa, M. and Tahvildari, L., Distributed computing Uncovered: A Research Landscape. *Adv. Comput.*, 86, 41–85, Elsevier: Amsterdam, The Netherlands, 2012.

108. Khan, Z., Anjum, A., Kiani, S.L., Cloud Based Big Data Analytics for Smart Future Cities, in: *Proceedings of the 2013 IEEE/ACM sixth International Conference on Utility and Cloud Computing*, Dresden, Germany, 9–12 December 2013, pp. 381–386.

109. Mahmud, R., Kotagiri, R., Buyya, R., Mist processing: A scientific classification, review and future bearings, in: *Internet of Everything*, pp. 103–130, Springer, Berlin/Heidelberg, Germany, 2018.

110. Verma, M., Bhardwaj, N., Yadav, A.K., Ongoing proficient planning calculation for load adjusting in haze registering condition. *Int. J. Comput. Sci. Inf. Technol.*, 8, 1–10, 2016. [CrossRef].

111. Atlam, H.F., Walters, R.J., Wills, G.B., Mist figuring and the web of things: A survey. *Large Data Cogn. Comput.*, 2, 10, 2018. [CrossRef].

112. Bhardwaj, A., *Utilizing the Internet of Things and Analytics for Smart Energy Management*, TATA Consultancy Administrations, Mumbai, India, 2015.

113. Sigfox, Inc., *Utilities and Energy*, Research Gate Publication, 2019, Accessible on the web: https://www.sigfox.com/en/utilities-vitality/ (gotten to on 27 September 2019).

114. Immelt, J.R., *The Future of Electricity Is Digital; Technical Report*, General Electric, Boston, MA, USA, 2015.

115. Al-Ali, A., Web of things job in the sustainable power source assets. *Vitality Proc.*, 100, 34–38, 2016. [CrossRef].

116. Karnouskos, S., The helpful web of things empowered keen network, in: *Proceedings of the fourteenth IEEE Worldwide Symposium on Consumer Electronics (ISCE2010)*, Braunschweig, Germany, 7–10 June 2010, pp. 7–10.

117. Lagerspetz, E., Motlagh, N.H., Zaidan, M.A., Fung, P.L., Mineraud, J., Varjonen, S., Siekkinen, M., Nurmi, P., Matsumi, Y., Tarkoma, S. *et al.*, MegaSense: Feasibility of Low-Cost Sensors for Pollution Hot-spot Recognition, in: *Proceedings of the 2019 IEEE seventeenth International Conference on Industrial Informatics (INDIN)*, Helsinki-Espoo, Finland, 23–25 July 2019.

118. Ejaz, W., Naeem, M., Shahid, A., Anpalagan, A., Jo, M., Effective vitality the executives for the web of things in shrewd urban areas. *IEEE Commun. Mag.*, 55, 84–91, 2017. [CrossRef].

119. Mohanty, S.P., All that you needed to think about shrewd urban areas: The Internet of things is the spine. *IEEE Consum. Electron. Mag.*, 5, 60–70, 2016. [CrossRef].

120. Hossain, M., Madlool, N., Rahim, N., Selvaraj, J., Pandey, A., Khan, A.F., Job of shrewd network in sustainable vitality: A review. *Restore. Support. Vitality Rev.*, 60, 1168–1184, 2016. [CrossRef].

121. Karnouskos, S., Colombo, A.W., Lastra, J.L.M., Popescu, C., Towards the vitality productive future manufacturing plant, in: *Proceedings of the 2009 seventh IEEE International Conference on Industrial Informatics*, Cardiff, UK, 23–26 June 2009, pp. 367–371.

122. Avci, M., M.E., Asfour, S., Private HVAC load control methodology continuously power evaluating condition, in: *Proceedings of the 2012 IEEE Conference on Energytech*, Cleveland, OH, USA, 29–31 May 2012, pp. 1–6.

123. Vakiloroaya, V., Samali, B., Fakhar, A., Pishghadam, K., An audit of various techniques for HVAC vitality sparing. *Vitality Convers. Manage.*, 77, 738–754, 2014. [CrossRef].

124. Arasteh, H., Hosseinnezhad, V., Loia, V., Tommasetti, A., Troisi, O., Shafie-khah, M., Siano, P., IoT-based keen urban areas: A review, in: *Proceedings of the 2016 IEEE sixteenth International Conference on Environment and Electrical Engineering (EEEIC)*, Florence, Italy, 7–10 June 2016, pp. 1–6.

125. Lee, C. and Zhang, S., Advancement of an Industrial Internet of Things Suite for Smart Factory towards Re-industrialization in Hong Kong, in: *Proceedings of the sixth International Workshop of Advanced Assembling and Automation*, Manchester, UK, 10–11 November 2016.

126. Reinfurt, L., Falkenthal, M., Breitenbücher, U., Leymann, F., Applying IoT Patterns to Smart Factory Systems, in: *Proceedings of the 2017 Advanced Summer School on Service Oriented Computing (Summer SOC)*, Hersonissos, Greece, 25–30 June 2017.

127. Kaur, N. and Sood, S.K., A vitality effective design for the Internet of Things (IoT). *IEEE Syst. J.*, 11, 796–805, 2015. [CrossRef].

128. Shaikh, F.K., Zeadally, S., Exposito, E., Empowering advances for green web of things. *IEEE Syst. J.*, 11, 983–994, 2015. [CrossRef].

129. Lin, Y., Chou, Z., Yu, C., Jan, R., Ideal and Maximized Configurable Power Saving Protocols for Crown BasedWireless Sensor Networks. *IEEE Trans. Horde. Comput.*, 14, 2544–2559, 2015. [CrossRef].

130. Anastasi, G., Conti, M., Di Francesco, M., Passarella, A., Vitality protection in remote sensor systems: A review. *Impromptu Netw.*, 7, 537–568, 2009. [CrossRef].

131. Shakerighadi, B., Anvari-Moghaddam, A., Vasquez, J.C., Guerrero, J.M., Web of Things for Modern Vitality Systems: State-of-the-Art, Challenges, and Open Issues. *Energies*, 11, 1252, 2018. [CrossRef].

132. Anjana, K. and Shaji, R., A survey on the highlights and innovations for vitality productivity of keen framework. *Int. J. Vitality Res.*, 42, 936–952, 2018. [CrossRef].

133. Boroojeni, K., Amini, M.H., Nejadpak, A., Dragičević, T., Iyengar, S.S., Blaabjerg, F.A., Novel Cloud-Based Stage for Implementation of Oblivious Power Routing for Clusters of Microgrids. *IEEE Access*, 5, 607–619, 2017. [CrossRef].

134. Kounev, V., Tipper, D., Levesque, M., Grainger, B.M., Mcdermott, T., Reed, G.F., A microgrid co-reenactment structure, in: *Proceedings of the 2015 Workshop on Modeling and Simulation of Cyber-Physical Energy Frameworks (MSCPES)*, Seattle, WA, USA, 13 April 2015, pp. 1–6.

135. Wong, T.Y., Shum, C., Lau, W.H., Chung, S., Tsang, K.F., Tse, C., Demonstrating and co-recreation of IEC61850-based microgrid insurance, in: *Proceedings of the 2016 IEEE International Conference on Smart Network Communications (SmartGridComm)*, Sydney, Australia, 6–9 November 2016, pp. 582–587.

136. Porambage, P., Ylianttila, M., Schmitt, C., Kumar, P., Gurtov, A., Vasilakos, A.V., The mission for security in the web of things. *IEEE Cloud Comput.*, 3, 36–45, 2016. [CrossRef].

137. Chow, R., The Last Mile for IoT Privacy. *IEEE Secur. Priv.*, 15, 73–76, 2017. [CrossRef].

138. Jayaraman, P.P., Yang, X., Yavari, A., Georgakopoulos, D., Yi, X., Security protecting Internet of Things: From security systems to an outline design and proficient execution. *Future Gener. Comput. Syst.*, 76, 540–549, 2017.

139. Roman, R., Najera, P., Lopez, J., Making sure about the web of things. Scientific Research, PC 44, 51–58, 2011.

140. Fhom, H.S., Kuntze, N., Rudolph, C., Cupelli, M., Liu, J., Monti, A., A client driven security chief for future vitality frameworks, in: *Proceedings of the 2010 International Conference on Power System Technology*, Hangzhou, China, 24–28 October 2010, pp. 1–7.

141. Dorri, A., Kanhere, S.S., Jurdak, R., Gauravaram, P., Blockchain for IoT security and protection: The contextual analysis of a savvy home, in: *Proceedings of the 2017 IEEE International Conference on Pervasive Computing and Interchanges Workshops (PerCom Workshops)*, Kona, HI, USA, 13–17 March 2017, pp. 618–623.

142. Poyner, I. and Sherratt, R.S., Protection and security of shopper IoT gadgets for the unavoidable checking of defenseless individuals, in: *Proceedings of the Living in the Internet of Things: Cybersecurity of the IoT—2018*, London, UK, 28–29 March 2018, pp. 1–5.

143. Li, Z., Shahidehpour, M., Aminifar, F., Cybersecurity in dispersed force frameworks. *Proc. IEEE*, 105, 1367–1388, 2017. [CrossRef].

144. Tune, T., Li, R., Mei, B., Yu, J., Xing, X., Cheng, X., A security saving correspondence convention for IoT applications in savvy homes. *IEEE Internet Things J.*, 4, 1844–1852, 2017. [CrossRef].

145. Roman, R. and Lopez, J., Security in the conveyed web of things, in: *Proceedings of the 2012 International Gathering on Trusted Systems*, London, UK, 17–18 December 2012, pp. 65–66.

146. Meddeb, A., Web of things measures: Who stands apart from the group? *IEEE Commun. Mag.*, 54, 40–47, 2016. [CrossRef].

147. Banafa, A., IoT Standardization and Implementation Challenges, 2016, Accessible on the web: https://iot.ieee.org/ bulletin/july-2016/iot-institutionalization and-execution challenges.html (got to on 10 May 2019).

148. Chen, S., Xu, H., Liu, D., Hu, B., Wang, H.A., Vision of IoT: Applications, Challenges, and Opportunitie With China Perspective. *IEEE Internet Things J.*, 1, 349–359, 2014. [CrossRef].

149. Al-Qaseemi, S.A., Almulhim, H.A., Almulhim, M.F., Chaudhry, S.R., IoT architecture challenges and issues Lack of standardization, in: *Proceedings of the 2016 Future Technologies Conference (FTC)*, San Francisco, CA, USA, 6–7 December 2016, pp. 731–738.

150. Kshetri, N., Can Blockchain Strengthen the Internet of Things? *IT Prof.*, 19, 68–72, 2017. [CrossRef].

151. Dorri, A., Kanhere, S.S., Jurdak, R., Towards an optimized blockchain for IoT, in: *Proceedings of the Second International Conference on Internet-of-Things Design and Implementation*, Pittsburgh, PA, USA, 18–21 April 2017, pp. 173–178.

152. Huh, S., Cho, S., Kim, S., Managing IoT devices using blockchain platform, in: *Proceedings of the 2017 19th International Conference on Advanced Communication Technology (ICACT)*, Bongpyeong, Korea, 19–22 February 2017, pp. 464–467.

153. Alladi, T., Chamola, V., Rodrigues, J.J., Kozlov, S.A., Blockchain in Smart Grids: A Review on Different Us Cases. *Sensors*, 19, 4862, 2019. [CrossRef].

154. Christidis, K. and Devetsikiotis, M., Blockchains and Smart Contracts for the Internet of Things. *IEEE Access*, 4, 2292–2303, 2016. [CrossRef].

155. Korpela, K., Hallikas, J., Dahlberg, T., Digital Supply Chain Transformation toward Blockchain Integration, in: *Proceedings of the 50th Hawaii International Conference on Ssystem Sciences*, Waikoloa, HI, USA, 4–7 January 2017.

156. Hawlitschek, F., Notheisen, B., Teubner, T., The limits of trust-free systems: A literature review on blockchain technology and trust in the sharing economy. *Electron. Commer. Res. Appl.*, 29, 50–63, 2018. [CrossRef].

157. Conoscenti, M., Vetro, A., De Martin, J.C., Blockchain for the Internet of Things: A systematic literature review, in: *Proceedings of the 2016 IEEE/*

ACS 13th International Conference of Computer Systems and Applications (AICCSA), Agadir, Morocco, 29 November–2 December 2016, pp. 1–6.

158. Boudguiga, A., Bouzerna, N., Granboulan, L., Olivereau, A., Quesnel, F., Roger, A., Sirdey, R., Towards better availability and accountability for iot updates by means of a blockchain, in: *Proceedings of the 2017 IEEE European Symposium on Security and Privacy Workshops (EuroS&PW)*, Paris, France, 26–28 April 2017, pp. 50–58.

159. Samaniego, M. and Deters, R., Blockchain as a Service for IoT, in: *Proceedings of the 2016 IEEE International Conference on Internet of Things (iThings) and IEEE Green Computing and Communications (GreenCom) and IEEE Cyber, Physical and Social Computing (CPSCom) and IEEE Smart Data (SmartData)*, Chengdu, China, 15–18 December 2016, pp. 433–436.

160. Zhu, C., Leung, V.C.M., Shu, L., Ngai, E.C., Green Internet of Things for Smart World. *IEEE Access*, 3, 2151–2162, 2015. [CrossRef].

161. Abedin, S.F., Alam, M.G.R., Haw, R., Hong, C.S., A system model for energy efficient green-IoT network, in: *Proceedings of the 2015 International Conference on Information Networking (ICOIN)*, Siem Reap, Cambodia, 12–14 January 2015, pp. 177–182.

162. Nguyen, D., Dow, C., Hwang, S., An Efficient Traffic Congestion Monitoring System on Internet of Vehicles. *Wirel. Commun. Mob. Comput.*, 2018, 2018. Hindawi. [CrossRef].

163. Namboodiri, V. and Gao, L., Energy-Aware Tag Anticollision Protocols for RFID Systems. *IEEE Trans. Mob. Comput.*, 9, 44–59, 2010. [CrossRef].

164. Li, T., Wu, S.S., Chen, S., Yang, M.C.K., Generalized Energy-Efficient Algorithms for the RFID Estimation Problem. *IEEE/ACM Trans. Netw.*, 20, 1978–1990, 2012. [CrossRef].

165. Xu, X., Gu, L., Wang, J., Xing, G., Cheung, S., Read More with Less: An Adaptive Approach to Energy-Efficient RFID Systems. *IEEE J. Sel. Areas Commun.*, 29, 1684–1697, 2011. [CrossRef].

166. Klair, D.K., Chin, K., Raad, R.A., Survey and Tutorial of RFID Anti-Collision Protocols. *IEEE Commun. Surv. Tutorials*, 12, 400–421, 2010. [CrossRef].

167. Lee, C., Kim, D., Kim, J., An Energy Efficient Active RFID Protocol to Avoid Overhearing Problem. *IEEE Sens. J.*, 14, 15–24, 2014. [CrossRef].

168. Marinakis, V.; Doukas, H. An Advanced IoT-based System for Intelligent Energy Management in Buildings. *Sensors*, 2018.

3

Energy-Efficient Routing Infrastructure for Green IoT Network

Pradeep Bedi¹, S. B. Goyal²*, Jugnesh Kumar³ and Shailesh Kumar⁴

¹*Department of Computer Science & Engineering, Lingayas Vidyapeeth, Faridabad, Haryana, India*
²*Faculty of Information Technology City University, Petaling Jaya, Malaysia*
³*St. Andrews Institute of Technology & Management, Gurgaon, India*
⁴*BlueCrest College, Freetown, Sierra Leone, West Africa*

Abstract

Smart world is envisioned as an era in which objects (e.g., watches, mobile phones, and smart devices) can automatically and intelligently collaboratively serve people. The Internet of Things (IoT) is a technology that connects everything to the smart world. To achieve a feasible smart scenario, this chapter discusses different technologies and their challenges to achieve the target of green IoT. While the implementation of energy-efficient communication in large-scale IoT systems has become a major challenge in recent years. The primary need in such networks is to minimize the overall power consumption of battery-powered devices to reduce data transmission costs and extend network life. In this work, there is a need for a scalable and energy-efficient scheme for heterogeneous nodes for green IoT. There is a need to design energy-efficient techniques for power conservation used by IoT nodes to guarantee a long-lived network. Particularly, in this chapter, an overview regarding IoT and Green IoT is discussed first. Then, an analysis of different energy-aware machine learning methodologies is performed for giving direction toward future enhancements in green IoT.

Keywords: WSN IoT, green IoT, energy efficiency, routing protocol, machine learning

**Corresponding author*: drsbgoyal@gmail.com

Roshani Raut, Sandeep Kautish, Zdzislaw Polkowski, Anil Kumar and Chuan-Ming Liu (eds.) Green Internet of Things and Machine Learning: Towards a Smart Sustainable World, (87–112) © 2022 Scrivener Publishing LLC

3.1   Introduction

The Internet of Things (IoT) can be regarded from a broad context as a prospect with technological and social impacts. IoT can be regarded from a technical standardization point of view as a digital infrastructure for the knowledge community, facilitating the interconnection of things (physical and virtually) based on established and evolving interoperable systems of information and communications [1]. The IoT uses materials to deliver resources to all customers using information management, collection, and communication methods while maintaining the required privacy. IoT is designed with the basic six elements described in Figure 3.1.

Identification is quite important for services as it plays a vital role while balancing the requirements of services. For example, ubiquitous codes (uCode) and electronic product codes (EPC) are for the identification of IoT services. Sensing is for the collection of data and to transfer it for storage to database, warehouse, data center, etc. [2]. The data collected was further analyzed to carry out effective measures depending on the requisite resources. Sensors can include moisture sensors, moisture sensors, portable sensors, and smartphones. Communication systems incorporate heterogeneous objects to provide advanced facilities. The network communication protocols required for the services of IoT are such as Bluetooth, Cellular,

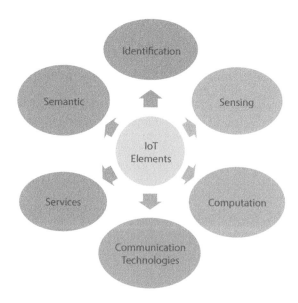

Figure 3.1 Key elements of IoT.

Z-wave, and IEEE 802.15.4. The role is performed in hardware process-ing units such as microcontrollers, microprocessors, chip systems (SoCs) and FPGAs, and computer software programs. A variety of hardware sys-tems were designed and software frameworks were used, such as Arduino, UDOO, Friendly ARM, Intel Galileo, Raspberry Pi, and Gadgeteer (e.g., TinyOS, Riot OS, and LiteOS) [3].

Generally, IoT services operate in four forms:

- Services of identity
- Services of aggregation of data
- Services of collaborative
- Ubiquitous services

Applications linked to identity set the basis for other services. So, the objects must first be identified in the virtual world for each application mapping real-life objects. It captures and summarizes raw data that needs to be gathered and documented for knowledge aggregation services.

In addition to making decisions, shared information resources use the data gathered to respond. Ubiquitous networks are intended to offer collaborative services to individuals on request, whenever and whenever [4]. Semantic displays the capability to collect information intelligently to have the neces-sary tools. This includes a description of resources, utilization of resources, simulation of information, object detection, and analysis. Semantic technol-ogies are widely used: Efficient XML interchange (EXI), resource description framework (RDF), web ontology language (OWL), etc.

3.2   Overview of IoT

IoT has transformed the world. One of the most relevant research subjects has been known to be IoT. The relationship between passive and active networked devices is characteristic of IoT. Communication between IoT devices is possible anytime and anywhere via some link with services as shown in the Figure 3.2. The IoT is a multi-faceted environment with several different nodes, including sensors, Radio Frequency Identification (RFID) tags, RFID scanners, and handheld devices. Moreover, in every area of our lives, numerous IoT innovations are available, including defense, market-ing, and healthcare. The IoT is also a framework that includes protocols, events, and big data analysis, and not only is a network for data transfer.

Moreover, the development of IoT does not require human intervention; it could therefore be used in artificial intelligence applications. The evolution of IoT brings both options and risks. IoT analysis challenges face multiple problems, including processing and storing of data, routing, distribution of

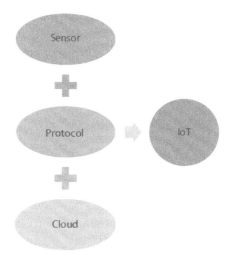

Figure 3.2 IoT system.

multimedia, anonymity, accessibility, and power management. It is common knowledge that IoT applications often need long-term battery-based nodes without human interference. This node will exhaust its batteries in a short time in the absence of energy conservation techniques. Furthermore, an IoT application can only accomplish its function until its nodes are alive [5].

The aim of every energy efficiency and control technology is therefore to optimize the entire life of the network. Energy intake thus poses one of the most relevant and multidimensional problems in the IoT world. The issue of energy saving without compromising IoT quality can be summed up in this challenge. The energy-dependent IoT nodes have various kinds of implementations, including the Wireless Sensors Network (WSN), the RFID network, and the mobile ad hoc network (MANET). Due to different existing techniques, this cannot be extended to the IoT climate. It is also difficult to find a solution to reduce energy consumption (if not impossible). The following thing could be demonstrated by each energy-based node's using various software and hardware specifications and functions.

An energy framework for smart homes was implemented by [6]. The heterogeneous existence of the IoT population is not considered important and only implemented for sensors along with the camera. Besides, it is not ideal for equipment that can move large volumes of data in the IoT network.

Ku, *et al.*, [7], designed a clever energy utility for IoT. This framework was designed to gather electricity knowledge. Apart from the faulty tests that take into account the IoT infrastructure, the drawback of this technique was low failure tolerance. The energy monitoring device was suggested by Ku *et al.* [8].

As it is designed for a specific open-source group only, this framework is known as a particular system of purpose. Moreover, the experiments are not structured intensely to yield detailed results that confirm the researchers' argument.

Prathik, *et al.*, [9], suggested a method for calculating energy utilized by IoT technologies. There was no suggestion for a solution to the IoT energy problem. In the study, a solution to the energy problem was not indicated in the IoT. The concept itself even struggled to reflect the IoT's design.

Srinivasan, *et al.*, [10], introduced smart technologies to use IoT-based energy approaches using smart plugs but encountered no energy-critical levels in IoT-based nodes.

Suresh Kumar, *et al.*, [11], developed a system for energy extraction using IoT. The issue of IoT energy consumption is not dealt with, especially for unrenewable energy knots.

Machine-to-machine mapping interaction and energy consumption for energy management schemes development are reduced by [9]. This is a special use computer due to its services.

Chaouch, *et al.*, [12], author proposed a clever way to wirelessly charge smartphone sensors using IoT. Because of their tension on the WSN climate, this intelligent strategy's virtual testbed is not suitable if other strong nodes i.e., RFID are ignored.

Panahi, *et al.*, [13], the author proposed only the procedure for real-time control of energy levels in the IoT device.

Alaudin, *et al.*, [14], the author showed a hardware architecture that can modify the rate of power usage. Since only mobile nodes in the IoT environment are envisaged, this is considered a solution for a particular reason. Moreover, it did not have a good testbed to prove the study point.

Tcarenko, *et al.*, [15], developed an IoT-based energy storage network. In the IoT setting, a small number of energy-based nodes were investigated. However, this analysis did not report installations, simulations, or observations.

Azar, *et al.*, [16], developed a method based on edges. To minimize the size of transmitted data in IoT words, data compression is considered a compulsory operation. In certain IoT implementations, this method can therefore be implemented when lacking in other applications. There are also several other routes, such as those that are called special use alternatives for the use of electricity.

3.3   Perspectives of Green Computing: Green IoT

The study, analysis, and implementation of sustainable and eco-friendly computing are called green computing. The environmental condition of

Figure 3.3 Components of green computing.

the earth is getting poor continuously and there is a need for design eco-friendly architecture components, hardware, technology, and the algorithm [17]. So, we have the requirement of green computing. On average, a huge amount of power more than need is consumed by the computers that emit CO_2 in a large amount. Moreover, the disposal of computers is very hard because it is made up of hardware components having toxic materials. Especially, Green IoT has technologies of communication like Green Machine-to-Machine (M2M), Green RFID, Green Cloud Computing (CC), Green Data Center (DC), and Green WSN (Figure 3.3) [18]. A special kind of software and hardware is required in the technologies of green internet that are designed especially for less consumption of energy without decreasing the performance as minimizing the resources of utilization.

3.3.1   Green Radio-Frequency

It is the most seminal technology and experienced abundant enhancements over the years. It is the technology used in the device identification using radio waves [19]. Shortly, it is a mechanism of sense. It operates radio waves, which is the fact that makes it as well as its architecture distinctive. There are four distinct components of RFID as shown in Figure 3.4.

The key element in the identification of devices is "Tag". It has two different varieties: active tags and passive tags. Active tags own their power source (like batteries) for transmitting and receiving the signals. The passive tags depend on other readers for power because they do not own any source of power. These signals are used in the production of electromagnetic energy utilized by the tags to power themselves. The sent information from the tag is fetched by the RFID reader. The component that establishes the communication between the reader and the tag is "Antenna". It is like the heart of the technology of RFID, so the reader and tag must be confines in the range of radio waves for suitable functioning. It is an easy circuit for receiving signals and converting them into the form of radiations. Antennas are also small as per the small size of systems of RFID.

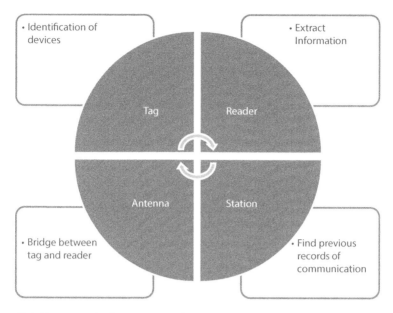

Figure 3.4 Components of green computing.

This results in a small bandwidth and small wavelength. The searching for tag or communication history between tag and reader are recorded by the "Station" which is the self-standing intelligent part of the system.

In multiple domains, RFID is used to track assets, in the commerce field, in retail applications, in inventory control, and in tracking the addition of new items and removal of the old item. It discovers the reason in the sector of access control for allowing access to the users of authority. Barcodes are used in place of magnetic strip to give control to users with the valid privilege. For example, the issued cards of the library require to place in front of the reader and after getting assuring feedback from a reader the owner of the card enter. RFID is an easy, efficient, and seminal technology. There are a lot of benefits; they impose many adverse impacts on the environment.

Green computing aims to develop and deploy a system of computers and their components that are environment friendly from the phase of manufacturing to the phase of disposal and not discard anything that cannot be roll backed. The components used in RFID cannot be recycled and are quite dangerous to the earth's environment. This results in a serious problem since recycling or disposal is the sector of the lifecycle of components of technology. Several organizations have taken already it for resisting and revealing the serious effect of components of primitive RFID and published by many papers for the revision of this fact. Barcoding is cheaper than RFID and, in several cases, the utilization of barcode readers can easily replace the RFID. RFID is a technology that is unique and requires high maintenance and frequent checking. The expert's installation, implementation, and monitoring of the reader are required. Components of RFID do not have the efficiency of energy in any way. The used protocols and algorithms required to focus on the collisions of the eliminating tag, overheating issues management, and use of algorithms that are dynamic and powerful for handling the reception and transmission of the signals.

3.3.2   Green Wireless Sensor Network

Wireless sensor network (WSN) contains several sensors connected from a distance over a network for monitoring and storing the information based on the reason of deployment, and chiefly, they record the humidity, temperature, etc. The possible first step is making the room capable of efficient power usage [20]. WSNs are inactive at a maximum time so the management of power in WSNs is not efficient. Keeping these sensors in the sleep mode at their idle time and getting them up at the time of reception or transmission is a very useful enhancement. This enhances the efficiency of the system as well as builds the system greener and smarter. Moreover, the sensors can take benefit from their deployment environment. For example, the solar energy can be used by the WSNs in place of the mobile WSNs and short-lived batteries.

3.3.3   Green Data Centers

The word data center is used commonly in the world of technology. All over the world, about 390–400 only DCs are established. That is why these centers are quite large that contain resources with trillions of capacities. According to the definition of DCs, it is considered to be a group of networked computer servers, storage services, and processing unit with high capacity (Figure 3.5). They contain either a large number of small servers or few numbers of large servers, all in a single room or a building [21]. These are termed as server farms.

DCs are divided into three distinct varieties [22]:

Centralized DCs: These are established in different areas all over the world with extra resources, for optimizing the usage of resources, these all are placed in a single location is called as consolidation of DCs.
Distributed DCs: A link of the distributed or interconnected DCs over a network for providing the services 24/7 wherever and whenever necessary.

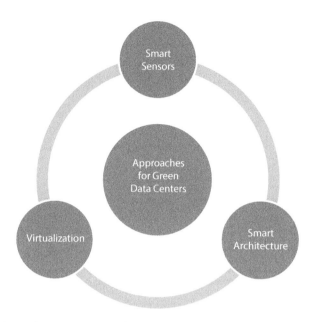

Figure 3.5 Green data center approaches.

Cloud-enabled DCs: These are current and trending technology linked with the centers of data satisfy services and needs dynamically, so Cloud-enabled DC are capable of providing services with the help of cloud from the centers of data, and the cloud is used as remote storage.

DCs required great resources and attention because they cause heat in a large amount and for cooling them, more resources are required. The centers of data can be constituted by changing them in the terminology of cooling mechanisms, used hardware equipment, in the used component in "chilling plants" or cooling towers and materials to supply power continuously. In short, we are finding ways to support the reduction in the consumption of power, better plans of architecture, new models implementing that architecture, and getting to bottom of searching alternatives of greener hardware. Finding the successful implementations renders us an idea of completing our goal, and different contributions are discussed in the following sections.

3.3.4   Green Cloud Computing

Cloud computing is used for accessing data in large amount remotely on the go, with no requirement of presenting physically and required an environment for classical work. Cloud term was used to represent the Internet because as the cloud is spread all over like that Internet is also available everywhere. Cloud computing is used to store, process, and control data from a remote location. The connection of the Internet is the primary need for cloud computing. Clouds are of four distinct kinds—private, public, hybrid, and community [23].

One of the categories of green computing is green cloud computing that transacts with the two major problems—reducing the consumption of energy and incrementing sustainability by installing effective algorithms, virtualization, and centers of green data. Green computing perceives the plan implemented for developing computers having 0 or little negative effect on the environment from the process of their manufacturing to disposal. Many findings and plans have already been raised some of them are, multi-method delivery of data linked with the sensors of cloud technology demonstrated to lower down the consumption of power and energy. The software of multi-method has more than one technique for analysing and collecting the data, to keep it simple, it has distinct techniques for handling the same activity and selects one of that technique suitable perfectly at that point of time. Cloud computing is dependent on the centers of data for its function [23].

Moreover, cloud computing focuses on the availability and flexibility of data, the centers of data take up large spaces, require the top resources or power, and eject CO_2 in huge amounts. So, the optimum solution for this issue is green substitutes. The green substitutes do not affect the service quality as much on being friendly to the environment.

3.3.5   Green Edge Computing

Green fog computing or green edge computing is a methodology that dispenses the load of required computation among different systems inside a fog or edge. It could rarely execute the sector of computation and remaining all the work is done via the cloud, or it could execute the complete job of processing by dividing it with other edges [24].

3.3.6   Green M2M

In IoT, Machine-to-Machine technology is the propensity of machines for intercommunication between them without any commands and actions directed by the human. The AI field is behind this, as we finding the techniques for building self-sufficient and intelligent systems, then we expect them to execute the tasks based on gained knowledge that results in better outcomes and actions than that of humans. Intelligent machines require a decided element for communicating with other machines, and few examples of that type of elements are wireless Internet connection with high speed, sensors for sharing the data on the area of discussion, RFID to sense juridical recipients, and required links of communication in the network. In several ways, M2M technology is very useful [25].

M2M can be implementable in the areas where the machines are useful or being used. In numerous places, the M2M technology changes the requirement of manual work; this is very beneficial in the dangerous areas where a human cannot go. At present, M2M technology is being already used in some industries or factories for manufacturing. It could also be installed in maintaining the regulation of traffic light and in preventing the jams of traffic on busy roads.

3.3.7   Green Information and Communication Technology (ICT) Principles

About 2%–2.5% of the global emission of CO_2 is caused by the technologies of communication and information, which is equal to industry carbon footprint [26]. Manufacture, design, in-use phases of servers, cooling systems, PCs, printers, decided and mobile telephony, and all government, IT, and commercial and infrastructure of telecommunications are covered in this calculation all over the world. On the other side, the technologies of communication and information are the main keys to the development of smart and efficient systems like cities, logistics, buildings, and smart grids. The sector of ICT could help in migrating the carbon footprint of sectors of other human activity like building, industry, logistics, and power transport by 15% and decrease the consumption of power by 10%. Using the best of ICT can enhance the energy efficiency of the environment of urban areas and services by implementing smart systems by considering three pillars: people, planet, and profit. Hence, the two very dominant theses of the approach of Green Economics can be formulated as follows:

- Greening ICT
- Greening by ICT

The following IEEE principles about green ICTs are presented by which the aforementioned introduction of greening ICT, greening ICT may be made possible [26]:

- Turn out equipment that is not needed: If the machinery works always, it uses a lot of electricity. However, power usage shall be minimized if used when necessary. For example, sleep programming is a common method of saving WSN energy consumption by dynamically control the active, idle, and sleep modes of the sensor nodes.

- Transmission when needed: Data transmission (e.g., high-scale multimedia data) uses a lot of resources. Transmitting only that required data for the user would significantly save electricity. Predictive data sharing is, based on an interpretation of user behavior, a feasible solution to presenting users with only the appropriate data.

- Minimization of the data path length: It is also considered a key aspect for reducing consumable energy. The energy-efficient routing systems which take into account the chosen data path length can be used. Network operating systems that follow the routing requirements are also possible for much shorter data routes in contrast.

- Minimization of wireless data path: Wireless networking networks should be known to minimize the duration of wireless data paths through energy efficiency technical architectures. Despite this, the shared transmission of wireless signals often promises to conserve resources by using relays to overhear and transmit the signal to the target node, leading to large increases in diversity.

- Processing trade-off: Data fusion prevents the sharing of similar data values by exchanging more complex data by combining the data from multiple sources. This increases energy efficiency. The modern approach to detect a signal with a much-reduced number of linear measurements will also improve energy consumption as the underlying signal is sparse.

- Advanced communication system: Advanced networking strategies are emerging for green communication. The Multi-Input Multi-Output (MIMO) signaling techniques employed by the transmitter and the receiver (Tx), for example, show increased spectral efficiency compared to their Single-Input Single-Output (SISO) counterparts in a fading environment in multi-way environments. Besides, a cognitive radio (CR) is aware of the environment through software and hardware manipulation will increase the spectrum's performance and reduce the problem of overcrowding by adapting its operating modes (working frequency, modulation scheme, waveform, transmission capability, etc.)

- Alternative renewable sources of green electricity: A resource that is automatically replaced and again available is a green resource, unlike traditional resources (e.g., biomass, solar energy, freshwater, wood, and oxygen). The use of renewable green energy sources also will have a fundamental impact on oil depletion and CO_2 emissions reductions.

3.4   Routing Protocols for Heterogeneous IoT

IoT is considered an intelligent network where a wide range of independent components such as control units, sensors, and wireless devices are integrated to accomplish difficult tasks [27–29]. Recently, the research community was very interested in IoT systems that are focused on developing heterogeneous networks for wireless sensors (WSNs). In several places, the WSN-based model IoT has been applied through easy access and connectivity with products and things, such as smart homes, smart buildings, smart grid, and smart city. Energy efficiency (EE) and energy usability are quite complicated issues related to such an IoT environment [30]. Frequent substitution of node battery in the exterior results in considerable running costs. In some circumstances, the power supply problem prohibits the construction of certain networks in a wide area. Consequently, battery power management by improving the EE of sensors and actuators is vital, effectively prolonging the existence of WSN-dependent devices in IoT Networks. The routing protocols have routing features (i.e., end-to-end packet transmission) to allow the connected devices' lifetime limit. Modules are heterogeneous in IoT networks [31–35]. Heterogeneity arises from power consumption, remaining energy, and capability of sense. Conventional routing protocols for homogenous networks cannot be tailored to the need for versatility in heterogeneous IoT networks. Energy harvesting (EH) has emerged as a primary enabler of field-deployable WSN and IoT technologies.

3.4.1   Energy-Harvesting-Aware Routing Algorithm

EH is considered the primary technology to allow the mass deployment of IoT products. Effective strategies for EH remove the requirements for regular substitution of energy sources, providing an almost lasting operating network environment. Advances in the technologies of EH have improved from "energy-aware" to "energetic-harvest-knowing" the routing protocol model for energy-harvesting IoT-based network wireless sensors applications [36]. It is intended by incorporating a new "energy-back-off" parameter to design an energy retrieval-conscious routing protocol for heterogeneous IoT networks in the presence of environmental energy supplies. Combined with various methods of energy collection, the algorithm increases the node's lifespan and network quality of service (QoS) under differing conditions of traffic and energy supply. Three energy recovery strategies listed below were applied by the author in [36].

Solar-based EH technique: The adaptably operated maximum power point tracker (MPPT) circuit has been introduced to provide a node architecture with solar-based energy capabilities. A tiny solar panel is used to capture sunlight energy.

Moving vehicle-based EH technique: In this EH-based model, moving vehicles were deployed. According to principle, every moving on-road vehicle creates pressure on the tire and creates weight that can generate a quantity of electricity on the surface of the road. The power harvest is composed of ceramic layers of lead zirconate titanate (PZT), a seismic mass at the middle, and a substrate. A cable connects the Harvester to the battery of the nodes available and it was assumed that energy loss was trivial.

RF-based EH technique: In this technique, the Long-Term Evolution (LTE) Frequency Division Duplex (FDD) physical downlink broadcast channel (PDBCH) and the physical downlink control channel (PDCCH) to follow an analysis of energy. Instead of data channels, the transmission sites were used to capture more resources. The transmitting rate and energy are set on the cable network while the power system was not necessary. Data sources also use electricity management equipment that absorbs energy harvested.

In this EH job, three separate scenarios were conducted. The first scenario offers three different types of harvesting processes simultaneously to produce electricity from the sun, traveling, and RF sources. In the second scenario, the domains are similarly split into three classes using EH from the solar system, EH from the driving vehicle, and EH from the RF system. In scenario 3, well, all nodes will take power from every form of electricity, either with a renewable EH or with an EH driving automobile or perhaps an EH dependent on RF. The findings of the simulation showed major changes in the accumulation of energy when fulfilling the QoS needs. The findings demonstrate that the use of several energy sources of the hybrid configuration represents a cost-efficient, effective, realistic approach that improves both EH and QoS problems at the same time and extends system life for diverse IoT applications.

3.4.2   Priority-Based Routing Algorithm

In [37], author studied the temperature heterogeneity energy (THE) apprised the protocol of routing for WBAN as standard's complement. "THE" targets to control the raising in temperature-induced sensors deployed on the body and enhance the comfortability of skin. "THE" maintains the conditions of the high-performance network in the terms of high packet output and long lifetime of a node. The data sensed is categorized into three levels of data with a priority of variable transmission to each level, emergency, namely, data priority 7, critical data assigned priority, and normal data assigned priority for satisfying these desired trade-offs. The protocol of "THE" is based on the function of utility that selects the WBAN's priority node (PN) having the remaining energy in the largest amount, least distance to the coordinator, the highest rate of data, and least temperature of sensor's. Looking for the data via PN is implementable for normal priority data while the data with high priority is transmitted to the coordinator in single-hop.

The algorithm frames several procedures:

Classification of Traffic: The two nodes [electrocardiography (ECG) and electroencephalogram (EEG)] are categorized from N nodes in the system as typical nodes and allotted the standard level of priority, which is applied for chief typical data transmitted periodically. But remaining, (N − 2) nodes are termed as normal nodes with the priority level of 5 and can be used for data transmitted periodically that may bear the delay.

Optimization of Hopping: The nodes categorized as critical directly transmit their data to cluster head node (CN) for fulfilling the requirement of minimizing latency in the protocol of "THE". In contrast, the nodes classified as normal transmit their data only to priority node (PN) nodes that are nearer to it for delivering it to the CN. However, the priority level of the normal node is set to 7, the level of emerging, where all other nodes are influenced suspend the operation on a temporary basis, thus enough resources are added for satisfying the necessities of emergency.

Selection of PN: PN node selection is a very typical problem for the protocol of "THE" because this node failure rapidly leads to loosing of earned data and was concerning to transmit to CN additionally for effecting far nodes performance. Therefore, the PN node selection is based on the function of a novel utility maximization. The results revealed the sensitivity in choosing the temperature allowed by nodes maximally which triggers the procedure of the node's sleeping.

3.4.3   Cluster-Based Routing Algorithm

In [38], author introduced an enhancement over the existing Stable Election Protocol (SEP) that executes the head section of cluster based on a threshold for heterogeneous network. The distribution of energy between nodes of cluster head and member nodes is maintained by the threshold. The sensor nodes are also classified into three distinct kinds called intermediate, advanced, and normal based on the supply of initial energy for evenly distributing the load of the network.

The sensing nodes link the CH based on information of their sent ADV message as the CH is elected in this algorithm. The clusters and CHs maintain changing for each cycle. The algorithm of Improved SEP (I-SEP) is perfectly fitted for monitoring the environment based on IoT in the terminology of lifetime and outcomes for different values of density of node. The changing of energy levels between member nodes and CH nodes which helps in the energy saving of the network is also done in this protocol.

The author in [39] designed an authentic rendezvous protocol of routing for the sensing infrastructure of IoT. First of all, an area for rendezvous within the middle of each vertical and horizontal direction is created. Then, a cluster within the area of rendezvous is created and created a structure like a tree within the rendezvous region additionally. Here, two methods of the transmission of information are designed between the IoT hub and sources. One path is via tree devices of resigns of rendezvous and the IoT hub modifies its information of location to tree device in the second path. The device at the source gets the information of the location of the hub from the nearest tree device and information is sent on the hub by the intermediate devices.

The terminology of Fuzzy-LEACH is introduced in [40] for optimizing the cluster head reorganization, incremented the network's lifetime, minimize the packet loss in wireless sink nodes.

3.4.4   Bioinspired Routing Protocols

There is a requirement for high and higher efficient algorithms and protocols that help in the superior functioning of the complete system with the development of IoT. In the network, the data routing can maintain the consumption of energy of the nodes of the network, network spreading, and also framing the smarter network so that it can be capable of making the decisions on its own based on previously collected data. Data Routing is a vital task in a network and energy can be saved in a valuable amount if the effectively routing in a network is done which is the problem of optimization with many prospects such as energy in node, path, traffic, and quality of the link. For solving these types of issues, GA (Genetic Algorithm) that consists of techniques of heuristic over the granted population of the network would give a convincing solution in an optimized manner. The execution of the algorithm of the type is obstructed because of the uncontemplated convergence, so these are not capable of search space traversing to have various solutions for saving the energy efficiently. For facing drawbacks of these types, improved GA operating of Local Search along with the mechanism of Sleep-Wake up was accepted by [41]. It optimizes the network of wireless sensor such that conservation of energy and network lifetime expansion occurs dynamically, via taking the constraints of communication and consumption of energy of sensors at the time of their communication and process.

In [42], author proposed a novel (routing protocol) based on optimization of ant colony for various agents that maintains the resources of network suitably in the conditions of real time. The method offered is used, both to search the next target of ants, and to maintain the pheromone modification and operators of evaporation rate. This methodology takes few parameters of key like buffer size, remaining energy, distance while choosing the next target under distinct conditions, and traffic rate into account. The methodology searches the optimal routes with the consumption of energy in a small amount thereby long-lasting the lifetime of the network in parallel and concurrent situations.

In [43], author proposed the routing protocol for the selection of multiple paths by deploying a tunicate swarm grey wolf optimization (TSGWO) algorithm for an IoT-assisted WSN scenario. With the application of this algorithm, multiple paths are selected for the transmission of data from source to destination IoT sensor nodes. This algorithm used clustering as a base routing protocol. In this, cluster head node is selected by fractional gravitational search algorithm (FGSA). The further multiple paths are selected by using TSGWO on multiple parameters such as fitness, trust factors, and QoS parameters. For optimal path selection, the fitness function selects the route with minimum distance.

In [44], author designed a hierarchical routing protocol for the lifetime improvement of the clustered network. For this, the algorithm used is termed as Fuzzy Multi-Criteria Clustering and Efficient Routing (FMCB-ER). This algorithm enhances the energy efficiency capability of WSN and results in green WSN. The robust clusters are formed using the TOPSIS method and further uses the Fuzzy-AHP for cluster head node selection. Three basic performance parameters are selected, i.e., QoS, energy, and node location. After optimal head node selection, the optimal path was selected by the algorithm, Emperor Penguin Optimization (EPO) for data transmission. This algorithm decreased the consumption amount of energy by 13%.

3.5   Machine Learning Application in Green IoT

IoT is considered to be one of the growing concepts that can directly connect several devices to communicate. The basic function of IoT devices is to sense, collect, and communicate the collected information over the internet from their environments. IoT devices consume energy while sending and receiving data among sensor nodes or devices. This results in the consumption of energy in large quantities and ultimately results in a decreased lifetime of the network. So, the placement problem of energy-harvesting IoT nodes and the determination of the best locations of the nodes are considered to be an issue. In the scenario of mobile IoT, there is a continuous change in the position of nodes and hubs.

This will cause a continuous update in the routing path which increases the overhead of energy consumption. Excessive energy consumption of such mobile nodes reduces the energy efficiency of the entire network. So, the optimal location needed to be decided that can prolongs the network lifetime. So, these issues have focused the researcher's interest in designing and developing such an algorithm that determines the optimal strategy to fulfil energy conservation requirements. For this Green IoT, is considered to be the most promising provision for a reduction in energy consumption by IoT devices. Apart from other conventional methods, the machine learning approach has proved to be one of the best solutions to achieve a feasible solution for Green IoT. Some of the applications of machine learning or deep learning in Green IoT scenarios are illustrated in Table 3.1.

Table 3.1 Contribution of machine learning or deep learning in Green IoT.

Approach	Application area	Description	Results	Ref
J48 machine learning	Smart Home	Analyzed the user behavior pattern along with the energy consumption pattern.	Approx. 13% energy saving.	[45]
ARIMA	Coffee Machine in Offices	Prediction of next week's usage. Reduced energy consumption.	80% of confidence level achieved.	[46]
Machine Learning	Green Building	Achieved QoS concerning energy efficiency.	-	[47]
Clustering	Green WSN	Detection of dead nodes in three conditions: first, half, and last. Focused on density in a region, relative distance, and residual energy for designing of energy-efficient WSN.	Network was alive for more than 10,000 rounds.	[48]
Dynamic clustering	Green WSN	The algorithm has equalized the demand power in the network.	BER = 10^{-1} to 10^{-4} Power consumption =approx. 5 MW	[49]

(Continued)

Table 3.1 Contribution of machine learning or deep learning in Green IoT. (*Continued*)

Approach	Application area	Description	Results	Ref
Deep Learning	Green WSN	Quality Prediction Phenomenon was used to select the cluster head node which enhances the network lifetime.	Execution time ~1 sec Throughput = 95%	[50]
Deep Belief Network	Green WSN	Balances the network load for efficient utilization of load and reduction in energy consumption.	Maximum execution time ~10 s.	[51]
Deep reinforcement learning	Green Edge	Optimal clustering of IoT users and results in optimal energy cost.	Cumulative system cost is between 10 and 15.	[52]
Greedy Q-learning	Green Edge	Task offloading scheme achieved a better trade-off performance between power consumption and task execution latency	Average service latency is between 10 and 20 ms.	[53]
Deep Reinforcement Learning	Green Edge	Energy-aware task offloading scheme	Average energy consumption is between 900 and 700 joule.	[54]

3.6 Conclusion

The IoT is considered to be an emerging technology that has gained the attention of researchers in the last few years. A large number of sensors and smart devices are connected to the IoT system that consumes a very large amount of power. Adaptation of IoT suffers constraints like limited energy and limited computation power. Therefore, these issues related to IoT adoption is an important focus of research. Many researchers focused their work to design reliable and energy-efficient routing protocols for routing data in the network. The concept of Green IoT resolves the issue of energy consumption of IoT devices that creates a sustainable working environment for IoT. So, the primary focus of this chapter is to analyze the power of machine learning for energy conservation for Green IoT communication.

References

1. Atzori, L., Iera, A., Morabito, G., The Internet of Things: A survey. *Comput. Networks*, 54, 15, 2787–2805, 2010.
2. Perera, C., Liu, C.H., Jayawardena, S., Chen, M., A Survey on Internet of Things from Industrial Market Perspective. *IEEE Access*, 2, 1660–1679, 2015.
3. Xu, L.D., He, W., Li, S., Internet of things in industries: A survey. *IEEE Trans. Ind. Inf.*, 10, 4, 2233–2243, 2014.
4. Perera, C., Liu, C.H., Jayawardena, S., The Emerging Internet of Things Marketplace from an Industrial Perspective: A Survey. *IEEE Trans. Emerging Top. Comput.*, 3, 4, 585–598, 2015.
5. Al-Fuqaha, A., Guizani, M., Mohammadi, M., Aledhari, M., Ayyash, M., Internet of Things: A Survey on Enabling Technologies, Protocols, and Applications. *IEEE Commun. Surv. Tutorials*, 17, 4, 2347–2376, 2015.
6. Salman, L., Salman, S., Jahangirian, S., Abraham, M., German, F., Blair, C., Krenz, P., Energy-efficient IoT-based smart home. *2016 IEEE 3rd World Forum on Internet of Things, WF-IoT*, pp. 526–529, 2017.
7. Ku, T.Y., Park, W.K., Choi, H., IoT energy management platform for microgrid. *2017 IEEE 7th International Conference on Power and Energy Systems, ICPES*, pp. 106–110, 2017.
8. Choi, C.S., Jeong, J.D., Lee, I.W., Park, W.K., LoRa based renewable energy monitoring system with open IoT platform. *International Conference on Electronics, Information and Communication, ICEIC*, pp. 1–2, 2018.
9. Prathik, M., Anitha, K., Anitha, V., Smart energy meter surveillance using IoT. *Proceedings of the International Conference on Power, Energy, Control and Transmission Systems, ICPECTS*, pp. 186–189, 2018.

10. Srinivasan, A., Baskaran, K., Yann, G., IoT Based Smart Plug-Load Energy Conservation and Management System. *International Conference on Power and Energy Applications, ICPEA*, pp. 155–158, 2019.

11. Suresh Kumar, S., Kaviyaraj, R., Jeni Narayanan, L.A., Saleekha, Energy Harvesting by Piezoelectric Sensor Array in Road Using Internet of Things. *2019 5th International Conference on Advanced Computing and Communication Systems, ICACCS*, pp. 482–484, 2019.

12. Chaouch, H., Bayraktar, A.S., Çeken, C., Energy Management in Smart Buildings by Using M2M Communication. *International Istanbul Smart Grids and Cities Congress and Fair, ICSG - Proceedings*, pp. 31–35, 2019.

13. Panahi, F.H., Moshirvaziri, S., Mihemmedi, Y., Panahi, F.H., Ohtsuki, T., Smart Energy Harvesting for Internet of Things. *Proceedings - 2018 Smart Grid Conference, SGC*, 2018.

14. Alaudin, A.H.B., Zan, M.M.M., Mahmud, A.R., Yahaya, C. K. H. C. K., Yusof, M.I., Yussoff, Y.M., Real-time residential energy monitoring device using internet of things. *ICSET 2018 - 2018 IEEE 8th International Conference on System Engineering and Technology, Proceedings*, pp. 97–101, 2019.

15. Tcarenko, I., Huan, Y., Juhasz, D., Rahmani, A.M., Zou, Z., Westerlund, T., Liljeberg, P., Zheng, L., Tenhunen, H., Smart energy-efficient gateway for Internet of mobile things. *2017 14th IEEE Annual Consumer Communications and Networking Conference, CCNC*, vol. 2017, pp. 1016–1017, 2017.

16. Azar, J., Makhoul, A., Barhamgi, M., Couturier, R., An energy-efficient IoT data compression approach for edge machine learning. *Future Gener. Comput. Syst.*, 96, 168–175, 2019.

17. Shaikh, F.K., Zeadally, S., Exposito, E., Enabling technologies for green internet of things. *IEEE Syst. J.*, 11, 2, 983–994, 2017.

18. Arshad, R., Zahoor, S., Shah, M.A., Wahid, A., Yu, H., Green IoT: An investigation on energy saving practices for 2020 and beyond. *IEEE Access*, 5, 15667–15681, 2017.

19. F. K. Shaikh, S. Zeadally and E. Exposito, Enabling Technologies for Green Internet of Things, *IEEE Systems Journal*, 11, 2, pp. 983-994, June 2017.

20. Lee, H.J., Wicke, M., Kusy, B., Gnawali, O., Guibas, L., Predictive data delivery to mobile users through mobility learning in wireless sensor networks. *IEEE Trans. Veh. Technol.*, 64, 12, 5831–5849, 2015.

21. Case, I. and Kitchens, F., The green data center: A modern solution to an old problem. *Iberian Conference on Information Systems and Technologies, CISTI*, 2019-June, 2019, https://doi.org/10.23919/CISTI.2019.8760948.

22. Patel, Y.S., Mehrotra, N., Soner, S., Green cloud computing: A review on Green IT areas for cloud computing environment. *2015 1st International Conference on Futuristic Trends in Computational Analysis and Knowledge Management, ABLAZE*, pp. 327–332, 2015, https://doi.org/ 10.1109/ ABLAZE.2015.7155006.

23. Muniswamaiah, M., Agerwala, T., Tappert, C.C., Green computing for Internet of Things. *Proceedings - 2020 7th IEEE International Conference on Cyber*

Security and Cloud Computing and 2020 6th IEEE International Conference on Edge Computing and Scalable Cloud, CSCloud-EdgeCom 2020, pp. 182–185, 2020, https://doi.org/10.1109/CSCloud-EdgeCom49738.2020.00039.

24. Goyal, Y., Arya, M.S., Nagpal, S., Energy-efficient hybrid policy in green cloud computing. *Proceedings of the 2015 International Conference on Green Computing and Internet of Things, ICGCIoT*, vol. 2015, pp. 1065–1069, 2016.

25. Shah, K. and Narmavala, Z., A Survey on Green Internet of Things. *14th International Conference on Information Processing: Internet of Things, ICInPro 2018 – Proceedings*, 2018.

26. Gorbenko, A., Tarasyuk, O., Kor, A.L., Kharchenko, V., Green economics: A roadmap to sustainable ICT development. *Proceedings of 2018 IEEE 9th International Conference on Dependable Systems, Services and Technologies, DESSERT*, vol. 2018, pp. 561–567, 2018.

27. Shu, L., Zhang, Y., Yang, L.T., Wang, Y., Hauswirth, M., Xiong, N., TPGF: Geographic routing in wireless multimedia sensor networks. *Telecommun. Syst.*, 44, 1–2, 79–95, 2010, https://doi.org/10.1007/s11235-009-9227-0.

28. Zhu, C., Yang, L.T., Shu, L., Leung, V.C.M., Rodrigues, J.J.P.C., Wang, L., Sleep scheduling for geographic routing in duty-cycled mobile sensor networks. *IEEE Trans. Ind. Electron.*, 61, 11, 6346–6355, 2014, https://doi.org/10.1109/TIE.2014.2311390.

29. Tombaz, S., Västberg, A., Zander, J., Energy- and cost-efficient ultra-high-capacity wireless access. *IEEE Wireless Commun.*, 18, 5, 18–24, 2011, https://doi.org/10.1109/MWC.2011.6056688.

30. Sheng, Z., Fan, J., Liu, C.H., Leung, V.C.M., Liu, X., Leung, K.K., Energy-efficient relay selection for cooperative relaying in wireless multimedia networks. *IEEE Trans. Veh. Technol.*, 64, 3, 1156–1170, 2015, https://doi.org/10.1109/TVT.2014.2322653.

31. Choi, K., Kim, M.H., Chae, K.J., Park, J.J., Joo, S.S., An efficient data fusion and assurance mechanism using temporal and spatial correlations for home automation networks. *IEEE Trans. Consum. Electron.*, 55, 3, 1330–1336, 2009, https://doi.org/10.1109/TCE.2009.5277996.

32. Choi, K., Kim, M.H., Chae, K.J., Park, J.J., Joo, S.S., An efficient data fusion and assurance mechanism using temporal and spatial correlations for home automation networks. *IEEE Trans. Consum. Electron.*, 55, 3, 1330–1336, 2009, https://doi.org/10.1109/TCE.2009.5277996.

33. Karakus, C., Gurbuz, A.C., Tavli, B., Analysis of energy efficiency of compressive sensing in wireless sensor networks. *IEEE Sens. J.*, 13, 5, 1999–2008, 2013, https://doi.org/10.1109/JSEN.2013.2244036.

34. Chen, J. and Pratt, T.G., Energy efficiency of space and polarization MIMO communications with packet erasures over wireless fading channels. *IEEE Trans. Wireless Commun.*, 13, 12, 6557–6569, 2014, https://doi.org/10.1109/TWC.2014.2322055.

35. Rahman, S., Green Power: What is it and where can we Find it? *IEEE Power Energy Mag., Institute Electrical Electron. Engineers Inc.*, 1, 1, 30–37, 2004, https://doi.org/10.1109/MPAE.2003.1180358.

36. Nguyen, T.D., Khan, J.Y., Ngo, D.T., A Distributed Energy-Harvesting-Aware Routing Algorithm for Heterogeneous IoT Networks. *IEEE Trans. Green Commun. Networking*, 2, 4, 1115–1127, 2018.

37. Selem, E., Fatehy, M., El-Kader, S.M.A., Nassar, H., The (Temperature heterogeneity energy) aware routing protocol for IoT health application. *IEEE Access*, 7, 108957–108968, 2019.

38. Behera, T.M., Mohapatra, S.K., Samal, U.C., Khan, M.S., Daneshmand, M., Gandomi, A.H., I-SEP: An Improved Routing Protocol for Heterogeneous WSN for IoT-Based Environmental Monitoring. *IEEE Internet Things J.*, 7, 1, 710–717, 2020.

39. Lenka, R.K., Rath, A.K., Sharma, S., Building Reliable Routing Infrastructure for Green IoT Network. *IEEE Access*, 7, 129892–129909, 2019, https://doi. org/10.1109/ACCESS.2019.2939883.

40. Van, N.T., Huynh, T.-T., An, B., An energy-efficient protocol based on fuzzy logic to extend network lifetime and increase transmission efficiency in wireless sensor networks. *J. Intell. Fuzzy Syst.*, vol. 35, no. 6, pp. 5845-5852, 2018 1–8, 2018. https://content.iospress.com/journals/ journal-of-intelligent-and-fuzzy-systems

41. Hampiholi, A.S. and Vijaya Kumar, B.P., Efficient routing protocol in IoT using modified Genetic algorithm and its comparison with existing protocols. *2018 IEEE 3rd International Conference on Circuits, Control, Communication and Computing, I4C*, 2018.

42. Seyyedabbasi, A. and Kiani, F., MAP-ACO: An efficient protocol for multi-agent pathfinding in real-time WSN and decentralized IoT systems. *Microprocess. Microsyst.*, 79, 103325, 2020.

43. Chouhan, N. and Jain, S.C., Tunicate swarm Grey Wolf optimization for multi-path routing protocol in IoT assisted WSN networks. *J. Ambient Intell. Hum. Comput.*, 1–17, 2020, https://doi.org/10.1007/s12652-020-02657-w.

44. Mehta, D. and Saxena, S., Hierarchical WSN protocol with fuzzy multi-criteria clustering and bio-inspired energy-efficient routing (FMCB-ER). *Multimed. Tools Appl.*, 1–34, 2020, https://doi.org/10.1007/s11042-020-09633-8.

45. Machorro-Cano, I., Alor-Hernández, G., Paredes-Valverde, M.A., Rodríguez-Mazahua, L., Sánchez-Cervantes, J.L., Olmedo-Aguirre, J.O., HEMS-IoT: A Big Data and Machine Learning-Based Smart Home System for Energy Saving. *Energies*, 13, 5, 1097, 2020.

46. Ventura, D., Casado-Mansilla, D., López-de-Armentia, J., Garaizar, P., López-de-Ipiña, D., Catania, V., ARIIMA: A real IoT implementation of a machine-learning architecture for reducing energy consumption. *Lect. Notes Comput. Sci. (Including Subseries Lecture Notes Artif. Intell. Lecture Notes Bioinformatics)*, 8867, 444–451, 2014.

47. Ghosh, P. and Ghosh, S., IoT and Machine Learning in Green Smart Home Automation and Green Building Management. *J. Alternate Energy Sources Technol.*, 10, 3, 8–36, 2020, https://doi.org/10.37591/JOAEST.V10I3.3443.

48. Chithaluru, P., Al-Turjman, F., Kumar, M., Stephan, T., I-AREOR: An energy-balanced clustering protocol for implementing green IoT in smart cities. *Sustain. Cities Soc.*, 61, 102254, 2020, https://doi.org/10.1016/j.scs.2020.102254.

49. Mukherjee, A., Goswami, P., Yang, L., Yan, Z., Daneshmand, M., Dynamic clustering method based on power demand and information volume for intelligent and green IoT. *Comput. Commun.*, 152, 119–125, 2020.

50. Sujanthi, S. and Nithya Kalyani, S., SecDL: QoS-Aware Secure Deep Learning Approach for Dynamic Cluster-Based Routing in WSN Assisted IoT. *Wirel. Pers. Commun.*, 114, 3, 2135–2169, 2020.

51. Kim, H.Y. and Kim, J.M., A load balancing scheme based on deep-learning in IoT. *Cluster Comput.*, 20, 1, 873–878, 2017, https://doi.org/10.1007/s10586-016-0667-5.

52. Liu, X., Yu, J., Wang, J., Gao, Y., Resource Allocation With Edge Computing in IoT Networks via Machine Learning. *IEEE Internet Things J.*, 7, 4, 3415–3426, 2020, https://doi.org/10.1109/JIOT.2020.2970110.

53. Chen, J., Chen, S., Luo, S., Wang, Q., Cao, B., Li, X., An intelligent task offloading algorithm (iTOA) for UAV edge computing network. *Digital Commun. Networks*, 6, 4, 433–443, 2020, https://doi.org/10.1016/j.dcan.2020.04.008.

54. Zhang, C., Liu, Z., Gu, B., Yamori, K., Tanaka, Y., A Deep Reinforcement Learning Based Approach for Cost- and Energy-Aware Multi-Flow Mobile Data Offloading. *IEICE Trans. Commun.*, E101B, 7, 1625–1634, 2018.

4

Green IoT Towards Environmentally Friendly, Sustainable and Revolutionized Farming

Ravi Manne[1]* and Sneha Chowdary Kantheti[2]

[1]Chemtex Environmental Lab, Port Arthur, Texas, USA
[2]Nemo IT Solutions Inc., Dallas, Texas, USA

Abstract

Agriculture is one of the major sources of greenhouse gas emissions. Changes in climate conditions are directly or indirectly impacted by agricultural sector which contributes to greenhouse gas emissions. Agriculture is one of the major sources that contributes to water pollution, soil pollution due to the use of fertilizers in large amounts to increase the crop productivity and yields. Along with that, genetic modification of crops has been causing issues as well, which has huge impact on biodiversity. Farmers working in the fields as well as, people consuming the foods, are facing illness, water, and airborne diseases due to polluted environment and foods. Increase of energy also increases the chance of pollution in environment because of presence of toxic pollutants and e-waste. Green-IoT helps overcome these issues with the help of latest techniques, leading to decrease in the environmental harms, more productivity and yields at low costs and less energy usage. In this chapter the role of G-IoT in the agricultural field is discussed in terms of, how it helps achieve precise, sustainable, and eco-friendly agricultural practices for crop management like less fertilizer usage, yield prediction, crop quality, less waste and many more.

Keywords: Environmental pollution, greenhouse gases, agriculture, farming, green IoT, green nanotechnology, crop yield

---

*Corresponding author: ravimannemr@gmail.com

Roshani Raut, Sandeep Kautish, Zdzislaw Polkowski, Anil Kumar and Chuan-Ming Liu (eds.) Green Internet of Things and Machine Learning: Towards a Smart Sustainable World, (113–140) © 2022 Scrivener Publishing LLC

4.1　Introduction

The role of agriculture is very crucial in the economy. As the population grows, pressure on the food production increases. United Nations Food and Agriculture Organization (FAO) estimated that world population might reach to 8 billion by 20125, and by 2050, it might reach to 9.6 billion. Agriculture sector and food sector are facing many challenges due changes in the climatic conditions and global population. To keep up with food production to the growing population, we have to overcome the problems that are present in the agricultural field. Technology evolvement helped overcome some of the problems which lead to improved yields, less environmental pollution, etc. Here, we will discuss about various Machine Learning (ML) techniques that can improve farming, and how it tis applied in farming. We also talk about what is IoT and its disadvantages and why Green IoT (G-IoT) has been introduced in to the farming and its advantages over IoT.

4.1.1　Lifecycle of Agriculture

Soil Preparation: Farmers in the first step make the soil ready for seed sowing. In this process, they will break large clumps in the soil and remove rocks, sticks, and roots, and depending on the type of the crop, they add organic matter and fertilizers to get the best productivity [5]. Figure 4.1 shows the life cycle of agriculture and each phase is described as below:

Sowing of Seeds: In this second stage, seeds are sowed at a particular distance between them and depth at which they are sowed will be taken care of.

Adding Fertilizers: In order to grow healthy and nutritious crops, soil fertility is important, and to ensure these farmers add fertilizers, as fertilizers contain plant nutrients like potassium, nitrogen, and phosphorous. Fertilizers ensure plants get the necessary nutrients and elements that are naturally found in the soil.

Irrigation: In this step, soil is maintained moist and humid. Crop growth can be hampered by underwater or overwatering, and it may even lead to crop damage.

Weed Protection: Weed protection is important as these are the plants that are unwanted which grow near crops or at the farm boundaries, and they decrease the yields which, in turn, increase the productions costs and also reduces the quality of the crop.

Harvesting: In this process, all the ripened crops are gathered, and to complete this process, a lot of laborers are required. In this stage, activities like cleaning, packing, sorting, and cooling are covered.

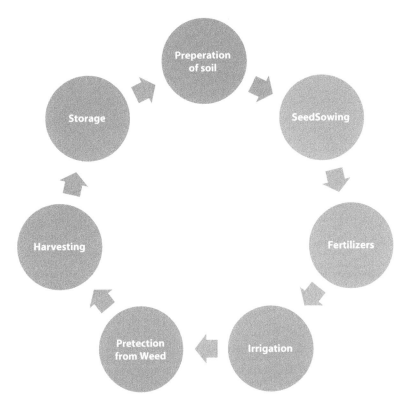

Figure 4.1 Lifecycle of agriculture.

Storage: In this stage, food is stored properly stored. It also means packing of crops and crop transportation.

4.1.2 An Overview on How Machine Learning Works

ML is nowadays a trending technology and is used in wide variety of industries including agriculture [1], healthcare- medical image analysis [2], drug designs, cybersecurity, speech recognition, data science, self-driving cars, online fraud detection, and many more. In the field of agriculture, the usage of artificial intelligence has significantly increased in wide number of projects. During the 20th century, due to low computing power, it did not let the automation of some processes in agriculture to grow. But later in the 21st century, role of Artificial Intelligence has increased in agriculture field. Figure 4.2 shows work flow of ML.

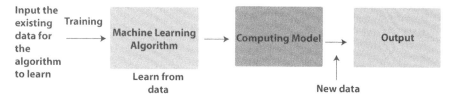

Figure 4.2 Machine Learning workflow.

ML is a subset of Artificial Intelligence. ML helps build applications which learn from the data and improve its accuracy in a period of time. In ML, algorithms make predictions and take decisions from the patterns based on the previous data, for the new input data. Algorithm is a bundle of statistical processing steps [3]. There are two types of data that is being fed to algorithms: labeled data and unlabeled data. Labeled data will have the tags to know features and classifications the model will have to identify. Other hand for the unlabeled data the model needs to extract the features and do the classification on its own. So, different types of algorithms are being used for labeled data vs. unlabeled data. Figure 4.3 shows relationship of ML with AI, neural networks, and deep learning.

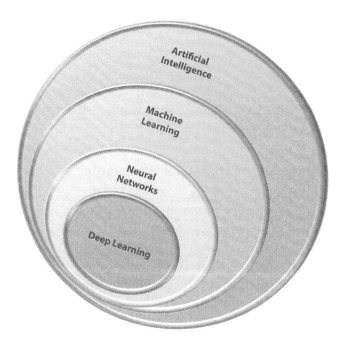

Figure 4.3 Machine Learning relation with others.

Algorithms used for labeled data are as follows:

- **Regression Algorithms:** Linear regression and logistic regression are few of the examples of regression and used to understand the data relationships. When the input data is binary, logistic regression can be used. To predict the dependent variable value depending on independent variable value, linear regression is used.
- **Decision Trees:** Depending on the set of decision rules, decision trees are used to classify the data to make recommendations.
- **Instance-Based Algorithms:** K-nearest neighbor (K-NN) is used for instance-based algorithm. Based on the proximity of the data to other points, it classifies how likely a data point in a member of one group or the other.

Algorithms used for unlabeled data are as follows:

- **Clustering Algorithms:** Clustering is like groups. Clustering will identify the groups that are similar and label the records depending on which group they belong to. This will be done without any previous knowledge of groups that they belong to [4]. Different types of this algorithm are k-means, two-step, and Kohonen.
- **Association Algorithms:** This algorithm identify if-then relationships by finding patterns and relationships in data, and these are called association rules.
- **Neural Networks:** A neural network will have different layers, and input layer, at least one hidden layer and the layer for output. A deep neural network which has one or more hidden layers, input of each hidden layer is the output of the previous layer. Inputs are fed into the input layer and based on its previous experience; an output will be generated through output layer. Calculations are performed at hidden layers.

Once you pick the type of data depending on your needs and the algorithm, you need to train the algorithm. Algorithm training is achieved by running variables through algorithm, and by comparing the output value with the predicted value, using weights adjustments in the algorithm, which will produce accurate results. There are three types of methods in ML.

- **Supervised machine learning:** Supervised ML is defined by using labeled datasets for algorithm training that is used to classify or predict the data accurately. When the input is fed into the model, it will adjust the weights using reinforcement learning process which we will discuss next, and that will ensure that model is perfectly fitted. Supervised learning helps many field and organizations solve variety of real-world problems. Supervised learning can be separated into classification and regression problems.

  Classification: Classification an algorithm is used to accurately classify and separate data into particular categories. It recognizes certain entities within the given dataset and tries to draw conclusions around those entities on how they should be labeled. Commonly used algorithms for classification are SVM, K-NN, and decision trees.

  Regression: To understand the relation between dependent variables and independent variables, regression is used. Some commonly used algorithms for regression are linear regression, polynomial regression, and logistical regression.

- **Unsupervised machine learning:** Unsupervised learning is when you have the variables for the input, but the corresponding variables for output are not there. The main aim of the unsupervised learning is to learn more about the data by understanding the distribution among the data. This can be further grouped into association and clustering.

  Clustering: In a clustering problem, you group the data depending on certain pattern or behavior.

  Association: In association, you want to discover rules which describe large part of your data.

- **Reinforcement machine learning:** In reinforcement learning, there is no pretrained data, the model decides what to perform to a given task. In reinforcement learning, as the training data is not available, the model learns from its experience. Reinforcement learning is of two types: positive and negative. When a certain behavior has happened, the event positive reinforcement will takes place, which increases the frequency and strength of the behavior. Advantage of positive reinforcement learning is it maximizes the performance, and it sustains change for longer time period. Negative reinforcement is strengthening the behavior when a negative event is stopped. Advantage of negative reinforcement learning is it increases the behavior of the model.

Deep learning is one of the types of ML. It is based on artificial neural network (ANN) which works similar to human brain. Deep learning will require large amount of data that passes through multiple layers where calculations are done and where weights are applied in each layer to adjust and improvise the outcomes.

4.2 How is Machine Learning Used in Agricultural Field?

4.2.1 Crop Management

ML shows a great impact on the crop effectiveness for classifying and quality of the crop, detecting disease and preventions and agrochemical production. One of the important factors of harvesting effectively is detecting more potent land and crops on a given day. These predictions are not only based on data from the past but also utilizes computer vision software combined with weather analysis in order to meet the demands in farming. Successful farming is based on some complex decisions like crop specifications, condition of soil, changes in climate, and more [6, 7]. ML helps farmers analyze these data for higher yields in the crop. Some areas where ML helps farmers are as follows:

1. **Identifying Species:** Plants are remarkably similar in many cases due very slight change in color or their shape, and so it given hard time to even experienced farmers in differentiating them. Image analysis can be done using ML and the images of plants can be classified and identified with the help of ML which saves time for farmers. By accessing the leaf vein map which contains the decisive information, ML algorithms will detect which plant it is.

2. **Selective Breeding:** To achieve desired features in crops breeding is done, and breeding is very time-consuming process and resource intensive. Currently various ML applications are being explored in achieving this breeding. Author [8] described how drones and on field sensors are used by researchers and large amount of data was gathered for soybean cultivation nuances. For selective breeding, more than conventional techniques ML techniques are superior, and

experience and knowledge of professionals in agricultural are also useful.

3. **Crop Yield Prediction:** In order to increase productivity yield estimation, crop management and matching crop supply with demand is very important. It is important to know crop yield prediction rates before harvesting and so it helps farmers to make decisions on what to grow when. ML is helpful in the situations where the relation between input variables and output is unknown. Assumptions about the construct of data model are not made by ML techniques, like traditional statistic methods do. This helps in describing complex non-linear behaviors like predicting crop yields. The accuracy of the model can be achieved by metrics like precision, recall, sensitivity, mean square error and root mean square error, sensitivity, and specificity. Through supervised, unsupervised, and semi-supervised learning crop yield prediction can be achieved using ML. Conditions like topography, soil conditions, precipitation, and socioeconomic factors are responsible for about 30% growth of crops. Data mining, regression, ANNs, and support vector machine (SVM) are used by many works in literature to predict the crop yields. Let us discuss some of the model approaches that are used to predict crop yield [9]:

   a. **Linear Regression:** Linear egression is based on supervised learning. By using linear regression, relation between dependent and independent variable could be measured. Linear regression has been used by multiple works and it is a statistical method that is applied over linear systems. During standard tests, this regression model shows consistent results. They are more used for linear data but they are not quite compatible with complex and non-linear data. If there is multiple co linearity between dependent and independent variables, this linear regression may not perform well due to the limitation it has with regression assumptions. Author [10] used Linear regression to predict the yield rates of Tea crop, and the results achieved were predicted correctly.

   b. **Multiple and Stepwise Linear Regression:** This is one of the most used and popular techniques and can be used to predict dependent variable Y_i using independent variables set X_{ij}, Equation (4.1) is used to predict the values as below.

$$Y_i = \sum_{j=1}^{K} B_j x_{ij} + \epsilon_r \qquad (4.1)$$

where K = Total number of independent variables;
B_j = regression coefficient;
X_{ij} = for the observation i, X_{ij} is the j value.

Stepwise linear regression models also work the same way as of multiple linear regression model. To improve and maximize the prediction efficiency of the model stepwise, linear regression does a semiautomated selection on independent variables.

c. **K-Nearest Neighbor:** Samples that are similar are assumed to have similar classification in K-NN. The parameter K is defined by samples that are similar and are used for assigning a classification to a sample that are not known. Clustering technique is used if there is no history of the samples that need to be classified, in order words if no training is provided to the model.

d. **K-Means Approach:** This is one among the important techniques. If there is no knowledge from before on the data aka training set, this technique is used. Parameter k is the number of clusters that are required for data partition [11]. The main idea behind clustering is basing on all the samples of a cluster, we can define one center for each cluster, and we can do K centers. All these centers need to be placed far away from one another and then each sample need to be associated to the cluster which has closest centroid. This process of finding K centers that are new and assigning samples to the closest clusters will carry out until there is no more samples left out to change the clusters. There are multiple training algorithms and ANN topologies.

e. **Support Vector Machines:** These are the binary classifiers which classify data samples in two classes that are disjoint. The two classes are separable linearly. SVM can build a model and decide whether the new sample falls into one category or other. It is a concept in statistics for a set of supervised learning related methods which analyzes data and recognizes patterns that are used for regression analysis and classification. For the given input data, it decides which two possible classes form the input, and this is a non-probabilistic binary linear classifier. For learning, SVM uses linear function. Main advantage of SVM over other models like ANN is it only needs few parameters for model optimization. This technique is applied variety of applications like weather prediction, in predicting crop productivity. The main issue in SVM is determining kernel functions, penalty coefficient and hyper parameters.

f.   **Artificial Neural Networks:** ANN solves nonlinearity and complex relations between various predictor parameters and crop production. They contain mathematical functions that are objective rather than rules subjective and easily automated. Simple processing units connected using direct and weighted interconnections are called as an ANN. The input to every processing unit come from other processing units. Weights of the interconnections are used to calibrate the input to the next processing unit. The inputs thar are calibrated are transmitted to other processing units using the correct interconnections [12]. Layers organize the units by hiding the intermediate layers from the users. nonlinear and nonadditive function represent this process and this function maps set of inputs to outputs. During the training stage, a continuous process is performed to form connections and is guided for error measure.

g.   **Regression Trees:** It is based on decision tree. The dataset is subdivided down into smaller datasets. This algorithm falls under supervised learning. This model is used for both continuous and categorical output variables. Nodes form the tree, and the first node is named as root node and it does not have incoming edges. Other nodes will have one incoming edge. A node which has outgoing edge is called as test node and node which does not have outgoing edge is called as leaf node. Samples are divided into more subspaces by each internal node in the tree based on input attribute values. If the attributes are numerical, the condition refers to range of values. Each leaf will be assigned to a class that represents appropriate target value. Classification of samples will be done starting from root of the tree down to leaf, depending on the outcome of the tests along the path down. To build regression trees, most common algorithms used are M5', CART, and M5.

h. **Biclustering Technique:** Biclustering technique is used when the data is in the form of rows or columns, like a matrix. Different biclustering algorithm types are as follows:

- Biclusters with values which are constant;
- Biclusters with rows which are constant;
- Biclusters with columns which are constant;
- Biclusters with values which are coherent.

i. **Metrics:** Various ML algorithms are used to predict the crop yield as we can see from above. Even though we have many algorithms available which algorithm to choose depends on application and accuracy of the model. This prediction accuracy is validated using different metrics and how to calculate these metrics are shown below.

Mean Squared Error: MSE (Mean Squared Error) is used to measure the average of squared error of predictions. It is the square of difference between actual value and the value that is predicted and then average of those values.

$$\text{MSE} = \frac{1}{N} \sum_{i=1}^{N} (y_i - \bar{y}_i)^2 \qquad (4.2)$$

where yi = output that is expected, i ranges from 1 to N
$\bar{y}_i$ indicates the output predicted for an ith data

Equation (4.2) is used to calculate MSE. If the value of MSE is low, it means that classifier accuracy is good. If the value of MSE is 0, then classifier is perfect.

Root Mean Squared Error (RMSE): Square root of MSE is the RMSE. It is expressed as. Equation (4.3) is used to calculate RMSE as below:

$$\text{RMAESE} = \sqrt{\frac{1}{N} \sum_{i=1}^{N} (y_i - \bar{y}_i)^2} \qquad (4.3)$$

First, the difference between model output and the actual targeted value is calculated. The difference is averaged and squared over all the data items and then rot of the mean value is calculated.

Mean Absolute Error (MAE): It is the average of the absolute difference between values that are targeted and the predicted. Equation (4.4) is used to calculate MAE as below:

$$\text{MAE} = \frac{1}{N} \sum_{i=1}^{N} |y_i - \bar{y}_i| \qquad (4.4)$$

4. **Soil Analysis and Disease Detection:** For the well-being of the crop, characteristics of soil like temperature, moisture, and levels of nitrogen play an important role and are a heterogenous natural resource with complex mechanism. Impingement in agriculture can be understood by properties of soil. By estimating soil conditions accurately can improve the soil management. Temperature of the soil alone plays and important role in the effects of climate change in a region. Farmers traditionally spread same amount of pesticides per each square meter. This affects farmers' budget by wasting resources and spoils flora and fauna, which also reduces number of pollinator species. There can also be other impacts like ground water side effects, impact on eco system and wild life, residues on crop products. Pest and disease control in open air is another significant concern in agriculture. ML helps farmers with precision agricultural management by helping on where chemicals need to be targeted in terms of time and place. Along with image analysis software ML can analyze health condition of each crop and soil erosion levels. The data that is obtained from this is used to identify what regions of fields are infected and by allowing farmers to know what parts of field need to be targeted by pesticides. When on large scale this is replaced by computer vision software oriented drones that are linked to IoT systems, which can collect thermal and visual data. The company in California called Trace Geonomics follows a different approach in assessing soil. Instead of detecting crops that are already infected, company would rather focus on disease prevention by providing in depth analysis of soil

with the help of ML. Farmers can send their samples to this company and get their results.

5. **Weed Detection:** Weed detection is one of the most important threats to the crop as it grows very fast, competing with the crop, which causes several plant diseases and by lowering the yield of the crop, and they are also difficult to discriminate from crops. Herbicides are used to control the weed, but they cause many economic and environmental concerns. Another bad thing is that, even these weeds are learning to adapt to chemicals that are used to kill them. By using ML, we can identify weed plants and spray only on them instead of spraying pesticides on the whole field thus by reducing use of chemicals and controlling their release into environment.

6. **Quality of Crop:** Proper detection along with classification of characteristics of crop quality is important to increase price of the product and to reduce the wastage. ML helps detect the crop quality. Author [19] introduced a new method for detecting and classifying botanical and non-botanical matter at the time of harvesting in the cotton lint. The main goal of this research is to improve the quality while reducing fiber damage. The algorithm they used was SVM, and the accuracy that was achieved was 95%.

4.2.2   Livestock Management

Livestock production system also needs data analysis and predictions to be done in order to create environmentally friendly and effective economy. For dairy production and cattle applications ML techniques can be used. It again consists of two categories: livestock production and animal welfare. ML in applied in animal welfare to monitor the well beingness of animals, by continuously monitoring behavior of animals and disease early detection. Another category livestock production deals with production system issue. ML is applied in this field to accurately estimate economic balances.

4.2.2.1   Animal Welfare

Some research papers used ML algorithms to observe the animal behavior. For example, author [13] has done research on animal species cattle, and features that were observed are grazing and walking and are recorded using devices like accelerometer and magnetometer. The algorithm that was used is ensemble learning, and the accuracy that was achieved was 96%. Similarly, author [14] has selected animal species calf, and they tried observing the chewing patterns in calves. The features that were observed are signals of chewing from ryegrass, rumination, and when supplying dietary. The model/algorithm they used is decision trees, and the accuracy they achieved is 94%.

4.2.2.2   Livestock Production

This subcategory relates to optimizing the economic efficiency of production system by accurately predicting and estimating farming parameters. Author [15] has chosen animal species cattle and they tried to find out the fermentation pattern prediction of rumen from milk fatty acids, and the feature they observed is milk fatty acids. The model/algorithm they used is ANN, and they calculated RMSE for Acetate which is 2.65%, propionate = 7.67% and RMSE for Butyrate is 7.61%. Another author [16] selected animal species Hens, and they tried to detect production curve warning for hen eggs. They used the model SVM and accuracy achieved was 98%.

4.2.3   Literature Review of Research Papers That Used Machine Learning in Agriculture

Author [8] did research on coffee crop. They observed color features in digital images that illustrates coffee fruits. The main aim of this research to count the coffee fruits on coffee branch, and the algorithm used here was SVM, and the results achieved are 82.5% to 87.83% for ripened and over-ripened fruits, and 68.25% to 85.36% for semi-ripened fruits, and 76.91% to 81.39% for unrepented fruits.

Author [17] did a research using BM/GNB model to detect branches of cherry trees with full foliage. The images that are used are digital images that are colored which depict leaves, branches, and cherry fruits and also background, and the accuracy achieved is 89.6%. Author [18] did research on green citrus crop to identify green citrus fruit that are immature under natural conditions, and the model used by this team was SVM model. Image features like directionality regularity, roughness, granularity, brightness, and smoothness are observed to identify immature green citrus fruits. The images used are of green citrus fruits that are not ripe and are digital with 20 * 20 pixel. The accuracy achieved was 80.4%. Authors researched on strawberry crop using SVM model for disease detection. They tried to classify parasites and automatically detect of thrips. The features they observed in the crop are region index, which is the ration of major to minor diameter, hue saturation, color index, and intensity [19, 20].

4.3   What is IoT? How Can IoT Be Applied in Agriculture?

Internet of Things (IoT) is first coined in 1998. There are three categories in IoT: hardware, software, and cloud. Hardware of IoT includes sensors, microcontrollers, and communication. Basic elements in IoT are as follows:

Internet: Communication between things or devices is provided using internet protocols.

Things act as sensors, which can be able to sense surroundings.

Processing: Producing an outcome based on the data received by sensor with the help of software is what processing does.

Sensors: Depending on the functionality, sensors collect the data and send them to microcontrollers which are connected to internet. It is important to make them environmentally friendly as sensors consumes huge amount of energy when the use of these sensors increase in number. Temperature sensors are of multiple types which are resistor temperature detectors and thermocouples. Gas sensors are hydrogen sensor, carbon dioxide, ozone monitor sensors, air pollution sensors, etc.

Technology is improving and developing and is being used a lot more in the society. With these developments in technology in day-to-day life, IoT has major role in allowing various opportunities and possibilities in these advancements. The main goal of using IoT is to simplify many processes in multiple fields to allow an improved efficiency of systems. In olden days, Ethernet which is LAN technology is being more used to connect to other devices and this is for short communication [1]. Due to fact of disadvantage of short distance communication, Internet was introduced as universal connection of computer to computer. Internet had many facilities over ethernet like World Wide Web, video calls, emails, VoIP, and instant messaging. The information is transferred from one system to another through two-way communication, one being wired and other is wireless. The use of IoT has now expanded to multiple areas, especially agriculture [21]. The surge in the population and need for goods has increased the need for different techniques that are modernized in agriculture. Farming mainly depends on factors like water, soil, temperature, and, mainly, by water. In the future years, the availability of water is reducing and it is going to get worse in very future years, especially in countries like India.

IoT is being used in agriculture for several reasons; some of them are to monitor change in climate conditions, automation of greenhouse, in management of the crop, monitoring and managing the cattle, precision farming, and drones for agriculture.

4.3.1   Monitoring Climate Conditions

As we have already discussed earlier, climate plays an important role in agriculture, and having poor knowledge on how climate deteriorates heavily will put the quality and quantity of crop production in trouble. Real-time weather condition updates are possible with hem help of IoT. Sensors could be placed in and outside of agricultural fields. They will help guide farmers, by collecting the data from environment and letting them know which crop would sustain that weather at that time. The whole IoT systems are made up of sensors that accurately detect temperature, rainfall, and humidity [22].

4.3.2   Greenhouse Automation

Using IoT to enable weather stations to adjust the climate conditions automatically depending on the set of instructions given to it. Human intervention is eliminated by adopting IoT in greenhouses, and making the process cost effective and improved accuracy. IoT sensors that are powered by solar power build inexpensive and modern greenhouses. These sensors help monitor the greenhouses by collecting real-time data.

4.3.3   Crop Management

Crop management is another element in precise farming. Products of IoT should be placed in field for them to collect data related to crop farming. It collects the data elated to precipitation and temperature to leaf water potential and overall health of the crop.

4.3.4   Cattle Monitoring and Management

Just like how crop management is done, these IoT sensors can be attached to animals in the farm to monitor their health and note their performances. These sensors can help identify sick animals and separate them the remaining animals to prevent contamination. Drone also can be used for real-time cattle tracking which, in turn, reduce expenses related to staffing.

4.3.5   Precision Farming and Agricultural Drones

Precision farming is one of most productive and widespread application of IoT in agriculture. It is all about taking accurate data driven decisions and efficiency. By using these IoT sensors, farmers collect information about humidity, temperature, and pest infections, which will let farmers estimate amount of water and pesticides and fertilizers they have to use. This will less pollute the crop and the environment and also saves money and time. Drones are also used in agriculture, to perform wide number of tasks which needs humans like pests fighting and infections, monitoring crops, and spraying in agricultural fields.

4.3.6   Contract Farming

Contract farming is a new type in agricultural management and production. With growing urban modernization and advancement, the gap between rural areas and urban areas is increasing. It is surveyed that 80% of the people who are poor extremely and 75% of the people who are moderately poor live in rural areas. Some of the reasons for this is, the dangers which are hidden in the safety of using products used for agriculture, and isolation of information in buying these agricultural products are the reasons. Contract farming emerged to solve these issues in farming. It helps farmers to outsource the supply demand of the agricultural products through the customer base, helps farmers avoid blind production by reducing planting and breeding risks, and improves the marketing model and production.

There is no doubt that use of IoT technologies will bring so many benefits to the life quality and to society, but every technology will have its disadvantages along with advantages [23]. Few of the long-term effects associated with IoT technologies and its fast development are as follows:

- The development in IoT technologies have caused a raise in the consumption of limited resources for example raw materials like metals for electronics which are already rare or becoming rare.
- Environmental impacts might be intense on the long term use of IoT devices, due to the amounts of energy that would be needed to support operation of these devices and also for their production.

- Due to estimated increase in the IoT devices number in the future, electronic waste is expected to increase.

Due to increase in the use of IoT, and poor rates of recycling materials which is about 20% makes it questionable regarding the resource availability to produce products related to IoT.

4.4   What is Green IoT and Use of Green IoT in Agriculture?

G-IoT, as per IFG (International Federation of Green) ICT and IFG Standard, it is practicing and studying sustainable computing environmental wise in IT. In other words, it is the study and practice of manufacturing,

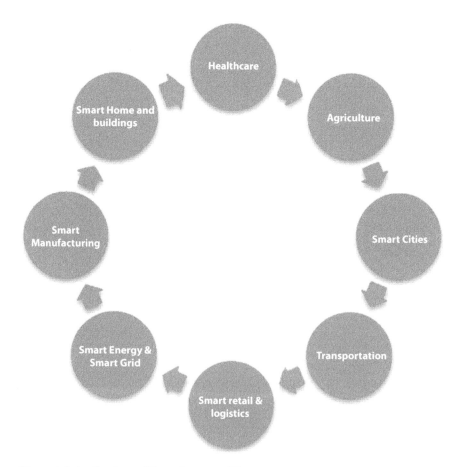

Figure 4.4 Applications of Green Internet of Things.

designing, disposing, and using servers, computers, and other subsystems, which are related like printers, storage devices, monitors, and any others effectively with no impact to the environment or with minimum impact. Figure 4.4 shows are the areas where G-IoT can be applied.

G-IoT is the extension of IoT which facilitates all the benefits and uses provided by the use of IoT in agriculture along with no harm to the environment.

G-IoT can be applied in multiple areas, and some fields where it can be applied to make the world a better place, as below:

The paths that need to be followed to effectively address the environmental effects of computing are as follows.

- **Green Use:** Reduce the amount of energy consumed by computers and other IT systems and utilizing them in an environmentally efficient manner.
- **Green Disposal:** Reusing and refurbishing computers that are old and also recycling the computers that are unwanted and any other electronic equipment.
- **Green Design:** Designing the electronics like computers and servers to function energy efficient and environmentally flexible.
- **Green manufacturing:** Manufacturing computers and any other electronic components with no impact or little impact on environment.

Application of G-IoT makes your house and lifestyle easier, by smoothing the control and usage of devices and appliances like heating systems, microwave, oven, and air conditioning. By using G-IoT, depending on weather sensing, a smart house will automatically shut the curtains and windows by regulating the energy burn. It helps with smart manufacturing by helping industries in multiple ways, like less human involvement, by using robotics, sensing devices which are used to automate the production tasks. Operations like machinery and productivity are checked automatically, and if there are any problems related machine failures, then the system will send maintenance request to the respective teams automatically. Also, by analyzing data related to timelines and other underlying factors using G-IoT, the production and manufacturing rates can be improvised. For smart healthcare, G-IoT can be used to monitor the patients and track their medications by integrating sensors and actuators. For example, by collecting data related to body conditions of patients and analyzing and sending the data to clinical care, they can monitor the physiological state for patients in real-time and take the appropriate actions, which enables patient care from any clinical location in the world. The use of G-IoT can make cities smart cities by helping people in cities to find the information of variety of services like transport utilities and health.

Communication components of Green IoT

The main technological components in G-IoT are Green Internet technologies, Green RFID, Green WSN, Green CC, Green M2M, and Green DC, where CC means Cloud computing, M2M means Machine to Machine, and DC is Data Centers.

Green Internet Technologies: Special hardware and software are required by green internet technologies which are designed to consume low energy without affecting performance along with minimal resource utilization.

Green RFID Tags: RFID tags can store data from any objects they have been linked to at small levels too. This transmission will require RFID systems of a few meter range. One of the types of RFID which is active tag has built in battery to continuously transmit their own signals, while the other type which is passive tags does not have that. The energy from the reader is stored by them.

Green Wireless Sensor Network: WSN has multiple sensor nodes that are small capacity and with small power. By using green conservation technique, green routing techniques, radio optimization technique green WSN could be achieved. By using these techniques, there is a reduction in mobility energy consumption and reduction in capacity to store the data as well as data size can be reduced by using smart data algorithms. Activate sensors can be used only when they are required.

Green Cloud Computing: In cloud computing, we have services like SaaS, PaaS, and IaaS. Policies which are energy efficient need to be applied in green scheme for hardware and software. Green computing–based technologies need to be used like networking and communication.

Green DC: To store manage, process, and disseminate, all types of data centers are used. These data centers should be designed based on energy consumption reduction. The routing protocol needs to be designed to make them turn off and be idle in the network and incorporate energy parameter for their routing of packets.

Green M2M: In the M2M communication as there are many machines involved, there need to be energy-saving–based transmission power and protocols for optimized communications and algorithms for routing.

The use of IoT in agriculture is using is utilizing wide number of sensors of different types and WSNs (Wireless sensor networks) which are capable of measuring parameters of interests like humidity gas concentrations, temperature and pressure. By utilizing Radio Frequency Identification (RFID) and Global Positioning System (GPS), we can track food products from anywhere. The information that is collected and measured on real-time basis, the information is then transmitted for further analysis and storage. For processing data which is diverse and voluminous, cloud and fog computing is enabled for easier processing of data. Data processing is important to obtain valuable insights inorder to understand and take decisions and to know updates of forecasting to perform appropriate actions to develop a good business model in different agricultural sectors. As we have already seen, utilizing IoT in agriculture gives us the opportunity to monitor various elements in fields and take appropriate actions regarding pesticide control, soil, temperature, plant breeding, food packaging, traceability, animal feeding, etc. By including G-IoT, these achievements can be achieved by revolutionizing the sector of agriculture and chain of food supply to be productive, with sustainable and agricultural practices that are precise. Use of G-IoT reduces the adverse effects on environment and negative influence by better management of soil fertility, effectively using resources like pesticides, fertilizers and herbicides, livestock diversification and crop production. The main benefits in including IoT in agriculture are as follows:

- Remote and to monitor water in real time, soil, fertilizers and pesticides, and animal health.
- Food safety improvement
- Protection of environment
- Decrease in production costs
- Sustainability
- Profitability increase, new opportunities, and development

It is very evident that inclusion of G-IoT enhances productivity, and effective utilization of resources like energy, at the same time reducing contamination and waste. It is estimated that with the utilization of G-IoT the CO_2 emissions per year could be reduced by 2030 along with reduction in global hazardous emissions by 16%. It is also anticipated that by intelligent detection, precise irrigation, and control cultivation by 2030, 1 billion MW of energy will be conserved, and land yield will increase by 897 kg/ha, and cost saving due to effective utilization of energy and resources and water could save up to 110$ billion [24].

Let us discuss about G-IoT in agriculture which is based on four layers.

- Agricultural sensor layers
- Fog Layer
- Core Layer
- Cloud layer

Agriculture Sensor Layer

This layer contains IoT enabled layers like sensor nodes and smartphones which are equipped with GPS for creating multiple types of IoT related to smart agriculture. Some of these are IoT for agriculture field, IoT for the greenhouse, IoT for photovoltaic farm, and solar insecticidal IoTs. So, there are two goals associated with adaption and integration of IoT devices into agriculture at various levels. The main important goal that comes first is to provide the nutrient solution distribution and manufacture reliability. Second goal is to lower the costs and reduce the loses by providing good control in consumption. Impact on environment will be greatly reduced along with the economic impact. Digital control system is used in the G-IoT–based agriculture by farmer in order to meet requirements for control of agriculture and process control. Sensors and meter nodes can be used for each equipment's inorder to integrate IoT for greenhouse and the details as follows [25]:

- For the water pumping system, IoT devices can be used which will consider the factors like surface to be irrigated, and the expected pressure and dripper flow rates.
- For water storage, we can use water meters to show real-time updates of water levels, etc.
- For the filtering equipment, IoT devices can be adapted which considers physical properties of water and drippers.
- To provide updates in the real-time for the storage and injectors of fertilizers, fertilizer meters can be used.
- To meet the value of nutrients solution at the desired levels, IoT devices can be used to control the pH and electrical conductivity.

- To control the moisture levels and temperature, IoT sensors can be used with small solar panels.

Fog Computing Layer

Fog computing layer is proposed inorder to process the IoT data related to agriculture IoT devices and meters, and this will reduce he process time significantly. This layer also can be called as edge computing layer. Agricultural IoT data is received by the fog nodes using the geo distributed devices which are controlled in a distributed network including gateway, router, access point, and switch. There are several advantages provided by fog computing layer like traffic overhead and data security. So, in G-IoT–based agriculture for the fog computing layer, there are three hierarchical architectures that can be used. The first basic architecture is of three layers which are Things/End devices for Tier 1, and Fog for Tier 2, and the third is cloud. The second architecture is four-tire hierarchical architecture combined with fog cloud. The last architecture is Software-Defined Networking (SDN) based. So, with the use of IoT in the greenhouse, nutrient solution could be calculated and processed at the fog computing layer. The IoT data used by nutrient solution is the data that is captured from sensor layer in agriculture.

Core Network Layer

Data from fog computing layer is transports by core network layer to cloud network layer. This layer is also called as foundation layer and is backbone to the network. High speed cables and switches which are high end are used by core layer to ensure packets are routed securely over the network.

Cloud Computing Layer

This layer is responsible for data access, delivery storage and synchronization. This layer consists of traditional cloud servers and data centers which has enough computing resources and storage, and it is like a centralized system.

4.5   Conclusion: Risks of Using G-IoT in Agriculture

There are some risks involved by using G-IoT in agriculture, for example, attacks on technological devices, let it be hardware or software. There are two possible attacks internal/external attacks or passive/active attacks. For examples, attacks can be against privacy, confidentiality, authentication, availability, and integrity.

Attack Against Privacy

This type of attacks is based on learning identity and accurate location of the IoT devices at the agricultural sensor layer, to obtain the data which is private and compromise the systems privacy. In G-IoT–based agriculture, the IoT data like humidity water and temperature are collected by IoT devices multiple times in an hour at the agricultural layer to get the minute information about the conditions and health of the plants status and improve nutrients. By accessing this private data, they can analyze farmers' next steps about the plant's health and nutrition. For example, let us consider the data regarding pH settings, if in the pH settings, it is known that pH is raised excessively and it means farmers might have to increase the ammonium supply, if pH decreases, which means farmers will reduce the ammonium supply. When attackers get to know about this information, they might disrupt the pH setting s by sending drones, and this form of data needs to be protected from unauthorized access [26].

Attack Against Authentication

This type of attack forges like another identity to impersonate as authorized nodes like cloud node or fog node or IoT device to gain the access to G-IoT–based agriculture. There are different types on how this can happen like replay attack, spoofing attack, masquerade attack, and impersonation attack. Replay attack is like a middleman attack. It works as middle person and interpreting the data packages between IoT devices or interrupts an IoT device which is access point at the agricultural sensor layer and relaying the data to the next layers without modifying the information that needs to be modified. Timestamp in encrypted data, pairing-based cryptography, and hash functions are used by IoT networks to protect against replay attacks. In the second type of attack which is masquerade attack, the attacker masquerade as legitimate node and logs into the server at fog computing layer or agriculture sensor layer. In order to secure the IoT networks, the authentication protocols used for securing against these attacks are human physiological-based techniques, behavioral feature-based biometric, pairing-based cryptography, hashing functions, and elliptic curve cryptosystem. These techniques use voice, fingerprint, face, eyes, or electrocardiogram gait to protect against these attacks.

Attacks Against Confidentiality

This type of attack tries to overhear the network traffic at the agricultural sensor layer between the IoT devices, to misguide the G-IoT agriculture system to take the wrong decisions and actions and compromise the confidentiality. To compromise the confidentiality, the attacker includes some attacks as expel tracing attack, known as key attack and brute force attack [27]. In tracing attack, attacker aims to collect the privacy information at the agriculture sensor layer from IoT devices to link the data to a real identity. In brute force attack, the attacker lists out all the possible passwords at the agriculture sensor layer that can be used by IoT devices and use them until they figure out the correct password. To protect against these attacks, security solutions that are developed need to contain nonce in session keys.

Attacks Against Availability and Integrity

Attacks against availability follows the denial-of-service attacks. This type of attack makes the service s in G-IoT–based agriculture unavailable by flooding the servers with large amount of data or making them busy enough to make them unavailable to provide services to IoT devices or sending false data injections. Attacks against integrity is a type of attack where unauthorized body modifies or access the unauthorized or private information. This category can be of multiple types like man in middle attack, Trojan horse attack, and biometric template attack [28].

Proper precautions need to be designed and developed and tested to overcome these attacks in G-IoT, and we can achieve good results in agriculture farming. With the help of ML and IoT, several factors in farming can be improved like soil analysis, disease detection, weed detection, crop yields, climate conditions monitoring, automation of greenhouse, managing crops, monitoring and management of cattle, and precision and contract farming. To overcome some of the disadvantages that are raised due to use of IoT and other techniques in farming like GHG emissions, harmful influence on land, biodiversity, and water resources, G-IoT was developed for smart and sustainable agriculture practices. So, G-IoT provides all the benefits provided by IoT plus sustainable agriculture. Use of G-IoT will contribute to agriculture practices and techniques which are modernized and revolutionized, making the agricultural sector and food industry more safe, efficient, and sustainable as never before!

References

1. Dokic, K., Blaskovic, L., Mandusic, D., From machine learning to deep learning in agriculture–the quantitative review of trends, in: *IOP Conference Series: Earth and Environmental Science*, 2020, December, vol. 614, No. 1, IOP Publishing, p. 012138.

2. Deshpande, A. and Sharma, R., Multilevel Ensembler Classifier using Normalized Feature Based Intrusion Detection System. *IJATCSE*, 7, 5, pp. 72–76, 2018.

3. Tsoraeva, E., *et al.* "Environmental issues of agriculture as a consequence of the intensification of the development of agricultural industry." E3S Web of Conferences. Vol. 215. EDP Sciences, 2020.

4. Louridas, P. and Ebert, C., Machine Learning. *IEEE Software*, 33, 5, 110–115, Sept.-Oct. 2016.

5. Talaviya, T., Shah, D., Patel, N., Yagnik, H., Shah, M., Implementation of artificial intelligence in agriculture for optimisation of irrigation and application of pesticides and herbicides. *Artif. Intell. Agric.*, 4, 58–73, 2020.

6. Liakos, K.G., Busato, P., Moshou, D., Pearson, S., Bochtis, D., Machine learning in agriculture: A review. *Sensors*, 18, 8, 2674, 2018.

7. Iflexion, Machine Learning in Agriculture: What It Can Do Now and in the Future, 2020. https://www.iflexion.com/blog/machine-learning-agriculture.

8. Parmley, K., Nagasubramanian, K., Sarkar, S., Ganapathysubramanian, B., Singh, A.K., Development of Optimized Phenomic Predictors for Efficient Plant Breeding Decisions Using Phenomic-Assisted Selection in Soybean. *Plant Phenomics*, 2019, Article ID 5809404, 15 pages, 2019.

9. Palanivel, K. and Surianarayanan, C., An approach for prediction of crop yield using machine learning and big data techniques. *Int. J. Comput. Eng. Technol.*, 10, 3, 110–118, 2019.

10. Sitienei, K.B.J., Juma, S.G., Opere, E., On the Use of Regression Models to Predict Tea Crop Yield Responses to Climate Change: A Case of Nandi East, Sub-County of Nandi County. *MDPI Sens.*, Sep;5(3):54, 2017.

11. Perpetua, N. and Shruthi, B.S., Comparative Study of Data Mining Techniques in Crop Yield Prediction. *Int. J. Adv. Res. Comput. Commun. Eng., IJARCCE*, 5(2), 132-135, 2016.

12. Gonzalez-Sanchez, A., Frausto-Solis, J., Ojeda-Bustamante, W., Attribute Selection Impact on Linear and Nonlinear Regression Models for Crop Yield Prediction. *Sci. World J.*, 2014, Article ID 509429, 10 pages, 2014.

13. Dutta, R., Smith, D., Rawnsley, R., Bishop-Hurley, G., Hills, J., Timms, G., Henry, D., Dynamic cattle behavioural classification using supervised ensemble classifiers. *Comput. Electron. Agric.*, 111, 18–28, 2015.

14. Pegorini, V., Karam, L.Z., Pitta, C.S.R., Cardoso, R., da Silva, J.C.C., Kalinowski, H.J., Ribeiro, R., Bertotti, F.L., Assmann, T.S., *In vivo* pattern classification of ingestive behavior in ruminants using FBG sensors and machine learning. *Sensors*, 15, 28456–28471, 2015.

15. Craninx, M., Fievez, V., Vlaeminck, B., De Baets, B., Artificial neural network models of the rumen fermentation pattern in dairy cattle. *Comput. Electron. Agric.*, *60*, 226–238, 2008.

16. Morales, I.R., Cebrián, D.R., Fernandez-Blanco, E., Sierra, A.P., Early warning in egg production curves from commercial hens: A SVM approach. *Comput. Electron. Agric.*, *121*, 169–179, 2016.

17. Amatya, S., Karkee, M., Gongal, A., Zhang, Q., Whiting, M.D., Detection of cherry tree branches with full foliage in planar architecture for automated sweet-cherry harvesting. *Biosyst. Eng.*, 146, 3–15, 2015.

18. Amatya, S., Karkee, M., Gongal, A., Zhang, Q., Whiting, M.D., Detection of cherry tree branches with full foliage in planar architecture for automated sweet-cherry harvesting. *Biosyst. Eng.*, 146, 3–15, 2015.

19. Zhang, M., Li, C., Yang, F., Classification of foreign matter embedded inside cotton lint using short wave infrared (SWIR) hyperspectral transmittance imaging. *Comput. Electron. Agric.*, *139*, 75–90, 2017.

20. Ebrahimi, M.A., Khoshtaghaza, M.H., Minaei, S., Jamshidi, B., Vision-based pest detection based on SVM classification method. *Comput. Electron. Agric.*, *137*, 52–58, 2017.

21. More, S. and Singla, J., Machine learning techniques with IoT in agriculture. *Int. J. Adv. Trends Comput. Sci. Eng.*, 8, 3, 742–747, 2019.

22. Nižetić, S., Šolić, P., López-de-Ipiña González-de-Artaza, D., Patrono, L., Internet of Things (IoT): Opportunities, issues and challenges towards a smart and sustainable future. *J. Cleaner Prod.*, *274*, 122877, 2020.

23. World Agriculture, 2021 IoT Architecture for Agriculture, https://www.biz-4intellia.com/blog/5-applications-of-iot-in-agriculture, 2018.

24. Ferrag, M.A., Shu, L., Yang, X., Derhab, A., Maglaras, L., Security and Privacy for Green IoT-Based Agriculture: Review, Blockchain Solutions, and Challenges. *IEEE Access*, 8, 32031–32053, 2020.

25. GeSi, *#SMARTer2030-ICT Solutions for 21st Century Challenges*, Global eSustainability Initiative (GeSI), Brussels, Belgium, 2015.

26. Maksimović, M. and Omanović-Mikličanin, E., Green internet of things and green nanotechnology role in realizing smart and sustainable agriculture, in: *VIII international scientific agriculture symposium "AGROSYM 2017*, pp. 2290–2295, 2017.

27. Ahmed, R., Asim, M., Khan, S.Z., Singh, B., Green Iot-Issues and Challenges, in: *2nd International Conference on Advanced Computing and Software Engineering (ICACSE-2019)*.

28. IBM, Models for machine learning, 2017, Available online at https://developer.ibm.com/technologies/artificial-intelligence/articles/cc-models-machine-learning/

5

CIoT: Internet of Green Things for Enhancement of Crop Data Using Analytics and Machine Learning

Sahana Shetty and Narayana Swamy Ramaiah*

Jain (Deemed-To-Be University), School of Computer Science, Faculty of Engg. and Technology, Computer Science and Engineering Department, Bangalore, India

Abstract

Indian farmers' primary concern is crop yields. The pH level of the soil, the water content of the crops, humidity, and micro- and macronutrients are all important for good crop growth. If any of these conditions are not met, crop growth may become unbalanced. Machine learning approaches can help with both prediction and categorization difficulties. The Crop Internet of Things (CIoT) is primarily used to monitor crop productivity and health on farmland. CIoT aids in the monitoring of humidity, soil pH, moisture content, type and quality of soil required for a given crop, and fertiliser type and content. Various sensors, such as humidity sensors, pH sensors, soil quality sensors, and temperature sensors, can be utilised to detect crop yields, as well as machine learning approaches for predicting crop yields while using descriptive analytics. Farmers will profit immensely from an early forecast of soil status using machine learning in the agricultural scenario in order to create a better environment for future agriculture. In the suggested work, we collect historical data and current live datasets from sensor data, and then we pass it via the preprocessing stage, where we perform and attempt to filter out irrelevant or missing data. It has been passed to the testing and training phase after the preprocessing stage has been completed. The data from this phase is subsequently passed to the analytic phase, where it is stored in the database using Spark. The model is trained using machine learning techniques, which will assist in making correct soil content and weed control decisions. Machine learning

Corresponding author: r.narayanaswamy@jainuniversity.ac.in

Roshani Raut, Sandeep Kautish, Zdzislaw Polkowski, Anil Kumar and Chuan-Ming Liu (eds.) Green Internet of Things and Machine Learning: Towards a Smart Sustainable World, (141–162) © 2022 Scrivener Publishing LLC

algorithms with multi-object parameters can be utilised to achieve accurate results by merging different crop-related characteristics. Big data paired with machine learning can help detect and control weeds and enhance performance. How much of each nutrient is required for crop production at different phases of the plant will aid in crop quality.

Keywords: KNN, Naive Bayes decision tree, adaBoost, random forests, support vector machine algorithms, multi-object parameters, big data, machine learning

5.1   Introduction

As the world's population grows, agriculture is increasingly responsible for feeding more than 7 billion people. As people's demands for food quantity and quality grow, increasing production efficiency becomes a challenge that must be addressed properly. The unpredictable nature of weather or humidity, soil types, and pesticide quality, which can result in a harvest that is entirely unusable, is the most important factor for a more profitable crop-based agricultural progress. If crop quality is poor or crops are killed by worms, farmers will suffer financial losses as well as a reduction in society's overall livability. Agriculture today is one of the sectors which advances in use of Internet of Things (IoT). Precision agriculture focuses on optimizing the crop productivity and contains faster and reliable growth for the overview of ongoing cultivation area and helps in automated system with the use of optimizing energy consumption along with water use and pesticide control and growth of plant. Precision farming has been used in agriculture for couple of years. As the name indicates precision, it is all about providing better accuracy and precise way. The main important components of precision farming are components of wireless sensors, robotics, and many more. To improve the farming, nowadays, drone geotagging is used which captures the field information and thereby improve the productivity of crops grown on the particular crop. Data captured from drone images are then stored on large repository. Big data techniques can be used for this purpose. Big data is all about collection of bigger amounts of data from various sources like the device data, surveillance data, internet data, and primary or secondary data. When we go for big data technologies, there are some drawbacks like security concern. Big data technologies can improve on capturing of data, storing, and analysis of data. IoT networks and IoT sensors are in the areas which connect all devices to internet. It also includes how the RFID usage is considered along with Wi-Fi and various sensors with internet stack that is in-built into the devices. These devices help in automated spraying of pesticides to the crops with the help of IoT along with huge data, use of mobile computing, associated with degreed detector network. To improve the precision in agriculture with the help of some of the entities like weather condition, soil health, temperature, humidity, and fertility of soil, IoT devices makes use of the sensors for checking the wetness of leaf, moisture content in soil, soil hydrogen content, and air strain sensors attached, pH values are sent to farmers' mobile devices with the help of SMS. Using the pH values, farmers then can be notified with the NPK level that can be used for crop pesticides to be sprayed. Later, with the help of soil properties that have been taken from land and environmental conditions which have been monitored through IoT devices along with number of users, enquiry about the details to the farmer after the crop has been harvested and the techniques that are used to store these details in a repository are then stored on cloud. It can produce huge data which then can be examined for chemical requirements on the present crop, mapping of crop production to soil properties, and then tell farmer the suitable time to cultivate the upcoming crop and type of crop. This multidisciplinary model depicts how the modules are linked, how all data is stored in big data, how all data retrieval from stored data is connected to the internet, how data from the field is updated from sensors, how similar data is manipulated with the help of a mobile app, and how farmers are notified on weather conditions, crop data, and specific pesticides that are required for crop growth. Farmers will be able to blend the solution, which will then be measured in a specific ratio of water and pesticides, as well as DC motors and power supply. After the solution has been thoroughly prepared, it is pumped to the sprinkler, where pesticides are sprinkled all over the crops, protecting them from pests and insects. To keep track of all of these tasks, we will use mobile devices to create a mobile app that is connected to sensors and sprays pesticides on the land with the help of automation, which helps farmers save time. All of the information about the farmers, the soil properties of the farmland, the chemical requirements for the crop, the quantity of pesticides used, and the amount of water needed will be stored on the system.

Huge information analysis on data is performed to convey the best crop sequences analysis, total production in use of pesticides and removal of insecticides on the farmland. Pesticide and insecticide control is done more automatically than in the past by using microcontrollers and the data obtained from all of the sensors and the pump, and everything is automated with the time limit set by the user. When the process is finished, an alarm signal will be sent to the farmer via message. If the required specifications are not delivered to the farm, the farmer will be alerted to make the necessary modifications, and the update will be performed by the mobile app via the app's admin. As we all know, soil is the foundation of agriculture, and it promotes crop growth by delivering necessary nutrients. Some of the chemical and physical properties of the soil, such as soil moisture, temperature, micro- and macronutrients, and soil type, can influence crop income. Weed control is also one of the most important standards for crop health. Minerals, water, air, and organic components such as manure and hummus are the most important soil components for agriculture. Micronutrients such as boron, copper, iron, zinc, manganese, and iodine should be present in fertile soil. Nitrogen, phosphorus, potassium, calcium, and magnesium are examples of macronutrients. For agricultural production, fertile soil must have a pH between 6.0 and 6.8. Fertile soil has a high-water retention capacity and supply characteristics. There are 16 essential nutrients for plant growth, of which hydrogen, carbon, and oxygen are derived from air and water.

Producers typically manage essential nutrients such as nitrogen, potassium, phosphorous, and magnesium, which are all important for crop development. Soil is categorized into many kinds [13]. Sandy soil has the most molecules of any soil type. It cannot retain water due to the heavier ions. The particles in silty soil are much smaller than those in sandy soil. Watermelon is a preferred plant that can be cultivated. Silty soil can hold water for longer periods of time, so it cannot hold much in the way of nutrients. Clay soil has a high capacity for storing water. Little air passes through its spaces due to the small size of its particles and their propensity to settle together. It has a stronger hold on plant nutrients because it drains slower. As a result, clay soil is high in plant food, allowing for better growth. Paddy is one of the crops that can be cultivated on this soil. Because of its high-water content, peaty soil is easily compressed and contains a lot of organic matter. It contains acidic water, but it is used to regulate soil pH levels and as a disease-control agent for all crops. Because of the organic matter content, loamy soil has a higher pH and calcium level. On loam soil, suitable crops such as wheat, gramme, sugarcane, and a variety of fruits can be cultivated. Improving soil parameters is the primary focus for increasing crop productivity through soil management. Due to terrestrial constraints and the decline of conventional soil management methods, soil fertility has decreased. Crop health is a critical component of modern agriculture's productive system. Adopting the right crop health management plan would result in large increases in crop production. Crop productivity can be increased through good soil management and the application of the right macro- and micronutrients. Decision makers (agricultural experts) and farmers will decide on adequate soil resource management and crop environment management if issues with crop yield pointers are detected and controlled in a timely manner. Prediction and classification problems would also benefit from machine learning methods. Different approaches, such as artificial neural networks and regression, can be used to predict soil fertility.

Water level capacity, silt loam, sandy soil, and electrical conductivity can all be predicted using regression techniques. Using KNN, Naive Bayes decision tree, different crops such as rabi crops and kharif can predict the amount of soil moisture, temperature, macro- and micronutrients needed. AdaBoost, Random Forests, and Support Vector Machine algorithms can be used to make decisions about the types of pesticides that are appropriate for specific crops, as well as the amount of nutrients that are necessary. In the agriculture scenario, farmers would benefit greatly from an early forecast of soil status using machine learning in order to create a better climate for future cultivation.

Machine learning is becoming more prevalent as a way to solve the problems of big data analytics. Machine learning is a collection of modeling methods or algorithms that can learn from data and make decisions without the use of humans. Machine learning methods are most useful when a vast amount of data is available and the output quantities of interest are known. Machine learning is a scalable and modular data analysis plan for massive or big data challenges. Crop protection and weed control would both benefit from big data analytics. To store and analyses datasets with various parameters, different methods such as Hadoop, Hive, and NoSQL can be used.

5.2 Motivation

In conventional farming, disease detection and weed control framers rely on previous expertise or experience, which can lead to incorrect disease detection or overuse of fertilizers that are unfit for crops, making disease and weed control impossible. Incorrect soil and crop management methods are the primary cause of significant soil quality degradation. Farmers overuse chemical fertilizers, resulting in nutrient imbalances in the soil. Worms are more common on cauliflower in our country, and caterpillars are more common on rice. These weeds devastate crops, resulting in no profit for farmers. As a result, constant monitoring aids in crop productivity, and early detection of soil parameters or crop disease aids in the timely implementation of preventative measures to protect the crop from serious diseases. As a result, we were inspired to pursue agriculture as a research topic. Even today, we see people doing manual soil nutrient testing, which takes more time.

An IoT-based device is used in a smart irrigation system to automate the irrigation process by analyzing soil moisture and weather conditions. Aside from that, the sensor data from the device is graphically displayed using the BOLT cloud platform. This has a number of advantages over classical cropping systems. Based on soil moisture and weather forecasting conditions, a smart irrigation system can help maximize water level contents. This can be handled with the help of wireless humidity sensors, which communicate with smart agriculture and allow the system to determine how much water is needed. Crop IoT (CIoT) also receives monitored local weather data, which aids in determining when the land was irrigated. This can be handled with the help of wireless humidity sensors, which communicate with smart agriculture and allow the system to determine how much water is needed. CIoT also receives monitored local weather data, which aids in determining when the land was irrigated. CIoT also receives controlled local weather data which helps us understand when the land was watered. The advantage of agricultural production is that the IoT is enormous. They allow for greater control over the land and the types of irrigations that are needed on a regular basis, allowing the systems to make autonomous decisions while the user is away at work. Because of intelligent control automation, this actually saves you money on your water bills. It also aids in resource optimization, ensuring that resources are not squandered. Furthermore, we have seen drought in certain parts of our world, resulting in the waste of water resources or their inability to be used in the future. The system includes two values that aid in the on and off of the system and can be safely automated with the use of a controller and solenoids. By creating an automated environment for agriculture or agricultural land, farmers would be able to apply the correct amount of water at the right time. CIoT has some advantages, such as saving water and money. The agricultural yard of framers offers a simple and comfortable climate. This system contributes to the reduction of facilities for water storage and transfer. This mechanism allows for the alteration of water resources for future crop generations. To train the model, machine learning techniques are used, which would aid in making informed decisions about soil content and weed control.

Machine learning techniques with multi-object parameters can be used to achieve exact results by integrating several crop-related parameters. Big data on machine learning can produce better results and aid in weed detection and control. How much percentage of nutrients needed for crop at various stages of plant would help to lead to good crop production quality.

5.3   Review of Literature

The paper [1] entitled "Improving the prediction accuracy of soil nutrient classification by optimizing extreme learning machine parameters" is by M.S. Suchithra and Maya L. Pai.

The scientists conducted a study of village-specific soil nutrients such as pH, phosphorus, organic carbon, and potassium. Using classification and prediction strategies for village-level soil parameters will help reduce fertilizer costs while also improving soil health and environmental quality. The authors used data from Kerala as a sample. The extreme learning machine classification methodology was used by the authors. When using ELM, precision has reach up to 80%.

The overall goal was to create a neural network model that could be used to classify and forecast soil fertility indices and pH values. The paper explains how the Kerala government was able to handle soil nutrient deficiency issues with the help of a machine learning algorithm. The ELM model was useful in improving the classification of soil fertility indices. The algorithm could not provide greater precision in classifying soil nutrients such as N2O, P2O5, and K2O. Advanced neural network methods can be used to suggest fertilizer for particular crop types.

In the paper [2], Anuja Chandgude, Nikita Harpale, and Diksha Jadhav present a review of machine learning algorithms used in crop monitoring systems in agriculture.

The paper delves into crop monitoring system ideas. Machine learning approaches are used to analyze data from the agricultural field. Data collected may be linked to weather conditions, temperature, sunshine, wind speed, soil moisture tracking, and other factors that could be the cause of crop diseases. The sensor's output will assist farmers in making the best decision regarding the use of pesticides control weeds at the appropriate time.

The authors employed an artificial neural network to aid in the forecast of soil data based on sensor data. The paper [2] aided farmers in making informed decisions about the profitability of the agricultural field. It will aid in disease prevention and prediction of how the outbreak will spread in the crop field. The paper's next step is to develop pesticides for illnesses that have been expected. The paper's major benefit is that it produces good results even though the output is distorted. Even if the neural network fails, it can still produce better results. The paper's major flaw is that it necessitates extensive training of various test cases, which can lead to poor results.

The paper [3] analyzes soil data using data mining classification techniques.

Soil is a key agricultural component. The purpose of this document is to predict the nature of the soil using various methods such as J48 and Naïve Bayes. These algorithms are used to extract knowledge from soil data and to obtain the algorithm of two soil types such as red or black.

The manually examined soil data set was obtained from the Virudhunagar District Soil Test Laboratory. For the exercise and testing of the data set, some parameters were used, such as village name, soil type, soil texture, pH value, EC, and phosphorous. Based on the value pH and EC, the system might predict the soil type in red or black. With J48, excellent results can be achieved and forecast statistics improved. The paper contributes to the resolution of big data issues. The paper's future scope is to increase the accuracy of the classification of large soil data sets. The average weighted positive rate was 0.97 based on the training dataset, and low 0.86. The paper helps in solving problems related to big data. The future scope of the paper is to enhance the exactness of classification of large soil data sets. Based on the training dataset, weighted average of true positive rate was 0.97 and low level as 0.86. A spectral analysis which was sensitive to soil fertility variation between different soil types was the primary drawback of the paper.

M. R. Bendre's paper [4] entitled "Big Data in Precision Agriculture: Weather Forecasting for Future Farming" discusses the use of big data in precision agriculture.

The organized and unstructured type of agricultural large-scale data was gathered. Historical data is referred to as precision farm datasets. Testing of soil, crop patterns, field surveillance, yield tracking, climatic conditions, weather conditions, GIS, and so on are all historical statistics. Agricultural sensor data included GPS reception systems, soil humidity, temperature sensors, and variable rate fertilizers. Social and web-based information contains input from producers and consumers, social media communities, search engine data, and stream data such as crop tracking data, wireless sensors, and security surveillance.

Paper [4] was about the use of the MapReduce data analysis algorithm. Machine learning algorithms and techniques can be used on a huge amount of data to grow the predictive model. The decision trees, means, K-nearest neighbor search, and neural networks can be used for the discovery of massive data sets using big data technology.

Akshatha and Shreedhara's paper [5] is entitled "Implementation of Machine Learning Algorithms for Crop Recommendation Using Precision Agriculture".

Precision agriculture is a contemporary agricultural approach that uses soil characteristics data, soil types, and crop yield data and offers farmers the right crop based on site-specific parameters. In precision agriculture, the wrong choice is thus reduced and the efficiency is higher. In document [5], a recommendation is proposed using an ensemble model with majority voting approach, based on the Random Tree, K-Nearest Neighbor, and Naive Bayes, and students to suggest crops for particular site parameters with high precision and effectiveness. This issue has also been addressed via a recommendation system.

Shivi Sharma, Geetanjali Rathee, and Hemraj Saini published paper [6] is entitled "Big Data Analytics for Crop Prediction Mode Using Optimization Technique".

Big agricultural data can be used to reveal new solutions that can provide a stronger decision-making process, by analyzing large-scale data sets. The authors focused on soil and environmental characteristics, including average temperature, average moisture, total precipitation, and output used for forecasting two classes, such as good performance and bad returns. As different classes are taken into consideration, the hybrid classification model has been used to optimize the selection of the feature. There are three phases of preprocessing, selection of features, and SVM GWO, which are used to increase accuracy and precision. The consistency of this outcome is around 77.09% and precision is of 75.38%. Other approaches like the artificial neural network, random forest, and hybrid approach are now being used for the future of the paper to obtain a greater range of feature results.

The paper [7] is about soil analysis and prediction of appropriate agricultural crops using machine learning, by S. Panchamurthi, Machine Learning. A. Syed Hameeduddin, P. Yuvaraj, and M. E, M. D. Perarulalan. M.

The farmers are supported by forecasting the appropriate crop for their agricultural purposes by using sensors that are very precise and that also indicate the fertilizers needed to grow the crops.

In paper [8] is about big data analytics framework to identify crop disease and recommendation a solution, by Rupinder Kaur, Raghu Garg, and Dr. Himanshu Aggarwal.

This huge amount of data cannot be stored or analyzed by traditional methods and techniques. Parallel computation and analysis of this type of data is necessary. As a solution, large data analytics are used. Because of its symptom's resemblance, a framework for agriculture is elaborated in the paper big data analytics, recommending a high-level solution. Hadoop and Hive methods were used for this purpose. Data are collected, purified, and standardized. Data is gathered from the laboratory reports and websites, and the data is then retrieved from unstructured redundant data. Data are cleaned. The next step is normalization, which is the extraction of characteristics from cleaned data. Normalized data is transferred to HDFS and saved in a hive-compatible file. HiveQL is a query language similar to SQL that is used to evaluate agricultural data. It determines the name of the disease based on crop disease symptoms and then proposes a solution based on evidence from historical data. The outcome is expressed in the form of graphs, which can be used to suggest a popular solution.

F. K. van Evert, S. Fountas, D. Jakovetic, and V. Crnojevic's paper [9] is about big data for weed control and crop protection.

Farmers should use a variety of data-intensive processes to monitor and control weeds and pests. Data collection, modeling, and interpretation, as well as data sharing, have emerged as critical problems in weed control and crop protection. We examine the problems and opportunities presented by big data in agriculture, including the nature of data gathered, big data analytics, and tools for presenting analysis that make for better crop management decisions for weed control and crop protection. Big data storage and querying present major challenges due to the need to distribute data across multiple machines, as well as the continuous growth and evolution of data from various sources. Semantic tools are useful when data is combined from several sources, which include identifying interactions of potential agricultural significance and creating relationships of significance and units between data items. Together with the numerical algorithms for their training, big data analysis models are summarized. Actionable information to farmers is examined on the developments and instruments to present the processed big data and a success story from the Netherlands. Finally, the potential uses of big data for weed control, particularly for invasive, herbicide resistant, and parasite weeds, are argued. This potential can be achieved only by working with data scientists in agriculture and by establishing organizational, ethical, and legal arrangements for data-sharing.

The paper [10] is about detection of weed using neural networks, by R. Dhayabarani.

In the response of the enormous population worldwide, improving agriculture's productivity would increase food resources. In the areas of weeds and plant diseases, we are faced with numerous problems. We need to find and delete the weeds. We do not now have more people in the fields to be able to work. In recent years, great attention has been focused on implementing machine learning techniques, such as neural networks of convolution on agriculture. To classify the plants, we use convolutional neural networks. The automatic identification process will provide a significant contribution to the application of pesticides, fertilization, and harvesting of various species in a short term to enhance food and pharmaceutical industry production processes. The cost of labor should be reduced. The architecture of the convolutional neural network is used to extract the characteristics of images after pre-processing.

The paper [11] is about automatic plant watering system, by Abhishek Gupta.

The author focused on crop watering which is done in automated way. The author implemented sensors that detect the soil humidity and water supply to the crop when the water requirement on crops goes down. PIC16F877A microcontroller was used for the same purpose. The microcontroller was responsible for controlling the water supply to the field that needs to be irrigated. Various sensors are used in field that gets activated when watering is required for plants. Once the field gets dried, sensors sense the water requirements and send a signal to microcontroller for watering of crops. Microcontroller then supply water to the field where the water is required until the required water is supplied the microcontroller will be activated, once the required water is supplied, it gets deactivated. The microcontroller is coded in such a manner that it detects or senses the moisture level of the plants and supplies water as needed. Such systems are usually implemented in small and large gardens where the microcontroller is placed inside the sensors. According to the author, as the crop requires watering twice a day, the microcontroller is programmed in such a way that it gets automatically watered as the time limit that is programmed. Such a microcontroller was designed for those people who are busy during their regular schedule and miss to water plants. The main problem with this system is it can be used for small or large garden and not for the crop systems.

The paper [12] is about IoT and agriculture data analysis for smart farm, by Jirapond Muangprathuba, Nathaphon Boonnama, and Aprirat Wanichasombata.

According to the authors, they suggested developing a system based on a wireless sensor network for optimally watering agricultural crops. The system's goal was to design and operate a control system using sensors on a crop field with a data management system using a web application for data management. The system is made up of three parts: hardware, a mobile application, and a web application. The primary components were defined and implemented in control box hardware that was linked to collect data on agricultural crops. Soil temperature sensors are used to monitor crops that are linked to the control box. The second component is a web-application that was designed and built to manage crop data and field data information. When developing the second component, data mining techniques such as a priori were used to analyze the data in order to predict the temperature, humidity, and soil moisture level, which are used to provide optimized crop management development in the future. The final component is primarily used to monitor crop watering, which can be done using a smartphone and a mobile application device. This system enables crop watering, which can be done either automatically or manually by the users. The system's automated control makes use of data collected from soil moisture and humidity sensors, which are necessary for crop watering. According to the authors, in the realistic control mode, consumers or farmers may choose manual management of agricultural crop watering. The system will then send a notification to the application through the LINE API. This system was developed and validated in Surattani, Thailand's Makhamtia District. The results showed that the implementation was beneficial to crop agriculture. The moisture content and humidity of the soil were also retained for crop growth, lowering costs and increasing agricultural crop productivity. Crop watering will be done automatically. The system went through many phases, including data pre-processing, data reduction, data modeling, and discovery. The association rule method was used in data modeling and discovery. The authors used a priori and periodic item selection procedures, as well as the Weka tool, to determine the accuracy of data on agricultural land crops. Data mining techniques that use association rules employ simple if else conditions as well as simple standards such as support and trust. The minimum level of support achieved was 0.75, and the level of trust was 90%. The writers' work assists farmers in undergoing digital transformation. As a result of this system, there has been a significant increase in the use of digital technology applications in agriculture.

According to author Sanjukumar "Advance technique for soil moisture automatic content for automotive organized land" was build and was successfully installed with sensors. Features of land requirements like temperature, water consumption monitoring, and automatic irrigation shutdown systems were the requirements. According to author, system can easily set the humidity content and is regularly updated with the values on the LCD screen. After this was implemented successfully, author also added additional features like pH of the soil, electric properties of soil components, and so on. Author also made use of wireless sensing network with ZigBee technology that helps regulate air humidity, moisture of the soil, and temperature required. The system also included groundwater sensor, humidity sensor, heat sensors, water pump system, a fan, and a transmitter. Here, wireless sensor network is integrated with ZigBee to transfer soil moisture and soil temperatures required. According to the system by author Sanjukumar, data gets transmitted to a web server using GPRS over a cellular network system. Data can be achieved through this system with the help of agricultural data and image classifications can be done through image processing system.

According to author Chethana "Automated Wireless Watering system" provides a user-friendly system. The system was designed in such a way that the users had two options, one with the default process and the other one with manual process option. The system was designed in such a way that the log file of various activities was also recorded. The system describes a wireless sensor network for sensing soil moisture level, temperature, and humidity values. The system also stores information about locations.

The user interface of the system was implemented using MATLAB for the data management.

All the authors with their proposal have done a good progress in their work. The only difference between all the authors is in communication technologies and the storage of data collected from different sources using sensor devices. Applications use more than one server to store the data collected. As the number of nodes increases, the servers will have more resource storage space which can result in more costly device.

5.4   Problem with Traditional Approach

In the traditional cropping system, crop cultivation is managed manually. As the water is directly irrigated on to the soil, they get a better soil pressure hence reduces the appearance of the plant. Due to the absence of automated system control, it would result in poor management of crop systems. The main problem is due to huge growth of the country's population. Nowadays, global water crisis is increasing where management of water scarcity has been emerging and increasing and this is the major issue. Hence, in traditional cropping system, irrigation of crops is the major problem.

According to the survey made, in the traditional approach, there were very few sensors like the soil moisture and the temperature sensors were used. But when we look ahead, our country is improving. Now, the irrigation system model uses main weather data for getter better crop yield. They use weather prediction to take decisions that result in better accuracy. In the traditional approach, neither machine learning nor deep learning techniques were incorporated. While we look into the current approach of our model, we use logistic regression along with ensemble techniques that can be implemented for better accuracy and precision. In the traditional approach, either complicated user interface or no user design was used for their referenced model. But in the current system, user interface with dialog box along with chat bot is build, so that users can better results for the query that is sent. In the traditional approach, they either used or operated the system at different location with the use of either Bluetooth or Zigbee protocols which had a problem that worked for only shorter distances. In the modern systems, use of flask application makes it easier to access the field data and what is the status of crop from anywhere the user can sit and get the information through internet connection. In the traditional approach, developers used Arduino board microcontroller for all the related sensors, but they had limited features for applications.

In the current system approach, Raspberry Pi was used, which had more features along with programming on Raspberry Pi which was much easier compared to traditional approach. Raspberry Pi was portable and includes built-in RAM, storage space, and software that are required to run the code on to it. Current sensors help in providing better results. UI sensors can be used that helps keep track of air ambience, UV ray intensity, and various gases released from industries that damages crop growth; all of these can be controlled using the Raspberry Pi.

5.5 Tool Requirement

5.5.1 Arduino UNO

Arduino UNO is an open-source hardware and software platform. It is made up of a programmable circuit board and Arduino IDE, which allows people to write code and upload it to a physical system. Arduino microcontroller was used to control and sense few parameters for the crops like the moisture of soil where resistors were used to check the moisture of soil. Resistors were used which gives the indication as when the value of

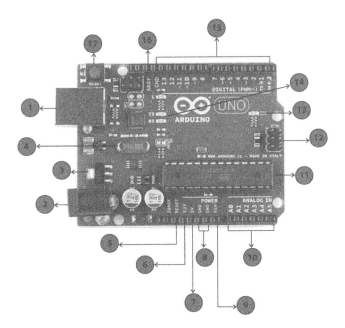

Figure 5.1 Arduino board.

resistance increases and when it decreases. When the moisture is more, the value of resistance will be more, and when the moisture of the soil is less, then the resistance value will be more. There were many features when using Arduino UNO. Se Arduino boards can read both analog and digital signals as input from various sensors and convert them to an output, like activating the motors, turning on or off the LED, connecting to the cloud, and many other functions. By sending a set of instructions to the board's microcontroller via the Arduino IDE, the user can control the board's functions. Arduino is a programmer circuit board that uses a USB cable to load new code onto the board. The Arduino IDE is written in C++, which makes it simpler to write programs. Arduino offers a standard form that breaks down the microcontroller's functions. Figure 5.1 shows the Arduino board.

5.5.2   Humidity Sensor

Light, water, soil, and air are all necessary for plants to flourish. All of these criteria aid in the growth of plants in a healthy way. Plant growth requires water as well. In order for crops to grow in a greenhouse, humidity and temperature are essential. The DHT-22 is a low-cost digital and humidity sensor with a digital output. To measure the air temperature, it uses a humidity sensor and a thermistor. It also has a capacitive humidity sensor which uses the data pin to transmit a numerical signal. The temperature range for the DHT-22 is −40°C to −80°C, with humidity levels ranging

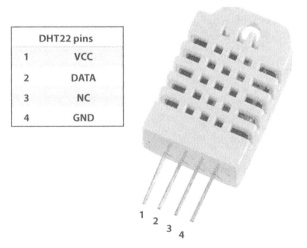

DHT22 pins	
1	VCC
2	DATA
3	NC
4	GND

Figure 5.2 Humidity sensor.

from 0%–99.9% RH. The sensor gets a 3.3- to 6-V DC power supply. The sensor has a high level of accuracy. Figure 5.2 shows a temperature sensor as well as DHT-22 pins.

A humidness sensor, also known as a hygrometer, measures and reports the humidity in the air on a regular basis. The humidity sensor detects the temperature and moisture content of the air. The sensing consists of two metal plates separated by a non-conductive compound film. The film absorbs moisture from the air, causing voltage fluctuations between the two plates. The changes in voltages are transformed to a digital representation of the amount of moisture in the air.

5.5.3   Relay

Relay is an electromagnetic device that is used for isolating two circuits electrically. It connects the circuits magnetically. Relays are useful in many ways and the circuits are allowed to switch to another one. These are used for interfacing an electronic circuit that works on low voltage with another electronic circuit that works on high voltage. For instance, a circuit of 5-V DC battery can be switched to 230 V. Alternative current main circuit uses a relay. Hence, the smaller circuit can be driven like fan and electric bulb. Relay switch has two parts: input and output. The input region contains a coil that helps in generating magnetic field when an electronic circuit provides a small voltage called operating voltage. Relays are commonly used and are present in various configuration of operating voltage like 6 and 9 V. Figure 5.3 shows the relay device.

Figure 5.3 Relay.

5.5.4   DC Motor

DC motor is an electronic device that is used to convert direct current energy to mechanical energy. It relies on the magnetic field's forces. Many types of motor have mechanism that internally changes the current direction. The speed of the DC motor could be varied over a wide range by varying the current strength or using variable voltages. Small DC motors have been used in a variety of gadgets. After the algorithm processes the data and if data tends to be fallen below a given thresholds value, then it gives high voltage to the motor and the motor gets turned on. DC motor has two leads positive and negative which can be connected to Arduino board; NPN transistor is used to control the switching process of motor. Figure 5.4 shows DC water motor used for agricultural crop.

5.5.5   pH Sensor and CO_2 Sensor

pH is a critical component of agriculture that ensures that crops remain healthy. Whether crops can flourish in acidic or alkaline soil, the highest hydrogen potential is between 5 and 6.5. pH sensors, such as the NodeMCU ESP8266, can be used in this way. Other sensors may be used to monitor the water quality of the soil. The pH of the soil indicates how acidic or alkaline it is. The potential of hydrogen is made up of hydrogen's attentiveness as well as ions in solution. It can also be counted using a sensor that detects the potential differences between two electrodes, one of which is a reference electrode made of silver or silver chloride, and the other of which is a glass electrode fine with hydrogen ions.

Figure 5.4 DC 12-V water motor.

5.6   Methodology

In the suggested work, we first gather previous data [15–17] and current live datasets from sensor data, and then, we pass it to the preprocessing stage, where we attempt to filter out irrelevant or missing fields. When the preprocessing stage has completed, it is passed on to the testing and training stage. This model has three connected modules; all of the data is stored in the big data storage and all of the data is retrieved from that store; it is all connected to the internet, and the data from the field is updated from the sensors, which are all in the sensor module; similar data is manipulated to the mobile app; and the farmer is notified on weather conditions, crop data, and other information. It also gives access to the farmer to mix the solution and then the solution will be mixed in a definite ratio of water and pesticide and then, with the help of power supply and DC motor, spraying pesticide on which time of the month and for how many times. To protect the crop from pests and insects, the solution is pumped into a sprinkler, and the pesticide is sprayed all over the crop. The data from the preprocessing stage is then sent to the analytic phase, where it is stored in the database using Spark. Machine learning techniques are used to train the model, which will aid in making proper soil content and weed control decisions. By combining multiple crop-related parameters with machine learning methods with multi-object parameters, precise results can be obtained. Big data combined with machine learning can help detect and control weeds, resulting in better results. What percentage of nutrients is needed for crop production at various stages of the plant will help to ensure good crop quality, preparation of data collection and formatting, as well as data conversion from one form to another. We should use machine learning and big data approaches in this case. The processed data can then be divided into two categories: training and testing datasets. Feature extraction is the process of selecting and extracting non-redundant data based on crop production. The end result will be improved precision and crop yield.

The system that we will be using here makes use of Raspberry Pi which captures different parameters like the weather condition, soil moisture conditions, temperature, humidity, and light intensity. These features are captured by the system. We can set the value to change the roof of the green house based on the type of crops. Any outliers or noise present can be removed by using convolutional neural network. The cropping system uses pH, humidity sensors, and data that are required to enter data from sensors. All the information that received through sensors is displayed on LCD and PC. Using artificial neural network techniques results in possible

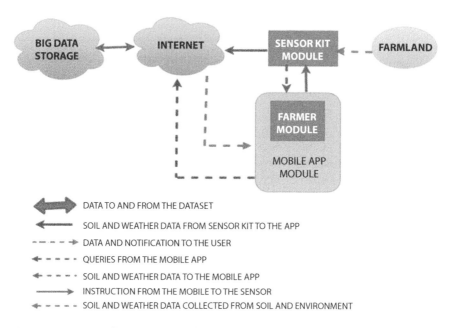

DATA TO AND FROM THE DATASET

SOIL AND WEATHER DATA FROM SENSOR KIT TO THE APP

DATA AND NOTIFICATION TO THE USER

QUERIES FROM THE MOBILE APP

SOIL AND WEATHER DATA TO THE MOBILE APP

INSTRUCTION FROM THE MOBILE TO THE SENSOR

SOIL AND WEATHER DATA COLLECTED FROM SOIL AND ENVIRONMENT

Figure 5.5 System architecture of CIoT. https://techatronic.com/smart-agriculture-using-iot/.

implementation of better and effective controls. The controller-based system does not require previous knowledge of system and provide better accuracy when artificial neural network is used on crop irrigation that in turn provide better optimized results for different types of agricultural crops (Figure 5.5).

The crop's most notable feature in the IoT includes a soil moisture sensor that detects the moisture level of the soil in crops. The detected values that are collected from sensors go to the cloud where the data values are saved are stored with the help of firebase. Values that are collected are then tested using ensemble model where the intelligent model helps in identifying the patterns in data set. The value accuracy is received in form of report and the predicted value is sent on to the cloud via the instruction received from Arduino board. Further, this model can be also connected to an app (web or mobile application) and the farmers can get the all the updates as when to water plants via the application.

5.7   Conclusion

CIoT helps to improve crop yields and improve the quality of crops. The system uses Arduino along with machine learning model like ensemble techniques to check for the accuracy of the crop yield. Using IoT on our system helps users to get the details of moisture level of soil, humidity of land, potential of hydrogen, and many more components. Further, big data framework like Spark can be used along with geotagging information.

References

1. Suchithra, and Pai, Improving the prediction accuracy of soil Nutrient classification by Optimizing Extreme Learning Machine Parameters. *Inf. Process. Agric.*, 7, 1, 72–82, 2019, March 2020.

2. Chandgude, A., Harpale, N., Jadhav, D., A Review of Machine Learning Towards Precision Agriculture in Crop Production. *J. Environ. Sci. Comput. Sci. Eng. Technol.*, 6, 4, 1468–1471, 2018.

3. Rajeswari, V. and Arunesh, K., Analysing Soil Data using Data Mining Classification Techniques. *Indian J. Sci. Technol.*, 9, 19, 2016, 2017.

4. Bendre, M., Thool, R., Thool, V., Big data in precision agriculture: Weather forecasting for future farming. *2015 1st International Conference on Next Generation Computing Technologies (NGCT)*, 2016.

5. Bondre, D. and Mahagaonkar, S., Prediction of Crop Yield and Fertilizer Recommendation Using Machine Learning Algorithms. *Int. J. Eng. Appl. Sci. Technol.*, 04, 05, 371–376, 2019.

6. Srinivasulu, D. and Vani, K., Big Data Analytics for Crop Prediction Mode Using Optimization Technique. *J. Adv. Res. Dyn. Control Syst.*, 11, 10, 1298–1310, 2019.

7. Panchamurthi, S., Soil Analysis and Prediction of Suitable Crop for Agriculture using Machine Learning. *Int. J. Res. Appl. Sci. Eng. Technol.*, 7, 3, 2328–2335, 2019.

8. Garg, R. and Aggarwal, H., Big Data Analytics Recommendation Solutions for Crop Disease using Hive and Hadoop Platform. *Indian J. Sci. Technol.*, 9, 32, 1-6, 2016.

9. van Evert, F., Fountas, S., Jakovetic, D., Crnojevic, V., Travlos, I., Kempenaar, C., Big Data for weed control and crop protection. *Weed Res.*, 57, 4, 218–233, 2017.

10. Dhayabarani, R., A.K., G.M., Detection of Weed using Neural Networks. *Int. J. Eng. Res. Technol. (IJERT)*, 6, 8, 1–5, 2018.

11. Murawwat, S., Qureshi, A., Ahmad, S., Shahid, Y., Weed Detection Using SVMs. *Etasr.com*, 8, 1, 2018, 2412-2416, 2019.

12. Muangprathuba, J., Boonnama, N., Kajornkasirata, S., Lekbangponga, N., Wanichsombata, A., Nillaorb, P., IoT and agriculture data analysis for smart farm. *Comput. Electron. Agric.*, available online 12 December 2019. 156, 467–474, January 2019.

13. Sirsat, M., Cernadas, E., Fernández-Delgado, M., Khan, R., Classification of agricultural soil parameters in India. *Comput. Electron. Agric.*, 135, 269–279, 2017.

14. Gao, J., Nuyttens, D., Lootens, P., He, Y., Pieters, J., Recognising weeds in a maize crop using a random forest machine-learning algorithm and near-infrared snapshot mosaic hyperspectral imagery. *Biosyst. Eng.*, 170, 39–50, 2019.

15. http://www.mospi.gov.in/statistical-year-book-india/2018

16. https://soilhealth.dac.gov.in/

17. https://data.gov.in/

6

Smart Farming Through Deep Learning

[1]Sandeep Mathur*, [2]Disha Vaid and [3]Ajay Rana

[1]GL Bajaj Institute of Management, Greater Noida, UP, India
[2]Amity Institute of Information Technology, Amity University, Noida, UP, India
[3]Shobhit University, Merrut, UP, India

Abstract

Machine learning is the ability provided to a machine to improve with experience and by using the accurate facts and figures. In the world that is preparing itself to get adapted to automated tools in the upcoming future, machine learning defines the core of dynamic fields such as robotics, various E-platforms, etc., and with the extent in the vision, it has a wider scope. History provides us with traces that our ancestors discovered the concept of civilization due to agriculture. In the modern world, the trending automation tools with traditional agricultural practices are blended. India is the largest producer of grains in the world. Being from the land of farmers and farmlands, a wide variety of crops are grown in respective seasons, but sometimes, the blessing turns out to be a curse for the farmers. There is a wide variety of challenges that farmers are facing such as climatic disasters, pests, quality of seeds, and land quality. Here, we are working on using modern machinery methods to solve these issues and paving the nation toward Jai Jawaan, Jai Kissan, and Jai Vigyan. In the present research work, we investigated the deep learning technologies that encompass traditional farming into smart farming.

Keywords: Deep learning, smart farming, image analysis, IoT, land quality check

6.1 Introduction

Machine learning is the ability provided to the machine to enhance with experience. It provides the computer the ability to adjust itself to a changing environment so that the programmer does not need to

---

Corresponding author: sandeep2809@gmail.com; smathur@amity.edu

Roshani Raut, Sandeep Kautish, Zdzislaw Polkowski, Anil Kumar and Chuan-Ming Liu (eds.) Green Internet of Things and Machine Learning: Towards a Smart Sustainable World, (163–188) © 2022 Scrivener Publishing LLC

think of all possible inputs. Since the last decade, AI and automated tools had been an area that has seen tremendous growth and popularity among many people. With the advancement of such technologies, life is becoming easier and machine learning provides the backbone to them. It helps in finding many solutions in vision, speech, database recognition, etc. It has been used to prevent fraud, the advancement of AI, medical sites, agriculture, etc. Machine learning has always been an area of keen interest for scientists as it provides them a hope that this tech can help them and creates a synthetic human brain or a super humanoid robot in the future. The practical application of machine learning can be seen in agriculture. India is known as the farmer's nation and has benefited from the improvement of technologies for the agriculture sector. The farmers of our country are getting well adapted to these techs which are safe and reliable, and enhance the quality of life. Agriculture does not only restrict the growing of crops but also means the growing of flowers, the recreation of a forest, animal husbandry, etc. There has been the development of many machineries with the rise of machine learning and AI that covers various aspects of agriculture ranging from the sowing of seeds to harvesting of grains. This machinery not only makes the agricultural practices easier but also prevents occupational hazards such as hazards occurring due to grain bins, contact of chemicals, excessive noise, musculoskeletal injuries, overheat, and others, and maybe exposure to animals that can transmit diseases. A large number of animal-related diseases have been discovered and cured with advanced tools, but the challenge still exists. All the farmers cannot afford technical practices over the traditional methods of farming to reduce the chances of crop failure. Hence, it is a great matter of concern for the inventor and needs to think about the ideas that make these gadgets affordable for large- and small-scale farmers.

The Internet of Things (IoT) is commonly known as "IoT", a new model that is transforming computing. It can be explained as the linkage between the individually distinguishable embedded computing instrument in the approachable internet framework. The "IoT" connects multiple different devices with the help of the internet as well as electronic sensors. Nowadays, many devices are connected to the web, whether it is mobile devices or appliances. There are many applications of IoT in different sectors:

- Elder care
- Smart city

- Smart home
- Medical and healthcare
- Home automation
- Agriculture
- Product digitalization, etc.

The IoT's biggest notable vogue in recent years is the increased number of gadgets connected to and supervised by the Internet. The large range of programs for IoT technology refers to that the details can vary from one device to other device but there are foundational features that are shared by most. The "IoT" generates chances for more straight combination of actual world into computerized systems which results in better improvements and reduced human efforts. The number of IoT devices has increased 31% every year to 8.45 billion in year 2017, and it has been calculated that there will be more than 30 billion devices by 2021. As we already know what is IoT and it is benefits now let us learn a bit about Green IoT. Green IoT represents the problem of bringing down energy consumption of IoT devices that attain a feasible environment for IoT systems [20]. Green IoT is identified as an essential skilled course in IoT to decrease the nursery impact brought about by existing applications. It is all about using the IoT to reduce the greenhouse effect and CO_2 emission.

When we are talking about the use of Green IoT in the environment, we mean using solar panels, IoT-based drones, soil moisture sensor, etc.

Benefits of Green IoT are as follows:

- Better health
- Healthier environment
- Smart energy-efficient system
- Cleaner water system
- Smart farming

6.2 Literature Review

Table 6.1 closely contrasts the various techniques for managing farm and different farming activities to enhance the productivity level with quality.

Table 6.1 Reviewing multiple authors previous research work.

Author's name	Outcome	Future work	Reference no.
Eugeniusz Herbut	"The aim of the paper discusses the connections among modern livestock production which includes its techniques and concentration with animal welfare demands".	"Precise production methods, as well as concentrated stocking density. This must be closely connected in providing the animals with necessary living conditions, which provide them with a base of welfare".	[1]
R.K.P Singh, K.K. Singh, and Abhay kumar	Blending the trend with tradition in the field of agriculture and providing their access to farmers in Bihar.	Self-driven system which will allow the enhancement of GPS locators and provide enough data for the monitoring system.	[2]
"Abdul Rehman, Luan Jindong, Rafia Khatoon, and Imran Hussain"	Focuses on farmers' adoption of modern agricultural techniques, their efficient usage and role.	Development of more efficient mobile apps to control the techs and can be available in all languages that provides even more better access and output through the devices	[3]

(Continued)

Table 6.1 Reviewing multiple authors previous research work. (*Continued*)

Author's name	Outcome	Future work	Reference no.
"Marianah Masrie, Mohammad Syamim Aizuddin Rosman, Rosidah Sam, and Zuriati Janin"	This project provides the methods to calculate the quantity of nutrients in soil at minimum cost. Minimizes the use of synthetic nutrients which are harmful for the resources.	More no. of pre-tests should be conducted to know the actual wavelength each nutrient signifies to enhance the precision and accuracy of the method.	[4]
N. Singh and A.Shaligram.	Provides the idea regarding the functionality of NPK managing robots in the field and How it calculates the NPK content of soil.	Introduction of a wide variety of sensors among one single robotic body to make things easier to operate even using a mobile app.	[5]
"Y. Kulkarni, K. K. Warhade, and S. Bahekar"	Information regarding the use of lights of different wavelengths in determining soil nutrients is mentioned in this paper.	Synthetic nutrients are harmful for the natural elements which support farming. So, it is very important of them to be used.	[6]

(*Continued*)

Table 6.1 Reviewing multiple authors previous research work. (*Continued*)

Author's name	Outcome	Future work	Reference no.
L.C. Garvade	Focuses on the methodology in which devices calculate the content of NPK in the soil.	Building up even better algorithms which will help in measuring the quantity of nutrients with even more precision.	[7]
"D.V. Ramane, S.S. Patil, and A. Shaligram"	Details regarding the use of optical sensors in the fields for even more precise data.	Planting the sensors in each corner of the field which later used in gathering collective information regarding the crops.	[8]
A. Rashid	Details regarding the soil health using electromagnetic radiation are described in this paper.	Even more different lights of various wavelengths should be tested to measure the soil health even more accurately.	[9]
D.Q. Huo *et al.*	Microfluidics can be used as a helpful tool for several machineries and has a wide area application in agriculture.	Advance systems need to be developed using the principles of microfluidics for proper analysis of agriculture fields.	[10]

6.3 Deep Learning in Agriculture

Deep learning refers to a subdivision of "Machine Learning" which is further a subset of Artificial Intelligence (AI). AI basically refers to any program that emulates the functions and working of the human brain. It works on various techniques and algorithms for creating different patterns and processing data which can be later used in process of decision making. It gradually selects useful data and information from the raw facts and figures. Deep learning AI is capable of learning and performing different tasks on various structured or unstructured data sets. The methods are based on artificial neural networks also known as neural networks. Artificial neural networks are computing structures that are roughly inspired by the human neural network. It is a collection of interconnected nodes also known as artificial neurons. Deep learning works on multiple layers in a network. Earlier the work was done on a linear perceptron but as the time passed, it was observed that new algorithms with more layers should be used. A modern alternative which was introduced for working on multiple layers was deep learning which grants practical application and advanced implementation. The data on which it is implemented is very vast and it is known as big data. This data can be found anywhere in different forms and structures from different zones of this world. Evaluating and comprehending this data and extracting the useful information manually can take decades, deep learning comes to rescue in these types of situations. Deep learning is a very powerful and effective tool whenever we are dealing with unstructured data. Deep learning algorithms easily become overfitted if the data we are working upon is very simple or incomplete, thus it fails to generalize the new data in a good manner.

"Deep learning" methods are based on "artificial neural networks" which can be grouped in the following types [18].

6.3.1 Feedforward Neural Network

"Feedforward neural network" is the easiest and first category devised of artificial neural network. In this type of neural network, the connections among the nodes do not form any cycle. It is totally different from the successor: recurrent neural networks (RNNs). The facts and figures progress in only a single direction forward from input nodes, across the hidden node and output node, in this network. No loops or cycles are formed in this network.

6.3.1.1 Single-Layer Perceptron

"Single-layer perceptron network" is the extremely basic type of neural network, which consists of a single (one) layer of output nodes; the inputs are sustained right to the outputs via a sequence of weights. In every node, the addition of the products of weights and the inputs is computed, and if the value is above doorway (typically 0), the neuron launches and takes the current activated value (typically, 1); else the disbanded value is taken (typically, −1).

Neurons with this type of simulation function are also known as false neurons or linear threshold units. A perceptron commonly known as algorithm that can be generated using any values for the currently activate states and deactivated states as long as the doorway value lies between the two.

Delta rule calculates the mistakes between calculated output and sample output data. A "single-layer neural network" computes a constant output instead of a single step function. A usual choice is the so-called logistic function:

$$f(x) = \frac{1}{1+e^{-z}}$$

The single-layer network is similar to the organizing regression model, commonly used in statistical modeling The derivative of this function is easily calculated:

$$f'(x) = f(x)(1 - f(x))$$

If its activation function is modulo 1, then it can solve XOR problem with exactly one neuron.

$$f(x) = x \mod 1$$

$$f'(x) = 1.$$

6.3.1.2 Multi-Layer Perceptron

In this type of networks, there are many computational units' layers that are connected to each other in a feedforward way. Every neuron in a layer has straight connections to neurons of the next layer. The units of these networks have a sigmoid function as a starting function. It uses a variety of learning approaches, and the most popular is back-propagation. In this, the output values are then contrasted with the actual right answer to compute the value of some already defined error-function, and after that, the error is then fed back again through the network. After repetition of this process for multiple times, the network normally converges to a state where the chances of mistake are less. To alter weights correctly, one applies a general method for non-linear development that is called "gradient descent." The issue of the back-propagation algorithm is the speed of merging and the chances of ending up in a local minimum of the error function. Today back-propagation in multi-layer perceptron's the tool of choice for various machine learning tasks.

6.3.2   Recurrent Neural Network

RNNs are a strong and robust type of neural network. It belongs to the most favorable algorithms in use as it is the only unique algorithm with an inner memory. RNN is the state of the artwork for consecutive.

In this, the relation among nodes forms a directed graph along a secular series.

This allows it to show secular dynamic behavior. Obtained from feed-forward neural networks, RNNs use their inner memory to process length of a variable series of inputs. This makes them relevant to tasks such as non-segmented attached handwriting recognition or speech recognition. It is used by Apple's Siri and Google's voice search feature. It is the first algorithm that recalls its input, due to an internal memory. Over the past years, impressive achievements were seen in the field of deep learning.

The filtering units in RNN form a cycle. The output from layer 1 becomes the input for the upcoming layer, which is typically the sole layer; hence, the output of the layer becomes an input to it, setting up a feedback loop. It permits the network to have memory about the earlier states and use that to affect the present output. One notable result of this contrast is far from feedforward neural networks, and RNN can have a series of inputs and create a series of output values as well, giving it very useful in applications which require filtering sequence.

$$\text{"St=f(Uxt+Wst-1)"}$$

Here,
xt is the input at time t.

U, V, and W are learned parameters (shared by every step).
Ot is the output at time t.
St is the state at time t.
f is the activation function.

6.3.3   Radial Basis Function Neural Network

Radial basis function neural network is a different kind of artificial neural network that is used in classification processes, faster learning techniques, and better universal approximation methods. It consists of three different kinds of feed forward neural network layers known as input layer, hidden layer, and output layers. In the first layer, it takes the inputs from the users, the second layer is a hidden layer which has some RBF non-linear activation units, the last and the final layer has the output of the network. Activation functions in RBFNs are typically executed as Gaussian functions [19]. For radial basis function, Gaussian function is generally used. We define radial distance $r = ||x - t||$.

"Gaussian Radial Function: =
$\phi(r) = \exp(-r^2/2\sigma^2)$
where $\sigma > 0$"

6.3.4   Kohenen Self Organizing Neural Network

Kohonen self-organizing neural network arranges the network model into the input data on its own using non manageable learning. In other words, it is also known as Kohenen self-organizing maps. It comprises two fully interconnected layers, known as input layer and output layer. The output layer is arranged as a 2D grid. There is no starting function, and the weights represent the characteristics (position) of the output layer's node. The Euclidean interval among the input data and each output layer node are computed. The weights of the nearest node and its adjacent from the input are updated to bring them near to the input with the formula below:

$$\text{"wi(t+1)=wi(t)+}\alpha\text{(t)}\eta\text{j}*\text{i(x(t)−wi(t))"}$$

Here, $x(t)$ is the input data at time t;
wi(t) is the ith weight at time t, and ηj*i is the adjacent function between the ith and jth nodes.

6.3.5   Modular Neural Network

A modular neural network is another artificial neural network that is distinguished by a continuous series of self-dependent neural networks decreased by some mediator. Each network obeys as a module and works on multiple different inputs to complete some subtask of the task in the network [1]. The mediator takes the results of each module and operates on it to generate the output of the network. The mediator accepts the outputs of the modules only—it does not respond nor otherwise signals. The modules do not interact with each other. Unlike one big network which can allocate to random tasks, each module in a modular network must be allocated a particular task and attached to other modules in particular ways by a designer. Example, the brain developed (rather than learned) to generate the lateral geniculate nucleus (LGN). In some cases, the generator can opt to go after biological models. In some cases, other models may be better. The standard of the output will be a function of the standard of the blueprint.

Food production is used to get processed through agriculture. History provides us the traces that our ancestor discovered the concept of civilization due to agriculture. In modern world, blending the trend, i.e., automated tools with traditional agriculture. Being from the land of farmers and farmlands, we come across a wide variety of crops that are grown in respective seasons. Agriculture sector shares 16% of total GDP of India and provides employment to around 60% of the population. But sometimes, the blessing turns out to be curse for the farmers. There are a wide variety of challenges farmers face such as climatic disasters, pests, quality of seeds, and land quality, and here, we are working on using the modern machinery methods to solve these issues. Agriculture might be seemed to be an easy task for an individual living in a high-tech city, but the reality just opposes this whole mirage of thoughts. The cycle mentioned below showcases the various steps taken to ensure the healthy crop production and quality. Figure 6.1 shows the distinctive crop cycle applicable across the world [18].

Each of these steps participates equally in the crop production and must be performed within the stipulated time and in almost accurate number of resources in use. Taking example of fertilizing, fertilizer is something which is a major resource and factor for a good quality of crop, but it should be applied during a phase of the crop growth that too in the adequate amount. Otherwise, it may lead to acidification of soil ultimately turning a fertile land into a barren one. Each of the crops required a certain type of climatic conditions and soil type to grow depending upon the nutrients and nourishment required by them for growth. Even, distance between the

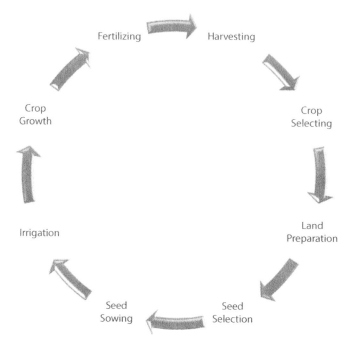

Figure 6.1 Typical crop cycle.

seeds while sowing plays a vital role so that there should be no conquest between plants for nutrients. Moreover, in last couple of years, some part of our nation especially regions of Maharashtra had been adversely affected by the shortage of rainfall that too leading to crop failure. As per the Jal Shakti Ministry, 42% of fertile land turned into barren due to shortage of rainfall and inappropriate irrigation methods since independence. On the other hand, farmers in Kerala adopted the modern farming methods that includes the machines that provides crops enough water that too in a proper way without any wastage. There are certain regions where sowing of seeds is done through drones developed using machine learning and there are many examples that prove that the agricultural sector needs to get even more help from researchers and investment to meet the requirements of the global population.

6.4   Smart Farming

The management using techs to increase the quantity and quality of agricultural products is known as smart farming. In the 21st century, many of the farmers have access to GPS, soil and weed scanning, and other technologies. With the change in climatic conditions, it is now important to precisely measure the variations for the farmers to improve the effectiveness of pesticides, fertilizers, and use them more selectively. In the field of animal husbandry, smart farming will help farmers to know about the needs of animals and adjust their nutrients. In the past years, there are certain techs developed which can measure the fodder quality which is provided to animals. All these developments are leading to the third green revolution using the advancement of genetics and application of ICT solutions such as exactness tools, the IoT, sensors and actuators, geo positioning systems, big data, unmanned aerial vehicles (UAVs, drones), and robotics. The experience proved that smart farming has huge possibility to carry a more productive and sustainable agricultural production. Smart farming provides key to save the resources from getting over exploited and ultimately leading to complete degradation. For example, if an excessive number of fertilizers are being added to soil, then it enhances the acidic content in it degrading its quality. Here comes the role of the new techs which calculates the number of fertilizers required over an area of land. Advancement in drone or aerial techs helps in sowing seeds too in a proper way by maintaining adequate distance among the plants which prevents clash of nutrients among them. It also provides a better geographical and territorial study of the land and helps farmers to decide the kind of crop and cropping pattern they should follow to maximize the yield. The farming

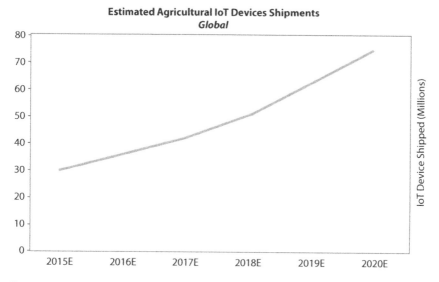

Figure 6.2 Graph showing the growth in purchase of IoT devices [15].

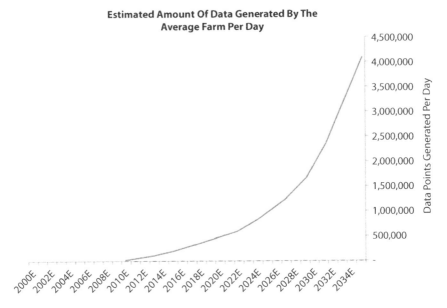

Figure 6.3 Graph showing the growth in data generation by IoT in agriculture [15].

industry will become more important than before in the upcoming years. The world needs to produce 70% more food in 2050 than we used to in 2006, to feed the growing population of Earth, according to the UN Food and Agriculture Organization. To meet this demand, farmers and agricultural companies are moving to the IoT for analytics and greater production capabilities. Figures 6.2 and 6.3 graphically represent applications of IoT technologies in agriculture.

6.5   Image Analysis of Agricultural Products

The following are the summarized points of previous research work done by different authors with publication references in Green IoT.

- Author Rushen Arshed found an investigation on energy saving practice. Its advantage is that it was about recycling and reusability of hardware components in order to reduce the impact of greenhouse effect [21].
- Faisal Karim found an Enabling technology for green IoT. It was a survey of the green perspective of IoT. It also gives a clear picture regarding the Green IoT [22].

- Kamalesh Sharma's smart system for universities. It gives an idea of controlling electrical devices from anywhere. In this, the sensor will sense if no one is present in the classroom so that the accountable person can switch the lights on and off from anywhere using a device [23].
- Prabhu Ramaswamy introduced an idea for smart parking IoT-based systems for reducing greenhouse gas emission. For that, the idea was to use a Raspberry Pi which will sense the free slot and send the details to the driver who has that application [24].
- Sheetal Valuri's idea was for greenhouse using IoT and cloud computing. The technology will sense the atmosphere and farmers can cultivate crops according to it with the information [25].
- Afgen Syeda proposed IoT by energy harvesting and trends and techniques for Green IoT. It accumulates energy from the surroundings and uses it for charging rechargeable batteries [26].

Image analysis has provided computers the ability to look in this world even more effectively and learn to adapt to the changes with respect to the environment. Emerging from the facial recognition system on mobile phones to the agricultural data collection, identification of weeds, soil type, and image analysis proved to be very vital in the agricultural sector. Through the imaging methods with various spectra such as infrared, hyper spectral imaging, and X-ray helps in deciding the vegetation indices, canopy measurement, irrigated land mapping, etc., with more accurate figures. Weeds which are the unwanted plants are said to be the biggest threat for the crops, can be correctly classified with the image processing algorithms. The approach of image analysis helps to save the cost and environment, but its accuracy of classification varies from 85% to 96% depending on the algorithms and limitations of image acquisition. The image processing techniques and better communication methods are being adopted by the agriculture sector and the data generated by them has increased with passage of time. The availability of multidimensional imaging combined with modern algorithms and increased possibility to fuse multiple sources of information from satellite imagery and sensors planted in fields. The major points to be taken care in agriculture are water stress, quality of yields and the use of pesticides. The satellite imaging provides the data regarding the amount of irrigation being done in an area over time providing additional means to analyze and monitor irrigation which provides cost benefits to the farmers. Another point is to be noted that large amount of water is as deadly for the plant as a shortage of water. Weeds in farms can also be detected by combining image processing and machine learning techniques. With development of herbicide applications and green color recognition algorithms, data regarding the texture of plants are integrated to enhance identification accuracy and helps in setting up farm management strategy.

6.6   Land-Quality Check

Traditionally, farmers have difficulties in calculating the soil's nitrogen level and dampness level of agricultural fields. These calculations will help them to evaluate and take necessary steps to get maximum productivities for their crops. Deep learning can be usable for measuring various parameters such as nitrogen and moisture status to convert the traditional farming techniques in smart farming methods with more accuracy and reliability.

6.6.1   Nitrogen Status

Nitrogen exists as a diatomic element in nature (78%). It is the most vital plant nutrient required by plants and mainly helps in the formation of chlorophyll, a pigment through which the plant produces food from sunlight and water by the process of photosynthesis. N_2 is also a major component of amino acids, the building blocks of protein without which the existence of plants is not possible. Nitrogen is consumed by plants mainly from two sources: nitrogen from atmosphere and nitrogen from soil. Existence of nitrogen in soil is known in three general forms: organic nitrogen compounds, ammonium (NH_4^+) ions, and nitrate (NO_3^-) ions. It is estimated that around 95%–99% of available nitrogen to the soil is in organic form, from animal and plant residues, organisms living inside the soil, and the microbes. Nitrogen exists in very inert form in the atmosphere and must be converted before it can be used by plants. Rhizobium is a genus negative soil bacterium that interacts with leguminous plants to form root nodules within which the conditions are made favorable for nitrogen fixation, this is known as the Rhizobium-legume symbiosis. When the amount of nitrogen exceeds more than what was required by Rhizobium bacteria, it is used by leguminous plants to produce food known as legumes. Hence, both bacteria and leguminous plants are dependent on each other for their survival. This provides the explanation why addition of extra nitrogen to legumes does not show much response as they are already receiving enough from bacteria in soil. Table 6.2 represents the list of multiple popular crops

Table 6.2 Different crops utilizes different amount of nitrogen.

Utilization of nitrogen by various crops		
Crops	Yield per acre	N
Alfalfa	80 tons	432
Corn	180 bu	180
Soybean	60 bu	294
Spring Wheat	80 bu	176
Winter Wheat	80 bu	152

with their nitrogen level utilization. It clearly indicates the high nitrogen is usable by traditional India crops.

Along with nitrogen, potassium, and phosphorus are essential requirements of the plant. The fertilizers which fulfill the deficiency of such nutrients are termed to be NPK fertilizers. NPK content of the soil can be known using an optical transducer. Figures 6.1 and 6.2 show the block diagram and functional diagram, respectively. It is a device formed by integration of techniques such as light transmission system and light detection system. The light source in the transmission system is controlled by the Arduino microcontroller. In fact, it also acts as a data collector from the light detection system and provides display along with the feature to control it [11–13, 16, 17].

Three different LEDs of different wavelengths are used in an optical transducer. The color of the LED is chosen as per spectrum absorption wavelength by the NPK present in the soil. Here, in the light detector system a photodiode sensor module is applied which converts light into current. The reflected light from the soil is received by photodiode and is converted into current, and then, the data was further sent to the Arduino controller for displaying procedure and further analysis using concepts of machine learning.

6.6.2   Moisture Content

The quantity of water that exists in the soil mass is termed as moisture content or water content. It defines properties such as compatibility and permeability of soil. With the increase in the moisture content, the permeability of the soil decreases, making it difficult for root nodules to breathe inside soil. Shear strength is another factor that is dependable on moisture content that too in an inversely proportionate manner. If the shear strength of the soil is high, the plant gets firmly held to the soil and it becomes difficult for agents such as running water and fast wind to uproot them. The tolerating capacity of the soil, that is, the capacity of the soil to support load, is directly proportional to the moisture content of the soil and is very important for the crop growth. For developing irrigation-based scheduling programs the main objective should be continuous gathering of data. Plant size and accurate measure of moisture content are some of the data which are an integral mechanism in the process of developing an irrigation scheduling program that allows a better understanding of plant, soil, and water relations. Based on gathered data, an appropriate computer interface is developed that helps in managing and implementing proper irrigation methods and scheduling to crops in the field. Proper irrigation methods can easily control the soil status by drainage and maintaining optimum levels of soil water for maximum plant growth. In the modern era, there are different tools available for obtaining soil moisture content through various techniques. The choice of instrumentation will be determined by the form of information required by the operator, the soil type, relative cost, reliability, and ease of use in the field. There is a well-known technique to measure moisture content called NEUTRON PROBE. In this, the fast-moving neutrons are slowed thermally in the soil by series of elastic collisions with the hydrogen particles in the soil. Hydrogen ion is nucleus of the hydrogen atom separated from its electron and is present in the soil in three ways:

1. Soil organic matter
2. Soil clay minerals
3. Water

The recordings gathered by the NP changes with respect to depths down the profile (For example, 20, 30, 40, 50, 60, 70, 80, 100, and 120 cm) with a sixteen second count.

The aluminum tubes are inserted in the soil and the water is stopped for proper measurement of moisture content. These aluminum tubes are used to mark depth intervals. Then, the neutron source starts releasing fast moving neutrons which are deflected by the hydrogen ion available from the water present in the soil and gets slowed down. The number of deflections showcases the moisture content of the soil [14].

6.7   Arduino-Based Soil Moisture Reading Kit

Many people are fond of gardening and planting small plants and even have nurseries, but as we all know that nowadays, the weather keeps on

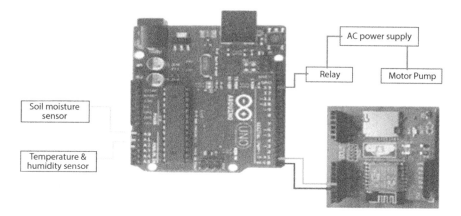

Figure 6.4 Connection of our prototype.

changing rapidly, in the morning, it seems hot, in the afternoon, it is rain-
ing, and at night, we feel cold so we are not able to identify that what type
of clothes should we wear similar is in the case of plants, people are not able
to decide that whether they should water the plants or not or how much
amount of water is required by a particular type of plant. So, to overcome
this problem, we can use soil moisture sensor which will take the reading
from the soil and whenever the water level will low it will send a message
to the person that "The water level is getting low, please water the plant" or
whenever the water level increases due to rain or overwatering it will give a
message "water overflow please store our plant in a dry place or save your
plant." Whenever the user will water the plants when humidity is high and
moisture in soil is already up to the required mark it will give the message
that "Do not water the plants as the water level is already up to the required
amount." Here, we are proposing the Arduino-based soil moisture reading
kit. The major idea is to create a product that can overcome the problems
listed below in an easy and cheaper way. Figure 6.4 represents prototype of
the proposed soil moisture reading kit.

6.7.1   Wastage of Water

As we all know that the water level of earth is declining day by day. Ground
water is continuously being exploited due to growth in population,
increased industrialization, and irrigation because of which ground water
levels in various parts of the country are declining. The latest groundwater
monitoring data of Central Ground Water Board indicates that out of total
wells analyzed, around 44% of the wells are showing decline in ground

water level in various parts of the country so saving water in every way possible has become a necessity. Overwatering not only wastes water, a valuable but limited natural resource.

6.7.2   Plants Dying Due to Over Watering

Not only this but, even plants die due to overwatering. Most of us have at least killed one plant or tree by overwatering it. In fact, overwatering the plants when they do not even require small amount of water is probably the number one problem we see. The roots of the plants absorb many minerals and nutrients along with air and water to support their stems and leaves above the ground. Watering the plants in excess cuts off the air and then the roots does not stay healthy and begin to suffocate, rot, and eventually die. The amount of fungus and mold in the increases in soil, which causes trouble for the leftover healthy roots. Wilting leaves and a pot that feels heavy due to soggy soil are the most common symptoms of an unhealthy and over watered plant. Yellow leaves and mushy or loose bark on the plant stems and molds that appear on the top of the soil are also indicators of overwatering.

6.7.3   Expensive Product

The product we have created will overcome both the above-mentioned problems as it will first save the plants from dying in both the cases either from the shortage of water or in the case of overflow. On the other hand, it will also save the water in case it is being wasted from overwatering plants and this product will do all these takes in a very less cost, that is that our product is very cost efficient. As we all know that water is a very essential resource and there cannot be life without it, so we should try to utilize it as much as we can. Soil moisture is an important factor in precision agriculture for enabling flexible and smart irrigation strategies. Measuring soil moisture through devices connected to the internet provides a centralized view of the water level present in the soil. Nowadays, sensor networks are the most used technology in this field. Soil moisture sensors can be used to check the moisture level present in the soil. This project senses soil moisture and actuates a relay to turn on the motor pump when the soil gets too dry. For deeper soil agriculture where moisture distribution will vary with depth, it is possible to bury the sensor, but care should be taken not to scratch the capacitive part of the circuit board and to protect the circuitry from corrosion.

We will pair this sensor with the temperature and humidity sensor to get the best results.

Products used in this kit are as follows:

- Soil moisture sensor
- Relay
- Jumper wires
- Temperature and humidity sensor—DHT11
- Wi-Fi nodule ESP8266
- Arduino Uno board
- Solar panel
- Motor pump

We will connect soil moisture, temperature, and humidity sensors with the Arduino Uno. Along with these, we must also connect the Wi-Fi module and the relay with it. An AC power supply will be provided to relay which will control the motor pump. The power supply given to relay will come from the solar panel attached to it. The reading of the water, humidity, and temperature level will be taken by the sensors, and in case of less water level, it sends a message to user to water the plants, and in case there is no response to it within 10 min, it will turn the motor pump on by itself using relay, and once sufficient water level is met, it will turn the motor off. In case of water overflow, it will send a message to the user to save the plants from overwatering. We feel that this prescribed product is very relevant and suitable for adoption to current market requirements as consumers always want a product which is more durable, has a long life, is pocket- friendly, and does not consume many resources. A product which is easy to install and eco-friendly is a product chosen by the consumer. The design of this product is accomplishing all the factors and fulfilling all the requirements as desired by the user, and hence, it makes itself more desirable and product of choice.

6.8   Conclusion

The days of hardship and non-profitable farming will be remembered as past if the modern machineries are used with efficiency and made affordable even to small-scale farmers. All these innovations have been supported by machine learning which enhances their skills and accuracy every day. The basic aim is to enhance the number of products without compromising the quality. A facial recognition system was first introduced as a security technology, but with the period, its applications increased. In today's digitalized world, it can be used to provide support to AI and machine learning to identify animals, to analyze their health and behavior analysis. It enhances the capabilities of the computer to create a proper database for a group of animals. Expanding such techs will completely change the scenario of agricultural and animal farms. An example related to such kind of technology can be seen in china. Companies like Alibaba manage pig farms using AI. Integrating all the requirements gathered by the various sensors, habits, and health of each pig is collected. They also use a voice-recognition system to trace diseases such as pig cough. Traditional methods of gathering data about the various crop healths are vivid and time-consuming. This led to the emergence of techs which are important to be intelligent enough to monitor, detect, and analyze the field of various data to study the status and feasibility of growing certain types of crops. The backbone of certain types of automated systems will be based on machine learning, hyperspectral images, and 3D laser scanning which will enhance the data collection and accurately provide the details about the crop disease if any found. This all will significantly minimize the use of pesticides and other insecticides which are harmful to the land as well as for consumers. Since the idea of robotics emerged several tech giants have invested in it. The evolution of robotics in each field has shown a positive sign that they have a vast capability to replace humans in each activity, including agriculture. Equipment such as drones, smart tractors loaded with sensors, radars, and GPS systems does not need human supervision. All this enhances the productivity and quality of living of a farmer.

6.9   Future Work

After having some research done, it is found that there are still many progresses needed in the machineries, and level of AI and machine learning still needs upgrades to work with even more precision and accuracy to eliminate the margin of errors while performing various functions such as, in image analysis, the embedded program or the AI sometimes gets confused among the crops and the weeds due to lack of proper skills that provides them the ability to differentiate between them. The main issue that stands in the center of all these inappropriate functions is the unavailability of a universal database that can be fed and updated in these devices with variance in the environment around them to make them work even more efficiently. A global database of farming can be created by taking the help of farmers from all around the globe and that will certainly make computers even smarter for farming related activities. This can also help gaining proper numbers of crop failures and other important data and providing a proper community for farmers to interact and exchange their ideas. Even in different regions, water cycle varies from place to place, and if the machine is connected to a proper global database, it knows how much it needs to dig up to achieve the desired water level preventing wastage of water and time and would be even more cost efficient for the farmers. A universal flu detector can be very useful for the farmers involved in animal farming as it can help them to exchange the ideas about the flu among them and help them to cure and take proper actions regarding them. As per the data, around 31.08% of the farmers directly or indirectly related with animal husbandry must suffer loss due to delay in detection of disease in their farm animals. As a result, it sometimes turns out to be a drastic pandemic not only among the animals but even to the humans consuming them and the products made of them. Having accurate data of various regions will help the computer to detect sudden rainfall or other calamities that can affect the crop quality adversely. It will help farmers to set up the action plans in case of emergency to reduce the crop damage. In India, various crops are destroyed due to Vermin, nuisance animals which get in the field and destroy crops, rather than pests. The farms in our country firstly require a good alarm system that makes the farmer aware if any vermin gets inside the farm. It must also contain a night vision camera to know about the animal as most of these animals are nocturnal. A proper and specialized team of people should be made to remove these animals to a safer place. Many of the small-scale farmers still have no idea about such advanced techs of agriculture and on the same side many of this machinery are electric or fuel driven which makes it cost effective for the farmers to afford them. To solve this issue, solar energy should be promoted which is cheap and even more reliable environment friendly.

References

1. Herbut, E., Modern animal production and animal welfare. *Agric. Eng.*, 22, 3, 5–10, 2018.
2. Singh, R.K.P., Singh, K.M., Kumar, A., A study on adoption of modern agricultural technologies at farm level in Bihar. *Economic Affairs,* 60, 1, 2015, 49–56, 2014.
3. Rehman, A., Jingdong, L., Khatoon, R., Hussain, I., Iqbal, M.S., Modern agricultural technology adoption its importance, role and usage for the improvement of agriculture. *Life Sci. J.*, 14, 2, 70–74, 2016.
4. Masrie, M., Rosman, M.S.A., Sam, R., Janin, Z., Detection of nitrogen, phosphorus, and potassium (NPK) nutrients of soil using optical transducer,

in: *2017 IEEE 4th International Conference on Smart Instrumentation, Measurement and Application (ICSIMA)*, 2017, November, IEEE, pp. 1–4.

5. Singh, N. and Shaligram, A.D., NPK Measurement in Soil and Automatic Soil Fertilizer Dispensing Robot. *Int. J. Eng. Res. Technol.*, 3, 7, 635–637, 2014.

6. Kulkarni, Y., Warhade, K.K., Bahekar, S., Primary nutrients determination in the soil using UV spectroscopy. *Int. J. Emerg. Eng. Res. Technol.*, 2, 2, 198–204, 2014.

7. Garvade, L.C., Detection of N, P, K using fiber optic sensor and PIC controller. *Int. J. Eng. Sci.*, 13787, 2017.

8. Ramane, D.V., Patil, S.S., Shaligram, A.D., Detection of NPK nutrients of soil using Fiber Optic Sensor, in: *International Journal of Research in Advent Technology Special Issue National Conference ACGT*, 2015, February, pp. 13–14, 2015.

9. Yusof, K.M., Isaak, S., Rashid, N.C.A., Ngajikin, N.L.E.D., Based Soil Spectroscopy. *Bul. Optik*, 3, 1–7, 2016.

10. Dan-Qun, H., Zhen, L., Hou, C.J., Jun, Y., Xiao-Gang, L., Huan-Bao, F., Jun-Jie, L., Recent advances on optical detection methods and techniques for cell-based microfluidic systems. *Chin. J. Anal. Chem.*, 38, 9, 1357–1365, 2010.

11. Kulkarni, Y., Warhade, K.K., Bahekar, S., Primary nutrients determination in the soil using UV spectroscopy. *Int. J. Emerg. Eng. Res. Technol.*, 2, 2, 198–204, 2014.

12. Masrie, M., Rosman, M.S.A., Sam, R., Janin, Z., Detection of nitrogen, phosphorus, and potassium (NPK) nutrients of soil using optical transducer, in: *2017 IEEE 4th International Conference on Smart Instrumentation, Measurement and Application (ICSIMA)*, 2017, November, IEEE, pp. 1–4.

13. Cull, P.O., Irrigation Scheduling–Techniques and Profitability, in: *National Irrigation Convention Proceedings*, Melbourne, Australia, pp. 131–170, 1992.

14. Patil, G.L., Gawande, P.S., Bag, R.V., Smart agriculture system based on IoT and its social impact. *Int. J. Comput. Appl.*, 176, 1, 0975–8887, 2017.

15. Kumar, A., Payal, M., Dixit, P., Chatterjee, J.M., Framework for Realization of Green Smart Cities Through the Internet of Things (IoT), in: *Trends in Cloud-based IoT. EAI/Springer Innovations in Communication and Computing*, F. Al-Turjman (Ed.), Springer, Cham, 2020.

16. Mathur, S. and Arora, A., Internet of Things (IoT) and PKI-Based Security Architecture, in: *Industrial Internet of Things and Cyber-Physical Systems: Transforming the Conventional to Digital*, Hershey, Pennsylvania, pp. 25–46, IGI Global, 2020.

17. Sehgal, A. and Mathur, S., Plant Disease Classification Using SOFT COMPUTING Supervised Machine Learning, in: *2019 3rd International conference on Electronics, Communication and Aerospace Technology (ICECA)*, 2019, June, IEEE, pp. 75–80.

18. Shrestha, A. and Mahmood, A., Review of deep learning algorithms and architectures. *IEEE Access*, 7, 53040–53065, 2019.

19. Buhmann, M.D., *Radial basis functions: theory and implementations*, vol. 12, Cambridge university press, Cambridge, England, 2003.

20. Tahiliani, V. and Dizalwar, M., Green IoT systems: An energy efficient perspective, in: *2018 Eleventh International Conference on Contemporary Computing (IC3)*, 2018, August, IEEE, pp. 1–6.

21. Jeyasheeli, P.G. and Selva, J.J., An IOT design for smart lighting in green building based on environmental factors, in: *2017 4th International Conference on Advanced Computing and Communication Systems (ICACCS)*, 2017, January, IEEE, pp. 1–5.

22. Shaikh, F.K., Zeadally, S., Exposito, E., Enabling technologies for green internet of things. *IEEE Syst. J.*, 11, 2, 983–994, 2015.

23. Sharma, K. and Suryakanthi, T., Smart system: IoT for university, in: *2015 International Conference on Green Computing and Interne of Things (ICGCIoT)*, 2015, October, IEEE, p. 15861593.

24. Ramaswamy, P., IoT smart parking system for reducing greenhouse gas emission, in: *2016 International Conference on Recent Trends in Information Technology (ICRTIT)*, 2016, April, IEEE, pp. 1–6.

25. Vatari, S., Bakshi, A., Thakur, T., Green house by using IOT and cloud computing, in: *2016 IEEE International Conference on Recent Trends in Electronics, Information & Communication Technology (RTEICT)*, 2016, May, IEEE, pp. 246–250.

26. Adila, A.S., Husam, A., Husi, G., Towards the self-powered Internet of Things (IoT) by energy harvesting: Trends and technologies for green IoT, in: *2018 2nd International Symposium on Small-scale Intelligent Manufacturing*, 2018, April.

7

Green IoT and Machine Learning for Agricultural Applications

Keshavi Nalla and Seshu Vardhan Pothabathula*

Bionicsol Bharat Private Limited, (R&D), Mogappair West, Chennai, India

Abstract

The Internet of Things (IoT) is a network of various sensors, software, and other technologies embedded into a system retaining flexibility and feasibility in human work. This involves the framework of various sensors and software in the form of an embedded system to perform either a single or multiple tasks simultaneously. IoT is a continuously building network of smart sensors and devices that are connected to the internet. However, the connected IoT devices require a huge amount of energy for high and efficient performance to provide a sophisticated environment to the users. This had become a huge concern and gained a huge focus on the upcoming research providing a pathway for the G-IoT, i.e., Green IoT. G-IoT represents the framework of connecting smart sensors and devices and creating automation by enabling energy conservation methods. Cloud Computing and Machine Learning techniques like Artificial Neural Networks, C-Means, K-Means, and Bayesian Model are used for creating IoT systems that are cost-effective and has low-power consumption. Energy consumption depends upon the system architecture and its requirements. The approaches like Green Computing and Green Wireless Sensor Networks make difference in the energy consumption criteria. G-IoT has many applications in agriculture, namely, smart agribots, machine navigation, harvesting robots, smart farming kits, material handling, agricultural drones, remote sensing for crop and weather conditions, monitoring and sensing soil quality, computer imaging techniques for quality control, sorting, and grading, and irrigation monitoring. Moreover, Machine Learning had become an emerging paradigm and the tools or models are quite widely used in various applications. In agriculture, Machine Learning tools are used for species

Corresponding author: director@bionicsol.in

Roshani Raut, Sandeep Kautish, Zdzislaw Polkowski, Anil Kumar and Chuan-Ming Liu (eds.) Green Internet of Things and Machine Learning: Towards a Smart Sustainable World, (189–214) © 2022 Scrivener Publishing LLC

management, field conditions management, crop management, and livestock management.

Keywords: Machine navigation, material handling, Bayesian model, machine learning, computer imaging, harvesting robots

7.1   Introduction

Internet of Things (IoT) is nothing framework of various things that are connected to things. This helps in building an automated network and building the cost-effective and advanced applications that are used in various sectors like agriculture, healthcare, medicine, smart cities, smart grid, transportation, and wearable technologies. IoT had become a unique and emerging paradigm in the recent world and also paved a path in building new technologies and applications. It involves the mechanism for connecting various sensors or devices, creating a need for a huge amount of energy for providing a sophisticated user experience with high and better performance. This issue had gained a huge focus perturbing the technologists and scientists in building the smart and advanced systems, especially for the industrial sector as it requires a large amount of energy and is expensive to work for. This paved a path toward Green IoT (G-IoT) which helps in solving all these issues. G-IoT is also a network of things that are connected with the Internet. This helps in building systems by enabling energy-saving methods or energy-conserving methods [1]. These methods might involve software tools like machine learning tools, namely, Artificial Neural Networks (ANNs) and Bayesian Model, and by selecting the hardware that promotes energy optimization. The energy consumption also depends on the architecture, hardware, and requirements. Sensor-cloud architecture is one of the promising options to reduce energy consumption and makes the device more feasible and cost-effective [2]. It provides the infrastructure that enables the real-time monitoring of data-intensive applications. Nowadays, the applications are being built with a combination of computing and hardware. IoT transforms the things or the devices from being too traditional to the advanced and smart systems by exploiting the underlying technologies like sensor networks, communication technologies, and computing. This drives away the conventional way of building systems and transforms them by adding modern technologies. G-IoT had gained a great focus for its cost-effective designs with energy conservative methods which help in obtaining a sustainable environment. Most of the G-IoT systems use the sensor-cloud architecture due to its flexibility while incorporating it in a system design. G-IoT has various applications such as smart agriculture, participatory sensing, smart logistic and retail, food and tracking retail, healthcare, smart industries, smart homes, smart grid, smart energy, smart transportation, smart cities, security and surveillance, and e-govern (Figure 7.1) [3].

Though there is a wide range of applications of G-IoT in various sectors, the applications in agriculture involve very unique and innovative applications and are said that it turned the hefty conventional practices into easy and handy devices that would perform all the tasks that need utmost pressure and strength. G-IoT is used in harvesting robots, machine navigation, material handling, crop monitoring and management, etc. The use of Machine Learning tools like Neural Networks and various statistical and mathematical models are used for energy conservation in advanced

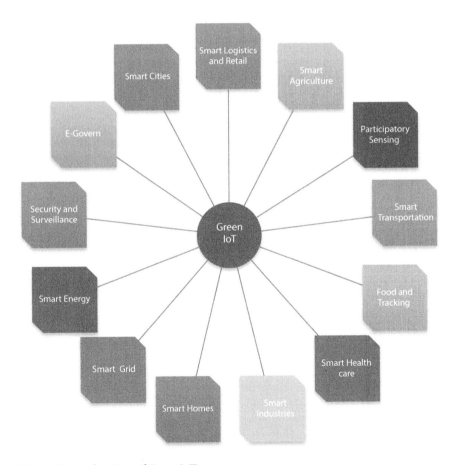

Figure 7.1 Applications of Green IoT.

systems [4]. Machine Learning had been an emerging technology that is being used in various sectors. It is an entity of Artificial Intelligence that is used to help computers learns through algorithms and data. This is mostly applied to various Bayesian approaches that are used for pattern recognition and learning. Machine Learning is a collection of a group of algorithms that are used to learn and make predictions according to the data collected in addition to the extra hidden structures or functions from the recorded data. There are various Machine Learning techniques that are used for multiple applications especially in IoT systems such as AdaBoost, Convolution Neural Networks (CNN), K-Means, and Q-learning [5]. Machine Learning algorithms provide a wide range of applications in various sectors, especially in agriculture. Techniques like ANNs and Support Vector Machines are used for species management, crop monitoring, field conditions and livestock monitoring and management, etc.

7.2   Green IoT

G-IoT is a pioneering technology that is widely used in the day to day systems in the current world. It helps in attuning the energy consumption issues in the systems for promoting a sophisticated and sustainable environment. We already discussed earlier that the implementation of the sensor-cloud–based architecture would reduce the energy consumption of the system and provide feasibility and flexibility to the user. This architecture is mainly used in G-IoT agriculture and also in healthcare applications. Therefore, this architecture is also known as GAHA (Green IoT Agriculture and Healthcare Applications) architecture (Figure 7.2) [6]. The physical sensors that are more reliable and available in the market are connected through the internet and the data from the sensors is collected and communicated to the cloud by the cloud service provider. This data obtained from the sensors can be controlled efficiently and this helps in monitoring various applications. This architecture provides ubiquitous computing of the sensors that are meant as an interface between the physiological environment and cyberspace where the internet is used as a communication medium. Moreover, the data is analyzed in clusters and is processed to provide the user with better monitoring results. It provides an idiosyncratic data storage, a remote management platform that provides excellent adjustability and rapid visualization with user amicable analysis. This kind of architectures is used for supporting the long deployment of wireless sensors. The sensors are connected to the internet and the data obtained from the sensors is collected by the sensor network provider. The collected data

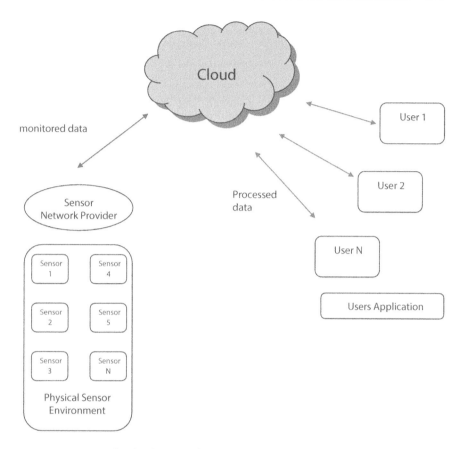

Figure 7.2 Sensor-cloud architecture for Green IoT [6].

from the various sensors is further communicated to the cloud by the cloud service provider and is given for processing, visualization, and storage. The raw sensory data is processed with the help of the data centers. The processed data undergoes delivery to the service user applications used. In this context, the network service providers act as the data sources to the cloud and the cloud service providers are used for the data requesters. The sensor-cloud interface provides the advantage to access the processed sensory data in the cloud anywhere and anytime only with the established network connection. The profitability of the Wireless Sensor Network (WSN) had increased the probability of serving the numerous applications simultaneously [7]. The ultimate use of cloud services enhanced the performance of the systems by decreasing the energy consumption to 36.68% and increasing the sensor activity and lifetime by 3.25%.

The main requirements of this architecture are that reducing the use of the dispensable facilities results in reducing the energy consumption by turning off the facilities in its non-working time. The transmission of the essential data significantly promotes an energy-saving mode as the data transmission requires a lot of energy. Moreover, minimizing the data path length reduces the energy usage which involves the better usage of routing energy-efficient schemes. Reducing the wireless data path would promote low energy usage by involving the relay nodes in a significant way. The framework of compressive sensing would enhance energy conservation. The competent use of advanced communication techniques would enhance the variation in the modes of operation such as frequency, amplitude, transmitting power, and modulation schemes. The use of renewable green power sources like biomass and solar energy would promote a sustainable environment and energy-efficient systems.

7.2.1   Components of GAHA

The main components of GAHA are Green Computing, Green WSN, Green RFID, Green Cloud Computing, Green Machine to Machine, and Green Data Center [8]. Green Computing is the practice or the interpretation of the design, manufacturing and use, disposal of the computers, and their constituents without creating any ill effects on the environment. Green Computing involves the four complementary pathways in achieving

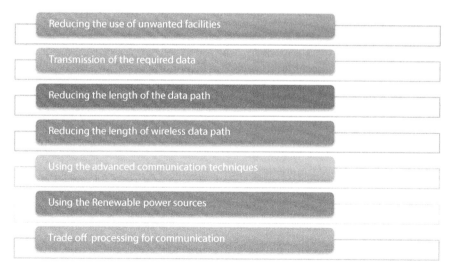

Reducing the use of unwanted facilities

Transmission of the required data

Reducing the length of the data path

Reducing the length of wireless data path

Using the advanced communication techniques

Using the Renewable power sources

Trade off processing for communication

Figure 7.3 Important factors supporting GAHA architecture.

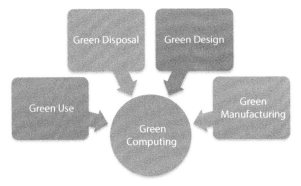

Figure 7.4 Complementary pathways for implementing Green Computing in computers and their subsystems [9].

the manufacturing of the computing systems without disturbing the environment (Figure 7.3). These pathways involve the following (Figure 7.4).

Green Use: This is an attempt to minimize energy consumption by a computing system by attempting the methods to use them sustainably without affecting the environment.

Green Manufacturing: This is defined as the process of fabricating or mass producing the electronic elements of a computer with the design promoting minimal energy consumption and a sustainable environment.

Green Design: This is an endeavour to design systems that promote energy conservation and is eco-friendly.

Green Disposal: This is a proposal for improving the motive of recycling and reusing the computers and their constituents with less or no impact on the biological systems.

Green WSN or Green WSNs constitute the sensor nodes and the base station where the sensor nodes will be working only in the necessary timeline and will be held in a sleeping mode to minimize the energy consumption and increase the lifetime of the sensors. These networks use techniques like wireless charging and utilize renewable energies like solar, wind, or other types of kinetic energies in case of energy depletion which enhances their flexibility to run in an environment. Green WSN makes use of radio optimization techniques like power transmission control, directional antennas, and cognitive radios for promoting energy conservation and better communication protocols. These WSNs follow various data reduction mechanisms such as aggregation, compression, and sampling for fast and energy-efficient transmissions. The use of energy-efficient routing techniques like cluster architectures and multipath routing for improving the shortest and energy-efficient pathway for communications [10]. Green Cloud Computing considers its resources as services such as PaaS, i.e., Platform as a Service. It provides computing services and storage with high capability. GCC requires the adoption of efficient hardware and software solutions enhancing energy conservation in a system. The use of power-saving virtual machines such as VM allocation and placement would provide high performance with minimal energy consumption. Numerous energy-efficient resource allocation mechanisms and evolving efficient models can be adopted easily [11]. Green M2M is a communication protocol with very powerful M2M nodes that could smartly pile up the processed or the monitored data in the M2M domain. The general M2M communication system requires a large amount of power for maintaining its stability. Green M2M is provided with smart transmission control and efficient design of communication protocols by applying various algorithmic and distributed computing techniques. Activity scheduling is one of the main functionality that comes up to switch the nodes in either on/sleeping modes depending on the necessity and priority providing the energy-efficient network. Applying joint energy-saving and energy-harvesting techniques like interference mitigation improve communications better [12]. Green Data Center is one of the key components of GAHA (Figure 7.5) as it provides the functionality to store, manage and

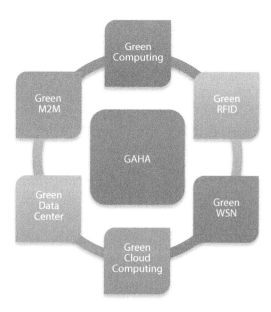

Figure 7.5 Components of GAHA.

process data from the various sensors. It helps in the generation and processing of data and sends it to the user applications. In general, it requires huge operational energy to perform better. The use of renewable resources like hydro and solar might be useful to control the use of a large amount of energy. Implementing dynamic power management technologies such as turbo boost would enhance the use of energy-efficient pathways. The efficient use of novel architectures and data center models would promote better data processing [13]. Green RFID is a package of RFID tag and a unique identifier with a low transmission range of 124–13 kHz. Decreasing the size of the RFID tags and the use of non-degradable material in the manufacturing process promotes a sustainable biosphere as it creates pollution. Applying energy-efficient algorithms would provide a pathway for tag estimation and transmission power level control efficiency [14].

7.2.2   Applications of Green IoT in Agriculture

G-IoT is one of the key technologies that is used for establishing an advanced and sustainable environment. G-IoT is used for a wide range of agricultural applications enabling low energy consumption techniques in building the systems.

7.2.2.1   *Livestock Tracking and Geofencing*

Livestock tracking and geofencing systems are mainly based on wireless networks. The IoT systems built for this application completely monitors the data regarding the location and health of their cattle from time to time. Green WSNs which are one of the components of the G-IoT systems play a vital role in this scenario. The trackers and sensors are set up to the cattle creating the sensor nodes and the monitored data is sent to the base station or cloud. The data processing is done by the data centers that processed data is shown in the user's application. Moreover, attaching the Green RFID to the cattle provides a unique identifier to that animal where the user gets a chance to take care of every animal and get complete data regarding any particular animal. This provides the user to identify the animal with infection and take necessary steps to stop the spread in case it is contagious. In this way, G-IoT helps in building systems with less power and high performance [15].

7.2.2.2   *Fisheries*

G-IoT systems can also be adopted in fisheries in a better way. The use of underwater sensor networks and waterproof energy-efficient hardware would help in monitoring the fish health and the oxygen and bacterial levels in the water. These systems can also be utilized to observe the behavior of the fish and can be used for many more applications [40].

7.2.2.3   Smart Crops

The G-IoT systems are also used for monitoring the crop and help the farmer to handle its fencing system. The G-IoT provides a network of various sensors like pH sensor, analog moisture sensor, gas sensors, temperature, and humidity modules and provides information regarding the environmental conditions and soil quality. The use of hardware that consumes less energy and the green sensor networks collects the data and is processed by the G-data center. The use of Cloud Computing provides the user with the facility to view and access the data anytime and anywhere. Sometimes, these systems come with the combination of remote sensing and IoT where the sensors are used for crop, weather, and soil monitoring. This kind of systems makes use of the sensor-cloud architecture which helps in energy conservation and highly efficient sensing, data analysis, storage, and data processing [16].

7.2.2.4   G-Drones

Agricultural drones are used for various application and fieldwork in agriculture. These are mostly used for spraying that protects the farmers from the health hazards created by pesticides, herbicides, etc. These are also used for irrigation purposes. The use of G-drones provides multiple solutions and help the farmer with physical work with accuracy. The drones also help in crop and field analysis, crop health monitoring, planting, and seed sowing. G-drones help in irrigation and adding fertilizers from time to time based on the plant health and environmental conditions. The implementation of sensor-cloud architecture provides the user with accurate data and feasible access.

7.2.2.5   Weeding Robots

Weeding robots helps in identifying the weeds using digital image processing and compares the image of the weeds to the crop plants and observe the similarities. Implementation of the G-IoT architectures makes use of energy-efficient and highly capable hardware and networks for weeding. Due to the increase in the weed plants that are resistant to weedicides and pesticides, the use of weeding robots helps the farmer to harvest in a better and simple way. This helps in building a sustainable environment and reduces the use of pesticides or herbicides that indeed cause pollution that affects the biosphere.

7.2.2.6 Machine Navigation

The latest technologies and the enabling of G-IoT brought the facility to control all the heavy equipment like tractors and ploughing implements with GPS at his comfy place. This kind of provisions can be obtained by applying the WSNs and hardware enabled with energy-efficient use techniques and models. This kind of systems provides control over the equipment and the agricultural practices can be performed at the ease of the user.

7.2.2.7 Harvesting Robots

Harvesting robots act as a great solution for the labor shortage, high labor charge, and high time-consuming issues. The use of harvesting robots promotes high productivity and better harvesting. This kind of robots is used to pick fruits and vegetable by using the combination of robotics and digital image processing technologies. The use of G-data centers and Green WSN provides the best data analysis and storage. Moreover, these robots can work 24/7 and helps the farmer with good productivity and low labor charges. These robots perform their tasks with the utmost accuracy and high efficiency.

7.2.3 Green IoT Security Solutions for Agriculture

G-IoT has influence and materialized three different aspects, i.e., precision agriculture, facility agriculture, and contract farming.

7.2.3.1 Precision Technology

Precision technology is a futuristic technology that employs better crop yield, in which, WSN is the critical source of its sophistication [27]. It viably decreases the possible risk in the production flow with appropriate information and interactions helping farmers via accurate and optimized farming and operate large functions within less power consumption. A sensor with a wireless communication system provides farmers with relevant data of livestock and crop yield [28, 29]. Current information technologies amalgamate remote sensing, global positioning system, and geographic information system. The sensing technology brings the crop monitoring crop spraying, monitoring cattle health, field condition analysis, etc., the sensing devices attached to the cattle will locate and update the health and stress conditions [30].

7.2.3.2 Facility Agriculture

It is a production model of industrial agriculture system defining good quality, rich yields under high input/output, capital, technology, and labor-intensive industry [31]. The expert decision system embedded in IoT enhances the services of agriculture management for providing traditional methods of farming such as minimal usage of pesticides and protects the environment is polluted, reducing the wastage of irrigational resources management, deciding the selection of crop in appropriate land and weather conditions, and updating the analyzed information of livestock growth and fall for improvement of product quality. G-IoT technology helps in engineering for production protection system facilitating the enhanced efficiency and automatic functions for appealing environmental stress factors. The seasonal disasters such as drought and flood conditions are predicted by the system and terminate the season distress to traditional and seasonal crops. For ages, the agriculture system information is available, and these statistical and predicted models' data provide decision management to farmers for selection of crop in appropriate conditions, for this understanding, there are interdisciplinary areas, i.e., agri-biotech, engineering, computer technology, and meteorology come into the picture to define a type of problems encountered [32].

7.2.3.3 Contract Farming

It is a novel idea of agriculture production and management. Due to urbanization trends, there is a wide gap between rural and urban development. The quality, safety, and standards of agricultural management are relatively backward compared to urbanized farming [33]. To overcome these problems, contract farming enables the outsourcing of the production demand for some products. It also helps in ignoring blind production by reducing risk via planting and breeding risk. It includes the supply chain management of products safety and trading system of agriculture monitored by IoT [34]. It employs as an information provider to the customer about the agricultural products. IoT monitors the food safety and quality throughout the process of the supply chain such as farm to fork traceability [35]. IoT also enhanced the e-commerce deliveries for the quality and freshness of the fruits, and throughout the process, it provides the information to the customer to enhance the purchase decisions [36–37].

7.3   Machine Learning

Machine learning is a part of artificial intelligence (Figure 7.6) that is used to process and analyze the data and promotes automatic model building. It provides great platforms that help the systems to learn from the processed data, patterns, and many more with minimal human intervention. It is a collection of various algorithms that helps in identifying the hidden structures and optimizes the recorded data.

Machine learning provides various types of learning approaches based on the type of data or task or problem. Supervised learning is one of the learning approaches used in machine learning. In this context, algorithms are designed to build a mathematical model that has a set of data where the inputs and the desired output are the constituents of the set. The data recorded or observed is said to be training data which consists of a set of examples. Supervised learning algorithms include active, learning, classification, and regression that are used mainly in the applications of agriculture. One of the examples of the above approach is a support vector machine which is a learning model that classifies or divides the recorded into various regions setting the linear boundary between the two regions [18]. Unsupervised learning

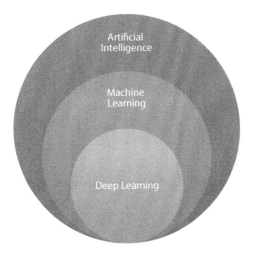

Figure 7.6 Machine learning as a subset of artificial intelligence [17].

is also an approach in machine learning that consists of algorithms that build a model that consists of only inputs and acquire the structures in data such as groups or clusters of data points. This kind of approaches is mainly used in statistics. Cluster analysis and clustering is an example of unsupervised learning [19]. Semi-supervised learning is also a kind of approach in machine learning which falls between the supervised and unsupervised learning approaches. In this context, the algorithms are designed to find the missing data or labels with the help of a small amount of labelled data. This approach improves learning accuracy and the labels are cost-effective. One of the approaches of machine learning is reinforcement learning which can be studied in various streams such as control theory, swarm intelligence, and genetic algorithms. Most of these algorithms are used in autonomous vehicles or game theory [20]. Self-learning is one of the most prominent approaches in machine learning which provides a facility for self-driving in machines. Both the inputs and the outputs of a consequence is computed with the help of the CAA self-learning algorithm [21]. Reinforcement learning is a process or a set of algorithms where the software agents take decisions in an environment to obtain the motive of cumulative reward. Feature learning is a unique machine learning approach that ain at preserving the data from the input and processing the data in a useful format. It is also known as a representation learning algorithm [22]. Anomaly detection is a promising approach that helps in identifying rare events or objects or observations from the recorded data. It is also known as outlier detection. Robot learning is also a useful approach to build bots for agriculture. The designed algorithms can generate their curriculum that could promote self-guidance for human-machine intervention. Associative rule learning is an approach that aims at utilizing the set of rules that could represent the data captured by the system. It is also known as rule-based learning that would learn, apply or evolve the relational rules to store and apply the knowledge obtained from the data. Various machine learning models could be used in various agricultural applications such as ANNs, decision trees, support vector machines, Bayesian networks, and genetic algorithms.

7.3.1   Applications of Machine Learning in Agriculture

7.3.1.1   *Species Breeding and Species Selection*

CNNs is mostly used for species breeding. This algorithm identifies the hidden structures from the data. The use of these kinds of data-driven models helps in interpreting the non-linear and unpredictable data sets. The neural network concepts are widely used for species selection. The species selection mostly depends upon the crop sequencing method where the crop is selected based on the difference between the current time and the end of the season and the select factor. CNN is mostly used in classification studies especially for image classification, feature extraction, object detection, etc. Approaches like ANNs, Support Vector Machine, and other supervised learning models can be adopted for species breeding and selection that helps the farmer by providing the predictive analysis of crop and the type of crop to be harvested at a current time [23]. Species selection is found to be one of the tedious tasks as it requires the identification of the certain genes that would have the abilities to adapt to the environment, disease resistance and measure of water and nutrient use. The use of the deep learning algorithms provides the predictive data of the crop that is yet to be harvested by analysing the data of the crop performance from the decades and delivers the model that interprets the probability of the gene that could accustom and give a high yield in current time, area, and climatic conditions [24].

7.3.1.2 Species Recognition

Species recognition can be performed by using the supervised and unsupervised models in machine learning. The machine learning models like CNNs, Random Forest Regression, and Support Vector Machine are used for identifying the hidden events in the obtained data and process them for species recognition. The physical parameters like vein morphology, shape, size, and color should be considered, compared to recognize the species.

7.3.1.3 Weed Detection

Weed detection requires the classification algorithms for better identification. Machine learning techniques such as ANNs, support vector machine, deep neural network concepts, and feature learning are most widely used for detection and classification purposes. The use of technologies like computer vision and machine learning algorithms would enhance the detection and removal of weeds in a cost-effective way. In this context, the use of these algorithms does not affect the environment in any way. The use of the algorithms minimizes the consumption or the use of herbicides and pesticides [25]. The implementation of the deep learning models facilitates simple object detection due to its efficient capabilities in extracting the features of the images automatically [41]. Deep learning provides two different strategic methods for achieving object detection. The first method provides the potential to detect or recognize the object by classifying its pixels. The other method is that the bounding boxes are drawn around the images. However, drawing the bounding boxes around the images is much easier than classifying the object pixels in the context of labelling. Although implementing the bounding boxes method is much easier, the most accurate object detection is achieved by pixel-wise classification. But the pixel-wise classification of objects is not completely exploited in agriculture applications due to the unavailability of the labelling at a pixel level [42]. Weed classifications involve the processes, namely, image acquisition, image segmentation, feature extraction, and image classification. Most of the machine learning models get involved in the image classification process. The classification and feature extractions steps are merged as one single process due to the advent of the deep learning techniques that are being used nowadays. CNNs play a vital role in performing the feature extraction before the classification and detection sections automatically. However, shelf deep learning architectures are used to classify images of sixteen different types of weeds. On the contrary, semantic segmentation is used to perform the individual weed classification and the estimation of the weed density. But semantic segmentation does not go well with the real scenarios with the training on the synthesized data. In this context, multilevel classification is adopted where the vegetation and the background in the crop images are separated as a part of the initial level and it is followed by the weed and crop partition as the second level [41]. Here, the neural network gets trained to label the dataset by using a small number of representative images. Later, the constituent models will be retrained by using the images from the entire dataset. CNNs had made a great revolution in the process of feature extraction with their ability to feature extraction automatically. The feature extraction is performed while the max-pooling layers are responsible for reducing the dimensions of the feature space. A large number of CNNs have been developed for image classification and feature extraction purposes. Whereas the architectures like VGG16, ResNet-50, Inception V3, and Xception are mainly used for feature extraction and classification. VGG16 is one of the CNN models that has a 3×3 kernel size in the convolutional layers and the size of 2×2 in max-pooling layers. In general, these two are connected with layers of the size of 4,096. When it comes to the semantic segmentation meta architectures, the layers are completely replaced by convolutional layers. VGG16 is named after the Visual Geometry Group [43]. It is also known as Oxford Net. The initial input of the convolutional layer 1 should be of a fixed size. The input image is set to pass through the pile of the convolutional layers with the filters used with the field of size 3×3. It is the smallest size that is used to capture the notion of directions left/right/u/down or center. In some of the configurations, it uses the 1 × 1 convolution filter which is utilized to see the linear transformation of the input channels. In this convolutional architecture, Rectified Linear Unit (ReLU) is used as an activation function. ResNet-50 is one of CNN models which is having 50 layers deep. It provides the facility to load the pretrained version of the trained network over a million images found in the Image Net. The mentioned pretrained network has the ability to classify millions of images into approximately 1,000 object categories. In this way, the network tends to learn good feature representations for a large number of images. The input image size is fixed to 224 × 224 in the network [44]. Inception V3 is one of the widely used image recognition models with great accuracy of 78.1% accuracy over the ImageNet dataset. This model consists of symmetric and asymmetric building blocks. This includes the layers of convolutions, average pooling, max pooling, concats, dropouts, and fully connected layers [45]. Xception is the advanced version of the Inception V3 architecture. It replaces the inception modules with the depthwise separable convolutions. It is mainly used for image recognition. The above mentioned convolutional models play a vital role in weed detection and can also be applied to detect the disease conditions in a plant [46].

7.3.1.4   Crop Quality

Support vector machine is mostly used for determining the crop quality. Support vector machine is a combination of the supervised and associative learning models that are used for classification and regression analysis. It works well with the clear margin of separation and can be plotted in n-dimensional spaces. It is memory efficient as it uses a subset of the training points with the decision function. It is a computational method used to converting quadratic optimization problem into a system of linear equation. Its intelligent method handles problems approximation based on data sets $\{(x_1y_1), (x_2,y_2,..(xn,yn)\}$ nonlinear functions [39].

$$f(x) = (w, \phi(x)) + b \qquad (7.1)$$

where $\phi(x)$ is the nonlinear function to perform regression, b is bias, and w denotes weight vector. Support Vector Machine provides the optimal study over the crop parameters such as soil quality, pH, texture, and many more and provides the data determining the crop quality.

7.3.1.5 Disease Detection

Support Vector Machine, K-Means, and Neural Networks are the most commonly used models for disease detection. Support Vector Machine helps in segregating the infected are and the uninfected area of a plant during the process of image processing. This helps in analysing the characteristics of the data. K means or K-means clustering is one of the unsupervised models which is a part of the vector quantization method. Here, the data is segregated or classified into various regions and is analyzed. The features of the image are taken as data and are divided into various clusters. The Euclidean distance will be calculated between the clusters and additionally new data clusters will be formed and no position will be changed. The repetition of this process gradually detects the infected cluster and goes for feature extraction [26]. ANNs also facilitate the best disease detection. The ANNs can be implemented along with digital image processing. The implementation of the ANNs involves two pathways, i.e., learning path and the testing path. The application of ANNs involves the accurate detection of the disease. The implementation of the ANN model proposes the use of the training model. The learning path involves the creation of the image database, image pre-processing, segmentation, feature extraction, weight adjustment, and classification. The testing path involves the acquisition of the input image, its processing, segmentation and feature extraction. The outcomes of both the training and testing paths are compared by also involving the process of edge detection (Figure 7.7) and the disease is diagnosed [40]. The different types of diseases can also be detected based on the symptoms and the patches over the infected areas.

Figure 7.7 Edge detection of a rice blast disease using the Robert cross method [55].

The implementation of the classifier also plays a vital role in detection. So, it is quite important to choose the classifier model and train it accordingly to perform the desired task [47].

7.3.1.6   Yield Prediction

Yield prediction requires a multidimensional analysis of a crop. Weather and climatic factors such as rainfall, temperature, humidity, and the soil factors like pH, texture and type of the soil, and its fertility are some of the factors that create an impact on the crop yield. Support Vector Machine and state-of-art approach with the association of computer vision technologies would provide the complete analysis of crop, weather, and economic conditions so far and provide the resultant predictive data. Moreover, these models include the data regarding the yield mapping, estimation from past decades, crop quality, and management and provide the analysis accordingly. Machine learning techniques provide a cost-effective predictive analysis for the crop by considering the factors like soil quality, temperature, and the previous yield data. ANNs, Support Vector Regression, M5-Prime Regression Trees, k-nearest neighbor, Adaptive Neuro-fuzzy Interference system, Data Mining, and Genetic programming are some of the machine learning methods that are used in the prediction of the crop harvest [48]. However, ANNs are considered to be the most effective solution for yield prediction among all. It is used to resolve the complex relations among the interrelated parameters and the crop yield. The algorithms in ANNs are set to analyze with their own examples to resolve a specific problem. ANNs has the capabilities to understand the factors and classification. They are familiar with non-linear problems. ANNs requires a minimum of three layers for performing the detection and as well as classification. The mentioned three layers are the input layer, the hidden layer, and the output layer. Initially, the first layer is responsible for receiving the raw data where they obtained is processed and transferred to the hidden layer and is reached to the output layer where the output is produced. ANNs consist of algorithms to optimize the training process. The most commonly used algorithms in ANNs are Levenberg-Marquardt, Bayesian Regularization, and Scaled Conjugated Gradient [49]. Levenberg-Marquardt Algorithm is a combination of the gradient descent method and the Gauss-Newton method. It is also known as Damped Least Squares method. It is mostly used to resolve the linear least square problems that arise in the least-squares curve fitting. The Levenberg-Marquardt method is known for its robustness over the Guass-Netwon method as it has the capabilities to find promising solutions in many cases even though it starts from the very final minimum [50]. However, the Levenberg-Marquardt Algorithm tends to be much slower than the Gauss-Newton Method in the case of the well-behaved functions and the reasonable starting parameters. However, the Levenberg-Marquardt Algorithm seems to be viewed as Gauss-Newton by making the use of the trust-region approach. Gauss-Newton Method is happened to express the backpropagation in a neural network providing the algorithm to have a higher probability to obtain the optimal solution [51]. Bayesian Regularization is one of the mathematical processes that use the method of rigid regression for converting the non-linear regression into a well-posed statistical problem. It is more robust when compared to the standard backpropagation nets. Bayesian regularized ANNs provide the advantage of robustness in the validation process. This algorithm provides the solutions to a large number of problems related to QSAR modeling [52]. It provides the solutions in an optimal way for the problems such as the optimization of the network architecture, robustness of the model, size and choice of validation set and effort, etc. These networks are difficult to overtrain and overfit. This is because the calculation and the training of Bayesian Regularization of ANNs depend on the effective parameters and the weights. The use of the Automatic Relevance Determination of the input variables with Bayesian Regularization of ANNs allows the network to estimate the importance and necessity of each input. The implementation of the Automatic Relevance Determination method in these algorithms ensures that the irrelevant and the highly correlated indices are neglected. It provides the advantage of highlighting the most important variable for the modeling of the active data. The scaled Conjugate Algorithm is one of the efficient algorithms for training the neural network. It is a second-order training algorithm with fast training and great test efficiency. It is one of the most widely used iteration algorithms. It is mostly used to solve the problems that arise in the large system of linear equations. It has the capability to reduce the purpose function over several variables. Moreover, it uses the step size scaling techniques in order to avoid the time consumption for a learning iteration [53].

7.3.1.7   Field Conditions Management

The machine learning algorithms are adopted to study the evaporation process that occurs in the plants and the soil moisture and temperature that a plant needs to sustain. The machine learning–based applications provide the estimated data of evapotranspiration that occurs in a plant from time to time. This estimated data helps in predicting the amount of water and nutrients required by the plant or a crop. The use of the ML algorithm enhances the efficient use of irrigation systems and temperature maintenance, expected weather phenomena in the field area. ANNs play a vital role in field conditions management. Artificial Neural Networks before process trend free data and normalized over [0, 1] range. The range is compulsory for the neuron transfer function to calculate the sigmoid function. This function relies on a limited range of consequent data. In any case of inappropriate scaling of the neural network, data lead to meaningless outcome [38]. The general method of normalization involves the mapping of the data linearly up to setup range, where variable x is prepared as follows:

$$Xn = x - \frac{xmin}{xmax} - xmin * (rmax - rmin) + Tmin \qquad (7.2)$$

where X = original data, Xn = normalized input/output, Xmax = maximum value, and Xmin = minimum value.

A standard range from 0.1 to 0.9 is suitable for transforming variables upon the sensitive range of the sigmoid transfer function. Moreover, the algorithms are designed to train the networks with the utmost efficiency. The neural networks are trained according to the field conditions and help in predictive analysis and as well as management.

7.3.1.8   Plant Seedling Classification

In general, Deep CNNs are used for plant seedling classification. Deep CNN provides ever-increasing speed and low-cost architectures. However, the availability of the hand-annotated datasets had also increased the demand for implementing the various Deep CNN architectures. In the context of the limited training data, the Deep CNNs could overfit the available training data within no time. In this instance, the expected output could be obtained at every single data point, whereas the model does not promote the general distribution of the data [54]. Deep CNNs provide an efficient pathway for the classification and detection protocols.

7.3.1.9   Greenhouse Simulation

Machine learning plays a vital role in the prediction of greenhouse cultivation environment; it provides optimized optimization, especially in cold and warm seasons, in which ANN and support vector machine estimate the inside environment such as air, soil, and plant temperatures.

7.4 Conclusion

This chapter is intended to depict available technologies and applications based on IoT and machine learning. Here, we extended the knowledge on G-IoT and machine learning for agriculture applications. In the 21st century, updated technologies facilitating the up-gradation of agriculture development as facility agriculture, greenhouse, and contract farming through rural to urban farming methods and moving forward to sustainable agriculture with energy conservation and data-driven management. The G-IoT provides an agriculture management system via Cloud Computing of farm data, security solutions, weeding robots, weather predictions, and disaster and irrigation management. It also facilitates harvesting robots, machine navigation, material handling, crop monitoring, etc. G-IoT technology is possible with the trained tools of machine learning via neural networks, statistical and mathematical modeling for energy conservation, and field and livestock monitoring systems. Future of agriculture system turns completely online to elevate the crop security, crop yield, risk management, robotic farming, greenhouse simulations, etc.

References

1. Tahiliani, V. and Dizalwar, M., Green IoT Systems: An Energy-Efficient Perspective. *2018 Eleventh International Conference on Contemporary Computing (IC3)*, 2018.
2. Alamri, A., Ansari, W., Hassan, M., Hossain, M., Alelaiwi, A., Hossain, M., A Survey on Sensor-Cloud: Architecture, Applications, and Approaches. *Int. J. Distrib. Sens. Netw.*, [online] 9, 2, 917923, 2013.
3. Lee, and Lee, K., The Internet of Things (IoT): Applications, investments, and challenges for enterprises. *Bus. Horiz.*, 58, 4, 431–440, 2015.
4. Zekić-Sušac, M., Mitrović, S., Has, A., Machine learning-based system for managing the energy efficiency of the public sector as an approach towards smart cities. *Int. J. Inf. Manage.*, 58, 102074, 2020.
5. Zantalis, F., Koulouras, G., Karabetsos, S., Kandris, D., A Review of Machine Learning and IoT in Smart Transportation. *Future Internet*, 11, 4, 94, 2019.
6. Nandyala, C. and Kim, H., Green IoT Agriculture and Healthcare Application (GAHA). *Int. J. Smart Home*, 10, 4, 289-300, 2016.

7. Al-Turjman, F., Kamal, A., Husain Rehmani, M., Radwan, A., Khan Pathan, A., The Green Internet of Things (G-IoT). *Wireless Commun. Mobile Comput.*, 2019, 1–2, 2019.

8. Ahmad, R., Asim, M., Khan, S., Singh, B., Green IoT — Issues and Challenges. *SSRN Electron. J.*, 2019.

9. Murugesan, S., *Harnessing green IT: principles and practices*, IT Professional, IEEE, Washington, DC, pp. 24–33, IEEE IT, 2008.

10. Sadiku, M.N.O. and O.G.K., Green Wireless Sensor Networks. *Int. J. Adv. Res. Comput. Sci. Software Eng.*, 9, 2, 2019.

11. Radu, L., Green Cloud Computing: A Literature Survey. *Symmetry*, 9, 12, 295, 2017.

12. Laya, A., Alonso, L., Alonso-Zarate, J., Dohler, M., Green MTC, M2M, Internet of Things. *Green Commun.*, 1, 217–236, 2015.

13. Nam, T., Thanh, N., Tuan, D., Green data center using centralized power-management of network and servers. *2016 International Conference on Electronics, Information, and Communications (ICEIC)*, 2016.

14. Duroc, Y. and Kaddour, D., RFID Potential Impacts and Future Evolution for Green Projects. *Energy Proc.*, 18, 91–98, 2012.

15. Ilyas, Q. and Ahmad, M., Smart Farming: An Enhanced Pursuit of Sustainable Remote Livestock Tracking and Geofencing Using IoT and GPRS. *Wireless Commun. Mobile Comput.*, 2020, 1–12, 2020.

16. Ali, T., Choksi, V., Potdar, M., Precision Agriculture Monitoring System Using Green Internet of Things (G-IoT). *2018 2nd International Conference on Trends in Electronics and Informatics (ICOEI)*, 2018.

17. S.V., An empirical science research on bioinformatics in machine learning. *J. Mech. Continua Math. Sci.*, 7, 1, 2020.

18. Talabis, M., McPherson, R., Miyamoto, I., Martin, J., Kaye, D., Analytics Defined, in: *Information Security Analytics*, pp. 1–12, 2015.

19. El Bouchefry, K. and de Souza, R., Learning in Big Data: Introduction to Machine Learning, in: *Knowledge Discovery in Big Data from Astronomy and Earth Observation*, pp. 225–249, 2020.

20. Zhu, X. and Goldberg, A., Introduction to Semi-Supervised Learning. *Synth. Lect. Artif. Intell. Mach. Learn.*, 3, 1, 1–130, 2009.

21. Bozinovski, S., Cognition-emotion primacy debate and Crossbar Adaptive Array in 1980-1982. *Proc. Comput. Sci.*, 145, 105–111, 2018.

22. Ghosh, D., Olewnik, A., Lewis, K., Application of Feature-Learning Methods Toward Product Usage Context Identification and Comfort Prediction. *J. Comput. Inf. Sci. Eng.*, 18, 1, 011004-1 to 011004-10, 2017.

23. Jain, N., Kumar, A., Garud, S., Pradhan, V., Kulkarni, P., Crop Selection Method based on Various environmental factors using Machine Learning. *Int. Res. J. Eng. Technol.*, 4, 2, 1530–1533, 2017.

24. Wang, H., Cimen, E., Singh, N., Buckler, E., Deep learning for plant genomics and crop improvement. *Curr. Opin. Plant Biol.*, 54, 34–41, 2020.

25. Yu, J., Schumann, A., Cao, Z., Sharpe, S., Boyd, N., Weed Detection in Perennial Ryegrass With Deep Learning Convolutional Neural Network. *Front. Plant Sci.*, 10, 2019.

26. Nalla, K., Pothabathula, S., Kumar, S., Applications of Computational Methods in Plant Pathology, in: *Natural Remedies for Pest, Disease and Weed Control*, pp. 243–250, 2020.

27. Srbinovska, M., Gavrovski, C., Dimcev, V., Krkoleva, A., Borozan, V., Environmental parameters monitoring in precision agriculture using wireless sensor networks. *J. Cleaner Prod.*, 88, 297–307, Feb. 2015.

28. Chen, K.-T., Zhang, H.-H., Wu, T.-T., Hu, J., Zhai, C.-Y., Wang, D., Design of monitoring system for multilayer soil temperature and moisture based on WSN, in: *Proc. Int. Conf. Wireless Commun. Sensor Netw.*, Dec. 2014, pp. 425–430.

29. Postolache, O., Pereira, M., Girão, P., Sensor network for environment monitoring: Water quality case study, in: *Proc. 4th Symp. Environ. Instrum. Meas.*, Lecce, Italy, pp. 30–34, 2013.

30. Ehsan, S., Bradford, K., Brugger, M., Hamdaoui, B., Kovchegov, Y., Johnson, D., Louhaichi, M., 'Design and analysis of delay-tolerant sensor networks for monitoring and tracking free-roaming animals. *IEEE Trans. Wireless Commun.*, 11, 3, 1220–1227, Mar. 2012.

31. Liu, D., Gong, Y., Wang, G., Chen, X., Zhang, X., Wu, G., Research advances in the mechanization of pesticide spraying technology for facility agriculture. *Asian Agric. Res.*, 10, 81–86, Jul. 2018.

32. Ram, V.V.H., Vishal, H., Dhanalakshmi, S., Vidya, P.M., Regulation of water in agriculture field using Internet Of Things, in: *Proc. IEEE Technol. Innov. ICT Agricult. Rural Develop. (TIAR)*, Jul. 2015, pp. 112–115.

33. Castañeda, A., Doan, D., Newhouse, D., Nguyen, M.C., Uematsu, H., Azevedo, J.P., A new profile of the global poor. *World Dev.*, 101, 250–267, Jan. 2018.

34. Talavera, J.M., Tobón, L.E., Gómez, J.A., Culman, M.A., Aranda, J.M., Parra, D.T., Quiroz, L.A., Hoyos, A., Garreta, L.E., Review of IoT applications in agro-industrial and environmental fields. *Comput. Electron. Agric.*, 142, 283–297, Nov. 2017.

35. Minbo, L., Zhu, Z., Guangyu, C., Information service system of agriculture IoT. *Automatika*, 54, 4, 415–426, Jan. 2013.

36. Liu, Y., Han, W., Zhang, Y., Li, L., Wang, J., Zheng, L., An Internet of Things solution for food safety and quality control: A pilot project in China. *J. Ind. Inf. Integr.*, 3, 1–7, Sep. 2016.

37. Wang, J. and Yue, H., Food safety pre-warning system based on data mining for a sustainable food supply chain. *Food Control*, 73, 223–229, Mar. 2017.

38. Lins, D., Araujo, M., Moura, M.D.C., Silva, M.A., Droguett, E.L., Prediction of sea surface temperature in the tropical Atlantic by support vector machines. *Comput. Stat. Data Anal.*, 61, 187–198, 2013.
39. Cao, H., Xin, Y., Yuan, Q., Prediction of biochar yield from cattle manure pyrolysis via least squares support vector machine intelligent approach. *Bioresour. Technol.*, 202, 158–164, 2016.
40. Janet, J., Balakrishnan, S., Sheeba Rani, S., IoT Based Fishery Management System, 1st ed. *Int. J. Oceans Oceanogr.*, 13, 147–152, 2019.
41. Jin, X., Che, J., Chen, Y., Weed Identification Using Deep Learning and Image Processing in Vegetable Plantation. *IEEE Access*, 9, 10940–10950, 2021.
42. Asad, M. and Bais, A., Weed detection in canola fields using maximum likelihood classification and deep convolutional neural network. *Inf. Process. Agric.*, 7, 4, 535–545, 2020.
43. Zhang, X., Zou, J., He, K., Sun, J., Accelerating Very Deep Convolutional Networks for Classification and Detection. *Comput. Vis. Pattern Recognit.* 2015, https://arxiv.org/abs/1505.06798v2.
44. He, K., Zhang, X., Ren, S., Sun, J., Deep residual learning for image recognition, in: *Proceedings of the IEEE conference on computer vision and pattern recognition*, pp. 770–778, 2016.
45. Gadkari, S., Analysis of Pre-Trained Convolutional Neural Networks to Build a Flower Classification System. *Int. J. Res. Appl. Sci. Eng. Technol.*, 7, 11, 489–495, 2019.
46. Chollet, F., Xception: Deep Learning with Depthwise Separable Convolutions. *2017 IEEE Conference on Computer Vision and Pattern Recognition (CVPR)*, 2017.
47. Kanjalkar, H.P. and Lokhande, S.S., *Detection and Classification of Plant Leaf Diseases using ANN*, 1st ed. *Int. J. Sci. Eng. Res.*, 4, 8, August-2013.
48. Chlingaryan, A., Sukkarieh, S., Whelan, B., Machine learning approaches for crop yield prediction and nitrogen status estimation in precision agriculture: A review. *Comput. Electron. Agric.*, 151, 61–69, 2018.
49. Jin, X., Che, J., Chen, Y., Weed Identification Using Deep Learning and Image Processing in Vegetable Plantation. *IEEE Access*, 9, 10940–10950, 2021.
50. Du, Y.-C. and Stephanus, A., Levenberg-Marquardt neural network algorithm for the degree of arteriovenous fistula stenosis classification using A dual optical photoplethysmography sensor. *Sensors*, 18, 7, 2322–2418, 2018.
51. Kayabasi, A., An application of ANN trained by ABC algorithm for classification of wheat grains. *Int. J. Intell. Syst. Appl. Eng.*, 1, 6, 85–91, 2018.
52. Burden, F. and Winkler, D., Bayesian Regularization of Neural Networks, in: *Methods in Molecular Biology™*, pp. 23–42, 2008.
53. Babani, L., Jadhav, S., Chaudhari, B., Scaled Conjugate Gradient-Based Adaptive ANN Control for SVM-DTC Induction Motor Drive, in: *IFIP*

Advances in Information and Communication Technology, pp. 384–395, 2016.

54. Asad, and Bais, A., Weed detection in canola fields using maximum likelihood classification and deep convolutional neural network. *Inf. Process. Agric.*, 7, 4, 535–545, 2020.

55. Homepages.inf.ed.ac.uk. 2021. Feature Detectors - Roberts Cross Edge Detector. [online] Available at: <https://homepages.inf.ed.ac.uk/rbf/HIPR2/roberts.htm> [Accessed 20 July 2021].

IoT-Enabled AI-Based Model to Assess Land Suitability for Crop Production

Aneesha Gudavalli, G. JayaLakshmi and Suneetha Manne

Department of Information Technology, V R Siddhartha Engineering College
Vijayawada, Andhra Pradesh, India

Abstract

With a burgeoning population over the world, food creation and cultivating needs to get progressively gainful and prepared to do exceptional returns in confined time. As per the UN Food and Agriculture Organization, the world should create 70% more food in 2050. To satisfy this need, ranchers and farming organizations should push the advancement furthest reaches of their present practices. Similarly as the Industrial Revolution took cultivating to the following level during the 1800s, arising advances, and even more fundamentally, the Internet of Things (IoT) is scheduled to similarly affect the horticultural business future. This progress from farming to agronomy is currently basic, to guarantee to put food on the tables of everybody around the globe while dodging ridiculous time and work necessities. This chapter gives a short study on IoT sensors utilized in horticulture and presents a survey of different machine learning (ML), artificial intelligence (AI), and deep learning (DL) strategies used to take care of the current issues of ranchers. With the examination of the study, troubles in past methodologies and recommending a superior answer for the current issues in the field of agribusiness are discovered. The review unveils that there are more prospects in recognizing an issue explicit model in a completely computerized way.

Keywords: Smart agriculture, IoT in agriculture, sensor statistics in agriculture, artificial intelligence, machine learning, deep learning, precision farming, artificial intelligence in agriculture

---

Corresponding author: gudavallianeesha@gmail.com

Roshani Raut, Sandeep Kautish, Zdzislaw Polkowski, Anil Kumar and Chuan-Ming Liu (eds.) Green Internet of Things and Machine Learning: Towards a Smart Sustainable World, (215–238) © 2022 Scrivener Publishing LLC

8.1   Introduction

Farming is considered as the significant wellspring of food grains and other crude materials. It is considered as the life of the living species. The biological limits, for instance, temperature, sun controlled radiation, relative tenacity, soil sogginess, and wind, impact the effectiveness of infrequent harvests, as they impact grain design and procure development. Drained soils, poor storerooms, and lacking information for ahead of schedule recognizable proof of plant sicknesses influence the rural efficiency. Modernizing the horticulture makes the harvest upkeep simpler. Brilliant agriculture alludes to utilizing mechanization and IoT in agribusiness. Besides, site-specific agriculture is the idea of utilizing novel advancements and gathering field data. The fundamental exercises of site-specific agriculture are information assortment, preparing along with variable rate uses of data sources. Moreover, IoT innovation is right now molding various parts of human existence. Exactness farming is solitary of the standards which can utilize the IoT focal points to enhance the creation effectiveness over the horticulture fields, upgrade the nature of the yields, and limit the negative ecological effect [1]. Soil readiness is the initial step prior to growing

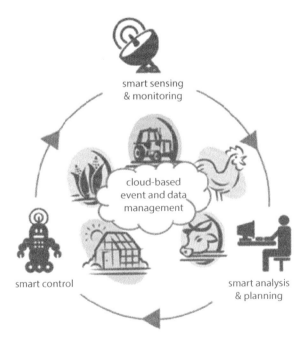

Figure 8.1 IoT-based precision farming cycle.

a harvest. A definitive target is to create a dense and sans weed seedbed for quick germination and development of the yield. One of the main undertakings in soil readiness is plowing whirling the dirt with slackening it. In addition, soil planning is one of the mainly energy burning-through pieces of agribusiness and necessitates critical contributions of fuel and time. Contingent upon the field's area, it might likewise expand the danger of soil disintegration. Nowadays, precision cultivating gear exists that encourages ranchers to utilize impressively a smaller amount fuel and time in soil planning by improving the precision, productivity, and also manageability of the cycle as shown in Figure 8.1.

8.2   Literature Survey

8.2.1   Internet of Things in Field of Agriculture

With the quick advancement of IoT purpose in the cloud stage, the number of connected gadgets has expanded in an exceptionally rapid way. It has been understood that the gadgets are further than the individuals on the Earth in 2011. Also, the associated gadgets are relied upon to arrive at 24 billion by 2050. These gadgets are associated by means of cloud stages for various purposes. IoT and distributed calculate working in joining makes another worldview, which have been named as Cloud of Things (CoT) [2]. In CoT, IoT things are stretched out from sensors to each front-end thing in the Internet. Furthermore, disseminated locales are associated with the overall body, for instance, a keen house, savvy manufacturing plant, perceptive city, and brilliant planet. In view of CoT, a legitimate engineering of a keen city is given. With the convergence of cloud stage and IoT, CoT is needed to improve the capacity for gigantic gadgets intuitive with interoperability in order to help keen as well as clever applications. At the position when the quantities of gadgets are growing, diverse information and direction will be associated through CoT. For further information and assets in a single viewpoint on cloud or existing IoT application, CoT will provide more contemplation in a business indulgent. The issues acknowledged with coordination of IoT with disseminated computing that entail a savvy door to cooperate out the rich errands with preprocessing, in which conventional sensors are not equipped for satisfying the task of information accumulation and processing, are shown in Figure 8.2.

Astute water framework [3] is good for giving the water to the entire ground reliably, schedule, and reins the water deftly indirectly so that each plant has the adequate proportion of water it needs, neither a ton of nor

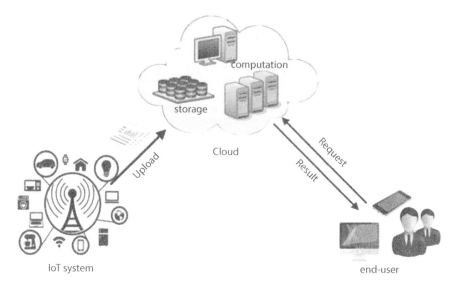

Figure 8.2 Cloud of Things.

exorbitantly slight, Water use capability in the ground can be directed by field water efficiency rate.

$$\textbf{WF\% = (WT of Crop / WA to Field)*100} \qquad (8.1)$$

WT is water efficiency is and WA is water added to ground, where WF is water efficiency. The architecture is intended to develop a programmed water system framework that adjusts the siphon engine ON/OFF to detect the dirt dampness material. The structure is intended to detect the dirt dampness substance. The organization of remote sensors has created comprehensive robotization events. This helps to obtain subtleties in the turf from assets such as water, soil, or air and analyze them to get the option to enhance the yield and spare assets. Inconsequential MQTT distributor endorser agreement is used for correspondence because of which harvests would be gracefully tested for soil dampness, mugginess, temperature, and water to crops. Observing these limits will help to understand and supervise land assortments for visible capitulation. For additional indication, the natural boundaries are put away in DynamoDB. To inform the client/rancher, AWS entryway with AWS Lambda is used. The advantage of using this method is that individual intercession is reduced and an adequate water system is still assured. Figure 8.3 demonstrates a genius irrigation framework using CloudIoT.

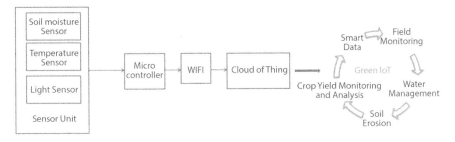

Figure 8.3 Irrigation system using CloudIoT.

The Green IoT (G-IoT) is expected to introduce considerable changes in everyday life and would facilitate realize the apparition of "green surrounded intelligence". Within the minority years, we will be surrounded by an immense amount of sensors, devices, as well as "things", which will be capable to communicate through 5G, act "intelligently", and supply green support for users in supervising their tasks [24]. G-IoT inducts cutting-edge sensor-based technologies for real-time accomplishment of micro-climatic data from farmers' field, timely measurement of crop situation, and personalized agro-advisory services to farmers.

The distinctive remote correspondence advancements have different reaches [4], which should be represented when planning the IoT arrangement, along with different factors, for example, information rate, power utilization, correspondence conventions, or expenses. In arable cultivating, because of the bigger homestead sizes and due to the work of portable sensors and gadgets on vehicles, this test turns out to be significantly more basic. Besides, depending on the inexact correspondence scope of a remote innovation can be misdirecting, for example, Wi-Fi is regularly depicted to have 100 m reach, however, a test investigating the parcel conveyance proportion regarding separation to door shows bundle misfortunes at ≥ 60 m. Notwithstanding the decision of remote technology, network geography in WSNs, for example, work geographies, can likewise build the correspondence range by utilizing hubs to speak with the focal hub. Contrasts in correspondence conventions can root specialized interoperability, which can prompt problems of compatibility and similarity between the equipment and programming used. Organization conventions are isolated into assorted layers shaping a convention stack, where errands are partitioned into more modest advances. In the foundation layer, some remote guidelines that characterize correspondence conventions are generally utilized by various remote technologies, e.g., IEEE 802.15.4, which is used by, among others, ZigBee, 6LowPAN, or 3GPP, which is used by, among others, GPRS, LTE, or 5G. Standards such as HTTP, MQTT, or XMPP are usually used in IoT applications within arable cultivation in the application layer, as shown in Figure 8.4.

As indicated by the applications that concentrate on QoS (Quality of Administrations) and push the board, the sensors for IoT purposes are relegated to unique functionalities. The administration of sensor arrangements is expected to advance regional control as well as energy usage and increase the length of the sensor center. In WSN, the LEACH shown in Figure 8.5 calculation was used to bring the organization together into groups in which each bunch contains a bunch head and a few group individuals are using the situation of WSN-based IoT applications consisting of sensor hubs, switches, and a descend. This modified the measurement of LEACH [5] to preserve geography to ensure the ideal degree intended to save the hub's transmission intensity. By sending HELLO messages and receiving the REPLY message, and afterward, benevolent and ideal decision of community individuals, the system learns the evolving organizational interface qualities.

The updated LEACH calculation aims to achieve the ideal K degree hub and also aims to ensure the organization's solid availability with the ideal geography chosen. The estimation involves two stages: the stage of setup and the stage of consistent state. The calculation is done consecutively in all sensor hubs at the arrangement level, which collect data from their neighbors. The sensor hubs will select the bunch head depending on the spread power and ideal degree of the hub at that point. At the consistent stage of conditions, the data is actually transmitted between the sensor hubs and the sink. The group head is selected by the degree of its ideal center,

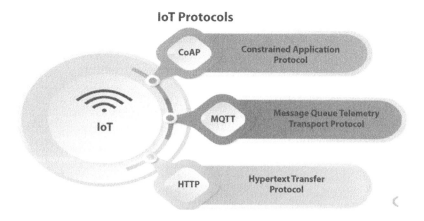

Figure 8.4 IoT protocols.

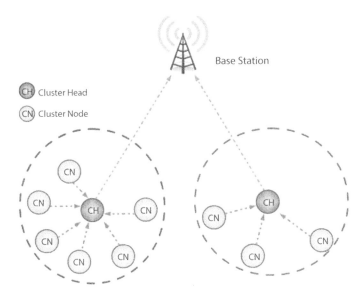

Figure 8.5 LEACH network topology.

separation from the sink hub, and lingering energy. The optimal degree of hub depends on the full utilization of resources or the group head's remaining energy. Expect that the head of the bunch is only affiliated with individuals of the K group, and the number of groups in the organization can be determined by

$$P_{opt} = \frac{N}{K}$$

The length of broadcasting expression can be controlled by

$$timeout = (N - 1)t_{hello}$$

In the setup process, each hub looks for the group leader, and the hub can choose to be a CH if there is no CH in the organization. Each hub will produce an arbitrary number selected anywhere in the range of 0 and 1 in the modified LEACH. If the irregular number is not as much as edges Pthr, the hub becomes CHs. The hub will communicate the HELLO message else, it will hang tight for the HELLO message. The limit to pick a group head is characterized by

$$P_i(t) = P_{opt} / 1-P_{opt} \left[r.\text{mod} \left[\frac{1}{Popt} \right] \right]$$

The head of the bunch is selected by its ideal degree of hub, separation from the downward hub, and remaining energy. The optimal degree of hub depends on the use of all out energy or the remaining strength of the head of the bunch. Accepting that the bunch head only interfaces with individuals of the K group, the number of groups in the organization can be determined by the number of groups

$$P_{opt} = \frac{N}{K}$$

The length of broadcasting expression can be controlled by

$$\text{Timeout} = (N - 1)t_{hello}$$

In Table 8.1, detailed analyses of the top level of IoT in cultivation are provided. Configuration, level, and geology of the agricultural network help to enable IoT spine and facilitate farmers to enhance the effectiveness of the reap. Similarly, this chapter offers a comprehensive overview of current and ongoing developments in IoT agricultural applications, devices/sensors, topologies, and protocols with various inventive developments that have been presented.

8.2.2 Machine Learning With Internet of Things in Agriculture

A forecasting engine has been developed that is important for an IoT-enabled frost prediction framework [6], which accumulates natural information to anticipate ice occasions utilizing artificial intelligence (AI) procedures. Expectation ability outflanks current proposition regarding affectability, accuracy, and F1 were appeared. Specifically, the utilization of SMOTE as shown in Figure 8.6 during the preparation stage has demonstrated an improved execution as far as review in both RF and Logistic Regression models. In explicit applicable cases, the incorporation of neighbor data assists with improving the accuracy or review of the estimated grouping model were noticed. Then again, relapse models have fewer errors, as well as neighboring data. In these instances, there is a corresponding enhancement in model execution with the spatial ties.

Table 8.1 Review on IoT in agriculture.

S. No.	Year	Researchers	Work	Description
1	2020	Anusha Vangala, Ashok Kumar Das, Senior Member, Neeraj Kumar, Mamoun Alazab [13]	Investigations of various cryptographic natives using the commonly known "Multiprecision Integer and Rational Arithmetic Cryptographic Library (MIRACL)" to estimate the usual time needed for primitives such as Texp, Tecm, Teca, Tsenc = Tsdec, Th, Tmul, Tadd, Tecsiggen, and Tecsigver to indicate the time required for a "bilinear blending", a "measured exponentiation", and a "elliptic bend point"	MIRACL is a C/C++ programming language-dependent cryptographic library that includes the "Elliptic Curve Cryptography Open Source SDK".
2	2018	Ahmed, A.N.; de Hussain, I.D [14]	1. In the current WSN-based solutions for covering longer ranges, implement the WiLD network with fog computing With a less important pause. 2. To minimize the delay, a cross-layer–based MAC with a routing response is used.	Wi-Fi–based long distance (WiLD) network with links up to 100 km can easily provide connectivity and is used efficiently to associate the provincial areas. With the all-inclusive scope, haze registration and distributed computing arrangements can be integrated into Wi-Fi gadgets for better and proficient IoT in such locations.

(Continued)

Table 8.1 Review on IoT in agriculture. (*Continued*)

S. No.	Year	Researchers	Work	Description
3	2019	Sudhir K. Routray, Abhishek Javali, Laxmi Sharma, Aritri D. Ghosh, Anindita Sahoo [15]	The ongoing structures of PA utilizing IoT were shown how it can help the agrarian areas of the agricultural nations in the long haul. The significance of IoT-based PA for better return. We mostly center the need of an IoT-based PA with regards to the agricultural nations are given	Precision agriculture (PA) is a way of working with ranch executives that employs data innovation (IT) to ensure that harvests and soil get what they need for optimum comfort and profitability in particular. PA seeks to ensure the benefit, manageability, and protection of the climate.
4	2018	Mohamed Abdel Basset1, Laila A. Shawky1, Khalid Eldrandaly [16]	For upgrading the zone inclusion level of WSN, an enhanced met heuristic calculation named multi-verse optimizer via overlapping detection stage (DMVO) is presented. The proposed calculation is attempted on various datasets with different data sets. Standards and contrasts and different calculations were discussed, as well as the first MVO, MVO, optimization of particle swarm, along with the algorithm of flower pollination.	Multiverse optimization (MVO) algorithm is an amazing meta-heuristic calculation dependent on laws of material science. Notwithstanding, it is anything but difficult to fall into a nearby ideal when taking care of complex multimodal advancement issues with high measurements.

(*Continued*)

Table 8.1 Review on IoT in agriculture. (*Continued*)

S. No.	Year	Researchers	Work	Description
5	2019	Tesfa Tegegne, Hailu Beshada Balcha, and Mebiratu Beyene [4]	ZigBee remote sensor organizations can achieve self-sorting remote information transmission, which has been commonly used in large-scale farming. RFID (radio-frequency identification) invention. RFID technology. It is usually used in creature distinguishing evidence that can be performed on creatures to perform astute perception, position, follow, observation, discernibility, and the managers are examined.	Radio transmission technology is transmission and discovery of correspondence signals consisting of electromagnetic waves that move through the air in an orderly fashion. RFID is an innovation that utilizes radio waves to inactively distinguish a labeled object.

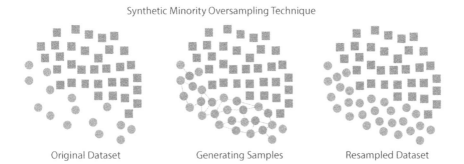

Figure 8.6 Synthetic Minority Oversampling Technique (SMOTE).

Regression models record the Mean Absolute Error (MAE) and Root Mean Square Error (RMSE). If, as stated in the test set, Yreal denotes the real minimum and Ypred denotes the expected form value, the metrics are defined as follows:

$$\text{Root Mean Square Error} = \sqrt{\frac{1}{n}\sum(Ypred - Yreal)^2}$$

$$\text{Mean Absolute Error} = \frac{1}{n}\sum_{t=1}^{n}|Ypred - Yreal|$$

For classification models, we can compute the following metrics:

Sensitivity: True Positive / True Positive + False Negative
Precision: True Positive / True Positive + False Positive
F_1-score: F_1 = 2 × precision × sensitivity / precision + sensitivity.

In order to achieve easy, reliable, and accurate agribusiness, drones equipped with suitable cameras, sensors, and coordination modules would make it easier. When combined with various [7] ideas for machine learning (ML) and the IoT, drones will help to extend the scope of additional enhancement, as shown in Figure 8.7.

For the grouping and examining of information that is transferred in the cloud, an uphold vector machine or SVM is utilized, which is an administered learning model, incorporated with AI calculations that chiefly centers around relapse and order issues. The fundamental target of the SVM is to prepare a model with the end goal that it allocates the new items to a particular classification. It begins by displaying the circumstance which

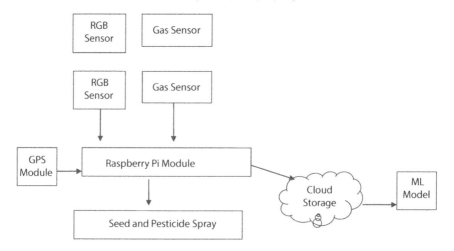

Figure 8.7 Block diagram of IoT-based drone for enhancement of crop quality in agricultural field.

makes a component space (vector space of limited measurement) wherein each measurement portrays a "highlight" of a specific article. SVM chooses the most ideal arrangement shown in Figure 8.8. The SVM can likewise be utilized in accuracy horticulture utilizing UAV.

IoT and ML-based ways to deal with soil dampness [8] levels ideal for the development of yields, regardless of the climate circumstances for the following 24 hours, were engaged. A savvy water system framework helping in appropriate water the board and giving ideal harvest recommendations dependent on noteworthy soil condition information and furthermore give the amounts of minerals should have been added to the dirt were clarified.

PART [9] classification procedure is proposed for crop profitability and dry spell prediction. This technique ends up being generally precise in giving dry season expectation just as the efficiency of harvests like Bajra, Soybean, Jowar, and Sugarcane. The WPART technique accomplishes the most extreme precision contrasted with the current incomparable standard calculations, and it is acquired up to 92.51%, 96.77%, 98.04%, 96.12%, and 98.15% for the five datasets for dry spell classification and crop profitability individually. Moreover, the proposed technique beats existing calculations with exactness, affectability, and F-score measurements. Given preparing vectors $X_i \in R_n$, i = 1, ..., l, and a name vector $Y \in R_l$, a choice tree recursively parcels the space with the end goal that the examples with similar marks are gathered. Leave the information at hub m alone spoken to by Q. For every up-and-comer split $_\theta$ = (j, t_m) consisting of a component j and limit tm, segment the information into and subsets $Q_{L(\theta)}$ and $Q_{R(\theta)}$.

$$Q_{L(\theta)} = ((X,Y) \mid X_j < t_m) \tag{8.2}$$

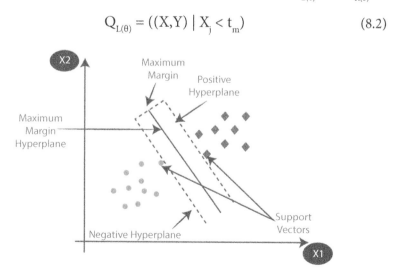

Figure 8.8 Support vector machine.

$$Q_{R(\theta)} = (Q \mid Q_{L(\theta)}) \tag{8.3}$$

The contamination at m is registered utilizing impurity function H (), the decision of which depends on the errand being tackled (classification or regression).

$$G(Q, \theta) = n_L / N_m \times H(Q_{L(\theta)}) + n_R / N_m \times H(Q_{R(\theta)}) \tag{8.4}$$

Table 8.2 Review on ML with IoT in agriculture.

S. No.	Year	Researchers	Work	Description
1	2020	Yemeserach Mekonnen, Srikanth Namuduri, Lamar Burton, Arif Sarwat, and Shekhar Bhansali [17]	A far reaching audit of the utilization of various AI calculations in sensor information investigation inside the rural environment. It further talks about a contextual analysis on IoT-based information driven brilliant ranch models as an incorporated food, energy, and water (FEW) framework.	Used the model of classification and regression trees (CART) to identify possible indicators of crop yield, FEW communications, and yield efficiency. Use the model of autoregressive integrated moving average (ARIMA) forever arrangement-based sensor data.
2	2016	Suyash S. Patil1, Sandeep A. Thorat [18]	The Hidden Markov Model is accustomed to observing frameworks which will distinguish the odds of grape illnesses in its beginning phases.	Hidden Markov Model (HMM) is a factual Markov model in which it is assumed that the structure being displayed is a Markov cycle with undetectable ("covered up") states. Well accepts that there is another cycle whose conduct "depends" on The objective is to find out about by noticing.

(Continued)

Table 8.2 Review on ML with IoT in agriculture. (*Continued*)

S. No.	Year	Researchers	Work	Description
3	2020	Uferah Shafi, Rafia Mumtaz, Naveed Iqbal, Syed Mohammad Hassan Zaidi, Syed Ali Raza Zaidi, Imtiaz Hussain, [19] and Zahid Mahmood	A coordinated methodology for observing yield well-being utilizing IoT, AI, and robot innovation is used. NDVI gives data about the harvest in light of the chlorophyll content, which offers restricted data with respect to the yield well-being. To acquire rich and itemized information about yield well-being, In order to construct crop well-being charts, the variable length time arrangement information of IoT sensors and multispectral images was changed to a fixed-size representation.	The Normalized Difference Vegetation Index (NDVI) is a simple graphical marker that can be used frequently from a space stage to break down distant detecting estimates, surveying whether live green vegetation is included in the goal being noticed.
4	2017	Rob Dolci [20]	In order to verify how CO2, temperature, humidity, and PH differ, AI algorithms such as Bayesian network analysis and multi-variant analysis are used.	Bayesian networks are a sort of probabilistic graphical model that utilizes Bayesian deduction for likelihood calculations. Bayesian organizations mean to display restrictive reliance, and hence causation, by speaking to contingent reliance by edges in a coordinated chart.

$$\theta^* = \mathrm{argmin}_\theta \, G\,(Q, \theta) \qquad (8.5)$$

Table 8.2 summarizes different ML algorithms used to solve agriculture related problems like odds of grape illnesses, food, energy, and water (FEW) framework and other such problems with the integration of IoT devices.

8.2.3   Deep Learning With Internet of Things in Agriculture

Codling [10] moth assault is the most widely recognized issue for apple plantations. Neural organization calculations of IoT sensors will naturally identify the codling moth: the system snaps a picture of the snare, preprocesses it, crops every creepy crawl for grouping, and, if any codling moth is detected, finally, sends a note to the rancher. The application is built on a low-energy stage fueled by a board of a few hundred square centimeters centered on the sun, recognizing an energy self-governing system suitable for consistently operating unattended over low-force large-area organizations. A quick part of this IoT arrangement is the low force stage for an AI calculation utilized for IoT quick prototyping. The machine relies on the Raspberry Pi 3 board and the Intel Movidius Neural Compute Stick [9], as shown in Figure 8.9, liable for the preprocessing strategy and the neural organization usage, separately.

On a Raspberry Pi 3 that provides the preprocessing step, the framework is implanted. At that point, an Intel Movidius neural register stick

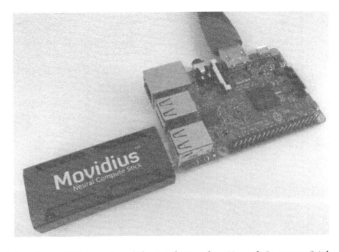

Figure 8.9 Raspberry Pi 3 board and the Intel Movidius Neural Compute Stick.

(NCS) with an Intel Myriad X neural quickening agent as a dream handling unit (VPU) groups the images obtained after the deep neural organization (DNN) preparation shown in Figure 8.10 using the model.

Table 8.3 summarizes different deep learning (DL) algorithms used in different agriculture related applications like hydroponics, soil health, and other such applications with the coordination of IoT gadgets.

To create an IoT structure for crop fine-grained sickness ID, IoT with DL is used. As a result, this system will classify crop infections and give ranchers indicative results. We propose the remaining neural organization (MDFC-ResNet) model for multidimensional portion remuneration for fine-grained disease distinguishing evidence in the system. From three metrics, in particular, organisms, coarse-grained disease, and fine-grained infection, MDFC-ResNet recognizes and creates a pay layer that uses a remuneration calculation to meld multidimensional recognition outcomes. Tests show that the neural organization MDFC-ResNet [11] has a stronger effect on recognition and is more enlightening than other popular DL models in genuine horticultural development exercises. MDFC-ResNet is an agricultural IoT device to accurately identify crop diseases, and MDFC-ResNet shown in Figure 8.11 recognizes species, coarse-grained sickness, and fine-grained disease from three measurements, in particular, and sets up a pay layer that uses a remuneration calculation to intertwine multidimensional recognition effects.

Two standards are embraced anticipating the reasonable harvest for the following yield pivot and ad libbing the water system arrangement of the field by particular water system. The above objective is accomplished by occasionally observing the field. The observing cycle includes gathering data about the dirt boundaries of the field. To collect this information and

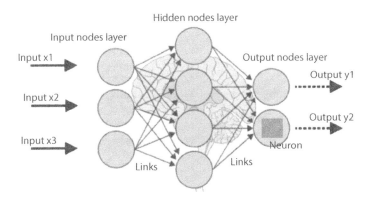

Figure 8.10 DNN.

Table 8.3 Review on DL with IoT in agriculture.

S. No.	Year	Researchers	Work	Conclusion
1	2019	Author: Kirtan Jha; Aalap Doshi; Poojan Patel; Manan Shahd [21]	Deep learning algorithms like **ANN** to identify the soil moisture.	This system presented an idea to develop a system with IoT and ML, to automate the traditional practices in agriculture
2	2019	E. Alreshidi [22]	A holistic forum for IoT/AI to cover all areas in the SSA ecosystem (Smart Sustainable Agriculture) to perform tasks like govern data flow, integration of components, sustainable storage, etc.	To fix issues arising from the fragmentary nature of the agricultural method, the AI/IoT framework for SSA is used.
3	2020	Disha Garg; Samiya Khan; Mansaf Alam [23]	**DNN** is used for hydroponic system development (multiple input parameters)	A comparison between two algorithms to make predictions for agricultural applications on agricultural data. DNN = 88% accuracy Deep CNN = 96.3%

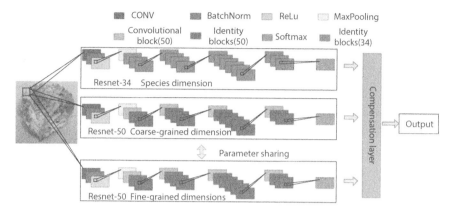

Figure 8.11 MDFC-ResNet.

have knowledge of the past, a remote sensor organization (WSN) is set up by uploading it to the cloud inconsistently. This information conveyed forms the justification for the inquiry. Long-Short Term Memory (LSTM) through experimentation, RNN, and GRU [12] networks shown in Figure 8.12 are discovered to be the appropriate calculation. The derived outcomes are contrasted and the ideal qualities and the most appropriate yield are suggested to the client through SMS administration.

A shrewd agribusiness IoT framework dependent on profound support realizing which incorporates four layers, to be specific horticultural information assortment layer, edge registering layer, farming information transmission layer, and distributed computing layer, is introduced. The introduced framework coordinates some serious data procedures, particularly computerized reasoning and distributed computing, with horticultural creation to build food creation. Uncommonly, the most exceptional computerized reasoning model, profound support learning is joined in the cloud layer to settle on prompt keen choices, for example, deciding the measure of water should have been inundated for improving harvest

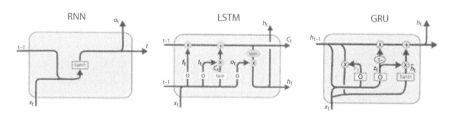

Figure 8.12 RNN, LSTM, and GRU structure.

development climate. A few delegate profound models learning models like progressive neural network are shown in Figure 8.13; single-task policy distillation and multi-task policy distillation are shown in Figure 8.14; and with their extensive applications that we explained, various memory-based deep Q-network is shown in Figure 8.15.

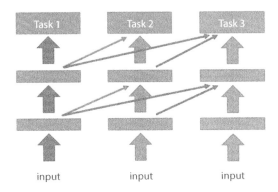

Figure 8.13 Progressive neural network.

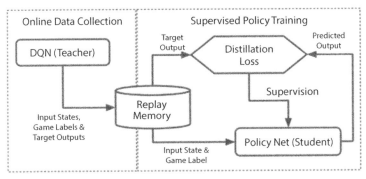

(**a**) Single-task data collection and policy distillation.

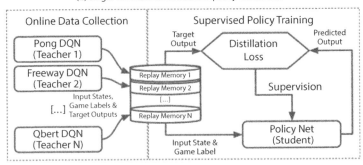

(**b**) Multi-task data collection and policy distillation.

Figure 8.14 Single-task and multi-task policy distillation.

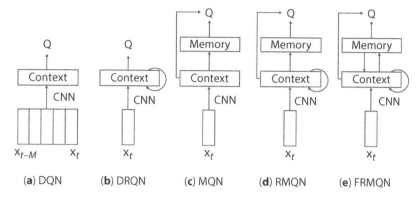

Figure 8.15 Different memory-based deep Q-network.

8.3 Conclusion

Agribusiness, similar to other businesses, is going through a computerized change. The measure of information being gathered from ranches is expanding dramatically. The utilization of remote sensor organizations, IoT, advanced mechanics, robots, and AI is on the rise. AI calculations allow useful data and bits of knowledge to be extracted from the information storm. The ML techniques commonly used by analysts in the previous 2 years relevant to remote sensor organizations were audited by this chapter. An increased use of further evolved processes such as distributed (or edge) DL may be seen in the coming years. In order to extend the computerization of errands in agribusiness and boost the yield while advancing the use of routine properties, computer-based intelligence must be used. This chapter has shown various models of IoT, ML, and DL implemented within the exact biological framework of agribusiness in numerous applications. The checked on work has been centered explicitly around IoT, conventions, cloud, ML, and DL-based exactness cultivating application. The engineering, equipment, correspondence convention, and information securing foundation are nitty gritty. The usage of cell phone applications and, furthermore, the back-end information investigation structure for forecast of climate, crop yield, and harvest quality, just as illness detection, irrigation, use of robots, and so forth, are introduced.

References

1. Dewi, C. and Chen, R.-C., Decision Making Based on IoT Data Collection for Precision Agriculture, Department of Information Management,

Chaoyang University of Technology, Taichung, Taiwan, Republic of China. Asian Conference on Intelligent Information and Database Systems Springer Nature Switzerland, ACIIDS 2019: Intelligent Information and Database Systems: Recent Developments, pp 31-42, AG, 2020.

2. Cai, H., Xu, B., Jiang, L., Vasilakos, A.V., IoT-based Big Data Storage Systems in Cloud Computing: Perspectives and Challenges. IOT-0592-2015,2327-4662 (c) 2016 IEEE *IEEE Sens. J.*, IOT-0592-2015,2327-4662 (c) 2016.

3. Raikar, M.M., Desai, P., Kanthi, N., Bawoor, S., Blend of Cloud and Internet of Things (IoT) in agriculture sector using lightweight protocol. *IEEE Sens. J.*, 978-1-5386-5314-2/18, 2018.

4. Villa-Henriksen, A., Edwards, G.T.C., Pesonen, L.A., Green, O., Sørensen, C.A.G., Internet of Things in arable farming:Implementation, applications, challenges and potential, *Biosystems Engineering*, 191, 60-84, March 2020, Elsevier, 2019.

5. Nguyen, T.N., Ho, C.V., Le, T.T.T., A Topology Control Algorithm in Wireless Sensor Networks for IoT-based Applications. *IEEE Sens. J.*, 2019.

6. Vangala, A., Das, A.K., Kumar, N., Alazab, M., Smart Secure Sensing for IoT-Based Agriculture:Blockchain Perspective. *IEEE Sens. J.*, 1558-1748 (c) 2020.

7. Saha, A.K., Saha, J., Ray, R., Sircar, S., Dutta, S., Chattopadhyay, S.P., Saha, H.N., IOT-Based Drone for Improvement of Crop Quality in Agricultural Field. *IEEE8th Annual Computing and Communication Workshop and Conference*, 2018.

8. Goapa, A., Sharmab, D., Shuklab, A.K., Rama Krishnaa, C., An IoT based smart irrigation management system using Machine learning and open source technologies, Elsevier, *Computers and Electronics in Agriculture*, 155, 41-49, December 2018.

9. Rezk, N.G., Hemdan, E.ED., Attia, AF. et al. An efficient IoT based smart farming system using machine learning algorithms. *Multimed Tools Appl*, 80, 773–797, 2021.

10. Syed, F.K., Paul, A., Kumar, A., Cherukuri, J., Low-cost IoT+ML design for smart farming with multiple applications. *10th ICCCNT IIT*, IEEE, Kanpur, 2019.

11. Brunelli, D., Albanese, A., d'Acunto, D., Nardello, M., Energy Neutral Machine Learning Based IoT Device for Pest Detection in Precision Agriculture, IEEE Xplore, *IEEE Internet of Things Magazine*, 2019.

12. Aruul Mozhi Varman, S., Baskaran, A.R., Aravindh, S., Prabhu, E., Deep Learning and IoT for Smart Agriculture using WSN. *IEEE International Conference on Computational Intelligence and Computing Research*, 2017.

13. Vangala, A., Das, A.K., Kumar, N., Alazab, M., Smart Secure Sensing for IoT-Based Agriculture: Blockchain Perspective. *IEEE Sens. J.*, 1558-1748 (c) 2020, 2020.

14. Ahmed, A.N. and de Hussain, I.D., Internet of Things (IoT) for smart precision agriculture and farming in rural areas. *IEEE Internet Things J.*, 5, 6, 2018.

15. Routray, S.K., Javali, A., Sharma, L., Internet of Things Based Precision Agriculture for Developing Countries. *Second International Conference on Smart Systems and Inventive Technology*, IEEE Xplore, 2019.

16. Abdel-Basset, M., Shawky, L.A. & Eldrandaly, K. Grid quorum-based spatial coverage for IoT smart agriculture monitoring using enhanced multi-verse optimizer. *Neural Comput & Applic*, 32, 607–624, 2020.

17. Mekonnen, Y., Namuduri, S., Burton, L., Sarwat, A., Bhansali, S., Review—Machine Learning Techniques in Wireless Sensor Network Based Precision Agriculture. *J. Electrochem. Soc.*, 167, 037522, 2020.

18. Patil, S.S. and Thorat, S.A., Early Detection of Grapes Diseases Using Machine Learning and IoT. *Second International Conference on Cognitive Computing and Information Processing*, IEEE, 2016.

19. Boursianis, A.D., Papadopoulou, M.S., Diamantoulakis, P., Liopa-Tsakalidi, A., Barouchas, P., Salahas, G., Karagiannidis, G., Wan, S., Goudos, S.K., Internet of Things (IoT) and Agricultural Unmanned Aerial Vehicles (UAVs) in smart farming: A comprehensive review, Elsevier, *Internet of Things; Engineering Cyber Physical Human Systems,*16,100187, 2020.

20. Dolci, R., IoT solutions for precision farming and food manufacturing Artificial Intelligence applications in Digital Food. *41st Annual Computer Software and Applications Conference*, IEEE, 2017.

21. Jha, K., Doshi, A., Patel, P., Shahd, M., A comprehensive review on automation in agriculture using artificial intelligence, KeAi, *Artificial Intelligence in Agriculture*, 2, 1-12, 2019.

22. Alreshidi, E., Smart Sustainable Agriculture (SSA) solution underpinned by Internet of Things (IoT) and Artificial Intelligence (AI), *arXiv, International Journal of Advanced Computer Science and Applications*, 10, 5, 2019. 93-102, 2019.

23. Garg, D., Khan, S., Alam, M., *Integrative Use of IoT and Deep Learning for Agricultural Applications*, Department of Computer Science, Jamia Millia Islamia, New Delhi, India P. K. Singh *et al.* (Eds.): Proceedings of ICETIT 2019, LNEE 605, pp. 521–531, 2020, Springer Nature Switzerland AG, 2020.

24. Al-Turjman, F., Kamal, A., Rehmani, M.H., Radwan, A., Pathan, A.-S.K., The Green Internet of Things (G-IoT). *Wireless Commun. Mobile Comput.*, 2019, Article ID 6059343, 2 pages, 2019, https://doi.org/10.1155/2019/6059343.

9

Green Internet of Things (GIoT): Agriculture and Healthcare Application System (GIoT-AHAS)

Anil L. Wanare[1*] and Sahebrao N. Patil[2†]

1JSPM's BSIOTR, Pune Dept. of Electronics & Telecommunication Engineering, Savitribai Phule Pune University, Pune, India
2JSPM's BSIOTR, Pune Dept. of Electrical Engineering, Savitribai Phule Pune University, Pune, India

Abstract

In the last couple of years, there are applications relevant to Green Internet of Things (GIoT) and the major focus on two development trending and admired technologies is upcoming: Green Cloud Computing Application (GCCA) and GIoT are current buzz discussions in the field of crop growing (agriculture) and medical related things, i.e., healthcare industry–based applications. Motivated by achieving a sustainable globe, this chapter discusses a variety of technology and issue concerning GCCA and GIoT and, additionally, further improves the conversation with the suppression of energy utilization of the combination of these two techniques (CCA and GIoT) in farming industry, i.e., one is agriculture-based and the other is healthcare industry–based system. The past and perception of the hot green information and communication technologies (GICTs) which enabled GIoT have been discussed rigorously. Green mathematical computational calculations opens first and, furthermore, or we can say, afterward focuses on the modern significant works completed concerning of these two upcoming emerging technologies in both agriculture and healthcare cases. In addition, this chapter has contributed significant information by presenting GIoT farming and healthcare applications linear time-invariant system (GIoT-AHAS) using digital wireless sensor cloud discrete integration or digital summation modelling. Finally, we have

Corresponding author: anilwanare15@gmail.com; alwanare_entc@jspmbsiotr.edu.in
†Corresponding author: jspmnarhepatil@gmail.com

Roshani Raut, Sandeep Kautish, Zdzislaw Polkowski, Anil Kumar and Chuan-Ming Liu (eds.) Green Internet of Things and Machine Learning: Towards a Smart Sustainable World, (239–268) © 2022 Scrivener Publishing LLC

summarized the limitations, advantages, challenges, and prospects of the research guidelines associated to emerging and advanced green-based application oriented development in relevant field. The aim of our chapter is to research and create broad green area and also to make contribution to sustainable application around the globe.

Keywords: Green Internet of Things (GIoT), green cloud computing applications, GIoT-based agriculture, healthcare, sensor cloud, ubiquitous computing

9.1   Introduction

The solar system now contains a number of components and relevant objects around it. Like the Internet of Things (IoT) [1, 2], so out of all, the most technologically advanced objects in world, it aims to connect various objects or objects via the internet (e.g., laptops, advanced computers, advanced cars, various digital gadget, and more functional objects) with different e-mail addresses or smart mobile phone application. Internet (IP) enables them to communicate with others and everywhere in world (worldwide). A lot of devices come up to develop a number of technological devices and objects are linked or joined to the internet with unusual levels of Internet of Things (IoT) imagination [2, 3]. The IoT-based on many applications are there, *viz.*, transportation from one place to another, advanced agriculture, recent health systems, programmable logic controller-based industrial automation, and emergency responses to natural disasters, disasters happened due to human beings, and combinations wherever human decision-making is extremely difficult in such situation. Among many applications are there to enable by IoT, which focuses mainly on two applications one is agricultural and the other is related to healthcare in this chapter. The many sensors connected to the network, through the wireless sensors network to human body or embedded in our environment, make it achievable to collect effective data that reflects a person's physical and mental health [3, 4].

The IoT empowers us to observe, pay attention to think and perform the tasks by enabling them to converse jointly, and share information and directives for the decision. Ultimately, all aspects of the human being cyber, substantial, societal, and psychosomatic world would be interrelated and rationally in the intellectual world (globally). As we know most recent stage in human times gone by, the intelligent world has received much attention from the world of education, business, industry, government, and many other organizations. In addition, the Green IoT (GIoT) is the raw material network aims at a robust (global) smart world device by suppressing the internet power utilization or consumption of components used in such applications [5, 6].

The green cloud computing (GCC) is one of the most popular and upcoming technologies, the upcoming and promise paradigm that offers computer use as an aid [7, 8]. It offers the most up-to-date software practice, mass data access, large data storage space services, and additional online mathematical computational calculations and helps customers payment resources based on the pay as you go representation system [5, 7]. Customers are only charged more for the way they use it properly. It is very expensive. The immense gain of cloud computing is that users can get computing for their statistics and huge data storage services on demand with no much investment in computer infrastructure (e.g., advanced computational tools). Díez, C. Hacia *et al.* provided statistics; all the world's data centers use 30 billion watts of electricity out of 2000, and 2000 is equivalent to the output of 30 nuclear energy and power generation plants [8]. Electrical energy that can be powered 5 million homes in 1 year is needed to cool all these servers and all big data centers in 1 year [9]. We should therefore look for new strategies to increase the energy demand of these large data centers, namely, cloud [8, 9]. Basic agricultural and networking methodology is described in Figure 9.1.

GIoT data–based computing is nothing but the environmentally friendly computer. It refers to efforts to suppress or to reduce energy consumption

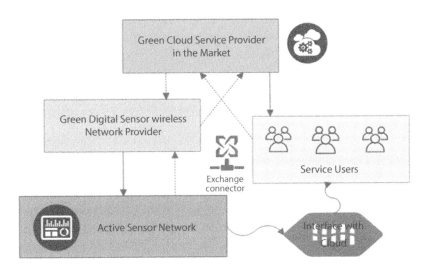

Figure 9.1 Basic Green IoT for both agriculture and health network.

and energy consumption issues and to reduce costs and emissions of carbon dioxide (CO_2) [10]. The sensor is connected to that, i.e., the digital sensor cloud architecture concept integrates cloud infrastructure and sensor network, thus enabling instantaneous monitoring of detailed applications that are often distributed in geographically distributed areas [11, 12]. Wireless digital-based networks are widely used to apply health related applications, as shown in Figure 9.1, to monitor the patients with diabetes mellitus, blood pressure, heart beats, mental condition, and sleep patterns [12, 13].

In such applications, the health facility take the essential steps or decision based on useful data collected from patients. It is very tricky task to observe the state of health condition of patient remotely, where the patient travels arbitrarily anywhere. Therefore, a well-organized computer system is very much needed to observe the situation of patients when they move at random. The most important information, time-varying sensor networks, can advantage from the complex incorporation of computer and storage space resources provided by cloud computing application for large statistics processing related to data collections [12, 15]. Therefore, green cloud sensor platforms are becoming increasingly popular in this era. This chapter presents the GIoT agricultural and healthcare system using the cloud-sensor integration model (GIoT-AHAS).

The GIoT is transforming things from conventional to highly intelligent by exploits its basic technology such, at the same time, as ubiquitous computers, advanced embedded equipment, communication technology, sensory network, and internet set of rules and application [14]. Through IoT, recent technologies which relate to cloud computing are extremely different prospect technologies coming from both that are already a part of our global life [15]. The IoT is over and over again characterized by small, extensively distributed real-world objects, with inadequate storage and handing out power, including concern about dependability, performance, safety, and confidentiality. In other ways, GCC has limitless storage capacity and processing power, highly advanced technology, and most of the IoT that are slightly solved using new IoT-related technology. Therefore, any application where cloud and IoT are both integrated technologies is predictable to disturb the existing and prospect and upcoming internet [15, 16]. This chapter is organized into section as follows. The second section provides a comprehensive introduction of computational statistics, ubiquitous usage necessities, and a brief introduction of the green computational devices and advanced computer. In the third section, we attempted to present the proposed construction, requirements, application of GIoT in the construction of the proposed buildings, and information and communication technology (GICT)–enabled green components such as green radio-frequency identity device (GRFID) frequency, green wireless sensor network (GWSN), GCC, green machine to machine (GM2M), green direct power supply (GDPC), and green infrastructure (GIoT-AHAS). Finally, we have completed the conclusion, and prospect indicators are discussed in the further section of this chapter in general.

9.2   Relevant Work and Research Motivation for GIoT-AHAS

9.2.1   Ubiquitous Computing

Computing everywhere is one of the best ways, lifestyle and engineering, new technologies at the same time: it basically refers to a type of technology that can access all aspects of the user's life and work behind their scenes, providing value without getting in the way. It is sometimes referred to as a full computer [17]. The concept of ubiquitous computing techniques began to emerge in 1988, when a scientist named Mark D. Weiser first introduced it to the council community [17, 18]. The ubiquitous computer has been described as "representing a powerful revolution in integration, in which people be alive, occupation, and engage in recreation in a seamless computer environment". An ever present computer lays the ground where public is enclosed by computer devices and the computer infrastructure we support everything [18, 19].

In the ubiquitous computer, individuals are surrounded by many computers that have networks, spontaneously but interoperable, a number of which are old or portable, some of which they encounter on the shift, many of which serve devoted purpose as part of the material, all using automatic, imperceptible, and limited human attention. In other ways, computing all over the place will carry the next epoch of more advanced computers around one user and become a more noticeable part of the substantial environment, and its mechanism will be disseminated on all scales day by day and usually turn to a clear quotidian edge. There are four key components that are everywhere in a computer: portable devices, customized nodes, network equipment, and smart labels related to the green internet (GIoT). To achieve ubiquitous computer services, rather than the so called five main goals of ubiquitous accessibility such as accessibility, transparency, shamelessness, awareness, and integrity (ATSAT). Presentation by the ubiquitous service from the ubiquitous computer view, by looking at five major GIoT-AHAS related methods: diversity, communication,

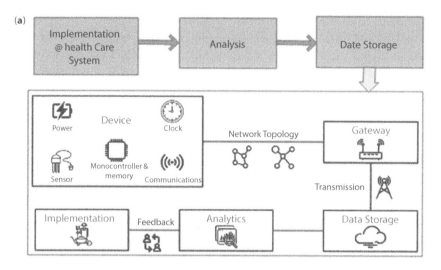

Figure 9.2 (a) GIoT-AHAS network platform with gateway.

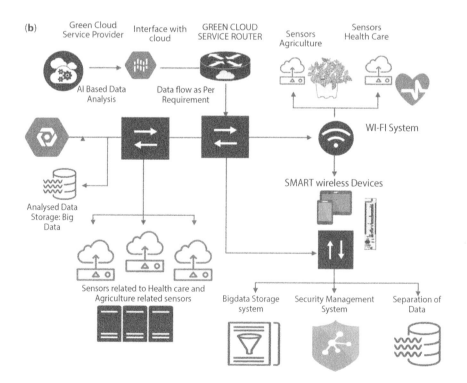

Figure 9.2 (b) GIoT AHAS network platform with security management system.

adaptability, credit, and easy to use (SCALE) [19, 20]. Network platform of GIoT-AHAS or, we can say, structure for GIoT Agriculture and Healthcare Application System (AHAS) is shown in Figures 9.2a and b to collect the significant data for analysis to take decision for corrective actions.

9.2.2   Ubiquitous Agriculture and Healthcare Application Requirement

By considering the universal applications, there are three objectives, namely, to reduce the time lost due to disposal, to reduce intermediate costs, and to reduce the inconvenience of conventional medical flow according to the literature [21]. The lag is a necessary time for printing by hand and paper delivery or by human-based information transmission which creates delays that could represent a major cause of possible financial losses in the medical field. The collateral reduction will suppress the gap between the information being recorded in linear time-invariant (LTI) system and when it is accessible for digital system out data or information analysis and processing using GIoT devices.

In addition, ubiquitous agricultural consumers and healthcare providers will send information from a variety of sources to get instantaneous information and expertise and seek relevant and useful information as shown in Figure 9.2. If the above conditions are met, then the application will be everywhere by using digital system. It will be a straightforward local program, performing one or a hardly any volunteer tasks. It will spread everywhere, connect digital green devices, and be embedded in such a way that communication is invisible and available in real time. It will get to know the context and link the change in the surroundings with digital computer programs. It will be transportable, using advanced technology while delivering [21]. It will have been worn out, using advanced digital devices while the human hands, voice, eyes, or awareness are aggressively involved in the corresponding physical surroundings. It will look good quality, see its nature, and respond appropriately [22]. It will also be good for ambient, working in concert to support community in day-to-day activities, activities and culture in a simple and recognizable way using information and cleverness hidden in the GIoT-based wireless digital network that connects these devices [22]. Figure 9.3 showed everything about the GIoT-based agriculture and healthcare network establishment using digital sensors network with platform and also described protocols which are required for the same. Requirement of software structure and highrarchical process is also shown in Figure 9.3.

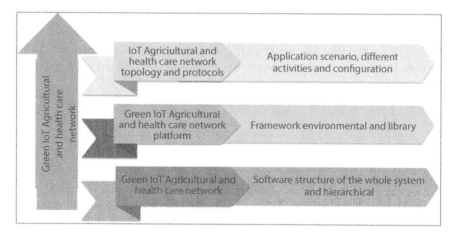

Figure 9.3 Green IoT agriculture and healthcare applications (GIoT-AHAS).

9.2.3   Green Cloud Computing

The idea of a green computer began to spread in the last few years, gaining popularity. In adding to the extensive compassion to ecological issues, such attention is also ambitious by financial requirements, as both the energy expenses and energy requirements of the IoT industry internationally replicate ever increasing trend [23]. Green computational process is the natural make use of advanced digital computer and other related resource as per compatibility. Such actions include the use of dynamic power plants, servers, and restrictions as well as the reduction of resource use and proper disposal of e-waste [22, 23]. The green computational analysis process must to study in details and operation of efficient and eco-friendly computing and the purpose of using energy-saving codes to get software before using less powerful hardware, rather than continuing to use the same code on a smaller amount powerful hardware.

Green computing, GICT according to the Internationally Federation of GICT and GIFG Standard, raw GIT, or GICT sustainability is the research and development of an environmentally friendly computer or IT [24]. V. Murugesan *et al.* describe GIoT and investigate and intend for the plan, manufacture, process and discarding of computers, servers, and correlated sub-LTI systems such as monitor, printer, storage space devices, and digital communication and digital communication systems professionally and efficiently without negligible environmental impact [25]. Also, it lists these four major parallel approaches to accurately and efficiently monitor the environmental effects of computer statistics that should be targeted at the green computer. Some of the terminologies used related to our GIoT-AHAS are described as follows:

1. Green Utilization: To minimize the energy utilization of computer systems and other information system and to use all of them in an eco-friendly ways.
2. Green Waste: Repairing and reuse of old computers and reuse of unwanted computers and other digital electronic-based equipment (reusable).
3. Green Intend: Designing power-efficient and environmentally forthcoming machinery, devices, digital computers, various faults, high capacity servers in terms of memory, and advanced cooling equipment consume low power in a day.
4. Raw Production: The production of digital-based electronic equipment and various relevant advanced components, digital computers, and other high-tech devices with negligible impact or very low-impact environmental programs.

GCC identifies many areas and functions, including ecological sustainability, power-efficient computer, power administration, archiving, construction, configuration and position, computer digital server performance, appropriate discarding and recycle, control compliance, metrics raw materials, testing tools, and methodology, to reduce environmental hazards, the use of advanced renewable power devices to get eco-friendly power from renewable process, and the labeling of GIoT-AHAS product.

9.2.4   Green IoT Agriculture and Healthcare Applications (GIoT-AHAS)

We focused on ubiquitous computer communication, the needs to achieve universal usage, and the basics of cloud computing to integrate with the GIoT-AHAS. In this part of this chapter, we have defined the fundamental concept of the GICT technology components associated with the GIoT-AHAS and introduced the construction of the GIoT-AHAS using the concept of cloud integration.

9.2.4.1   GIoT-AHAS Architecture

Green Sensor cloud computing (GScS) is considered one of the most powerful advanced agricultural technology and healthcare monitoring systems.

GScS is a new green cloud computational model that can be utilized visual digital sensors to collect its information and transfer all sensory data to advanced cloud computing infrastructure. Control sensor statistics can be used by many monitoring system. Initially, we will try see the definitions of cloud sensors as below.

In the concept presented by Intelli Sys *et al.*, it is an infrastructure that allows for complete statistics computation using digital advanced sensors as a visual associated between substantial and comprehensive sets of statistics such as cyber core and the GIoT as a source of communication [26].

From another available book by Micro Strains *et al.*, sensor cloud definition is a unique, visually sensitive information and remotely managed audio amplifier that uses commanding cloud computing technology to provide the best statistical information, visualization, and comprehensible analysis. Innovative advances are designed to compatible reliable long-term transmission of microstrain wireless digital active sensors, and green sensor cloud now supports any IoT-based web connected to other network device, wireless digital sensor, or digital wireless active sensor network using the open facts application programming interface (API) [27, 28]. To attract ever increasing attention from both educational and engineering industrial communities, sensor cloud computing (SCC) is actually a new paradigm, driven by the fulfillment of 1. ability to get ubiquitous statistics and significant information collection for wireless network networks and 2. the ability to store data and process GSCC data.

Specifically, the basic sensor-based cloud application model has ubiquitous digital sensors or body sensors; it is easily accessible and commonly worn sensors such as accelerometer digital wireless sensors, digital proximity sensors, and luminosity and temperature lamps [28, 29] provided by the wireless sensor network (WSN) provider to collect a variety of sensory monitored information from various locations. Combined all sensor information is also transferred to the cloud provide by a cloud service contributor for storing and further processing of information. After the cloud has stored and processed raw digital wireless sensor statistics with data center, the used or value sensor data is delivered to the user's applications for each service and requirement. In this full scenario, the network providers act as information sources for cloud service provider for analysis purposes (GIoT-AHAS). Users of the service are the ones asking for large data from cloud service providers. With the integration of cloud sensor (SCI), there are many interesting benefits [31, 32], which benefit users and the WSN and cloud like this: Users can access their required data or information collected by sensors from the cloud whenever and wherever there is a GIoT system connection get established, instead of clinging to their desks, that is, 24/7. The utilization of a green digital WSN can be increased, allowing it to run various relevant applications. The cloud of services provided is able to be greatly improved, by being capable to recommend the services provided by the digital WSN (e.g., agriculture and healthcare monitoring in this system which is GIoT-AHAS). Specifically, to improve the performance (e.g., information processing speed, impulse response time, and visibility) of a large storage network and cloud performance, investigative results have shown that the green cloud sensor can make a conventional wireless network, by ever increasing sensory lifetime by 3.35% and reducing power utilization by 37.55%. All of this is very appealing to the smart world and the green HEIs in India when used in the right ways [33].

9.2.4.2   GIoT-AHAS Requirements

We have written down and summarized the GICT requirements for the construction of GIoT-AHAS as follows:

1. Turn off unwanted areas: If the buildings remain functional, then it will consume a lot of power. However, if buildings are opened only when necessary, then power consumption will get reduced in such applications. For example, sleep planning is one of the most extensively used way to save energy on digital WSNs, by making the wireless digital sensor nodes wake up stronger and fall asleep.
2. Launch only the necessary information: Transferring big data (e.g., multimedia statistics) consumes a lot of power. Sending data only needed to users can accumulate a maximum of power utilization or consumption by the system. The prediction of data prediction is based on user performance analysis; it is one of the ways to make available information needed to user.
3. Reduce the distance end to end of the data pathway: This is as well a straightforward way to decrease the power consumption. Route scheme in view of the length of the selected data pathway can be very well energy efficient. In adding together, setup of network operating systems that meet route requirements is, in addition, an effective way to obtain a to a great extent shorter data pathway.
4. Suppress the distance end to end of the wireless data transmission pathway: In terms of reducing the length of the wireless data transmission path within network in the wireless

network, energy-efficient construction designs for wireless communication systems can be considered. In addition, a collaborative transmission system must be present for wireless communication also promises efficient power, through the transmission nodes to hear the broadcast and digital signal transmission to the target node, which has resulted in significant gain of diversity.

5. Trade in communication processing: As new sensible ways to hear the signal at a much lower rate of relative proportions as long as the causal signal is small, the pressing sensation is also capable of improving energy efficiency in both systems.

6. Improved communication: In terms of green communication, sophisticated communication methods are emerging. For example, recent trends of cognitive radio system (CRS) that is knowledgeable about its nature and can change its operating systems (frequency, voice fluctuations, wave form, and transmitting power). With advanced software and hardware deception, it is possible to improve frequency spectrum band efficiency and reduce the difficulties of overcrowding by using appropriate algorithms.

7. Renewable green energy sources: Unlike traditional sources, renewable energy sources, namely, oxygen, clean water, solar energy, timber, biomass, fuel cell, and geothermal energy, are natural resources that can be replaced and can be reused. Therefore, the use various types of renewable green energy source will have a significant impact on reducing oil dependence and emissions of carbon dioxide.

Table 9.1 summarizes of impact by adapting some important things to get significant result related to reduce energy consumptions to get efficient results while constructing the GIoT and healthcare application system.

9.2.4.3   Applying Green Internet of Things to Agriculture and Healthcare System

While discussing the GIoT, we should first see a variety of GIoT-related definitions, and it is considered the subsequently wave when cloud deployment is expected to be outside the conventional desktop area [34]. By considering the same, in line with this awareness and thinking of available literature, a new concept called the GIoT gained momentum in the last

Table 9.1 Impact of requirement in GIoT-AHAS.

Requirement	Impact to GIoT-AHAS
Shutdown the services that are not really required	If the some part of buildings remains functional, then it will consume a lot of power. However, if buildings are opened only when necessary, then power consumption will get reduced in such applications. For example, sleep planning is one of the most extensively used ways to save energy on digital WSNs, by making the wireless digital sensor nodes wake up stronger and fall asleep.
Keep active system when the data that are really required/ needed	Transferring or communicating the digital information or relevant data (e.g., multimedia computation statistics) consumes a lot of power. Sending data only when required or really needed to users can accumulate a lot of power consumption.
Reduce data transmission path as per requirement in the digital wireless sensors network	This is as well a straight forward way to decrease the power consumption by low power generation devices required. Route scheme in view of the length of the selected data transmission pathway can be very well energy efficient. In adding together, setup of wireless network operating systems that meet route requirements is, in addition, an effective way to obtain a to a great extent shorter data pathway.
Minimization of length of wireless data broadcasting path (Transmitter and Receiver)	In terms of reducing the length of the wireless data path in the wireless network, energy-efficient construction designs for wireless communication systems can be considered. In addition, a collaborative transmission system must be present for wireless communication also promises efficient power, through the transmission nodes to hear the broadcast and digital signal transmission to the target node, which has resulted in significant gain of diversity.
Trade off processing for communications in IoT-based system	As new sensible ways to receive the signal at a much lower rate of relative proportions as long as the causal signal is small, the pressing sensation is also capable of improving energy efficiency in both systems.

(Continued)

Table 9.1 Impact of requirement in GIoT-AHAS. (*Continued*)

Requirement	Impact to GIoT-AHAS
Advanced digital communication techniques adaptation in such applications	In terms of green communication, sophisticated communication methods are emerging. For example, recent trends of Cognitive Radio System (CRS) that is knowledgeable about its nature and can change its operating systems (frequency, voice fluctuations, wave form, transmitting power). With advanced software and hardware deception it is possible to get better frequency spectrum band efficiency and reduce the difficulties of overcrowding by using appropriate algorithms.
Renewable green power sources which are easily available in the market specially for agriculture and healthcare applications	Unlike traditional sources, Renewable Energy Sources, namely, oxygen, clean water, solar energy, timber, biomass, fuel cell, and geothermal energy, are natural resources that can be replaced and can be reused. Therefore, the use various types of "Renewable Green Energy Source" will have a significant impact on reducing oil dependence and emissions of carbon dioxide.

not many existence. GIoT refers to a universal global digital network of connected objects that is specially designed according to the common rules of communication its purpose is to connect to the Internet. The best GIoT is inspired researchers by the most recent development in various digital devices and advanced digital communication technology, but GIoT facilitates devices that are not only as multifaceted as smart transportable phones devices but also contains everyday substance [34]. They are able to work together to achieve the same objectives in this applications related to GIoT to AHAS [35, 36].

A key quality characteristic in GIoT is, without any doubt, its impact on the daily lives of probable consumer. GIoT has significant special effects in the workplace and the home environment, wherever it can play very significant role in the future prospect such as assisted livelihood, physical condition, crop growing, transports, and many other applications. Significant business outcomes are expected (e.g., logistic, industrial automation, advanced logistics, agricultural surveillance, security, and health employment). Factors in the IoT environment [37, 38] are presented in

Figure 9.4. Particularly, there are six sub-blocks in GIoT such as recognition, hearing, communication or broadcasting technology based on advanced green digital coding techniques, and arithmetic, various relevant services and semantics. Connectivity of all subsystems related to GIoT-based GIoT-AHAS is shown in Figure 9.4.

Classification and identification play a very important position in designing and comparing various services and their needs. Example of diagnostic techniques is used in GIoT digital electronic device product codes, digital codes everywhere. Pay attention to collect a variety of information from related substance and send it to the database, database, and data analysis center. The data collected also analyzes the data based on the necessary services [39]. Sensors can be wetness or moisture detecting sensor, high sensitive temperature detecting sensors, sensing reading devices, cell phones, etc. Advanced digital communication devices are installed by

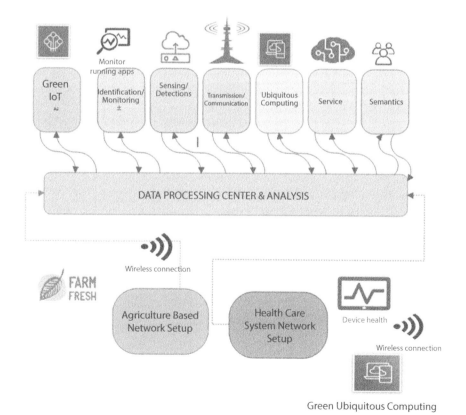

Figure 9.4 Building blocks of GIoT to AHAS connected to IoT-based system.

using IoT-based techniques to connect diversified substances together to provide precise services as per the prerequisite. The accessible GIoT communication protocols are wireless fidelity (Wi-Fi), standard IEEE 802.15.4 protocol, Bluetooth, Z-wave which is one of the best wireless communication protocol, long-term evolution (LTE) advanced, Near Field wireless broadcasting or Communication (NFC), ultra bandwidth wide frequency protocol (UWB), etc. [40].

For cloud computing, hardware-based digital signal processing units [e.g., sophisticated microcontrollers, emerging microprocessors, and required various LTI system on chips (SoCs, RC, etc.), field planning gateways (FPGAs), and software-based algorithms and applications highly developed numerous hardware (cards) platforms (e.g., Arduino, UDOO, Friendly ARM, Intel Galileo, Raspberry PI, and Gadgeteer)] are being built and using a variety of software platforms (e.g., Tiny OS, Lite OS, and Riot OS) [34, 35]. The cloud platform is an integral part of GIoT computation calculation, as it has great potential for the processing of large amounts of data in real time and extracts all kind of important information from the collected statistics.

GIoT-based services can be divided into three categories: proprietary-related services, integration services, and known mutual ubiquitous services. Proprietary-related services place the establishment for various types of services, because all applications that map real-world substance to the physical world need to recognize objects primarily. Data collection or integrating services gather and summarize raw information that needs to be processed and report to required sections of the system. The information obtain is also used by mutual services to build decision and act in response properly. The ubiquitous services tender common services to everywhere on require, anytime wherever required. Semantic refers to the ability to take out information significantly and intelligently to provide the essential services applications [41].

This development more often than not includes resource acquisition, resource utilization, data modeling, data identification, and analysis. The most normally used semantic technologies are resource development framework, i.e., RDF interpreting frameworks (RDF), web language ontology (OWL), and active XML exchange (EXI) [42, 43].

9.2.5   Green IoT for AHAS (GIoT-AHAS)

To simplify raw GIoT, IoT should be separated by energy efficiency. In particular, all agricultural equipment and health applications must be there prepared with emotional and communication additives so that they can hear and correspond well in a timely manner, and they will need a lot of power. In adding together, determined by increasing interest rates and sustain from various organization, the requirement for energy will be to a great extent greater than before. All of these create the GIoT focused on dropping the utilization of GIoT energy as a requirement, in provisions of satisfying the elegant world through sustainability. If you consider energy effectiveness as a key feature throughout the expansion, then expansion of GIoT, raw IoT can be defined as below [43].

The well-organized process for energy consumption (hardware or software) adopt by GIoT possibly will either reduce the thermal impact of presented application or decrease the impact of GIoT's thermal effect. In the previous case, the utilization of GIoT will assist to decrease the impact of heat, at the same time as in the further development of IoT conservatory printing will be taken care of. The lifelong cycle of raw GIoT should focus on raw materials, raw production, raw resources, and, ultimately, green waste discarding/recycle with little or no environmental impact [44, 45].

9.2.5.1   GIoT to AHAS Components

In this particular section, the GICT framework and the raw technology for the G-AHAS are discussed. GICT is an umbrella term linked with several relevant applications, coming up technology and application for information and data broadcasting communication, enabling users to access, store with memory devices, broadcast, and use a variety of information. Any required items are listed below, with regard to the identification, hearing, communication, and calculation of IoT devices presented in this chapter.

1. Radio-Frequency Identification (RFID): A very tiny advanced electronic device consisting of a very large-scale integrated circuits and aerial as an antenna, which automatically identifies and tracks tag attached to objects, operating at a certain frequency.
2. Wireless sensor network (WSN): A digital network consisting of independent distributed sensors that work together to supervise physical or ecological circumstances such as temperature, sound, vibration, pressure, and movement.
3. Wireless local area network (WLAN): A groundless wireless network of digital devices connected to an individual's workplace.

4. Wireless physical network (WPAN): A wireless digital network consisting of portable computer devices (e.g., sensors and actuators) available on or off the body.
5. Local area network (LAN): A type of LAN, which connects existing digital devices within or within the immediate neighborhood of the system.
6. Neighborhood Network (NAN): A network contains wireless fidelity hotspots and WLAN, enable users to connect to the Internet faster and to make it a much cost effective system.
7. Machine to Machine (M to M): This is one of the advanced technologies that allow both guided communication and digital wireless devices to proper communicate with other devices which are compatible with the same.
8. GCC: One of the advance computing models of a novel to enable easy network access, required for configuration resources (e.g., various network, big servers, big data storage memory devices, relevant applications, and many relevant services). To integrate GCC into a portable environment, green transportable cloud computing (MCC) can continue to load large amounts of digital information and data processing for analysis and storage functionality from smart mobile devices to the cloud.
9. Big Data Center (BDC): A database (visible or virtual) for storing, managing, and disseminating data and information.
10. Green Radio-Frequency Identification Model (G-RFIDM): RFIDM incorporates high-frequency RFID tags and an extremely small separation of tag reader. The G-RFIDM, or we can say, tags, is a small microprocessor-based integrated circuit (i.e., microchip) attached to the radio (used to receive and broadcast signal), with only one of its kind identification code.

Summary of the methods for optimization of the efficient energy of a variety of components at different positions in GIoT-based agriculture and healthcare applications LTI systems is described in Table 9.2.

The purpose of the RFID tags is to store information related to the attachment [46, 47, 49]. The fundamental procedure is that the flow of information caused by the readers of the RFID models or tags by transmitting the self-generated signal for questions followed by the answers of the RFID models [48].

Table 9.2 Typical class of components used for energy-efficient techniques toward GIoT in agriculture and healthcare applications.

Components used	Cause of power consumption	Energy-efficient techniques
Digital active and passive sensors	Sensing data on site and continuous sensing and storing the information	Selection of sensing devices, self-powering digital sensors, sleep mode scheduling as per need, compression sense about the information
Radio Frequency Identification Device (RFID)	Detection of sensed information and data on site for specific purposes	Green passive sensing device to utilize whenever needed or required
Sink nodes in digital wireless network	Distribution and analyze the information	Optimization utilization of processing at sensing end task to core mapping
Data center connected to cloud	Processing the data or information in cloud, high-computational task perform	Need to distribute the load to node as per requirement, reducing the data transmission pathway to collect or to send the data within network
Gateway nodes by combining the both the system agriculture and healthcare system	Broadcasting between digital wireless sensors and WSN N/W	Controlled storage space and setting up with triggered events as per requirement
Resource allocation as per need and priority	Distribution of information/ statistics to resources from gateway in the GIoT-based agriculture and healthcare system	Modification and allotment of sensing devices and processing mechanism to access the scheduling throughput, interoperability

(Continued)

Table 9.2 Typical class of components used for energy-efficient techniques toward GIoT in agriculture and healthcare applications. (*Continued*)

Components used	Cause of power consumption	Energy-efficient techniques
Processors and cloud system	High-computational tools, relocate the different task to different central part of the linear time-invariant system, circumstance aware allotment of servers	Use of vapor computation and edge computation, dynamic redundant data packets downloading, suppressing the data path dynamics task distribution and scheduling for quality-of-service cost

In general, the broadcasting range of radio-frequency detection systems is very low down range radio system (i.e., a few distances in meter). In addition, it is used to perform multi-band transmission (for example, it is very low frequency range from 124 to 135 kHz up to ultra high frequencies at 860 to 960 MHz). Two types of RFID tags [i.e., Active Tags and Passive Tags (ATPT)] are available. Active markers have battery that facilitate signal transmission by using digital signal processors and increase transmission range, while entry tag do not have internal battery and require harvesting power from the student signal with the goal of input [50, 51].

- Reducing the size of RFID tags should be considered as reducing the number of non corrosive materials used in their production (e.g., visible RFID models and printed RFID tag), because that models themselves are easier said than done to reproduce often.
- Energy-saving algorithms and processes are supposed to be used to increase tag proportions, to adjust the power transfer capacity, to keep away from tag collisions, to avoid hearing.

9.2.6   Green Digital Wireless Sensor Networks

Green digital wireless sensor networks (GWSNs) usually contain a definite number of digital active sensor nodes and a base station (e.g., wireless sensor nodes). The sensor nodes have low down processing power, partial power, and required memory devices or, we can say, storage capacity, and the base channel has high power [52, 53]. The sensors nodes are connected to each other with several active and passive sensors in the system, take the reading (e.g., temperature, humidity, and speed) from the first circuit. They then collaborate and transmit sensory information to a standard ad-level channel. The most commonly used WSN solution for sale is based on the standard IEEE 802.15.4 benchmark, which includes low and medium access control (MAC) levels of low power and low level of communication [53, 54]. Agriculture-based farm remote monitoring in agriculture and low-power GWSN topology have been shown in Figures 9.5 and 9.6 in details to get clear idea about the green WSN which is used for agriculture and healthcare-based application system. It shows how to connect all the required sensors to WSN and advanced microcontroller-based connectivity embedded system prototype, and it shown in Figure 9.5.

In the system which relates to green wireless sensors network (GWSN), the following methodologies must be adopted:

- Build the sensors node work only when desirable, while spending their entire lives in sleep mode saving energy consumption in that span.
- Decrease in energy utilization (e.g., unguided wireless charging, energy harvest methods like renewable energy system [54], for example, wind and solar, kinetic energy, and vibration, by using some material like negative temperature coefficient variations, etc.). Radio production methods [e.g.,

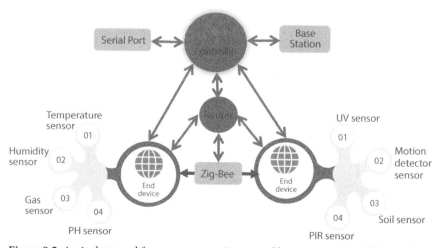

Figure 9.5 Agriculture and farm remote monitoring and low-power green WSN topology.

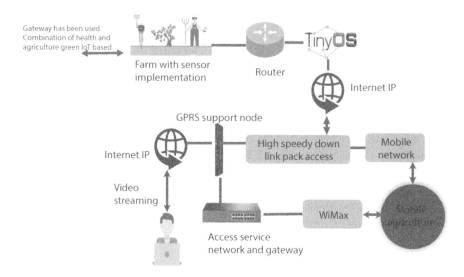

Figure 9.6 Remote monitoring in healthcare system and low-power green WSN topology.

     power manage, voice fluctuations, collaborative communication, directional horns, and high efficiency radio (CR)];
- Ways to reduce unnecessary statistics (e.g., integration, dynamic model, compression, and network coding)
- Power saving routing strategies (e.g., group configuration, power such as traffic flow metrics, duplicate route, transmission node setting, and node flow).

9.2.7   Green Cloud Computing

At G-CC, resources have been managed to get proper functionality of the system, namely, Infrastructure Services (IS), Platform as Service (PS), and Software as a Service (SS). Depending on the needs of the users, the GCC provides a variety of resources (e.g., high-end computer and high-capability storage) to user. Instead of owning and organization their resources, the user shares a more number of resources and also manages resource with easy access. As increasing applications are deployed in the cloud, more resources need to be distributed and used more energy, leading to more ecological issues and emission of CO_2 [55, 56].

1. Acceptance of early advance hardware and recent software that reduces power consumption in such system. In this look

upon, advance hardware solutions are supposed to focus on the design and production of low power devices. Necessary software solutions must try to provide effective software implementations that use a smaller amount power with a smaller amount of resource use;

2. Energy-saving equipment strategies (e.g., VMT integration, VMT migration, VMT placement, and VMT distribution);
3. Various forms of energy resource allocation (e.g., auction equipment distribution and gossip-based resource allocation);
4. Effective and accurate working models and testing methods with respect to energy-saving policy;
5. G-CC scheme based on cloud support technology (e.g., digital wireless sensors network N/W, advanced communications, and location and allotment of nodes in network).

9.2.8   Green Machine-to-Machine

In requisites of Machine-to-Machine (M to M) interactions, large M to M nodes intelligently collect the specified statistics used in the M to M domain. On a wireless set of connections domain, the unguided network transfers data collected to the processing center for processing [56]. The processing station also supports a variety of M to M applications via the network in the application area: M to M machine.

In this case, the Green M to M and the more number of machines get involved in the M to M interaction digitally will use a lot of energy, especially from the M to M applications [57].

1. Cleverly adjust the broadcasting relevant transmission power (e.g., at the required stage).
2. Design well-organized significant communication protocols (e.g., tracking channels) and algorithmic computer distribution and distribution strategies.
3. Functional configuration, where the purpose is to control other nodes to less energy consumption/inactive mode so that only a set of interconnected various nodes are used when maintaining the working system, i.e., functionality of the system (e.g., data/information collection) of the original wireless sensors digital network.

4. Shared power or energy conservation measures (e.g., over safety and resource allotment).

5. Use energy harvest relevant and aesthetics (e.g., frequency band sensitivity, frequency band management, minimization distortion, use of electrical energy) for green perception radio (GPR).

9.2.9   Green Data Processing Center (GDPC)

The main function of Green Data Processing or handling Center (GDPC) is to store the such a big data or information, manage big data, and process and distribute a variety of statistics and applications, user generated, objects, systems, etc. Typically, to deal with a wide range of specifications and applications, in some cases, GDPC devices consume more amounts of power with expensive operating manpower with their costs and huge amounts of CO_2. Furthermore, with the ever increasing generation of big data with a extensive range of widely available and all GIoT-based advanced equipment (e.g., smart phones and digital sensors) by considering world scenario, the energy efficiency of GDPCs becomes more imperative in such applications [58].

With regard to GDPCs, existing strategies for improving use of energy utilization effectiveness can be found in the following factors [15, 59, 60].

1. Use of renewable or green energy sources
   - (e.g., wind, water, solar energy, heat pumps, geothermal, and fuel cell)
2. Use dynamic and efficient energy control technology
   - (e.g., turbo development and location [61])
3. Create the most effective hardware tools for different strengths and styles
   - (e.g., exploits the benefits of dynamic energy system and time span, i.e., frequency measurement [61, 62])
4. Construction of energy-efficient data center buildings to achieve energy efficiency
   - (e.g., raw data centers)
5. Design advanced power transmission capabilities to integrate traffic flow into a sub-network set and turn off idle device
6. Build large, efficient, and accurate electrical equipment with highly efficient performance [63]

7. Highly supportive advance digital communication system and highly configured computer systems
   - (e.g., improved visual broadcasting or communication system, machine migration in machine migration, and installation performance [64]).

9.3   Conclusion

In this chapter, we have discussed the statistics of ubiquitous computational process, the needs of ubiquitous tools and applications, and the green computer. Continuing to review technologies such as green information and computer technologies that allow emerging technologies, the Green Internet Material (GIoT) for GIoT-AHAS architecture using a combination of SCC and the benefits that outlined sensor cloud and GIoT-AHAS are introduced. As per the theory given in this chapter as a literature review and conducting some surveys and by visited some typical places, we have overcome the some important challenges to establish the GIoT system for agriculture and healthcare system. Typical or major five challenges category-wise correspond to architecture and healthcare system of GIoT system: (i) green measurement equipment, (ii) GIoT-based information broadcasting system, (iii) big data storage space and predictive analytics by computing system, (iv) significant performance and development of GIoT-AHAS, and (v) assignment understanding and support. WSNs alone have some of the traditional challenges that digital sensor cloud green infrastructure can offer: 1) green data management system, 2) well-organized and significant uses of resources, and 3) high GIoT-AHAS operating costs. Green semi-conductive material equipped infrastructure is a very cost effective method, where the accessible GCC-based platform can be utilized. In conclusion, prospect identified indicators associated to the GIoT for both, one is agriculture and other is healthcare application system (GIoT-AHAS) for buildings with digital green sensor cloud integration, are presented as follows:

1. The design of the system should be close to the GIoT-AHAS with a view to energy efficiency, in terms of satisfactory service, superior superiority and critical performance.
2. Personality features and the use of various applications require a better understanding.
3. Models for the real-world use of the (GIoT-AHAS are required.

4. Cost issues and access to the digital sensor cloud service require both a green digital service contributor and a mathematical computer and a GIoT-based cloud system provider. GIoT-based cloud system provider must have independent user controls, services and efficient management, payment and pricing advanced techniques, and pricing system.

References

1. Abid, A., Abid, K., Naeem, M.A., A Survey On The Role Of Iot In Agriculture For The Implementation Of Smart Farming. *IEEE Access*, 07, October 25, 2019.
2. Takruri, M., Attia, H.A., Awad, M.H., Wireless charging in the context of sensor networks. *Int. J. Appl. Eng. Res.*, 11, 12, 7736–7741, 2016.
3. Khodr, H., Kouzayha, N., Abdallah, M., Costantine, J., Dawy, Z., Energy-efficient IoT sensor with RF wake-up and addressing capability. *IEEE Sens. Lett.*, 1, 6, 1–4, 2017.
4. Atzori, L., Iera, A., Morabito, G., The Internet of Things: A survey. *Comput. Netw.*, 54, 15, 2787–2805, 2010.
5. Perera, C., Liu, C.H., Jayawardena, S., Chen, M., A survey on Internet of Things from industrial market perspective. *IEEE Access*, 2, 1660–1679, 2014.
6. Hassanalieragh, M., Page, A., Soyata, T., Sharma, G., Aktas, M., Mateos, G., Andreescu, S., Health monitoring and management using Internet-of-Things (IoT) sensing with cloud-based processing: Opportunities and challenges, in: *Services Computing (SCC), 2015 IEEE International Conference on*, pp. 285–292, 2015.
7. Da Xu, L., He, W., Li, S., Internet of Things in industries: A survey. *IEEE Trans. Indr. Inform.*, 10, 4, 2233–2243, 2014.
8. Díez, C., *Hacia una agricultura inteligente (Towards and intelligent Agriculture)*, vol. 60, pp. 4–11, Cuaderno de Campo, 2017.
9. Al-Fuqaha, A., Guizani, M., Mohammadi, M., Aledhari, M., Ayyash, M., Internet of things: A survey on enabling technologies, protocols, and applications. *Commun. Surv. Tutor. IEEE*, 17, 4, 2347–2376, 2015.
10. Zhu, C., Leung, V., Shu, L., Ngai, E.C.H., Green Internet of Things for smart world. *IEEE Access*, 3, 2151–2162, 2015.
11. Zhou, J., Leppanen, T., Harjula, E., Ylianttila, M., Ojala, T., Yu, C., Jin, H., Cloudthings: A common architecture for integrating the internet of things with cloud computing, in: *CSCWD*, IEEE, 2013.
12. Weiser, M., The computer for the 21st century. *Pervasive Comput. IEEE*, 1, 1, 19–25, 2002.
13. http://www.koreaittimes.com/story/defining-perfect-ubiquitous-health-care-information-system.

14. Gubbi, J., Buyya, R., Marusic, S., Palaniswami, M., Internet of Things (IoT): A vision, architectural elements, and future directions. *Future Gener. Comput. Syst.*, 29, 7, 1645–1660, 2013.
15. Evangelos, A.K., Nikolaos, D.T., Anthony, C.B., Integrating RFIDs and Smart Objects into a Unified Internet of Things Architecture. *Adv. Internet Things*, 1, 2011.
16. Weiser, M., The computer for the 21st century. *Pervasive Comput. IEEE*, 1, 1, 19–25, 2002.
17. Botta, A., de Donato, W., Persico, V., Pescapé, A., Integration of cloud computing and internet of things: a survey. *Future Gener. Comput. Syst.*, 56, 684–700, 2016.
18. Shaikh, F.K., Zeadally, S., Exposito, E., Enabling Technologies for Green. *Internet Things*, 11, 2, 2015.
19. Juels, A., RFID security and privacy: A research survey. *IEEE J. Sel. Areas Commun.*, 24, 2, 381–394, Feb. 2006.
20. Zhu, C., Shu, L., Hara, T., Wang, L., Nishio, S., Yang, L.T., A survey on communication and data management issues in mobile sensor networks. *Wireless Commun. Mobile Comput.*, 14, 1, 19–36, Jan. 2014.
21. Gutierrez, J.A., Naeve, M., Callaway, E., Bourgeois, M., Mitter, V., Heile, B., IEEE 802.15.4: A developing standard for low-power low-cost wireless personal area networks. *IEEE Netw.*, 15, 5, 12–19, Sep./Oct. 2001.
22. Han, S.-H. and Park, S.K., Performance analysis of wireless body area network in indoor off-body communication. *IEEE Trans. Consum. Electron.*, 57, 2, 335–338, May 2011.
23. Saif, U., Gordon, D., Greaves, D.J., Internet access to a home area network. *IEEE Internet Comput.*, 5, 1, 54–63, Jan./Feb. 2001.
24. San Murugesan, BRITE Professional Services and University of Western Sydney, Australia, G.R. Gangadharan, Institute for Development and Research in Banking Technology, India, Harnessing Green It Principles and Practices, John Wiley & Sons, Ltd., USA, 2012.
25. Khan, J.Y. and Yuce, M.R., *Internet of Things (IoT); Systems and Applications*, Taylor & Francis group, Jenny Stanford Publishing, Singapore, 2019.
26. Mediwaththe, C.P., Stephens, E.R., Smith, D.B., Mahanti, A., A dynamic game for electricity load management in neighborhood area networks. *IEEE Trans. Smart Grid.*, 7, 3, 1329–1336, May 2016.
27. http://www.ntu.edu.sg/intellisys.
28. Weyrich, M., Schmidt, J.-P., Ebert, C., Machine-to-machine communication. *IEEE Software*, 31, 4, 19–23, Jul./Aug. 2014.
29. Dayarathna, M., Wen, Y., Fan, R., Data Center Energy Consumption Modeling: A Survey.
30. Namboodiri, V. and Gao, L., Energy-aware tag anticollision protocols for RFID systems. *Mob. Comput. IEEE Trans.*, 9, 1, 44–59, 2010.

31. Li, T., Wu, S.S., Chen, S., Yang, M.C.K., Generalized energy-efficient algorithms for the RFID estimation problem. *IEEE/ACM Trans. Netw.*, 20, 6, 1978–1990, 2012.

32. Klair, D.K., Chin, K.-W., Raad, R., A survey and tutorial of RFID anti-collision protocols. *IEEE Commun. Surv. Tutor.*, 12, 3, 400–421, 2010.

33. Anastasi, G., Conti, M., Di Francesco, M., Passarella, A., Energy conservation in wireless sensor networks: A survey. *Ad Hoc Netw.*, 7, 3, 537–568, 2009.

34. Rault, T., Bouabdallah, A., Challal, Y., Energy efficiency in wireless sensor networks: A top-down survey. *Comput. Netw.*, 67, 104–122, 2014.

35. Farahnakian, F., Using ant colony system to consolidate VMs for green cloud computing. *IEEE Trans. Serv. Comput.*, 8, 2, 187–198, 2015.

36. Chang, C.H., Chang, R.Y., Hsieh, H.-Y., High-fidelity energy-efficient machine-to-machine communication, in: *Proc. IEEE 25th Annu. Int. Symp. Pers., Indoor, Mobile Radio Commun.*, pp. 91–96, 2014.

37. Tian, X., Zhu, Y.H., Chi, K., Liu, J., Zhang, D., Reliable and energy-efficient data forwarding in industrial wireless sensor networks. *IEEE Syst. J.*, 11, 3, 1424–1434, 2017.

38. Basnayaka, D.A. and Haas, H., A new degree of freedom for energy efficiency of digital communication systems. *IEEE Trans. Commun.*, 65, 7, 3023–3036, 2017.

39. Qureshi, F.F., Iqbal, R., Asghar, M.N., Energy-efficient wireless communication technique based on cognitive radio for the Internet of Things. *J. Netw. Comput. Appl.*, 89, 14–25, 2017.

40. Yi, G., Park, J.H., Choi, S., Energy-efficient distributed topology control algorithm for low-power IoT communication networks. *IEEE Access*, 4, 9193–9203, 2016.

41. Zhu, C., Leung, V.C., Wang, K., Yang, L.T., Zhang, Y., Multi-method data delivery for green sensor-cloud. *IEEE Commun. Mag.*, 55, 176–182, 2017.

42. Maksimovic, M., Greening the future: Green Internet of Things (G-IoT) as a key technological enabler of sustainable development. 283–311, 2018.

43. Hiraj, A. and Alvi, Energy efficient green routing protocol for internet of multimedia things, in: *IEEE International Conference on Intelligent Sensor, Sensor Networks and Information Processing (ISSNIP)*, IEEE, 2015.

44. Jain, A., Mishra, M., Peddoju, S.K., Jain, N., Energy efficient computing green cloud computing, in: *International Conference on Energy-Efficient Technologies for Sustainability*, 2013, April, IEEE, pp. 978–982.

45. Shuja, J., Ahmad, R.W., Gani, A., Ahmed, A.I.A., Siddiqa, A., Nisar, K., Zomaya, A.Y., Greening emerging IT technologies: techniques and practices. *J. Internet Serv. Appl.*, 09, 2017.

46. Lee, I. and Lee, K., The Internet of Things (IoT): Applications, invest- ments, and challenges for enterprises. *Bus. Horiz.*, 58, 4, 431–440, 2015.

47. Chen, S., Xu, H., Liu, D., Hu, B., Wang, H., A vision of IoT: Appli- cations, challenges, and opportunities with china perspective. *IEEE Internet Things J.*, 1, 4, 349–359, Aug. 2014.

48. M., Vaněk, J., Masner, J. and Pavlík, J., Internet of Things (IoT) in Agriculture - Selected Aspects, *Agris On-Line Pap. Econ. Inform.*, 8, 1, 83-88, 2016.

49. Ray, P.P., Internet of Things for smart agriculture: Technologies, practices and future direction. *J. Ambient Intell. Smart Environ.*, 9, 4, 395–420, 2017.

50. Kamienski, C., Soininen, J.-P., Taumberger, M., Dantas, R., Toscano, A., Cinotti, T.S., Maia, R.F., Neto, A.T., Smart water management platform: IoT-based precision irrigation for agriculture. *Sensors*, 19, 2, 276, 2019.

51. Ojha, T., Misra, S., Raghuwanshi, N.S., Wireless sensor networks for agriculture: The state-of-the-art in practice and future challenges. *Comput. Electron. Agric.*, 118, 66–84, Oct. 2015.

52. Elijah, Rahman, T.A., Orikumhi, I., Leow, C.Y., Hindia, M.N., An overview of Internet of Things (IoT) and data analytics in agriculture: Benefits and challenges. *IEEE Internet Things J.*, 5, 5, 3758–3773, Oct. 2018.

53. Zhang, X., Zhang, J., Li, L., Zhang, Y., Yang, G., Monitoring citrus soil moisture and nutrients using an IoT based system. *Sensors*, 17, 3, 447, 2017.

54. González-Amarillo, C.A., Corrales-Muñoz, J.C., Mendoza-Moreno, M. Á., Hussein, A.F., Arunkumar, N., Ramirez-González, G., An IoT-based traceability system for greenhouse seedling crops. *IEEE Access*, 6, 67528–67535, 2018.

55. Windsperger, B., Windsperger, A., Bird, D.N., Schwaiger, H., Jung-meier, G., Nathani, C., Frischknecht, R., Greenhouse gas emissions due to national product consumption: From demand and research gaps to addressing key challenges. *Int. J. Environ. Sci. Technol.*, 16, 2, 1025–1038, 2019.

56. Shirsath, D.O., Kamble, P., Mane, R., Kolap, A., More, R.S., IoT based smart greenhouse automation using Arduino. *Int. J. Innov. Res. Comput. Sci. Technol.*, 5, 2, 234–238, 2017.

57. Corkery, G., Ward, S., Kenny, C., Hemmingway, P., Monitoring environmental parameters in poultry production facilities, in: *Proc. Comput. Aided Process Eng.-CAPE Forum*, pp. 1–12, 2013.

58. Cowlar, Accessed: Jun. 24, 2019. [Online]. Available: https://www. cowlar.com/store/product.

59. Cow Intelligence, Accessed: Jun. 24, 2019. [Online]. Available: http:// www.scrdairy.com/cow-intelligence/sensehub.html.

60. Hi, X., An, X., Zhao, Q., Liu, H., Xia, L., Sun, X., Guo, Y., State-of-the-art Internet of Things in protected agriculture. *Sensors*, 19, 8, 1833, 2019.

61. Zhang, Y., Chen, Q., Liu, G., Shen, W., Wang, G., Environment parameters control based on wireless sensor network in livestock buildings. *Int.J. Distrib. Sensor Netw.*, 12, 5, 2016, Art. no. 9079748.

62. Chen, W.-L., Lin, Y.-B., Lin, Y.-W., Chen, R., Liao, J.-K., Ng, F.-L., Chan, Y.-Y., Liu, Y.-C., Wang, C.-C., Chiu, C.-H., Yen, T.H., AgriTalk: IoT for precision soil farming of turmeric cultivation. *IEEE Internet Things J.*, 6, 3, 5209–5223, Jun. 2019.

63. Wanichsombat, A. and Nillaor, P., IoT and agriculture data analysis for smart farm. *Comput. Electron. Agric.*, 156, 467–474, Jan. 2019.

64. Krishna, K.L., Silver, O., Malende, W.F., Anuradha, K., Internet of Things application for implementation of smart agriculture system, in: *Proc. Int. Conf. I-SMAC (IoT Social, Mobile, Anal. Cloud) (I-SMAC)*, Feb. 2017, pp. 54–59.

10

Green IoT for Smart Transportation: Challenges, Issues, and Case Study

Pradnya Borkar[1]*, Vijaya Balpande[2], Ujjwala Aher[3],
Roshani Raut[4] and M. Sulas Borkar[5]

[1]Jhulelal Institute of Technology, Nagpur, MS, India
[2]Priyadarshini J.L. College of Engineering, Nagpur, MS, India
[3]Govt. Polytechnic, Sakoli, Bhandara, MS, India
[4]Pimpri Chinchwad College of Engineering, PCCOE, SPPU, Pune, MS, India
[5]GNIET, Gurunanak Institute of Technology, Nagpur, MS, India

Abstract

The number of devices and network use on the Internet of Things has exploded in this modern era. But due to usage of large number of network devices, the more energy consumption is required. Energy consumption is now became the state of art in the view to achieve the green IoT consistency and the implementation of smart world. Intelligent transportation is one of the important aspects of technically smart world. To develop a viable agile world, an energy efficient environment must be created to decrease the carbon dioxide (CO_2) emissions by sensors, devices used in the application, and services of IoT. The use of IoT is also increased in smart transportation (car, train, bus, etc.). Nowadays, most of the transportation vehicles are Wi-Fi enabled which also needs energy consumption. In order to prevent more energy consumption, some effective ways should be provided. This chapter overviews the Green IoT, challenges and issues in Green IoT, various technologies used in Green IoT, and need of Green IoT in smart transportation, and also it focuses on the case study.

Keywords: Green IoT, smart transportation, challenges of IoT and Green IoT, Green IoT case study

*Corresponding author: pradnyaborkar2@gmail.com

Roshani Raut, Sandeep Kautish, Zdzislaw Polkowski, Anil Kumar and Chuan-Ming Liu (eds.) Green Internet of Things and Machine Learning: Towards a Smart Sustainable World, (269–296) © 2022 Scrivener Publishing LLC

10.1   Introduction

In recent years, the Internet of Things (IoT) has exploded in popularity. This had an effect on the performance of network and energy resources used by IoT devices. There has been a massive transition in almost every field of work as a result of rapid advancements in digital technology. The IoT has grown in popularity as a result of a growing trend toward the use of technologically advanced and networked devices. The IoT is a global network infrastructure made up of sensors, actuators, and equipment integrated in physical devices that can monitor, process, and share data over the internet. IoT models waste energy by remaining ON even though they are not in use because they are not built for energy consumption. As a result, a large amount of energy is consumed when it is turned ON and transmitting data 24 hours a day, all days in a week.

10.2   Challenges of IoT

The IoT is a leading-edge and hi-tech technology that has the potential to revolutionize the IT industry, but it comes at a price [1]. Security and privacy, which are described in [2] and [3] as one of the key areas on which experts must concentrate in order to gain users' trust, are one of the various challenges faced by IoT technologies.

According to the mentioned paper, RFID tags can track an individual without their permission or knowledge, which could cause widespread mistrust among the public. However, energy would be the most significant obstacle in the implementation of IoT. The National Intelligence Council of the United States has estimated that by 2025, everyday things such as food, pens, and other related items incorporated in the internet. This means that the internet will be accessible to billions of users [4]. Depending on its functionality, each active RFID needs a very little quantity of power to operate, and active RFIDs are critical for efficient services. Consider how many billions of such devices consume energy every day; sensors relay millions of gigabytes of data, which must be processed or edited by huge data centers, necessitating massive processing and analytical capabilities. Furthermore, CO_2 emissions from ICT products are steadily increasing, causing harm to our atmosphere [5] and are expected to continue if appropriate steps are not taken to resolve this issue. The Green IoT is a crucial subject for resolving these vital issues.

10.2.1   Green IoT

The Green IoT is focused on energy conservation in IoT principles. Green IoT refers to IoT methods that are energy-efficient and can minimize or eliminate the greenhouse gas emissions emitted by current applications. The environmentally friendly and energy-efficient characteristics of the IoT are referred to as "GREEN". These characteristics are achieved by the use of energy-efficient methods and techniques on both the hardware level and software level, which aids to reduce energy demand, CO_2 emissions, and the greenhouse effect associated with current IoT systems, goods, and services. Green IoT guarantees that the system is only switched on when it is needed and that it is inactive or turned off when not needed.

Proper ventilation of heat produced by servers and data centers, as well as energy efficiency using smart IoT technology, are two examples of Green IoT solutions that can save a large amount of energy. In order to achieve green IoT reliability and a smart environment, energy use is being state of the art [6]. The planet is becoming more sophisticated as science and modern technology progress at an exponential rate. In such a smart world, smart and intelligent devices (e.g., computer systems, mobile phones, and watches), smart environment (e.g., workplaces, factories, and homes), smart mobility (e.g., trains, cars, and buses), and so on will serve people automatically and collectively [7].

For example, a Global Positioning System (GPS) can constantly upload a location of an individual person to a device, which will immediately return the quickest path to the travel destination of individual, preventing traffic jams. Furthermore, any abnormality in an individual's voice will be immediately identified and sent to a server, which will compare the abnormality to a series of collected voiceprints to decide if the person is sick. In a smart society, all facets of people's cyber, physical, emotional, and mental environments would be inevitably interconnected and intellectual.

Green IoT Techniques are based on the following:

- Hardware
- Software
- Habitual
- Awareness
- Recycling

10.2.1.1   Hardware-Based

The majority of IoT energy consumption models [1] depend on algorithm used and hardware improvements, but categorizing objects in an IoT network can be very useful in making it "GREEN". The MECA algorithm [8], which is used to solve the optimization problem, uses a three-layer architecture to construct the network of GREEN Technology goals. Although Active RFID Optimization was discussed in [9], advances in Passive RFID [10] and the Wireless Identification and Sensing Platform (WISP) [11] will result in to more effective and low power computation in the IoT. A series of energy-efficient commands can also trigger communication delays between sensor nodes and interrogators, resulting in substantial energy waste. In an IoT network, designing of IC's, i.e., an Integrated Circuits are important in terms of energy conservation. Green Sensors on Chip (SoC) [12] enhance IoT network architecture by integrating sensors and computing power on a single chip, resulting in lower traffic carbon footprint, e-waste, and overall energy consumption. While the Sleep Walker model saves energy through the use of a Green SoC, this model can save even more energy through the use of recyclable materials.

10.2.1.2   Software-Based

Although data centers are critical components of an energy-efficient IoT network, they must be properly maintained before being used for IoT. In [13], researchers introduces a Policy-Based Architecture, i.e., E-CAB, that employs an Orchestration Agent (OA) in a Client-Server Model, which is responsible for context assessment of servers in terms of utilization of resources, as well as management.

The stored data is then sent back to client devices via intelligently chosen servers. This design, however, necessitates the installation of OA on each client-side computer, as well as the use of backup servers, which can lead into a very high energy consumption. To boost energy efficiency, C-MOSDEN [14], a context-aware sensing device, uses selective sensing. The results show that energy consumption has decreased, but there are a few minor overheads that, if eliminated, might make this model extremely efficient.

10.2.1.3   Policy-Based

The various policies and approaches focused on real-time data from IoT sensors will aid in large-scale energy savings. Monitoring (different contexts of energy consumption), knowledge processing, customer input, and an automation mechanism are all stages of developing policies for achieving energy efficiency. We may use data obtained from various areas of a building where occupants' behavior is observed. Automation systems can assist in identifying the position of a building's occupants as well as environmental improvements, allowing us to make energy-saving choices. City Explorer [15], the home automation solution used in [16], is divided into three levels, each of which is responsible for storage of data, processing of data, and providing services such as energy efficiency. As the previously discussed, policy-based system is used in real-life situations, and energy demand is decreased by 20%.

10.2.1.4   Awareness-Based

While public awareness campaigns are effective at reducing energy consumption, their effectiveness varies by culture and country, making it difficult to guess how many people will respond, listen, and support such campaigns. Using Smart Metering Technology, we can provide homeowners with real-time reports on their energy use from various sources in their homes, workplaces, and buildings, and then advise them on how to track and minimize their energy use based on the real-time data. This results in saving 3%–6% of the energy consumed [17].

10.2.1.5   Habitual-Based

Another strategy for improving energy quality and lowering carbon emissions is to implement a few basic practices that reduce energy consumption in our daily lives. While this is a small-scale measure, when the small savings are added up on a global scale, it adds up to a significant difference. One solution is to monitor energy use patterns in workplaces, homes, and factories using the automation systems suggested in [18–20] and then alleviate energy losses in our everyday activities. Though we should not rely too heavily on this technique, it can be useful.

10.2.1.6   Recycling-Based

Recyclable materials are used in the design of IoT network equipment would aid in its environmental friendliness. Mobile phones, for example, are manufactured by using some of the most costly resources available naturally, such as copper, and contain non-biodegradable materials that, if not properly disposed of when no longer in use, will contribute to the greenhouse effect. According to reports, there are 23 million no longer used mobile phones in drawers and cupboards in Australia [21], and 90% of the material used for making phones is recyclable, and therefore, recycling is becoming increasingly important if we have to address the problem of greenhouse gas emissions and huge energy consumption. Although 90% waste recovery is a lofty goal, it has the potential to save a significant amount of energy. Many strategies for improving the smart phone's power usage and performance were proposed in [22]. EEE (electric and electronic equipment) has recently used the efficient collection and recovery mechanism of the basic feature for each EEE type as a source of metal [23]. When the charger is connected, solar energy is favored more than 20% of the time, according to the sensitivity study [24].

10.3 Green IoT Communication Components

Green IoT is primarily comprised of networking technologies [25] such as Green RFID [26], Green WSN [27], Green CC [28], Green Machine to Machine (M2M) [29], and Green DC [30]. Cloud computing is abbreviated as CC, Machine to Machine is abbreviated as M2M, and data centers is abbreviated as DC. Figure 10.1 shows the cycle.

10.3.1 Green Internet Technologies

Green Internet Technologies necessitate the use of specially designed hardware and software that consume less energy without losing performance while optimizing power use.

10.3.2 Green RFID Tags

RFID tags can hold data or information at a low level for any items that are connected to them. RFID transmission necessitates RFID systems with a few meter radius. Passive RFID tags lack support of an active battery

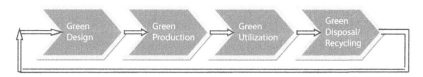

Figure 10.1 Green cycle.

source, whereas active RFID tags have built-in batteries that allow them to continuously transmit their own signal. The reader's energy is stored in them. An RFID tag's size can be decreased, which aids in the reduction of non-biodegradable waste.

10.3.3   Green WSN

The Wireless Sensor Network (WSN) has a large number of sensor nodes, but their power and storage capacity are limited. Green energy management, radio optimization, green routing techniques that minimize mobility energy consumption, and smart data algorithms that reduce storage space and data size requirements can all contribute to the development of a green WSN.

10.3.4   Green Cloud Computing

We are aware that there are cloud computing frameworks such as IaaS, PaaS, and SaaS. In a green system, hardware and applications have to be used in such a manner that energy demand is reduced. Energy-efficient policies must be implemented. Green cloud computing scheme–based technologies such as communication and networking are also to be used.

10.3.5   Green DC

Data centers are in charge of collecting, handling, sorting, and disseminating all forms of data and software. Data centers should be built with clean energy resources in mind. Aside from that, routing protocols should be configured to be energy sensitive, turning off idle network devices and incorporating energy parameters into packet routing.

10.3.6   Green M2M

Since a huge number of computers are involved in M2M communication, there should be energy-saving transmitting capacity and streamlined communication protocols, as well as routing algorithms. There should be search passive nodes in order to save resources.

10.4   Applications of IoT and Green IoT

The numerous applications of IoT and Green IoT are as follows in Figure 10.2.

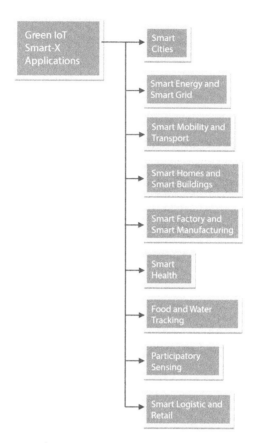

Figure 10.2 Green IoT applications.

- Smart Home
- Smart Industries
- Smart City
- Smart Healthcare
- Smart Transportation

Out of these, this chapter mainly focuses on the smart transportation.

10.4.1   Green IoT in Transportation

In recent years, the number of cars on the road has steadily increased. By 2030, it is estimated that it will rise to two billion people. This is due in part to global urbanization. In coming years, there will be significant change in transportation modes [31], particularly as demand of electric cars grows in the market [32] due to enormous increase in fuel prices. The impending ban of diesel-powered vehicles due to environmental concerns [33] and the introduction of new energy technologies such as hydrogen-powered vehicles [34] would alter the future shape of transportation systems. More environmentally friendly transportation options are needed in general, and these are being built incrementally with market penetration in mind. Vehicles, bicycles, buses, trains, and highways have recently received sensors, actuators tags, and the processing power required to relay vital information to traffic control websites. Modern smart transportation systems make it easier to better route traffic, provide visitors with accurate transportation statistics, and track the status of goods or products being transported. To ensure desirable vehicle autonomy, unique vehicle technologies require the construction of transportation infrastructure. The internet of vehicles definition [35] has recently emerged, demonstrating the IoT's potential in this important field. In the case of the automated smart car (vehicles) model, IoT is the most important application field [36]. The smart car idea takes into account the use and optimization of various internal functions in the vehicle that are enabled by IoT technologies. The driver's experience, as well as their comfort and safety, will be enhanced by the use of IoT. The smart car gathers data and correlates it with key operating parameters such as tyre pressure, charging, early detection of potential faults, and routine maintenance indicators, among others. A modern vehicle has evolved into a sensor network that gathers data from the surrounding environment. Data processed by a computer which is on-board and used for navigation, pollution control, and traffic management, among other items. Fast data processing, on the other hand, necessitates the use of a powerful computer which is on-board. This is one of the reasons why high-end vehicles with advanced driver assistance systems are so costly. Heavy computing activities should be able to be uploaded to the cloud through the Internet to prevent the use of costly equipment. As a result, in addition to the data already gathered by cars, IoT will assist traffic control centers in gathering additional data. In general, the targeted use of IoT technologies can result in improved service and added value for customers, which can help car manufacturers compete more effectively in the automotive industry. The most challenging part of IoT deployment when it comes to self-driving vehicles is in [37]. The autonomous vehicle's location, path, and planned route could be aided by the IoT in general, as well as autonomous vehicle safety system monitoring [38]. The production of fully autonomous vehicles is rapidly increasing, fueled by automotive industry competition and electro mobility. Vehicles must use local and global V2V communication in this context to allow for smoother, more efficient, and comfortable driving, as the vehicle would be able to detect hazardous situations ahead of time, even if they are out of sight due to a curve or other vehicles in front. Crash prevention and avoidance is the most challenging problem with automated vehicles, which could be addressed by strategically deploying IoT devices [39]. In recent years, the growing availability of vehicles has created a problem of finding vacant parking spaces, especially in major cities. This condition leads to emissions, fuel waste, and dissatisfaction among motorists. Smart Parking Systems, which provide real-time information and are a cost-effective and safe solution based on IoT technologies [40], can help solve this issue. Traffic issues, such as traffic congestion, are becoming more common as the world's population grows. Using the technology of vehicular ad hoc networks (VANETs), it is possible to avoid traffic congestion, which allows vehicles to communicate with one another and share road data in order to gain a better understanding of road conditions [41, 42]. Again, sensor technology advancements, such as smart parking sensors, are crucial for delivering reliable and accurate service [43]. The important issues that must be addressed, such as the rising number of people killed in car accidents and global environmental degradation. As a result, for using ICT to solve transportation problems, designing intelligent transportation system application is important so that it must have the potential to improve safety. IoT could help with vehicle maintenance and failure prevention [44], which could increase vehicle protection and lifespan. Taking all into account, IoT innovations have the potential to fully transform the driving experience and increase the overall efficiency of transportation systems in a variety of ways. Real-time supply chain monitoring is mainly owing to data collected via RFID, NFC, and sensors. These technologies can also capture product-related data in real time, enabling companies to respond as quickly as possible to changing consumer dynamics. In most cases, a typical company requires about 120 days to fulfil a customer's request. Enterprises that use innovative technology, such as Wal-Mart and Metro, on the other hand, just require a few days to meet consumer demands [45, 46].

Intelligent Transportation, in which vehicles are regarded as intelligent mobile devices capable of connecting to the network and exchanging knowledge about their environment, is a topic that has a big impact on how a smart city allocates resources intelligently. In fact, for governments and modern economic growth in general, improving the transportation management system and promoting sustainability is crucial. Lower environmental impacts, energy savings, and time and money savings will all benefit from transportation system optimization. Despite the many benefits of the 5G era and the IoT, there are still technical challenges to overcome.

10.5   Issues of Concern

10.5.1   End User Viewpoints

Though various IoT devices used for autonomous vehicles, its acceptance and adaptation depends on its users. End user viewpoints, i.e., simplicity and user friendliness are needed to be consider while designing and developing IoT devices and applications.

10.5.2   Energy Conservation

As various sensors used in autonomous vehicles, sensors' continuous sensing often causes them to rapidly deplete their resources. Various sleeping strategies have been suggested in the past to save space. In certain cases, extrapolating from previous data is a viable option [47], and this is an area that has the potential to save significant amounts of energy for sensor devices and deserves more research in the upcoming years.

10.5.3   Data Security and Privacy

There is a risk of unauthorized access to users' personal information, just as there is with self-driving cars in cities, where all of our data is shared in the cloud. Security threats exist, but they are tackled from the perspectives of preventing deadly accidents in one case and protecting private information in the other.

10.5.4   Preserving Contextual Data

The IoT aims to link billions or trillions of smart devices to the Internet, ensuring a bright future for smart cities. These objects can generate massive amounts of data or information and send it to the cloud for processing, which is especially useful for finding information and taking subsequent action. Detecting all possible data items collected by a smart object and then sending the entire recorded data to the cloud, on the other hand, is less useful in practice. In addition, such a tactic would be a waste of money (e.g., network bandwidth and storage space). Collecting massive volumes of data without context would be of no benefit in the future and will waste a enormous time. Out of the most complex and difficult issues that IoT faces is maintaining the context or background of the data generated so that further research can provide more meaningful and useful results.

10.5.5   Bandwidth Availability and Connectivity

The growing number of IoT devices on the market would result in increased competition for usable bandwidth, including increased interference [48]. Future IoT devices must be designed to operate in congested environments while minimizing interference from other IoT devices and using the least amount of resources possible.

Previously, system extensions were often hardware-based and not very versatile. Thanks to today's advancements in network technology, high speed processors, and cheaper memory, expanding the functionality of a computer, such as an IoT system, is now as simple as uploading a smartphone application to the device. As a result, it is easier and quicker to link to new products as they hit the market. This ensures that future IoT devices can take advantage of the variety and user-friendliness of various mobile applications.

10.6   Challenges for Green IoT

Around the world, transportation and traffic have become a major concern. Congestion is bad for public health, efficiency, and the environment, and reducing dependence on private cars will help solve many interconnected problems in these areas. Green transportation alternatives would also help to reduce the need for expensive infrastructure investments and contentious traffic regulations. Implementing new types of programs that provide community members with situational conscious information in multiple ways is one way to do this. Green technology will be critical in enabling an energy-efficient IoT. There are several difficult topics that must be tackled.

10.6.1   Standard Green IoT Architecture

The present and potential visions for smart cities are of modern urban development that integrates knowledge and the IoT to manage and track the majority of the city's activities and resources. Smart city infrastructure is required as IoT devices are dispersed throughout the city and information is shared through various sensors attached to it. Energy consumption though these devices should be less to prevent environment from CO_2 emission.

It is essential to develop such an architecture which is energy efficient and based on existing standard TCP/IP model. So developing standard

Green IoT architecture is a research area to be considered on priority. WSN plays vital role in IoT.

10.6.2   Security and Quality of Service

Huge data flows in network hold a lot of personal privacy data, including identity, location, and private content. Privacy breaches may have serious consequences in some situations. When it comes to IoT implementation, security or safety and privacy are major issues to be considered. The implementation of protection algorithms necessitates a significant amount of processing on the part of computers. The promise of energy-efficient and safe mechanisms, which are still in their infancy, could entice further research and development [49]. As the huge amount of data is store and shared on cloud, security of data is of primary concern to maintain confidentiality and privacy of users' data from hackers. Data integrity must be preserved by delivering high-quality service.

10.6.3   Data Mining and Optimization

Millions of IoT devices are increasing in coming years in the internet leading to increase in data stored on clouds. Storing data is not a big deal but to extract useful content from data is important. So developing data mining algorithm that provides optimal solution is an area of research to be considered by academicians and scientists.

10.6.4   Various Traffic Management and Scheduling-Based Smart Public Transport Solutions

The traffic monitoring system [50] contains many IoT-enabled devices. These complex interconnected devices needs interoperability that depends on alteration and self-administering actions is one of the challenges of overall transportation. Interoperability between different standards, data collection, heterogeneous gear, customs, resource create, programming, and database frameworks is the key problem in IoT. Another problem is the need for a user experience as well as access to different organisations and applications. This gives an idea that adaptable administrators are a valuable device for dealing with these problems to handle IoT interoperability and communication among such devices. In cases of low bandwidth, insignificant messages through systems to undefined objectives, and handling IoT interoperability, a versatile administrator is an excellent option. The TCP/IP Protocol is used to set up all notification exchanges among administrators. An expert of product is an independent executable program that monitors and responds to circumstances while acting to achieve predetermined goals. The operators should be able to move between organized devices, sharing their knowledge, implementation states, and should be possible to converse with other expert or humans. New approach involves implementing operator creativity during the period allotted for traffic monitoring and control. Such inventions are elegantly suits for traffic monitoring and regulating system as it follows self-ruling, adaptability, structurally, and flexibility. Experts are also helpful to send messages through proper networks where the actual position of the targeted traffic device is not known. A product expert (an operator) is used to answer to every traffic query. In this system, an astonishingly large number of devices would be linked and communicated to by their own smart operator who collects data and responds to other devices. Operators may demonstrate their worth as administrators. Every device contains an operator, and each device must support all professional capabilities, such as relocation and execution. The system as a whole can be regulated by a specific application. The system's portable specialists inside the device move from one center to the next, allowing the devices to send and receive data, retrieve data, and locate available assets.

10.6.5   Scheduling and Admission Control for Independent Vehicle Public Transportation System

The Autonomous Vehicle Transportation System (AVTS) focuses on the system's two main issues [51]:

1. Scheduling—to create the most cost-effective plan to meet transportation demands
2. To maximize benefit, admission control determines the collection of admissible requests among all requests.

A control center coordinates all vehicles, handles all service activities, and assigns vehicles to respond to requests. To evaluate arrival time and configure travel schedules, Dijkstra's algorithm is used to analyze the scheduling problem. The admissions control problem is addressed by considering that all timetables are capable of transporting such solicitations with the shortest possible ride time. The above problem is addressed using a Genetic Algorithm–based methodology.

The study discovered that profit is highly dependent on the various parameters focusing on the individual demands, and its benefits from various cases cannot be exactly comparable, despite the fact that more benefit can be gained if the number of vehicles increases.

10.6.6   Impacts on Public Transportation Management by Applying AVLs

The paper [52] describes the various characteristics of monitoring framework and analyzing public transportation not in big but particularly for area of a medium sized. In this application, it is planned to implement and test a model for predicting bus positions and arrival times based on real-time data as well as past data from previous transportation operations for the same route as the forecast.

The investigation was carried out in the Nis's Siberian city. A server was installed in the transportation system of city to collect positional updates from vehicles. A monitoring system was mounted on 150 buses, and an information monitor was installed at a specific bus stop. The prediction algorithm was found to be more specific than previous Kalman filters for transport data.

10.6.7   Lisbon and Portugal's Bus Ride Study and Prediction of Transport Usage

The focus of the research paper [53] is mainly on accuracy with which people use public transportation. It finds out the data of accessibility of large trip records from large number of transport clients in Lisbon, Portugal through an electronic ticketing system. An electronic access history associated with the cardholder is registered once an explorer loads a transport. This data of bus transportation are being mined to analyze the scope and prediction of bus rider's transport behavior. The prediction algorithm is used for the purpose as follows:

1. To analyze the extent of user rides prediction.
2. Depending on the prediction accuracy, categorization of bus according and bus usage behavior characteristics [53].

As per the data collected from Automatic Fate Collection Systems as well as Automatic Vehicle Location system, it is observed that for buses which run in regular fashion can be predicted with a high degree of accuracy for a maximum number of trips.

10.6.8   Smart Assistance for Public Transport System

This section explains the concept of transparent smart assistance in the public transportation system. The project has been carried out in favor of public transportation (for example, Pune Municipal Transportation in Pune). It includes the entire smart assistance system that is needed for public safety and well-being. The elegant structure also provides security for women. The accident site and the observing office are two additional modules in this mission. It was also simple to use the app for customers to monitor their transportation on their mobile phones. Both GSM and GPS modules can be used to plan the structure. In this case, to get the accurate coordinates for the disconnected (GSM) structure framework, the GPS structure is mostly used. People can get the information about the availability of seat in the transport, similarly stop information and the time when the transport arrives at the next stop. It also provides the facility for handicapped and older people to allow them a straight entry to take advantage of the vehicle. It also has an RFID-based driver verification system [54]. The framework additionally has several extra highlights to make people most familiar and to provide easy going transport facility.

10.7   Green IoT in Smart Transportation: Case Studies

10.7.1   Smart Traffic Signal

As it we see, most of the people do not follows rule especially at traffic signal. As a result, accident happened on traffic signal. Due to this, many people loss their life. According to NDTV repot 400 people loss their life every day in road accident. The main reason behind this is to violate rules. One smart system should be there which will automatically note the vehicle number which has violated rules. To avoid this, a smart chip has been designed. Once this chip inserted in the vehicle as shown in Figure 10.3, if any vehicle driver did not follows traffic signal, then the vehicle number is automatically display on screen. Once the unique number of vehicle gets catches now the system can send E-chalan to that driver. As the E-chalan application is already is there we directly transfer the unique to code to control room. Control room identifies the driver and E-chalan can issue to him. In this

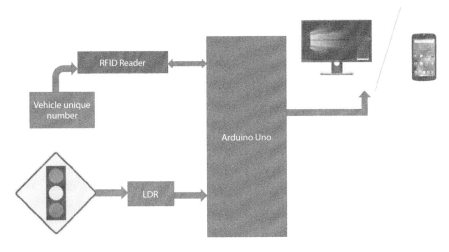

Figure 10.3 Smart traffic signal system.

system, we use Arduino Uno as a microcontroller, passive RFID chip, and RFID sensor. RFID chip contains the unique code (engine number) of vehicle and to sense the unique code RFID sensor is used. To uniquely identify an object, animal, and person, the RFID (Radio Frequency Identification) uses electromagnetic or electrostatic coupling in radio frequency portion of electromagnetic spectrum, and it comes under the wireless communication.

The working of this model is based on microcontroller. The RFID reader collects the unique code from RFID chip and displays it on screen. The RFID sensor is ON when the traffic signal is RED and get OFF when it get GREEN. When any vehicle driver break signal when traffic light is RED, RFID sensor read the unique code from RFID chip and display it on screen.

10.7.1.1   Description

A RFID reader is a device that collects data from a tag of RFID that is used to monitor a vehicle's unique id number. Radio waves play an important role for transmission of data from the tag to the reader. Because of high cost and the need to mark each object individually, RFID tags have not yet replaced bar codes. An RFID tag is used to store digital data in RFID technology. RFID consists of integrated circuits with a small antenna for transmitting data to an RFID transceiver. Since water absorbs wavelengths in the 2.4 GHz range, they are restricted. The Light Dependent Resistor (LDR) is made up of a piece of uncovered semiconductor material, such as cadmium sulfide, that changes its electrical resistance from thousands of Ohms in the dark to only a few hundred Ohms when light shines on it, causing hole-electron pairs to form in the material. It is made up of semiconductor substrates such as lead sulfide (PbS), lead selenide (PbSe), and indium antimonide (InSb) that detect light in the infrared range, with cadmium sulfide (CdS) being the most widely used of all photoresistive light sensors (CdS).

10.7.1.2   Application

1. It reduces the human effort in traffic control.
2. It is used to take immediate action against the violation of rules.
3. It is economic to use because the cost of chip is less.
4. Lost vehicle can be identified.

10.7.1.3   Advantages

1. The cost of chips as well as reader is less.
2. RFID chip life is 10 years.
3. Work of traffic police get reduces.
4. No power supply is required for chip.
5. Size of chip is compact.
6. In case of accident when it unable to find of the owner of vehicle, at that time by scanning the unique code the details of owner can be get.

10.7.1.4   Disadvantages

1. The chips should be inserted in vehicle and should have its engine number as its unique code.
2. The reading range is only 3 ft.

10.7.2   Cloud-Based Smart Parking System

The application described in [55] has different components. The simple slot detection is achieved with infrared sensors that are used to send data to a database. The user must register and book a slot, and payment must be made online. RFID tags are used to detect entries and exits at the entrance.

The Rpi3 microprocessor is used in the device. In a large parking lot, the proposed system reduces waiting time and helps to ensure more effective usage of the entire parking lot. This method is also efficient in terms of reducing paper use and lowering costs. A prototype including an Android application on the MIT app inventor was linked to cloud storage via firebase as a proof of concept (POC). Once the reservation is done, the hardware system which is implemented at the car parking will wait for the user's arrival and, after identification at the doors, will let them in. To retrieve the data, the RPi3 connects directly to the firebase. Every parking bay's IR sensors, LEDs, and LCD are all connected to the NodeMCU. On the LCD at the entrance, the NodeMCU shows the total count inside the parking lot as a way to be reminiscent customers looking for parking. The overall block connectivity diagram for two parking lots are operated by the same system as shown in Figure 10.4.

Two Arduino Uno are used at Parking 1 [Car Parking (CP1)] and [Car Parking 2 (CP2)], one at each entry and exit of CP1 and CP2. In addition, infrared sensors have been introduced in place of ultrasonic sensors. If the scanned RFID tag is approved, at the entrance, Arduino Uno controls the RFID tags and the servo motor that lifts the gate. It also checks the length of the vehicle and shows messages on the various LCDs. Similar features are available on the Arduino Uno at the exit, but it lacks the length sensor. To share data about number plate authentication and RFID anti-pass-back-values, the Arduino Uno communicate serially with the RPi3.

The proposed framework is more integrated and linked with each other using serial and cloud networking, as seen in the overall block diagram as shown in Figure 10.5. The system's inner working is described in detail below.

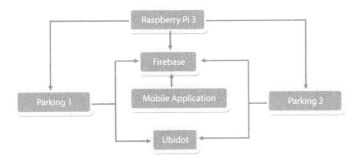

Figure 10.4 Overall architecture of cloud-based parking system.

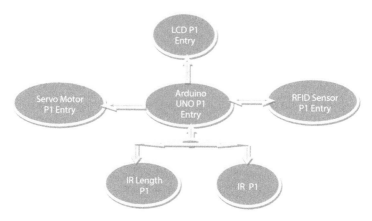

Figure 10.5 Overall block diagram.

10.7.2.1   Hardware—Car Parks CP1 and CP2

Once the car enters the parking and after detecting as a light vehicle (based on length), the access card get checked by the Arduino Uno with its RFID tag and if the card is flashed, the Arduino Uno checks with the RPi3 to see if the card has been used to enter the parking before closing the gate. With this process a pass back get avoided. If the card is not flashed, the Arduino Uno sends the checking command to RPi3 to activate image processing portion.

10.7.2.2   Smart Airport Management System

Airport management is a dynamic structure that is separated into phases. In this part, we suggest an IoT-based airport management application [56, 57]. Each component of the device is regarded as a thing. In this smart airport application system, the terms are described the following: the object of the operations office, the object of the desk for check-in, the object of the departure lounge, the passengers, baggage, the aircraft, and the crew member.

Each device object is self-contained and communicates with other components. Figure 10.6 depicts the system's elements and their relationships.

The different steps for airport management described as follows:

- The airport's important section is the operations room. It is in charge of the check-in counters, departure lounges, and flights. As a result, the assignment of check-in desk to a flight

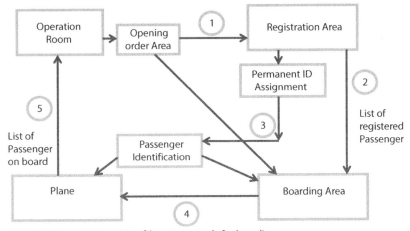

Figure 10.6 Architecture of airport management system.

is carried out by the operations room, and the list of already booked passengers is also provide to the officers. The flight's departure lounge is also assigned by the operations room.

- When passengers with their baggage arrive at the check-in counter, each passenger is given an electronic access key, and on each suitcase, an electronic sticker is placed. Passengers with their baggage are now treated as objects by the machine.

- Passengers and their baggage can take two separate routes to the aircraft. In this article, the main focus is on passenger routes.

- The registered passenger's list will be sent to the departure lounge by the check-in-desk assigned to the flight at the conclusion of the check-in process.

To find the appropriate departure lounge, the registered passenger's list is very useful. If the passenger ID does not appear on the list of departure lounges, then he is led to the correct one.

- A warning is sent prior to boarding (usually 20 minutes) to notify screened passengers who are not available in the departure lounge.

- Prior to boarding, the passenger's list who are available in the departure lounge is provided to the plane.
- Each member of the crew wears an electronic badge that allows him to be seen in the system.
- Passengers on board the plane are added to the list of enplaned passengers.
- Prior to take-off, the number of passengers on board get compared to the passenger's list preparing to board. If a traveller does not return, then his baggage is withdrawn and the luggage inventory is revised.
- When the plane lands at the destination, it sends passenger's list present in plane to the destination airport's operations room.

10.7.2.3   Intelligent Vehicle Parking System

Sensors are really important in this application [57]. It helps in gathering information about the vehicle's geographic location, parking lot capacity (as shown in Figure 10.7), prior reservation data, parking status, vehicle details, and information of current traffic. As a result, big data plays a significant role in this case, as it requires real-time implementation with the capability of providing a smart transportation infrastructure. The outcome factors such as occupied or free component influence the vehicle parking

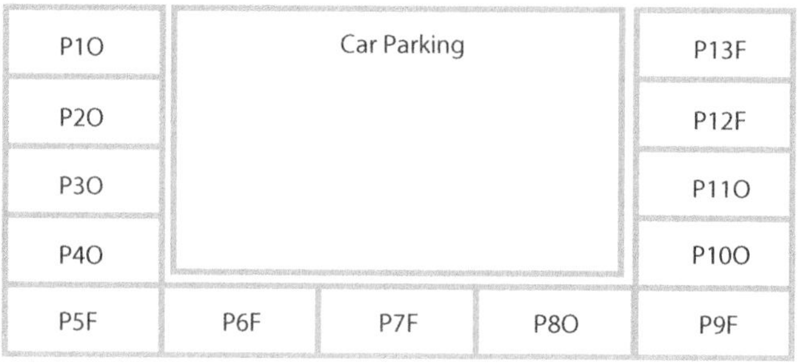

P1O	Car Parking			P13F
P2O				P12F
P3O				P11O
P4O				P10O
P5F	P6F	P7F	P8O	P9F

Figure 10.7 Architecture of intelligent vehicle monitoring system.

judgment. If the location is free and open for parking, then it is labeled as such. If there are cars present, then the position is identified as inhabited. The parking decision is dependent on the implementation of the conclusion, which will be modified over time through sensors. Then, the server is updated with the decision. For the final decision on the parking slot, these features are compared to the specified threshold value.

10.7.2.4   IoT-Based Smart Vehicle Monitoring System

The SVSM [58] was not a straightforward method, but rather a tool for quickly detecting serious injuries. SVMS also allows the driver to remotely disable the car after a burglary. It also helps the driver to find the location of the car from anywhere in the world. To support all of this, the SVMS contains a Raspberry Pi, as well as various sensors, a GSM/GPRS module, and a GPS module.

Figure 10.8 depicts the overall architecture of the SVMS system. Figure 10.9 depicts the internal architecture of the IoT system. The Raspberry Pi IoT device includes several sensors, a camera, a GSM/GPRS module, and a GPS module.

Any change in acceleration in any direction, as well as any tilt or rotation, can be observed. The impact sensor has been used in cars to detect crashes and deploy airbags in recent years. SVMS uses these two sensors to detect any injuries. The accelerometer readings are continuously monitored when the acceleration or deceleration reaches a threshold value or the sensor is tilted. It will detect an accident if acceleration exceeds the threshold value.

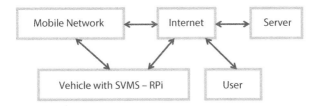

Figure 10.8 Overall architecture of the SVMS system.

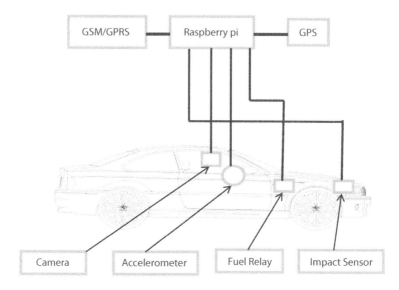

Figure 10.9 Internal architecture of IoT system.

10.8   Conclusion

Intelligent transportation is one of the important aspects of technically smart world. The use of IoT is also increased in smart transportation (car, train, bus, etc.). Nowadays, most of the transportation vehicles are Wi-Fi enabled which also needs energy consumption. Similarly, Green IoT is used nowadays in smart transportation. But it has issues such as energy conservation, data security and privacy, preserving contextual data, bandwidth availability and connectivity, and challenges such as security and quality of service are discussed here. The various technologies used in Green IoT are discussed here. The case studies related to various transportation issues are also described in this chapter. The case studies which are discussed here are implemented by focusing on cloud-based parking, smart traffic signal, smart airport management system, etc.

References

1. Arshad, R., Zahoor, S., Shah, M.A., Wahid, A., Yu, H., Green IoT: An Investigation on Energy Saving Practices for 2020 and Beyond, *Special Section On Future Networks: Architectures. Protocols, and Applications,* IEEE ACCESS, Received February 1, 2017, accepted February 26, 2017, date of

publication July 31, 2017, date of current version August 22, 2017. Digital Object Identifier 10.1109/ACCESS.2017.2686092. pp. 15667-15681.

2. Weber, R.H., Internet of Things–New security and privacy challenges. *Comput. Law Secur. Rev.*, 26, 1, 23–30, 2010.

3. Singh, D., Tripathi, G., Jara, A.J., A survey of Internet-of-Things: Future vision, architecture, challenges and services, in: *Proc. IEEE World Forum Internet Things*, Mar. 2014, pp. 287–292.

4. Lee, C.-S., Kim, D.-H., Kim, J.-D., An energy efficient active RFID protocol to avoid overhearing problem. *IEEE Sens. J.*, 14, 1, 15–24, Jan. 2014.

5. Gelenbe, E. and Caseau, Y., The impact of information technology on energy consumption and carbon emissions, in: *Proc. Ubiquity*, Jun. 2015, pp. 1–15.

6. Zhu, C., Leung, V.C.M., Shu, L., Ngai, E.C.-H., Green Internet of Things for Smart World. *Special Section On Challenges For Smart Worlds* Received IEEE ACCESS, October 9, 2015, accepted October 17, 2015, date of publication November 3, 2015, date of current version November 16, 2015. Digital Object Identifier 10.1109/ACCESS.2015.2497312. pp. 2151–2162.

7. Han, Q., Liang, S., Zhang, H., Mobile cloud sensing, big data, and 5G networks make an intelligent and smart world. *IEEE Netw.*, 29, 2, 40–45, Mar./Apr. 2015.

8. Caragliu, A., Del Bo, C., Nijkamp, P., Smart cities in Europe. *J. Urban Technol.*, 18, 2, 65–82, 2011.

9. Weber, R.H., Internet of Things New security and privacy challenges. *Comput. Law Secur. Rev.*, 26, 1, 23–30, 2010.

10. Occhiuzzi, C., Caizzone, S., Marrocco, G., Passive UHF RFID antennas for sensing applications: Principles, methods, and classifcations. *IEEE Antennas Propag. Mag.*, 55, 6, 14–34, Dec. 2013.

11. Sample, A.P., Yeager, D.J., Powledge, P.S., Smith, J.R., Design of a passively-powered, programmable sensing platform for UHF RFID systems, in: *Proc. IEEE Int. Conf. RFID*, Mar. 2007, pp. 149–156.

12. Boll, D. *et al.*, Green SoCs for a sustainable Internet-of-Things, in: *Proc. Faible Tension Faible Consommation (FTFC)*, pp. 1–4, 2013.

13. Peoples, C., Parr, G., McClean, S., Scotney, B., Morrow, P., Performance evaluation of green data centre management supporting Sustainable growth of the Internet of Things. *Simul. Model. Pract. Theory*, 34, 221–242, May 2013.

14. Perera, C., Talagala, D.S., Liu, C.H., Estrella, J.C., Energy-efficient location and activity-aware on-demand mobile distributed sensing platform for sensing as a service in IoT clouds. *IEEE Trans. Comput. Soc. Syst.*, 2, 4, 171–181, Dec. 2015.

15. Zamora-Izquierdo, M.A., Santa, J., Gómez-Skarmeta, A.F., An integral and networked home automation solution for indoor ambient intelligence. *IEEE Pervasive Comput.*, 9, 4, 66–77, Oct./Dec. 2010.

16. Moreno, M.V., Úbeda, B., Skarmeta, A.F., Zamora, M.A., How can we tackle energy efficiency in IoT based smart buildings? *Sensors*, 14, 6, 9582–9614, 2014.

17. McKerracher, C. and Torriti, J., Energy consumption feedback in perspective: Integrating Australian data to meta-analyses on in-home displays. *Energy Effic.*, 6, 2, 387–405, 2013.

18. Occhiuzzi, C., Caizzone, S., Marrocco, G., Passive UHF RFID antennas for sensing applications: Principles, methods, and classifcations. *IEEE Antennas Propag. Mag.*, 55, 6, 14–34, Dec. 2013.

19. Fensel, A., Kumar, V., Tomic, S.D.K., End-user interfaces for energy efficient semantically enabled smart homes. *Energy Effic.*, 7, 4, 655–675, 2014.

20. Moreno-Cano, M.V., Zamora-Izquierdo, M.A., Santa, J., Skarmeta, A.F., An indoor localization system based on artificial Neural networks and particle filters applied to intelligent buildings. *Neurocomputing*, 122, 116–125, Dec. 2013.

21. Foteinos, V., Kelaidonis, D., Poulios, G., Vlacheas, P., Stavroulaki, V., Demestichas, P., Cognitive management for the Internet of Things: A framework for enabling autonomous applications. *IEEE Veh. Technol. Mag.*, 8, 4, 90–99, Dec. 2013.

22. Falaki, H., Lymberopoulos, D., Mahajan, R., Kandula, S., Estrin, D., A rst look at traffic on smartphones, in: *Proc. 10th Annu. Conf. Internet Meas. (IMC)*, p. 281, 2010.

23. Oguchi, M., Murakami, S., Sakanakura, H., Kida, A., Kameya, T., A preliminary categorization of end-of-life electrical and electronic equipment as secondary metal resources. *Waste Manage.*, 31, 9-10, 2150–2160, 2011.

24. Zink, T., Maker, F., Geyer, R., Amirtharajah, R., Akella, V., Comparative life cycle assessment of smart phone reuse: Repurposing vs. refurbishment. *Int. J. Life Cycle Assess.*, 19, 5, 1099–1109, 2014.

25. Ahmed, R., Asim, M., Khan, S.Z., Singh, B., Green IoT—Issues and Challenges. *2nd International Conference on Advanced Computing and Software Engineering (ICACSE-2019)*.

26. Namboodiri, V. and Gao, L., Energy-aware tag anticollision protocols for RFID systems. *IEEE Trans. Mob. Comput.*, 9, 1, 44–59, 2010.

27. Lin, Y.-H. *et al.*, Optimal and maximized configurable power saving protocols for corona-based wireless sensor networks. *IEEE Trans. Mob. Comput.*, 14, 12, 2544–2559, 2015.

28. Farahnakian, F. *et al.*, Using ant colony system to consolidate VMs for green cloud computing. *IEEE Trans. Serv. Comput.*, 8, 2, 187–198, 2015.

29. Chang, C.-H., Chang, R.Y., Hsieh, H.-Y., Highfidelity energy–efficient machine–to–machine communication. *Personal, Indoor, and Mobile Radio Communication (PIMRC), 2014 IEEE 25th Annual International Symposium on. IEEE*, 2014.

30. Shuja, J. *et al.*, Survey of techniques and architectures for designing energy-efficient data centers. *IEEE Syst. J.*, 10, 2, 507–519, 2016.

31. Jonkeren, O., Francke, J., Visser, J., A shift-share based tool for assessing the contribution of a modal shift to the decarbonisation of inland freight transport. *Eur. Transport Res. Rev.*, 11, 1, 1–15, 2019.

32. Capuder, T., Sprčić, D.M., Zoričić, D., Pandžić, H., Review of challenges and assessment of electric vehicles integration policy goals: integrated risk analysis approach. *International journal of electrical power & energy systems* (0142-0615) 119 (2020); 105894, 12.

33. Li, J., Han, Y., Mao, G., Wang, P., Optimization of exhaust emissions from marine engine fueled with LNG/diesel using response surface methodology. *Energ. Source. Part A Recovery, Util. Environ. Eff.*, 42, 12, 1436e1448, 2020c.

34. Ajanovic, A. and Haas, R., Economic and environmental prospects for battery electric- and fuel cell vehicles: a review. *Fuel Cells*, 19, 5, 515e529, 2019.

35. Shen, X., Fantacci, R., Chen, S., Internet of vehicles. *Proc. IEEE*, 108, 2, 242e245, Article number 8967259, 2020.

36. Chugh, A., Jain, C., Mishra, V.P., IoT-based multifunctional smart toy car. *Lect. Notes Netw. Syst.*, 103, 455e461, 2020.

37. Padmaja, B., Narasimha Rao, P.V., Madhu Bala, M., Rao Patro, E.K., *Proceedings of the International Conference on I-SMAC (IoT in Social, Mobile, Analytics and Cloud), I-SMAC 2018*, 26 February 2019, p. 18e21, Article number 8653736, 2019.

38. Bylykbashi, K., Qafzezi, E., Ikeda, M., Matsuo, K., Barolli, L., Fuzzy-based Driver Monitoring System (FDMS): implementation of two intelligent FDMSs and a testbed for safe driving in VANETs. *Future Gener. Comput. Syst.*, 105, 665e674, 2020.

39. Abdou, M., Mohammed, R., Hosny, Z., Essam, M., Zaki, M., Hassan, M., Eid, M., Mostafa, H., *Proceedings of the International Conference on Microelectronics, ICM*, December 2019, vol. 2019-December, p. 103e107, Article number 9021613, 2019.

40. Luque-Vega, L.F., Michel-Torres, D.A., Lopez-Neri, E., Carlos-Mancilla, M.A., Gonzalez-Jimenez, L.E., Iot smart parking system based on the visualaided smart vehicle presence sensor: SPIN-V. *Sensors*, 20, 5, 2019. DOI: 10.3390/s20051476

41. Xu, Y. *et al.*, Data collection for the detection of urban traffic congestion by vanets, in: *Proc. APSCC*, pp. 405–410, 2010. DOI: 10.3390/s20051476

42. Xu, Y., Wu, Y., Xu, J., Sun, L., Efficient detection scheme for urban traffic congestion using buses, in: *Proc. 26th Int. Conf. WAINA*, pp. 287–293, 2012.

43. Perković, T., Solic, P., Zargariasl, H., Coko, D., Rodrigues, J.J.P.C., Smart parking sensors: state of the art and performance evaluation. *J. Cleaner Prod.*, 262, 121181, 2020a.

44. Saki, M., Abolhasan, M., Lipman, J.E., A novel approach for big data classification and transportation in rail networks. *IEEE Trans. Intell. Transp. Syst.*, 21, 3, 1239e1249. Article number 8701707, 2020.

45. Yuan, R.. Shumin L., Baogang, Y., *Value chain oriented RFID system framework and enterprise application*, Science Press, Beijing, 2007.

46. Hugl, Ulrike, Smart Technologies and Privacy: Running a close race?, 2006.

47. Patterson, D., Liao, L., Fox, D., Kautz, H., Inferring high-level behavior from low-level sensors, in: *Proc. UbiComp*, pp. 73–89, 2003.

48. Tragos, E., Zeadally, S., Fragkiadakis, A.G., Siris, V.A., Spectrum assignment in cognitive radio networks: A survey. *IEEE Tutor. Surv. Commun.*, 15, 3, 1108–1135, Third Quarter 2013.

49. Caviglione, L., Merlo, A., Migliardi, M., What is green security?, in: *Conf. Rec. IEEE 7th IAS Annu. Meeting*, pp. 366–371, 2011.

50. Jalaney, J. and Ganesh, R.S., Review on IoT Based Architecture for Smart Public Transport System. *Int. J. Appl. Eng. Res.* 14, 2, 466–471, 2019.

51. Lam, A.Y.S., Leung, Y.-W., Chu, X., Autonomous-vehicle public transportation system: scheduling and admission control. *IEEE Trans. Intell. Transp. Syst.*, 17, 5, 1210–1226, 2016.

52. Shalaby, A. and Farhan, A., Prediction model of bus arrival and departure times using AVL and APC data. *J. Public Transp.*, 7, 1, 3, 2004.

53. Foell, S., Phithakkitnukoon, S., Kortuem, G., Veloso, M., Bento, C., Predictability of public transport usage: A study of bus rides in Lisbon, Portugal. *IEEE Trans. Intell. Transp. Syst.*, 16, 5, 2955–29, 2015.

54. Rathod, R. and Khot, S.T., Smart assistance for the public transport system, in: *Inventive Computation Technologies (ICICT), International Conference on*, vol. 3, IEEE, pp. 1–5, 2016.

55. Mukadam, Z. and Logeswaran, R., A Cloud-Based Smart Parking System Based On Iot Technologies. *Journal of Critical Reviews*, 7, 3, 105-109, 2020.

56. Bouyakoub, S., Belkhir, A., Guebli, W., Smart airport: an IoT-based Airport Management System. *ICFNDS '17*, Cambridge, United Kingdom, July 19-20, 2017.

57. Muthuramalingam, S., Bharathi, A., Rakesh kumar, S., Gayathri, N., Sathiyaraj, R., Balamurugan, B., IoT Based Intelligent Transportation System (IoT-ITS) for Global Perspective: A Case Study, in: *Internet of Things and Big Data Analytics for Smart Generation, Intelligent Systems Reference Library*, vol. 154, V.E. Balas and *et al.* (Eds.), Springer Nature Switzerland AG, 2019, https://doi.org/10.1007/978-3-030-04203-5-13.

58. Mallidi, S Kumar Reddy., IoT Based Smart Vehicle Monitoring System. *International Journal of Advanced Research in Computer Science*, 9, 738–741, 2018.

11

Green Internet of Things (IoT) and Machine Learning (ML): The Combinatory Approach and Synthesis in the Banking Industry

Prakashkumar Hasmukhbhai Patel[1*], Chetan K Rathod[2]
and Karan Zaveri[3]

[1]*Department of Commerce and Business Management, Faculty of Commerce, The Maharaja Sayajirao University of Baroda, Vadodara, Gujarat, India*
[2]*Apex Chemical Company, Vadodara, Tarsali, Vadodara, India*
[3]*Co-owner of Shalibhadra Enterprise, Partner at Baseline Corporation Proprietor of Padmavati Enterprise, Karelibaug, Vadodara, India*

Abstract

People are cognate beings living in a digital world, facing a quantum future, and the Internet of Things (IoT) is one thing that connects everything in the smart world. As a result, the biggest challenge faced by researchers is to minimize the energy consumption of these IoT technologies. The digital world is developing with such force and such a pace that you simply can't ban or control it. Taking inspiration in achieving low power consumption IoT, a GIoT is proposed. On the other hand, innovative technologies like Artificial Intelligence (AI) and Machine Learning (ML) provide enhanced customer experience, drastic reduction in costs for the institutions, and increased profit margin which is of utmost importance considering the cutthroat competition in the market. In this chapter, we aim to share an overview as to how the institutions in the banking industry are making use of GIoT and its life cycle. Also, we would and how to leverage the power of AI and ML in the banking industry. More so, this chapter has scrutinized the

Corresponding author: prakashkumar.patel-cbm@msubaroda.ac.in

Roshani Raut, Sandeep Kautish, Zdzislaw Polkowski, Anil Kumar and Chuan-Ming Liu (eds.) Green Internet of Things and Machine Learning: Towards a Smart Sustainable World, (297–316) © 2022 Scrivener Publishing LLC

important role of AI and ML in the banking sector and identified the latest technologies which can be adopted for reducing the carbon footprints because of the IoT.

Keywords: Artificial Intelligence (AI), Green Cloud Computing (GCC), Green Data Center (GDC), Green Internet of Things (GIoT), Green Wireless Sensor Networks (GWSN), hazardous emissions, Internet of Things (IoT), Machine Learning (ML)

11.1   Introduction

The Internet of Things (IoT) is being termed as the judicious tool which will help financial institutions, especially banks, to grow in the financial market which is the heart of the customer services industry [1]. Moreover, in the present unprecedented times, digital transformation is vital. The most important challenge at present is to update the legacy business software and revamp the existing banks without hindering the working system and the least inconvenience to the customer. This is where Artificial Intelligence (AI) and Machine Learning (ML) come into the picture and play a crucial role in executing hassle- and risk-free digital migration [2].

IoT encompasses the projected growth network consumption and the number of nodes in the future. Hence, it is of utmost importance that the network components being used are reduced along with the reduction in the energy consumed in the entire process [3]. The world is transforming itself in terms of the processes used in having a Green IoT (GIoT). The process in itself is a state of the art that leads to a smart world implementation. The IoT should be known for its self-capacity to minimize the greenhouse effects and reducing carbon footprints. The smart world would become more sustainable only when the carbon dioxide (CO_2) emission from the sensors, technology devices, applications, and services is automatically reduced [4]. When these changes are implemented the life cycle of the GIoT should have no impact on the environment concerning the Green Generation, Green Utilization, Green Architecture, and Green Disposal.

At present, there is enormous competition in the banking industry which has brought together the inherent pressure of managing the risk. Moreover, there is regulatory pressure in maintaining the standards of regulatory requirements and the government which the banks are required to improve. All this results in providing a different and unique customer service, which is pleasant.

11.2   Research Objective

The prime objective of this research is as given below:

- To understand and study different ways in which the life cycle of GIoT can be adopted by the existing banking industry.
- To understand how to maximize the inherent strength of AI and ML for working with data science acceleration this can be used for elevating the customers' portfolio offerings in the banking sector.
- To understand the major role of AI and ML in the banking industry.
- To determine the modern technologies this can be embraced in developing methods for reducing the carbon footprints arising as a result of the IoT.

11.3   Methodology

We have used exploratory research design and collected secondary data to derive analogies concerning how GIoT can be deployed in the existing banking sector. Also, how we can leverage the inherent power of AI and ML in banking. External data has been collected from various websites for inspecting the major role of AI and ML in the banking sector. Upgraded and modern technologies have been identified for implementation in the banking sector which will, in turn, play a pivotal role in reducing the carbon footprints because of the Internet of Thing.

11.4   Result and Discussion

As time passed by, the average time spent by people on digital devices has increased manifolds. In terms of quantity, it ranges stupendously from millions to billions. Recent studies have projected that almost 75% of the world population having access to the internet; together connect more than 6 million devices along with an average of 4.5 billion people penetrating the internet in 2019 alone [5]. With the quantum of gadgets connected via the internet increasing, the IoT automatically becomes interesting. With the help of IoT data, banking institutions are at present developing various

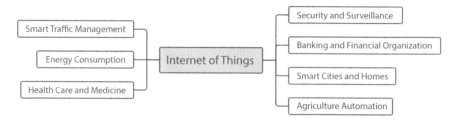

Figure 11.1 Some potential application domains of Internet of Things.

apps by assigning them to the various IoT developers. These apps end up transforming the banking experience of the customers. To partner with different business affiliates and FinTech services for embracing present-day demands and regulations while at the same time maintaining the security standards, this so-called AI and ML will play a pivotal role.

Few major application domains of IoT are highlighted in Figure 11.1. These are security and surveillance, banking and financial organization, agriculture automation, healthcare and medicine, energy consumption, smart traffic management, and smarts cities and homes.

11.4.1   Internet of Thing (IoT) in the Banking Industry

IoT can be defined as an interrelationship between solely referable and ingrained computing accessories within the current Internet framework. It is assumed that IoT will be able to provide the banking industry with a network of accessories, structure, system, and services which will go away from the routine machine-to-machine conversation along with enveloping an array of rules, domain and different functions [3]. The enormous traditional software and procedures which are present in the present banking and finance sector are bound to escort itself toward computerization because of these ingrained accessories. The banking and financial market is flooded with new commodities and new core strategies because of the conversion of data and process which is powered by the IoT [6]. This has resulted in a generation of new opportunities and process which will change the way the client interacts with the banks. A benchmark will be created for the banks to match and whichever entity fails to match the standards will end up losing the market share [7]. IoT contains the ability to define a new method of working with the existing systems in banking related to Know Your Customer, Credit Disbursement, Security Administration, Risk Controlled Self-Assessment, Forex Business, Alternate Delivery Channels, and Bank Assurance. With the help of other evolving automation in the market such as digital banking and biometrics, the IoT has the potential to develop innovative peer-to-peer business processes which can rattle the traditional money lending procedures in many places.

11.4.1.1   Internet of Things Facilitating Banking

An intelligent and robust system is formed when billions of devices are interconnected with each other. This is how the world is getting digitalized and modernized in every aspect. These intelligent systems transfer data using the cloud which is then scrutinized in different ways to help modify the businesses, the lifestyle of people, and the world in general [8]. As the lifestyle of the peoples change with modern technology and the smart devices they use in banking, the real-time details of the customer in terms of their finances are received by the banks. This vital data is shared by the bank from the customer's side with the help of the various devices which the customers use. Effective use of this data enables the banks to project the customers' needs and accommodate them with new solutions which, in turn, help the customer in making a correct decision with the effective use of their finances. Hence, the "Bank of Things" turns itself into a competent tool for adding value to the customer loyalty for the banks. This results in more business for the bank. In addition to this, banks also communicate with their customers through cell phones and provide the necessary guidance as per their needs. This results in a change in the behavior of the customers' spending and purchasing habits. Banks can also build customer loyalty by communicating with them in various ways which may not necessarily be in finance but by offering advice and service in many spheres of life.

11.4.1.2   Benefits of Internet of Things (IoT) in Banking

IoT has numerous advantages when we talk in terms of banking. It provides value-added services to both its debt customers and credit card customers. Based on the patterns and volume of transactions through ATM kiosks by the customers, banks can either increase or decrease the number of ATMs in a particular area [9]. On the other hand, banks can also effectively use the IoT to introduce on-demand services by introducing need bases kiosks which can help in increasing the accessibility of banking services for the customer [7]. IoT can provide the banks with customer data which can, in turn, be utilized in identifying the business needs of the customers along with their preferred value chain of retailers, suppliers, and distributors [10]. This helps the bank in gaining customer insights. This vital information provided by the IoT supports the bank in introducing various value-added services, customized banking services and products, and need to be based on financial assistance to the customer. This ends up becoming a win-win situation for both the customer and the bank.

The IoT solutions have also been very beneficial in the agricultural sector for the farmers who are the customers of the banks. For instance, using modern technology the banks can project farming outputs in addition to the various other factors of crop farming. This has resulted in enabling the banks to forecast the output of the actual value of the crops being cultivated. With the help of the crop yield which is forecasted by the IoT, the banks are in a position to provide flexible financial benefits to the customers in terms of the conventional yield as well as the constancy and crop output. This results in developing a greater bond between the farmer and the bank.

Moreover, banks can also anticipate frauds in financial transactions and develop methodologies to prevent such occurrences beforehand [3]. Whenever a customer uses the card on a point of sale, the verified details of the customer flow to the bank through the device location. Now depending on the volume of the transaction and the concurrence of the customer the bank is in a position to confidently decline or process the transaction. Also, various sensor devices may be installed around the warehouses and storage points of the borrowers to note and track the inventory which flows in and out [11]. This crucial information can help the bank in monitoring the account which ensures that the credit taken by the customer is repaid promptly as and when the inventory is liquified by the customer. This results in reducing the manual tracking costs and denying the borrowers indulging in any dishonourable practices.

11.4.1.3   Other Benefits Benefits of the Internet of Thing (IoT) in Banking

The optimum application of connected devices can result in the customer taking a wise decision in changing the financial habits of overspending. As an example, one of the first IoT banks, Interact IoT, started implementing shock wearables as a constituent of an inculcation program for the users. As and when the customer sets a credit card limit, the wearable device would start tracking the spending habits every hour throughout the day and immediately raise an alert as and when the limit approaches. If the customer continues the spending without paying attention to the alert, then a shockwave is triggered by the wearable through the device on the wrists, indicating to the customer that the daily limit will be consumed shortly. That way, the user can take a cognitive approach toward the spending.

11.4.1.3.1   Improved Banking Experience

There are many ways in which the Internet of Thing affects the services provided in banking. It promptly provided customers with various insights and personalized exposure. The device connectivity with a network allows the customer to take a token beforehand and keep a check on it by using their smartphone. This provides them with a regular update with the exact time remaining for their turn in availing the service at the bank, rather than waiting in a line. The bank collects and stores the footfalls of the customers in their centralized database along with their preference of services which are utilized by them at the time of their bank visit. They also store the patterns of the questions being asked by them. This in return helps the bank customers to have an enhanced banking experience at every visit.

11.4.1.3.2   Expanded Range of Service Beyond Beyond Banking

At present, banks can make use of the IoT mechanism to broaden the variety of services and products available for their customers which are different from the regular features. For example, banks in the United Arab Emirates (UAE) have initiated fitness programs linked with their accounts with the bank which excites them to stay healthy. When the customers achieve a certain benchmark set by the bank they are rewarded in the form of a preferential rate of interest in accounts and free shopping vouchers. This process results in the customer thinking that the banks care about their fitness and, in turn, results in building a strong relationship with the bank.

11.4.1.3.3   Efficient Branch Banking

The public sector banks are finding it difficult to cater to branch banking in this era of mobile banking. The banks on one hand want to preserve the traditional system of banking which always used to add value to their business and old customers, whereas, on the other hand, to meet the ever-growing demands of the young generation, they have to make use of the technology where more emphasis is given to smart devices.

All the traditional banks are making full use of the IoT and other technology-driven banking applications to bridge this gap between the traditional banking at branch because of mobile banking [12]. For example, biometric sensors are being utilized to collect data whenever a customer enters the branch and transmit the same data to the primary system. Using the technology and creating lobby's where all the IoT products are available in one single place the branches can reduce the number of employees and reduce the cost. This also results in reducing the turnaround time for the customer in availing the service. The back offices where the footfalls from the e-lobby are recorded can be used to link various branches in different locations.

11.4.1.3.4 Enhance Credit Card Ecperience

IoT has facilitated the evolvement of an interactive credit card. Instead of using the traditional plastic card, the customer talks and gets engaged with a digital display which allows them to strike a question to the bank branches in real-time and modify the features of the credit card upfront without any delay. Such instant modifications are very useful at the time of online shopping and other instant purchasing requirements.

11.4.2 Artificial Intelligence and Machine Learning in Banking

A recent survey by research conducting organization Autonomous Next has found out that banks around the globe can minimize the operating costs by around 22% by 2030 by effectively using technology driven by AI [13]. To minimize the frauds in the credit card sector, banks shall use face recognition technology which will then trigger an increase in the annual revenue growth by over 20% in 2021.

The extraordinary level of automation can be achieved with the effective use of AI and ML in reducing the repetitive and routine tasks done by

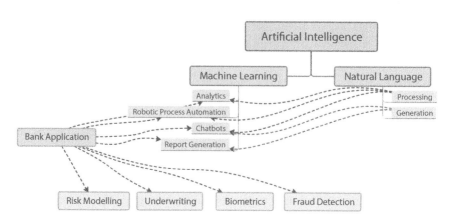

Figure 11.2 Artificial Intelligence in banking.

humans by either taking over the human experts, or by intensifying their conduct while at the same time assisting them with the mundane jobs [14].

The different application in the banking sector where AI can be used effectively is mentioned above in Figure 11.2. Apart from these, there are many reasons behind the incorporation of AI and ML in the banking industry:

- Heavy competition in the banking and financial industry.
- Demand for process-driven services.
- Introduction of customized service at banks.
- Need for customized solutions.
- Ensuring operational efficiencies.
- Escalating employee efficiency.
- Increase profitability and acquiescence.
- To trim down maladies and safety risks.
- To deal with a huge amount of business data.
- To bring in effective decision making.

11.4.2.1 Significant Roles of Artificial Intelligence and Machine Learning in Banking and Finance

The extraordinary level of automation can be achieved with the effective use of AI and ML in reducing the repetitive and routine tasks done by humans by either taking over the human experts, or by intensifying their conduct while at the same time assisting them with the mundane jobs [15].

11.4.2.1.1 Mitigate Risk Management

Dealing with risk management is one area where the practical benefits of AI and ML can be demonstrated [16]. At the time of sanction and disbursement of credit limits to the clients, banks have to trust the creditworthiness of the customer by believing their history with them. In reality, the process is not smooth and correct every time, and the banks have to counter many challenges in approving the credit limits to the customer. With the advent of ML algorithms that analyzes and presents a better picture to the banks, the process of loan sanctioning has become much more convenient. This is the power of digital transformation.

11.4.2.1.2 Preventing Fraudulent Activities

Without any doubt, banks are looked upon as regulated institutions which are guided by strict government regulations and policies to prevent and safeguard financial frauds in the system [16]. It is no doubt that because of this reason it has become more important than ever for the banks to migrate in becoming complete digital as early as possible. The utmost important activity on the part of the banks is to be aware of the risks beforehand and not wait for any suspicious activity which may result in fraud. In the traditional process, banks were required to deviate from the set rules to avert fraudulent activity. ML technology can predict any doubtful movement even before the external hazard breaches the client's account. These tasks which are infeasible for humans to perform can be easily achieved by the machines by operating at high precision in real-time.

11.4.2.1.3   The Functionality of Chatbots

Chatbots are the latest AI and ML-based software that can clone human conversation. It becomes easier for the banks to reply to queries raised by the customer with the technology ingested chatbots and they have resulted in serving the banking sector on a large scale instantly.

11.4.2.1.4   Algorithm-Based Marketing

This technology of using algorithms to classify the client's past actions and design special operation is a blessing for both the client and the bank. New age clients prefer such specially crafted services as it reduces their time and effort in searching for it manually as it brings all the necessary information directly to them. This augments their experience of banking.

11.4.2.1.5   Greater Automation and Improved Productivity

All the repetitive tasks can easily be taken over by AI and ML which, in turn, provides ample time for the staff to concentrate on many important and crucial tasks on hand. Full automation reduces manual jobs and eventually leads to higher profits.

11.4.2.1.6   Personalized Customer Service

When the tasks which have higher storage capabilities are automated, they provide a larger picture of the customers' transaction habits and provide the most appropriate and personalized exposure. Effective use of the footfalls of the customer allows a bank to make the maximum use of the analytical capacity of AI and ML which helps in identifying the most ingenious tendencies in the customers' action. This supports in creating a perfect personalized action for each customer.

11.4.2.1.7 More Precise Precise Risk Assessment

The staff who interact and work directly with the client can also benefit by minimizing the uncertainty when the correct digital footfall of each client is known. When it comes to scrutinizing the loan and avoiding any human mistakes, this automated system turns out to be more authentic than human intelligence.

11.4.2.1.8 Advanced Fraud Detection and Prevention

Without any doubt, the best feature of AI and ML in banking is to detect and prevent fraud from taking place beforehand because there is no dearth of criminals and innovative ways in which they commit fraud. Because of AI and ML at present, there are many ways in which we can identify and detect fraud before taking place.

11.4.2.2 *Machine Learning for Safe Bank Transactions*

Since the ML systems are continually learning, fraud avoidance in the financial institution is its. primary advantage [8]. If we have to put it in simple words, any same idea of committing fraud will never work in the same manner again. This work perfectly in the frauds committed with credit cards in banking institutions.

11.4.2.2.1 How Artificial Intelligence Makes Banking Safe

The prime spot nowadays where the financial transaction takes place is when the customer makes online spending, which makes it the perfect place for committing the fraudulent transaction under the influence of purchasing something. This fraudulent transaction can be prevented from taking place with the help of AI and ML. For instance, when a customer who is at a point of sale has a camera with face recognition then it can be used to identify the correct holder of the credit card. Moreover, in the frauds wherein discount coupons are offered with fraudulent intent, the Internet Protocol (IP) addresses can be easily tracked as and when the financial transaction takes place.

11.4.2.2.2 Market Research and Prediction

When ML is used in concurrence with big data, then it can assist in finding certain impressions along with assembling information. It becomes feasible to envisage currency variations, project the most profitable investment decisions, minimize risk, find the optimum position where the risk is lowest, identify the most perfect credit portfolio for the client, survey competitors, and identify security lapses.

11.4.2.2.3   Cost Reduction

The jobs done by the employees can be done more effectively with the help of ML which facilitates the financial institutions to predict deficiency in processes and organize it proficiently. For example, a chatbot can profitably handle the customers who have the most common and routine issues. Chatbots never demand any remuneration for their duty, in fact when we are working with ML it drastically cuts the costs of the institution. Without a doubt, it generates profit and raises the bar of customer service.

11.4.2.2.4   Machine Learning for Bank Transactions Monitoring

When it comes to keeping an eye on electronic payments and receipts, without a doubt, ML is far ahead of any other ground breaking technology [17]. ML is the ultimate solution to all future voluminous digital transactions [18]. Over the years in the existing traditional transaction system, it is difficult to set limits on the number of alerts. When the benchmark is set too low, if the institutions end up with a higher number of alerts then it demands scrutiny. When after setting the benchmark too high if the doubtful transactions are missed then the whole process of setting up alerts is of no use. The false alerts which look true at the first instance also require redressed as the effectiveness of the entire monitoring system depends on it. These tasks can be monitored and processed by humans only up to a certain level.

The ability to monitor financial transactions by ML in the banking industry is its most important feature. ML has proved to be very beneficial in discovering abnormality in financial transactions with many industries. ML can be very useful in fortifying the decision support system when offering a completely new automated analysis and examination, either by reinstating or assisting the expert [13]. This assistance can be in the form of security efficiency or operational efficiency.

11.4.3   Application of Machine Learning in Banking will Expand in 2021

Capital in billions is expected to be invested in the banking, finance, and insurance sector this year which is far ahead then the investment in other sectors [18]. Projections that were made in favour of AI and ML before the disastrous pandemic of Covid-19 have proven to be correct and the industry is deemed to grow more in the coming times.

11.4.4   Technologies that Can Be Adopted for Reducing Carbon Footprints

With the advent of technology and astounding growth in the area of the IoT, how we do our job and live our daily life has also changed. Even though the community has gained a lot from the benefits of the IoT, it has to be kept in mind that the Internet of T absorbs energy, brings in toxic pollution, and generates huge volumes of E-waste [19]. This thing puts a lot of pressure on nature and the smart world. This is why there is a huge appeal to shift toward the Green IoT to maximize its benefits and minimize the damage of the IoT. Green IoT is the environmentally benevolent future of the IoT [20]. This can be achieved by minimizing the CO_2 footfalls, utilizing fewer reserves, and advocating competent techniques for using the available energy [21]. Hence, the electronic machines, communication devices, cloud storage, sensors, and internet have to be moved toward a Green IoT where the energy efficiency is improved and CO_2 footprints are reduced.

With the internet, the whole world has become a small community wherein everything is connected and the entire world with the help of Global Communication Network using the TCP/IP Protocol [4]. The way we live our lives and communicate with different things including personal and professional affiliations is remarkably changed with the advent of the internet. Everything ranging from daily objects like home appliances, cars, motorbikes, electrical appliances, and communication devices are under the control of wireless communication networks. The IoT consists of smart connectivity of the present network and computation of awareness with ambience. Hence, the IoT is each and everything surrounding us which needs to be connected. In simple terms, it is anything that is connected to the internet. IoT technology makes all the instruments and machines smarter and enables them with the capability of storing and processing data brilliantly. IoT also makes technical communication between the instruments more adequate and accurate. Additionally, the IoT consists of an array of devices. It includes devices such as RFID (Radio Frequency Identification), sensors, smartphones, smart appliances, drones, and many more. These devices communicate with each other and work toward a mutual target of providing effective transmission [3]. Hence, many applications will foresee a wide change in their real-time recording and monitoring of data. A few of the applications which will undergo these changes are home automation, environmental and weather monitoring, e-healthcare, transportation sector, and industrial automation. Moreover, the IoT is also a boon for many applications which are in the area of wireless communications wherein brilliant handlers are deeply associated with the distribution of information, making collective decisions and completing jobs most favourably. IoT is nothing but the process of accumulating data, using data and its bilateral communication. IoT becomes omnipresent for big data which requires a huge capacity to store data, cloud computing (CC), and broad channel bandwidth for transmission [6]. Nonetheless, the processing of big data demands high power consumption which will indirectly put pressure on the surrounding environment and the society at large. Hence, to minimize carbon emission and reduce power usage, the Green IoT has been brought into the picture to accomplish the evolution of the smart world and its feasibility.

Keeping in mind the environmental damages taking place around the globe because of the CO2 footfalls, Green IoT initiatives needs to be given attention. Green IoT refers to the latest advancement in the modification of the IoT technology wherein the IoT is modified to become more environmentally friendly by utilizing the facilities and the storage capabilities which enables the users to collect, store, access, and supervise various collected information [22]. This modification in the existing technology and enabling for Green IoT is known as Information and Communication Technology (ICT). Green ICT means the storage capabilities which enable the users to collect, store, access, and supervise various collected information. This ICT can bring changes in the climate of the world at large primarily due to higher power and energy consumption. The present discussion on the stability of ICT has concentrated on data centers optimization, using different processes of allocation of framework and the infrastructure, which primarily maximizes energy competence. The focus should be on minimizing Carbon discharge and e-waste of material demolition. Greening ICT means enabling technology for the Green IoT which encompasses RFID, Green Cloud Computing (GCC), Green Data Center (GDC), green internet, and green communication network. Hence, Greening ICT plays a major role in the Green IoT and accommodates numerous benefits to the environment by minimizing the power and energy consumptions utilized for designing, manufacturing and distributing ICT accessories, machinery, devices, and types of equipment.

11.4.4.1   Green Internet of Things (Green IoT)

IoT encompasses an unseen communication chain and a computing ambience which is built on smart cameras, sensors, various software and data

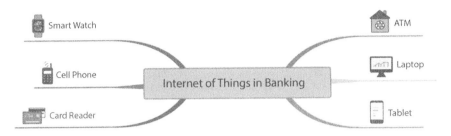

Figure 11.3 Internet of things in banking.

center which stores the entire data. Its scrutiny has embraced the possibility of utilizing the IoT for building a green grounds climate that is focused on energy saving. Notwithstanding earlier proof surrendered, IoT components were talked about in, where the upsides of IoT design concerning how to make green grounds by using the trend-setting innovations astutely and proficiently were portrayed [23]. The areas where GIoT should be incorporated in banking are as given in Figure 11.3.

Green Internet of ThingsIoT has three ideas, in particular, plan innovations, influence advancements, and empowering advances. Plan advances allude to the energy productivity of gadgets, correspondences conventions, network models, and interconnections. Influence advances allude to cutting fossil fuel by-products and upgrading the energy effectiveness [24]. Because of gres, the Green Internet of ThingsIoT turns out to be more proficient through lessening energy, decreasing dangerous emanations, diminishing assets utilization and diminishing contas, the Green Internet of ThingsIoT prompts saving regular assets, limiting the innovation sway on the climate and human wellbeing and decreasing the expense essentially.

11.4.4.2   *Green Cloud Computing Technology*

At present CC is fast materializing in a virtualization technology used across the internet. Limitless computational capacity, unrestricted storage capacity, and prompt service delivery through the internet come along with it [25]. CC is omnipresent, whereas the IoT is universal. CC and the IoT both go hand in hand in providing an enhanced research study [26]. The basic target of GCC has always been in advocating the usage and utilization of products that are eco-friendly and which can be easily recycled and reused without delay. Another aim of GCC is to minimize the hazardous nature of the materials being used, optimize and maximize the consumption of energy and increase the recyclability of the old products and the wastes being generated from them. Additionally, it can be achieved by product durability appropriation of resources and paperless virtualization. The same idea is supported by research and study in the field for GCC by minimizing energy utilization.

The main goal of GCC which is to reduce the carbon footprints is backed by utilizing numerous techniques and ideas to reduce the usage of power in its application [25]. The Public and Private Clouds were examined and they constituted energy consumption in switching, data processing, transposable, and data storage along with electronic data processing. In terms of the percentage of total energy utilization in CC, the actual energy utilization in transportation and circuit, switching forms a major chunk. GCC the optimum and likely solutions can be summarized as follows:

(I) Acceptance of hardware and software for reducing energy utilization.

(II) Power conservation by adopting VM techniques such as VM amalgamation, VM migration, VM placement, and VM allocation.

(III) Different energy capable means allocation and mechanisms and tht risks.

(IV) Capable and Productive productive methods for energy-saving systems.

(V) GCC procedures positioned on CC backend technologies such as communications, network, etc.

11.4.4.3   Green Data Centre (GDC) Technology

The latest technology for data management, data dissemination, and data storage are commonly known as GDC [27]. The prime components of these data are users, systems, things, etc.

In the process of working with distinct and different data along with the various applications, the data center absorbs a substantial quantity of energy with high working cost and substantial releasing of carbon footprints [28]. Moreover, the production of big data is soaring by numerous universal things, namely, cell phones and sensors. With this path of moving toward a digital and smart world, the energy capability for data center becomes more compelling.

Additionally, GDC has a provision of accommodating the data services for cloud supported mobile ad-hoc networks in 5G. Progressive technologies are utilized for reducing the paints used in structures and carpets, a low emanation of building products, imperishable landscaping and utilizing substitute of regular form of energy like heat pumps, solar cells, and evaporative cooling [28]. The process of saving energy in data servers using cloud technology is reducing routing and searching transactions. Engineers have examined the mechanism combined capability into the energy capable context-aware broker framework (more commonly known as e-CAB) to govern next-generation data center. The examination has resulted in a GDC wherein the air conditioning is supported by cloud procedures and techniques wherein two sub-processes are there, namely: (1) Data Center of Air Conditioning System and (2) Cloud Management Platform. The prime function of the Ant Colony System was to search for a feasible clarification and solution. Additionally, the dynamic virtual machine is generally utilized for minimizing the energy and power consumption of the cloud data center while preserving the perfect Quality-of-Service. Hence, every device is utilized by multiple users and a virtual machine is utilized to access those physical devices.

11.5   Conclusion

With an increase in the popularity of the various online tools by the customers, the banks have been forced to utilize the IoT data with the intent to modify and upgrade their experience of banking with the new services and products. This is where the banks will have to leverage the power of AI and ML in banking along with data science acceleration to enhance customers' portfolio offerings. In the present scenario, the banks need to convert the data generated from the IoT into information that gives them some value and which, in turn, can help them in making informed and qualified decisions. This will, in turn, help them in increasing their market share resulting in a pleasant experience of better services to the customer and this will be possible only with the help of the introduction of AI and ML in the banking sector. With this increased use of AI and ML, the utmost important thing will be to make the optimum use of the Green IoT which contains green design, green production, green utilization, and green recycling. Its effective use can result in reducing carbon footprints because of the IoT. This reduction in the carbon footprints will be beneficial for society and it has its benefits and its social implications and industrial implications for the society. Hence, the Green IoT means concentrating on Green Production, Green Usage, Green Architecture, and Green Demolition.

- Green Production: Developing electronic peripherals and computers along with the correlated subsystems with minimum or no impact on the environment and society at large.

- Green Usage: Reducing the energy consumption of computers and their peripherals and making their optimum use in an environmentally friendly manner.
- Green Architecture: Energy-efficient designs for Green IoT sound peripherals, computers, and servers and its cooling technology.
- Green Demolition: Remodeling and reusing old computers and recycling rejected computers and other electronic equipment.

Concerning ML, it was not going to take long for AI and ML to take hold in modern banking because of the rapid pace with which the technology is getting used in the banks. This has, in turn, redefined the existing dynamics existing in the banking industry forever. The data provided by AI and ML can be utilized and analyzed for forecasting consumer behavior in terms of patterned data sets of customers' behavior and spending behavior. This will result in providing them with better services utilizing modern technology. The effective and early adoption of AI and ML will play a major role in providing the banks with a competitive edge with their peers and will ultimately result in providing a pleasant experience to their customers in terms of speed which will be fast, a trust which will be secured and banking experience which will be personalized.

References

1. León, O., Hernández-Serrano, J., Soriano, M., Securing cognitive radio networks. *Int. J. Commun. Syst.*, 23, 5, 633–652, 2010.
2. Cioffi, R., Travaglioni, M., Piscitelli, G., Petrillo, A., De Felice, F., Artificial intelligence and machine learning applications in smart production: Progress, trends, and directions. *Sustain.*, 12, 2, 1–26, 2020.
3. Kumar, S., Tiwari, P., Zymbler, M., Internet of Things is a revolutionary approach for future technology enhancement: a review. *J. Big Data*, 6, 1, 1–21, 2019.
4. Byoung-Oh, G., Kim, T.C., Yang, S.E., A Study on Internet of Things Implementation. *J. Knowl. Inf. Technol. Syst.*, 12, 6, 845–856, 2017.
5. Kemp, S., *DIgital2019: Global Digital Overview*, 2019. https://datareportal.com/reports/digital-2019-global-digital-overview, 2019.

6. Hussein, A.R.H., Internet of Things (IOT): Research challenges and future applications. *Int. J. Adv. Comput. Sci. Appl.*, 10, 6, 77–82, 2019.

7. Malali, A.B. and Gopalakrishnan, S., Application of Artificial Intelligence and Its Powered Technologies in the Indian Banking and Financial Industry: An Overview. *IOSR J. Humanit. Soc Sci. IOSR-JHSS*, 25, 6, 55–60, 2020.

8. Kaur, N., Sahdev, S.L., Sharma, M., Siddiqui, L., Banking 4.0: 'The Influence of Artificial Intelligence on the Banking Industry & How Ai Is Changing the Face of Modern Day Banks'. *Int. J. Manag.*, 11, 6, 577–585, 2020.

9. Salunkhe, R.T., Role of Artificial Intelligence in Providing Customer Services with Special Reference to SBI and HDFC Bank. *Int. J. Recent Technol. Eng.*, 8, 4, 12251–12260, 2019.

10. Pareek, A., Internet of Things (IoT) in Banking: Examples of IoT Solutions In Finance, https://customerthink.com/internet-of-things-iot-in-banking-examples-of-iot-solutions-in-finance/, 2020.

11. Adam, A., Internet of things in the supercool game of B2B marketing, 2017. https://customerthink.com/internet-of-things-in-the-supercool-game-of-b2b-marketing/, 2017.

12. Vijai, C., Artificial Intelligence in Indian Banking Sector: Challenges and Opportunities. *Int. J. Adv. Res.*, 7, 4, 1581–1587, 2019.

13. Chuprina, R., Machine Learning in Banking – Opportunities, Risks, Use Cases, https://spd.group/machine-learning/machine-learning-in-banking/, 2021.

14. Shouval, R., Fein, J.A., Savani, B., Mohty, M., Nagler, A., Machine learning and artificial intelligence in haematology. *Br. J. Haematol.*, 192, 2, 239–250, 2021.

15. Das, P., AI and Machine learning are redefining the banking industry, https://www.analyticsinsight.net/ai-machine-learning-redefining-banking-industry/, 2020.

16. Leo, M., Sharma, S., Maddulety, K., Machine learning in banking risk management: A literature review. *Risks*, 7, 1, 1–22, 2019.

17. Dey, A., Machine Learning Algorithms: A Review. *Int. J. Comput. Sci. Inf. Technol.*, 7, 3, 1174–1179, 2016.

18. Carbo-Valverde, S., Cuadros-Solas, P., Rodríguez-Fernández, F., A machine learning approach to the digitalization of bank customers: Evidence from random and causal forests. *PLoS ONE*, 15, 10, October, 2020.

19. Baliga, J., Hinton, K., Ayre, R., Tucker, R.S., Carbon footprint of the internet. *Telecommun. J. Aust.*, 59, 1, 05.1–05.14, 2009.

20. Ferrag, M.A., Shu, L., Yang, X., Derhab, A., Maglaras, L., Security and Privacy for Green IoT-Based Agriculture: Review, Blockchain Solutions, and Challenges. *IEEE Access*, 8, 32031–32053, 2020.

21. Uddin, M., Okai, S., Saba, T., Green ICT framework to reduce carbon footprints in universities. *Adv. Energy Res.*, 5, 1, 1–12, 2017.

22. Alsamhi, S.H., Ma, O., Ansari, M.S., Meng, Q., Greening internet of things for smart everythings with a green-environment life: A survey and future prospects. *arXiv*, 1–14, 2018.

23. Gadre, M. and Gadre, C., Green Internet of Things (IoT): Go Green with IoT. *Iciot - 2016*, 4, 29, 1–6, 2016.

24. Bashar, D.A., Review on Sustainable Green Internet of Things and Its Application. *IRO J. Sustain. Wirel. Syst.*, 1, 04, 256–264, 2019.

25. Atrey, A., Jain, N., Iyengar, N.C.S., A Study on Green Cloud Computing. *Int. J. Grid Distrib. Comput.*, 6, 6, 93–102, 2013.

26. Chowdhury, C.R., Chatterjee, A., Sardar, A., Agarwal, S., Nath, A., A Comprehensive study on Cloud Green Computing: To Reduce Carbon Footprints Using Clouds. *Int. J. Adv. Comput. Res.*, 3, 8, 78–85, 2013.

27. Varde, A., Robila, S., Michael, P., Energy Green Data Centers for Sustainability White Paper. *Technol. Innov. Progr. (TIP) Natl.*, Usepa, 2007, 2011.

28. Uddin, M. and Rahman, A.A., Techniques to implement in green data centres to achieve energy efficiency and reduce global warming effects. *Int. J. Glob. Warm.*, 3, 4, 372–389, 2011.

12

Green Internet of Things (G-IoT) Technologies, Application, and Future Challenges

Komal Saxena[1]*, Abdul Basit[1] and Vinod Kumar Shukla[2]

[1]*Amity Institute of Information Technology Amity University, Noida, India*
[2]*Department of Engineering and Architecture Amity University, Dubai, U.A.E*

Abstract

The Internet of Things (IoT) appends everything in the keen world, and consequently, the utilization of IoT advancement is a test and engaging investigation district. Enlivened by accomplishing a low power usage IoT, a Green IoT (G-IoT) is proposed. The paper reviews an investigation into worry about G-IoT. It fundamentally discusses the existence procedure of G-IoT which contains green development, green reprocess, green execution, and green improvement. Likewise, G-IoT degrees of progress, for example, green imprints, green perceiving systems, and green web improvements, are examined. The G-IoT is anticipated to show enormous adjustment in our normal day by day presence and would help in caring the view of "green including data". Under a few years, we as a whole will be fused by a huge extent of sensors, gadgets, and "things", which will have the decision to concede by techniques for 5G, act "particularly", and give green help to clients in dealing with their errands. This paper displays an analyze inspiration to G-IoT, plots pivotal energy about G-IoT and its structure, with generally hardly any examination applications, at long last, and proposes a section of the examination great and fit reactions for greening IoT.

Keywords: Green IoT, Internet of Things (IoT), cloud computing 5G, wireless sensor networks, energy, efficiency, smart cities

Corresponding author: ksaxena1@amity.edu

Roshani Raut, Sandeep Kautish, Zdzislaw Polkowski, Anil Kumar and Chuan-Ming Liu (eds.) Green Internet of Things and Machine Learning: Towards a Smart Sustainable World, (317–348) © 2022 Scrivener Publishing LLC

12.1   Introduction

With every passing day, there are constant changes in the internet. Low-cost and efficiently available internet connections have provided easy access to the data. This has prompted an expansion in the number of gadgets or devices utilized by people across the world. It is estimated that by the end of the year 2021 every individual will be using seven devices. Today, the number of gadgets that are being used is 50 billion [9] and it will be 100 billion arriving in the year 2030 [29]. At this moment, we can count on a huge transmission rate and an immense substance extent (on various events it will be more than in 2030, than what it was in the year 2010) at the estimation of extraordinary carbon transmissions into the planet. In [12], the extent of CO_2 outpourings as shown from the telephone systems is going to be around 346 million tons constantly by the year the 2020s and it is needed to support in the up and coming years. A conjecture of all-out discharges continuously 2020 is given in [10]. Under these enormous CO_2 emissions, present climate situations, and flourishing matters, prudent or green improvement is winding up being pulled in to explore the region in the progress of headway. Furthermore, the present battery headway of devices is another basic matter that prompts a green advancement technology [14]. The fifth-generation (5G) of remote communication has been open in the year 2020, and it will have the choice to oversee various events with more minimal information than the current cell skeleton [4]. Figure 12.1 shows the sustainable development of the Green Internet of Things (G-IoT).

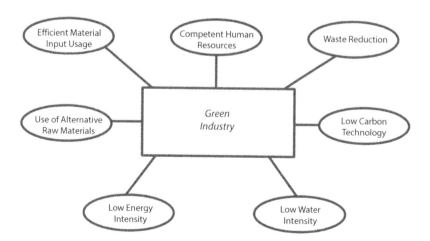

Figure 12.1 Green Internet of Things (G-IoT) for sustainable development.

The expanding awareness of environmental issues across the globe has led to G-IoT advancement activities that ought to be studied. G-IoT allows the IoT technologies to be environmentally friendly by the use of the offices and stockpiles that allow the contributors to collect, accumulate, connect, and regulate different forms of data. The empowering innovations for G-IoT are known as the Data and Correspondence Technology (DCT) innovations. Green DCT advances allude to the offices and stockpiles empowering endorsers to collect, accumulate, connect, and regulate different forms of data. DCT advances can cause environmental change on the planet because with the establishing utilization of DCT extra energy has been utilized. The understanding for manageability of DCTs has zeroed in on server centers improvement through strategies of distributed foundation, which led to the increment of the energy proficiency; lessen CO_2 outflows and electronic waste of element removals. Greening DCT is empowering advances for G-IoT that incorporates green RFID, green remote sensor networks (GRSN), green machine-to-machine (GM2M), green cloud computing (GCC), green server center (GSC), green web, and green correspondence network. Consequently, greening DCT advances play a fundamental job to G-IoT and give numerous advantages to the community, for example, diminishing the energy utilized for planning, fabricating, and disseminating DCT gadgets and, what is more, hardware.

The principal ambition of this study is to give an outline of G-IoT in the matter of approach, applications, advances, and, what are more, challenges and advantages. Section 12.2 portrays the fundamental ideas of IoT and evolution. Section 12.3 presents the elements which are associated with IoT. Section 12.4 defines the existence pattern of G-IoT. Section 12.5 explains the technologies of G-IoT. Section 12.6 gives an outlook on the applications of G-IoT. Section 12.7 examines the aspect of the IoT in 5G technology. In Section 12.8, we will talk about the use of IoT in various smart cities. In Section 12.9, the architecture of G-IoT is discussed. In Section 12.10, we have the advantages and disadvantages of G-IoT. Section 12.11 defines the challenges that are linked with G-IoT technology and the opportunities that are provided. Section 12.12 discusses the future of the G-IoT. At last, Section 12.13 finishes up the study with the conclusion.

12.2   The Internet of Thing (IoT)

The "Internet of Things" (IoT) word was earlier composed by Mr. Kevin Ashton [6] in 1999 where he affirms that the IoT can modify the world, similarly, what the web did possibly so far. *The term "Internet of Things (IoT)"*

Figure 12.2 Internet of Things (IoT) [34].

can be determined as the interconnection between various computing devices such as smartphones, routers, laptops, and tablets, to send and get information by the usage of the web (Figure 12.2).

In other words, we can say that "The IoT passes on the ability of the web, data figuring, and data assessment to the current truth of actual gadgets. For purchasers, this recommends associate with the comprehensive information network without the messenger of a reassuring and display; an impressive parcel of their normal things and devices can take rules from that network with immaterial human cooperation."

In large corporation settings, IoT can transmit the very efficiencies to genuine creation and scattering that the web has since an old-time back send on for data activity. Millions of fixed web-enabled sensors in most cases are offering an awesomely valuable course of action of information that organizations can utilize to gather data about the inflation of their errands, record resources, and diminish manual methods. Researchers can moreover utilize the IoT to amass information about people's decisions and mentalities, notwithstanding that can have certifiable influence for assurance and security.

12.2.1   How IoT Works

The fundamental segments of the IoT are contraptions that gather data. To make that data significant it ought to be gathered, processed, pervaded, and assessed, all of which can be managed in an arrangement of ways.

Social affair the data is done by sending it from the contraptions to a gathering point. Moving the data ought to be conceivable distantly using an extent of advancements or on wired associations. The data can be sent over the web to a working community or a cloud that has the limit and register power or the trade can be coordinated, with go-between devices gathering the data before sending it along.

Dealing with the data can happen in worker communities or the cloud, nonetheless, some of the incomprehensible time. On account of requesting contraptions, for example, shutoffs in mechanical assembly, the deferral of transmitting data from the device to an inaccessible worker station is unreasonably unprecedented. The complete trip time for transmitting data, taking care of it, looking at it, and returning rules (close that valve ahead of the lines blowout) can take unnecessarily lengthy. In those cases, threshold-management can turn out to be potentially the main aspect, where an insightful threshold device can boost up to data, analyze it, and design responses if crucial, all innards by and broad adjacent real distance, thus decreasing deferment. Threshold contraptions furthermore have an onerous organization for transmitting data to be also arranged and handled.

12.2.2   Evolution of Internet of Things

The year 1999: Bill Joy in the "Six Webs" structure at the World Economic Forum composed Device to Device (D2D) correspondence.

The year 2000: Envision of LG Internet Digital DIOS, the elementary Internet-related container on the globe. For IP accessibility the container used a LAN port.

The year 2001: David Brock, co-boss at the Auto-ID Center, MIT, suggested an "alternative article identification plan, the Electronic Product Code (EPC), as opposed to the common Universal Product Code (UPC or 'normalized tag') for exceptional identification and finishing off things all the thing life cycle using the establishment/web".

The year 2003: Bernard Traversat conveyed the "Undertaking JXTA-C: Enabling a Web of Things" at the 36th Annual Hawaii International Conference.

According to them, Project JXTA's goal is to show a standard plan of shows for improvised, unavoidable, shared figuring as a foundation of the approaching Web of Things.

The year 2003: At the McCormick Place gathering center a phenomenal kind of association to interface an enormous number of the huge quantities of marks that are currently on the globe was dispatched.

The dispatch of electronic thing code (EPC) network was gone to by different specialists from across the universes of retail, advancement, and the academic world.

The aim was to supersede the overall normalized tag with a comprehensive system that will deliver a novel count to each dissent on the globe. Some have quite recently started calling this association "the snare of things".

Also, some more equivalent turns of events and investigations later.

The year 2005: The staff at the Interaction Design Institute Ivrea (IDII), Italy, comes up with a singular board microcontroller that can be utilized in natural exercises being developed by their understudies.

At the end of the year, "The Internet of Things" named report was appropriated by the International Telecommunications Union, one of the seven segments that write about the web.

The year 2008: Distant industry collectively shapes the IPSO Alliance to progress related gadgets. It was a momentous bounce toward having the IoT realized for tremendous degree organizations in real incineration plans.

The year 2016 and further: smart homes, smart vehicles, solar-based trackers, and IoT-based gadgets for everyday use.

IoT has escalated across the endeavors and a newer term (E-IoT) is introduced that unite devices utilized in trade and corporate plans. As indicated by market subject matter professionals, there have been around 50 billion related devices in 2021.

Though the significance of IoT has transformed from what Kevin Ashton had thought it to be with different advancement improvements, the setting up the guideline of having an association of interconnected devices that are interfacing and the natural variables to accumulate and take apart information using the web has proceeded as in the past.

For the duration of the time, the RFID-based IoT model fails to procure adequate thought due to limited organization decisions, the massive cost of contraptions, and structure. Additionally, the RFID-based structure was not viewed as fit for huge extension cremation arrangements, for instance, the cutting edge robotization. Regardless, IoT continued creating as a result of movements in IP-based association organizations and diverse other particular headways that made the machine-to-machine (M2M) affiliation possible over a more broad region.

12.3 Elements of IoT

The six components in IoT, i.e., recognition, detecting, transmission machinery, computing, assistance, and semantics [27], are discussed in Figure 12.3.

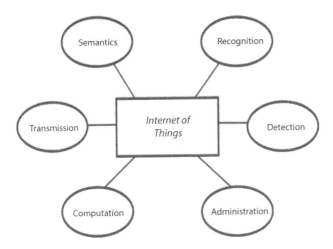

Figure 12.3 Elements of IoT.

> Recognition is designating and planning organizations accompanying their advantage for instance assembling data at an action of activity. The information can be gotten by a machine, a wearable gadget, an affiliate mounted control or many for the most part found gadgets.

> Detecting is for gathering diverse information from similar articles and transmitting it to an information collection, information storage, worker focus, etc. The collected information is moreover inspected to operate express exercises subject to required organizations. The sensors can be humidity sensors, wearable distinguishing devices, temperature sensors, mobile phones, etc. The distinguishing can be biometric, natural, environmental, visual, or detectable (or all the previously mentioned).

> Transmission machinery interfaces heterogeneous items composed to offer explicit administrations. That needs either Wi-Fi which is a remote Local Area Network (LAN)–based connection or WAN (Wide Area Network) interchanges. The correspondence conventions accessible for the IoT are Bluetooth, Z-wave, Wi-Fi, LTE-Advanced, and Near Field Communication (NFC), Ultra-wide data transmission (UWB), and so on.

> Computing, the hardware taking care of units [e.g., microcontrollers, central processor, a structure on chips (SoCs),

and field programmable entrance shows (FPGAs)], and programming applications play out this endeavor. Various hardware stages (e.g., Arduino, UDOO, Friendly ARM, Intel Galileo, Raspberry PI, and Gadgeteer) are made and diverse programming stages (e.g., Tiny OS, Lite OS, and Riot OS) are used. The cloud stage is a particularly huge computing piece of IoT because it is unfathomable in getting ready distinctive data progressively and eliminating a wide scope of necessary data from the collected information. Collected information is imparted to cloud-based help where the data coming out of the IoT contraption is amassed with alternative cloud-based information to give necessary data to the end customer. The information secured can be data from other web authorities similarly as from alternative purchasing with practically identical IoT contraptions. Information readiness is expected to give supportive data.

Administrations in IoT can be sorted into four different classes:

- Character relevant administrations
- Data collection administrations
- Community mindful administrations
- Ubiquitous administrations

Character-relevant administrations give the base to different sorts of administrations since each application planning true articles into the virtual world requirements to recognize the items first.

Data collection administrations assemble and sum up the crude data which should be handled and revealed. The got information is additionally used by the collective mindful administrations to settle on choices and respond subsequently. Ubiquitous administrations are for administrations to anybody on interest, whenever and anyplace.

> Semantic methods the capacity to remove information wisely to offer the necessary types of assistance. This cycle typically incorporates: finding assets, using assets, displaying data, and perceiving and breaking down information. The regularly utilized semantic advancements are OWL (Web Ontology Language), EXI (efficient XML interchange), and RDF (Resource Description Framework), and so forth [23].

12.4   The Green IoT: Overview

IoT is a worldwide, imperceptible, striking, encompassing correspondence association and handling habitat built reliant on cameras, splendid sensors, databases, programming, and worker focuses in a globe-navigating data surface structure. G-IoT fixates on diminishing IoT power use, a requirement for accomplishing the keen globes with the reasonability of insightful entirety, and decreasing CO_2 transmissions. G-IoT contains arranging and using points of view. G-IoT demonstrates a green climate as well as conserves time and power. It gives a methodical arrangement that empowers green and supportable development of the general public. It upholds advancements and applications for tending to cultural difficulties, for example, savvy transport, practical city, and effective usage of energy to make a G-IoT climate.

G-IoT aims at Green Production, Green Utilization, Green Design, and Green Disposal/Recycling [20] (Figure 12.4).

1. **Green Utilization:** restricting power use of PCs and other information systems similarly to using them in a naturally strong aspect.

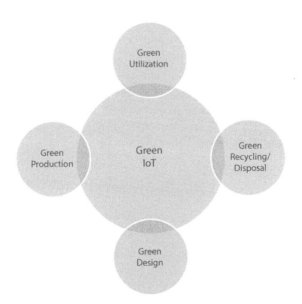

Figure 12.4 Key component of Green IoT.

2. **Green Disposal/Recycle:** fixing and restating old and unfortunate PCs and alternative electronic stuff.
3. **Green Design:** arranging power capable for G-IoT sound portions, PCs, and laborers and freezing equipment.
4. **Green Production:** conveying electronic sections and PCs and alternative similar subsystems with least or zero significance on the climate.

12.5   Green IoT Technologies

For G-IoT, a few green advances should be joined, for instance, green RFID tags, Green Sensing Networks, and, what is dynamic, Green Internet Technologies.

12.5.1   Green RFID Tags

The term RFID is the combination of RF and ID [RF intends to Radio Frequency (Wireless Communication Technology), and ID determines Identification (Tag Information)]. It is concentrated as perhaps the most favorable far-off association frameworks used to engage IoT. Besides, it does not need a Line of Sight (LoS) and can design this current reality into the visual world incredibly basic. Moreover, RFID is a modernized data variety and enabling items to relate through the web which uses radio waves to recuperate, perceive, and store data indirectly. The utilization of electromagnetics in the recurrence of radio and the utilization of scanner labels to track things in a depot is suggesting RFID solidification. Collecting information embedded in the things is the point of RFID. We can order RFID into active and passive RFID. Detached things do not have power backups mounted on them, and the transmission repeat is restricted. Of course, dynamic RFID has power backups that power the transmission signal (Figure 12.5).

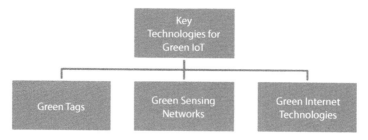

Figure 12.5 Key technologies for Green IoT [37].

Radio Frequency Identification (RFID) has an important part in helping the globe to become greener by decreasing the discharges of automobiles, saving power utilization and advancing garbage removal, and so forth. RFID use impacts emphatically and precisely regulatory dexterity which emphatically and precisely impacts both planning and operational achievement. The focus is on improving the life period of Unmanned Aerial Vehicle (UAV) power storage and RFID scanner detecting range. The consolidation of UAV and RFID is to give extra data that can be executed in the inventory conglomerate administration framework. UAV restriction and following have been mulled over for accomplishing straightforwardness also, cost productivity. UAV is utilized for information assortment from RFID sensors through dissipated all through the region utilizing downloading estimated information, straightforwardly drawing nearer them and hovering above them. UAV and RFID sensors cooperate appropriately while labels can be amazing observing instruments. Prominently, observing is required for a huge territory/brutal climate.

Certain recommended techniques that are necessary for green RFID:

➢ Recycling the tags is not an easy task therefore, reducing the size may help.
➢ Tag concussion, tag evaluation, overheating prevention and accommodating communication power level, etc., should be prevented using a power-competent approach and protocols.

There are countless applications for FRID, for example, transportation, creation following, dispatching, getting, stock control, administrative consistency returns, and reviews the board. Besides, FRID points of interest incorporate normalized, versatile methodology, dependable, and financially savvy.

12.5.2   Green Sensing Networks

Green Wireless Communication (GWC) plays an important role in providing interconnection between the devices in G-IoT. The power utilization used by the connecting devices or gadgets should be taken into attention. Green Sensing Networks refers to continuous, power receptive, power-efficient, and environment friendly. The thought of a Green Sensing Network (GSW) means that it should have low CO_2 emissions, less exposure to radiation, and power-efficient. We have taken the prior proposal of the genetic method optimization for the development of network preparation where less CO_2 emissions, energy-efficient, and low exposure to radiation [35] into consideration.

The feasibility of connecting the green and soft is to examine the five fields of innovation associated with each other, i.e., power efficiency, amend controlling, hidden base sites, and full-duplex radio. The examination minutiae of the power proficiency of 5G versatile correspondence networks are examined from three parts of hypothesis models, innovation improvements, and applications. The requirement for embracing energy effectiveness and CO_2 outflow are in procedure to satisfy the requests for expanding the limit, upgrading information rate, and giving high QoS (Quality of Service) of the NGN (Next-Generation Networks). Numerous kinds of specialists have been accomplished for saving power by utilizing cosmic powered and improved QoS. Applying web coding-based correspondence and dependable stockpiling helps save power for G-IoT. A stochastic math method for displaying different traffic examples can run proficiently and accomplish a huge upgrade in power productivity while keeping up QoS prerequisites. Utility-based versatile obligation cycle (UADC) calculation has been suggested to diminish delay, increment energy proficiency, and preserve a long life period. Hypertext move convention is utilized to improve the life period and abbreviate the deferral for giving the dependability. 5G consistently centers on diminishing energy usage and prompts green correspondence and sound conditions.

Today, 5G may affect our nature and life extensively as IoT vowed to make it productive. 5G is a significant innovation for upgrading the unwavering quality and QoS of the connection between machines and humans. Besides, 5G innovation empowers to give the enormous inclusion of availability, decrease the idleness, saving power and uphold higher information rate and framework limit. The 5G applications and its administrations for our general public are counting e-health, advanced mechanics correspondence, communication between human and advanced mechanics, media, transport and coordination, e-learning, e-administration, public health, auto, and modern frameworks, and so on.

12.5.3   Green Internet Technologies

In recent times, the Green web has gotten a fundamental concern. The web hypotheses and advancements contributed are used to develop a keen and green structure. Green web expects to diminish the force utilization of various gadgets that are related to IoT through the web. The use of power in the web network apparatus is dark because of the significant power. The assessment of the force use of association hardware has especially been treated for assessing the certainty and restraint. There is a colossal capability to reduce the internet power necessities besides, decrease the complication utilizing synchronized movement of engaging traffic and switches. Dynamic Geography Management Structure segment in the green web (GWDGMS) is created and perceived as the center development and association framework for energy use in association contraptions. The Greening web of Wired Connection Systems (WCS) in the information network is analyzed the force usage of wired association frameworks anticipated. Besides, Suh, Yuhwa, *et al.* [30] examined the consequence of the improvement equipment of data networks for greening the web. The appraisal power usage and saving power ability of information network gears are taken into thought.

12.6   Green IoT Applications

The IoT is associated with big data analysis and cloud computing to foresee the performance of smart gadgets, give helpful business experiences, and operate as input control. Likewise, a large portion of the associations would adjust to the developing significance of the smart globe which thus energy request builds all the more quickly. Additionally, there is a ceaseless expansion in the number of sellers and clients of different advancements. G-IoT conspicuously centers around diminishing the natural issues and establishing a maintainable climate identified with IoT [22]. There are numerous applications of G-IoT. We offer a few application situations.

12.6.1   Smart Homes

Smart homes advance the individual lifestyle of your home by encouraging and easy control and use of machines and devices (microwave, oven, cooling, warming systems, etc.). For example, according to the environment measure, an adroit house can normally cut and close the window disguise.

12.6.2   Modern Automation

With negligible human contribution, mechanical gadgets are computerized to perform creation errands. Machine tasks, capacities, and profitability are naturally checked. For instance, if there is an issue with the machine, then the framework quickly sends an upkeep solicitation to the support division to determine the issue. Also, profitability increments by investigating creation information, time, and reasons for creating issues. The IoT can bolster coordinated effort and correspondence between objects consequently. Be that as it may, with the expanding number of included gadgets, IoT frameworks may expend considerable measures of vitality.

The general engineering toward vitality effective IoT is delineated in Figure 12.6, which include a sense elements area, RESTful help facilitated systems, a cloud server, and client applications. Shrewd gadgets and hubs are conveyed in the sense of substance space. To additionally enhance vitality investment funds, they are ordered into sense hubs (SNs), passage hubs (GNs), and control hubs (CNs). The system has RESTful web benefits and associates the sense substances with the cloud server. The cloud server virtualizes objects, which at that point are moved to the server applications. Handling and calculation for the extricated information from the sense

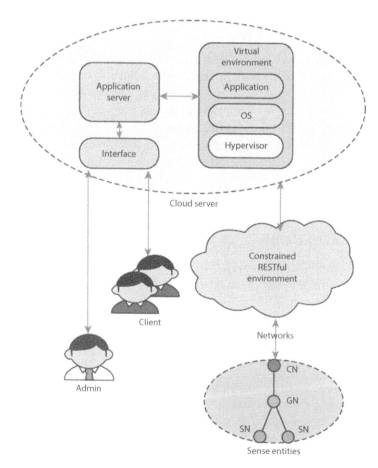

Figure 12.6 Green industrial IoT architecture: an energy-efficient perspective [18].

elements area are additionally made on the "cloud server". The application server associate helps the customer to speak to the application server without access to the server-side codes, while direct access can be made by the organization (administrator) hub.

Sense Units: IoT systems include sensor hubs and keen gadgets that are Internet Protocol (IP) empowered and RFID connected. Contrasted and brilliant gadgets, sensor hubs have severe vitality imperatives because they relied upon batteries. Even though there are contrasts between their capacities regarding memory and handling, for the comfort of conversation and without loss of consensus, we exclude these distinctions. We embrace a novel arrangement for these hubs focusing on the vitality effectiveness issue, which will be talked about later. SNs gather the ideal data information from their intrigued territory and deliver them to GNs. At that point, GNs save the information in the cradle and promote them to CNs. Additionally, GNs perform a convention to ascertain the rest intermissions of SNs, which will be examined in a later area. CNs fill in as the administrator to dispense assets under them and divert the collected information to the systems. Assignment of SNs to explicit GNs is additionally chosen by the CNs.

RESTful Service Hosted Networks: These days REST reasoning has been considered in various IoT suggestions since it makes the blend and accessibility of the heterogeneous contraptions less difficult and progressively beneficial. In like manner, our framework has RESTful help where functionalities and data are seen as resources that can be gotten to with uniform resource identifiers. For resource-constrained conditions, this RESTful assistance makes the applications lightweight, clear, and speedy. Our proposed RESTful help frameworks may fill in as an augmentation between physical sense components and virtual articles. They get the assurance data from the sense components side, for instance, thing ID, device IP address, or contraption incorporated, and prompt the cloud slice off to make the virtual articles with the semantic depiction of the sense substances.

- Cloud Server: In our essentialness gainful IoT plan, the cloud server fuses the going with two sections.
- Virtual Environment: Physical things, associated with the sense components space, are virtualized for organization questions in the virtual condition. By then the virtual things are encouraged and composited as applications performed inside the virtual machine.

- Application Server and Associate: The application server licenses SNs to talk with the client with the help of the associate or by methods for direct access from the executive. The library is made by following the organizations and physical components that are open inside the entire IoT.
- Customer Applications: Working as client-side applications, the customer applications can be orchestrated into the going with two orders as shown by the check instruments.
- Client Applications: To use virtual things encouraged as applications in the virtual condition, the client utilizes the application associate to send sales to the server. An explicit approach is not allowed inside this affirmation.
- Executive Applications: Unlike the client application, a manager application has the benefit to get to the server. By then, the chairman can quickly make significant changes following the structure and screen the introduction of the whole system.

12.6.3   Smart Healthcare

Smart healthcare improves the exhibition of medicinal services applications by coordinating sensors and actuators for inmates and their prescriptions to track and screen inmates. For instance, collecting and dissecting torso states of patients with sensors and sending broken down information to a treatment place, clinical consideration can screen the physiological condition of patients continuously and take important measures.

12.6.4   Keen Grid

Essential suppliers get support for an advantage the board and the administrators with the objective that imperativeness can be given according to mass improvement. As such, the imperativeness usage of houses and structures can be improved. For example, building meters can be related to an arrangement of imperativeness suppliers. Imperativeness suppliers could improve their organizations by the social affair, researching, controlling, checking, and regulating essentialness usage. In the meantime, potential dissatisfactions can be decreased.

12.6.5   Smart City

Improving personal satisfaction in the city, making it simpler for individuals to discover helpful data. For instance, contingent upon the requirements of the populace, diverse interrelated frameworks cleverly offer alluring administrations (for example, transport, utilities, and well-being) to individuals.

12.6.6   Green Cloud Computing Technology

Dispersed processing (CC) is the new digitalization advancement utilized on the web. It offers endless handling, vast limits, and internet benefits as it saves a lot of (essentialness usage) and is more capable than standard server ranches. CC development is inescapable, while IoT is in all cases. The blend of CC and IoT, when all is said in done, is a sweeping field of research. The fundamental goal of the GCC is to propel the usage of environmentally neighborly things that can be viably reused and reused. The basic goal of the GCC is to lessen the utilization of risky materials, increase imperativeness use, and improve the reusing of venerable things and waste. Also, this target can be cultivated by apportioning.

12.7   IoT in 5G Wireless Technologies

During the previous decade, the IoT has improved the unavoidable handling with countless applications worked around various types of sensors. A gigantic proportion of development is seen in IoT-based item contributions and this development is needed to fill in years to go with projections as high as billions of contraptions with on typical six to seven devices for every person constantly in 2020 [8]. With by far most of the issues at the contraption and show levels established during the previous decade, there is by and by a developing design in the compromise of sensors and sensor-based frameworks with computerized genuine systems and device-to-device (D2D) exchanges [8]. Fifth period distant systems (5G) are not very far away and IoT is tolerating the center stage as contraptions are needed to shape a huge digit of this 5G association perspective. IoT propels, for instance, M2M correspondence enhanced with keen data examination is depended upon to change the location of various endeavors. The ascent of dispersed figuring and its growth to fog perspective with the development of sharp "splendid" contraptions are depended on to prompt expedite headway in IoT. These headways stimulate us and design an encouragement to outline extant work, propose new systems, and observe new utilizations of IoT. Subject matter experts, specialists, and architects face developing difficulties in arranging IoT-based systems that can capably be facilitated with the 5G distant exchanges.

It is estimated by the experts that the 5G of the fifth period of remote likeness 5G will be talented to oversee various events with more adaptable information than the current cell structures. It will accomplish client requests at reasonable rates, much consistent quality likewise to unfathomable applications [8]. It will in like way change into a mainstay of the IoT progression, interfacing up repaired and telephones finishing being a bit of another mechanical and cash-related change. IoT and 5G are two of the most sizzling instances of progression. They are consolidated to change our future by interconnecting everything [25]. Regardless, many rising difficulties are not too far off in masterminding IoT-based structures that can adequately be gotten together with remote compatibility [21]. Security is the best test considered by IoT in 5G. In like manner, IoT improvement is depicted by little information packs, the epic relationship of contraptions with the restricted force source, and suspension tolerant similarity. In 5G, a compelled band structure proposal can advance framework joining, power use, and diminishing of terminal costs [13]. IoT in 5G systems to benefit the huge affiliation quantity of low-rate and less power consuming contraptions have been suggested.

Fifth generation (5G) remote correspondence frameworks are expected to deliver uncommon difficulties to adapt to a serious level of heterogeneity regarding:

> ➤ Administrations (portable broadband, huge machine and mission basic correspondences, wide/multicast administrations, and vehicular correspondences).
> ➤ Gadget classes (low-end sensors to top-of-the-line tablets).
> ➤ Organization types (full scale and little cells).
> ➤ Conditions (low-thickness to super thick metropolitan).
> ➤ Portability levels (static to fast vehicle).

Accordingly, 5G will give a significant degree improvement in some critical qualities to productively back such heterogeneity with an assorted arrangement of necessities including, however, not restricted to, limit/client rates, inertness, unwavering quality, inclusion, portability, an enormous number of gadgets, and cost/energy utilization. All the more explicitly, 5G air-interface will accomplish:

> ❖ 1,000 × higher portable information volume per topographical territory.
> ❖ 10 to 100 × more associated gadgets.

❖ 10 to 100 × higher ordinary client information rate.
❖ 10 × lower energy utilization.

12.7.1   Internet of Things and 5G: The Future of 5G Communications

Because of the momentum, immense cutoff, and unreasonably small lethargy of the Verizon 5G Ultra-Wideband system, the capability for imaginative progression is immense. Discover how 5G Ultra-Wideband and IoT can perform two by two, comparably to how 5G headway is needed to influence business taking everything into account.

12.7.1.1   5G and IoT: The Possibilities

5G is essential to the IoT due to the demand for a snappier system with greater limits that can deliver coordinated necessities. The 5G territory develops the recurrence that will move data by mechanized cell progressions. This increasingly broad range applicable for use assembles the general information move limit of cell frameworks, thinking about additional contraptions to relate. Another domain where 5G Ultra Wideband could influence the IoT is overhauling digital and expanded reality (AR/VR). 5G Ultra-Wideband's ultra-low inertia can advance the AR/VR experience and open doors for such advancement in business and guidance.

12.7.1.2   5G and Business IoT

5G-facilitated IoT is dependent upon not only to facilitate inventive turn of events; it is furthermore foreseen to benefit in providing 22 million career opportunities the world over. To start computerization of transport, cultivation, creation, and alternative physical endeavors, this action is required. 5G can drive movements in canny mechanical assembly similarly to a sharp gathering. Thinking a lot more prominently, 5G could facilitate IoT to run in every way that matters, flashing traffic examinations, improving security and open prosperity, and possibly enable remote clinical systems.

12.8   Internet of Things in Smart City

It is approximated that the smart city budget is going to be estimated at 2–3 billion dollars by the year 2020, with yearly spending appearing at practically 16 billion [31]. It will be depending on the combined structure, where a massive and dissimilar strategy of outskirts contraptions orchestrated over the urban region makes different sorts of information identified with any framework organization system. At present, getting some information about IoT is going on recognizing and tweaking control, sorting out infrastructure and likeness, and tremendous data analytics [3]. IoT associated with the smart cities are especially enchanting, such as astonishing parking [24], standard observing [19, 24, 32], traffic-the specialists [17], squander administration [28], maintaining the quality and management of water, and importance usages. In, an agreement of the IoT phases and a standard IoT working for sharp metropolitan systems has appeared. Supportive game plans have appeared to the key complications looked at during the collusion and the head of a metropolis-scale IoT structure in the downtown of Santander, Spain. In, the appraisal presents the particular reactions for the squares in the Padova Smart City experience, Italy. In, the association between beast information appraisal and IoT is examined. It takes after way another arrangement for an epic IoT information assessment looked out for.

12.8.1   Physical Experiences of Smart Cities Around the World

12.8.1.1   In Netherlands (Amsterdam)

Various undertakings were moved in the year 2006 in Amsterdam, including related open lighting inside the mindful city. Counterfeit lighting expects a focal action in urban zones not just for the dull time task yet in like manner for the significance of the city which picks the city's level of capacity to invite others there for business or the progression business. Considering, LED lighting was applied with sharp controllers for diminishing the utilization, which can make massiveness spare resources of up to 80% and experience resources of around 130 billion euro while giving an authentically irrefutable idea of achievement for inhabitants and coherently noticeable perceptible quality. In like manner, these structures have been interconnected by joining controls by techniques for the Internet which prompts a more noteworthy vitality hypothesis. From this time forward, rather than physical disappointment evaluation as in standard lighting assignments, the lighting thwarted expectations are consequently proclaimed by remote finding in a novel strategy. In like manner, vitality use was as a rule evaluated starting at now, regardless by and by astonishing meters completely discovering the centrality use. Besides, lights are reduced during low traffic hours to spare centrality or improved when expected to improve the flourishing.

12.8.1.2   In France (Nice)

Here, the potential for execution of the snare of centrality (IoE) was examined, furthermore, the IP-connected with progression structure, cash related model, and social focal points of IoE were endeavored and avowed. By then, four shrewd city associations were created including keen, stunning flow, shrewd waste association, and brilliant. Acting as information got by sensors for traffic models can serve for awe-inspiring and trademark observing.

12.8.1.3   Padova (Italy)

In this city, the central university, in a joint exertion with the region of the city, started an endeavor called Padova Smart City, which is an obvious case of a private and open joint effort for running a sagacious city. The area as a budgetary help gives the fundamental structure and monetary arrangement and the school as a hypothetical social gathering completes the amazing city thought. As showed by this experience, various sorts of sensors are set out to street light shafts and connected with the Internet through passages for get-together trademark and open street lighting data by methodology for remote for instance, and elasticity, vibrations, change, and so on are gathered, while giving a basic yet unequivocal framework to check the correct action of the open structure by assessing the light force. Despite the way that experience is prompt, it consolidates different contraptions and layer degrees of progress that are descriptive of most of the vital issues which should make sense of how to plan an urban IoT.

12.9   Green IoT Architecture for Smart Cities

The G-IoT is envisioned to produce a unique modification in our day-by-day activity and will help us understand the perception of "green surrounding knowledge". In the coming time, we will be embraced by a gigantic assessment of sensors, gadgets, and "things", that will have the preference to convey through 5G, perform "brilliantly", and offer green help for clients in dealing with their assignments. These latest smart things will likewise be setting mindful and ready to play out specific capacities self-sufficiently, calling for advanced types of green connection among individuals and things and also between the things themselves, where the power utilization is streamlined and data transfer capacity usage is expanded. This improvement would be significant not exclusively to specialists yet in addition to enterprises and people the same. Thinking about these realities, the point of this uncommon issue was to concentrate on both hypothetical and usage perspectives in green cutting edge systems that can be used in giving green frameworks through IoT empowering advances [5].

In smart cities, gadgets can cleverly speak with individuals through the IoT. This will cause smart cities a greener spot by perceiving contamination through IoT and natural sensors. To keep up the supportability of the green spot in brilliant urban areas, the developing innovation, for example, G-IoT consequently and brilliantly cause smart cities manageable in a communitarian way. Authorities and a lot of associations everywhere in the globe are accomplishing a ton of endeavors to battle the signs of the decrease of vitality utilization and carbon creation just as stress on the G-IoT for keen urban areas. In any case, this endeavor suggests the idea of the "G-IoT" to make a green situation that will capture the possibility of vitality sparing in brilliant urban areas. Right now, G-IoT design is projected for keen refers to the concentrate to diminish vitality utilization at each level and guarantee acknowledgment of IoT toward the green. The proposed G-IoT engineering depends on the cloud-based framework which lessens the equipment utilization [15].

There are three layers in the proposed architecture of G-IoT (Figure 12.7):

> Perception Layer
> Network Layer
> Application Layer

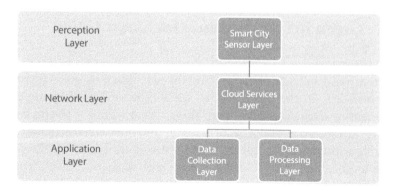

Figure 12.7 Green IoT architecture for smart city.

The design characterizes the principle correspondence standards for the interfacing substances [7].

12.9.1   Perception Layer

Perception layer detects the object and collects information through 2D Barcode, RFID, Camera, Sensor Network, etc. [26].

12.9.1.1   Smart City Sensor Layer

The smart city sensor layer has an altered set of IoT centers that are escalated over metropolitan territory. These centers gather information about different exercises in physical condition. An IoT center is a bundle that contains microchips, power delivery, sensors, and system components. IoT centers are sorted into two distinct classes dependent on their working situations.

12.9.1.1.1   Constrained Hub

These centers work in low consumption of power situations. They have an uninformed move rate and small planning power.

12.9.1.1.2   Unconstrained Hub

These centers have no operational imperatives regarding power utilization, handling rate, and information move rate.

An IoT center can go about as both obliged and unconstrained relying upon the operational situations. For instance, a closeness sensor center in a little office stopping compound might be compelled, while a similar nearness sensor center in huge stopping edifices can be unconstrained.

IoT centers with the assistance of sensors perceive the exercises everywhere in the globe and send information to server centers in the information layer. Right now process, unconstrained hubs send information in an Extensible Markup Language (XML) position. Notwithstanding, this arrangement is not good with obliged centers, because the overhead in portraying the moved information makes it too long to even think about parsing. Moreover, the literary idea of an XML portrayal makes parsing hard for CPU-constrained hubs.

As a response to this issue, the World Wide Web Consortium (W3C) proposed the Efficient XML Interchange (EXI) position. This grants constrained Hubs to locally bolster and produce messages by utilizing an open-data plan that is acceptable with XML [33].

There are two types of encoding techniques in EXI:

1. Construction less encoding: The data is encrypted straight-forwardly from the XML information and afterward deci-phered by any EXI processor with no earlier information about the information.
2. Pattern educated encoding: Ahead of the encoding or deci-phering measure begins the XML framework is divided among two EXI processors. This common planning licenses the EXI processor to distribute numeric identifiers to the XML marks and assembling EXI accentuation upon such coding.

The composition-educated EXI processor can be consistently coordi-nated with any obliged IoT Hub. This empowers the compelled IoT hub to peruse an EXI position as well as advance into a multipurpose IoT hub (Figure 12.8).

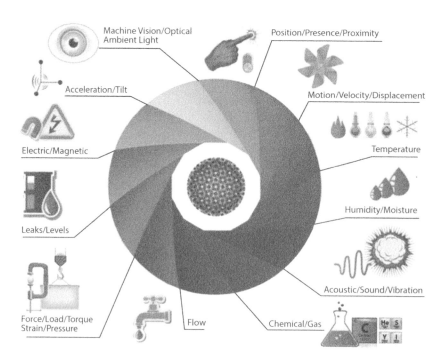

Figure 12.8 IoT sensors [35].

12.9.2 Network Layer

The network layer is liable for preparing the collected information. Furthermore, it is culpable for transferring data to the application layer by distant system advancements, such as obscure/connected systems and Local Area Networks (LAN). The principal medium for communication incorporates Wi-Fi, Bluetooth, 3G/4G, FTTx, Zigbee, UMB, infrared innovation, etc. Gigantic measures of data will be passed on by the framework. To show up at this level-headed, appropriated registering is a fundamental development at present. To be sure, inquire about and developing on the handling part is significant for the future improvement of IoT [1]. Network layer consists of a sub-layer known as cloud services layer.

12.9.2.1 Cloud Services Layer

With the assistance of cloud computing, many services can be accessed on the cloud, and residents of a smart city can utilize these services effectively through the internet on their smartphones, workstations, PCs, tablets, and so on. Right now, the essential meanings of Smart city and cloud computing are incorporated. What should the fundamental highlights, essential criteria, necessities of a smart city is likewise included? Presently, cloud computing is generally utilized in different fields. Cloud is only the similitude of the internet. Everything is accessible on clouds and clients can utilize all applications, information as and when they need it. The residents of a smart city can survey all applications on their advanced mobile phones through the cloud without any problem [2].

12.9.3 Application Layer

The application layer is culpable for handling the information forwarded by the preceding layer. Indeed, the application layer comprises the front finish of the unified IoT engineering utilizing which IoT capability will be exploited. Besides, this layer gives the necessary instruments (for example, inciting gadgets) for developers to understand the IoT vision. Right now, the scope of potential applications is great (for example, inventive transportation, coordination administration, personality verification, location-based administrations, and well-being). Application layer Comprises of two sub-layers.

12.9.3.1   Data Collection Layer

In this layer, information collected from different sensors is taken care of for further approach. A part of the associations in which heterogeneous data is accumulated is CSV, tweets, data set outlines, and texts. The assembled designs are then dealt with using semantic web headways to change over them into an exemplary game plan. The accompanying level portrays the methods used in the difference in data into an average game plan [11].

12.9.3.2   Data Processing Layer

Information collected from the data variety level is consolidated before transmission, assessment, and mix in the further levels using semantic web advancements. The key objective of this level is to change over the assembled heterogeneous information into a normal design, for instance, RDF. RDF11 is the most fundamental way to deal with exchange information over the web and it energizes heterogeneous data sharing and fuse for particular Smart City spaces. RDF moreover helps in portraying metadata about the resources on the web. Interesting programming applications would then have the option to utilize RDF data for savvy thinking exercises. Pre-arranged RDF data delivered at this level will be abused using semantic data and problematic intuition rules in the accompanying level for raised level setting careful information restoration [11].

12.10   Advantages and Disadvantages of Green IoT

12.10.1   Advantages of Green IoT

- ➢ It does not emanate anything hurtful for nature.
- ➢ It has gotten well known as purchasers of the innovation are turning out to be greater condition cognizant. This will offer advantages to financial specialists since a long time ago run in specific regions.
- ➢ It requires less expense for support. This lessens working expense and subsequently by and large expense on the since a long time ago run.
- ➢ As it utilizes sustainable normal assets, and thus, we will never come up short on indispensable assets, for example, water and power.

➤ It will hinder the impacts of a dangerous atmospheric deviation because of the decrease in CO_2 outflows.

12.10.2   Disadvantages of Green IoT

➤ The introductory investment or usage cost is very high.
➤ The individuals associated with the innovation are less experienced and will not take interest in the innovation until it has gained popularity.
➤ The innovation is still in the development phase and a large number of components are Research and Development (R&D) organized. Henceforth, individuals are unknown with the execution results.
➤ The shortfall of talented HR is available to present or complete the green advancement-based things or systems.
➤ In an enormous segment of the countries, approaches have not been agreed to the green advancement-based structures [36].

12.11   Opportunities and Challenges

Notwithstanding the path that there are colossal investigations endeavors to accomplish a green headway, G-IoT advancement is still in the beginning sort out. Here are some constraints and tests that need to be addressed. The following are the main difficulties that are found:

➤ Unified ability over IoT working to accomplish an admirable presentation.
➤ Applications are requisite to be green to confine their implications for nature.
➤ The validness of (G-IoT) with intensity use models.
➤ Context-care with intensity competent IoT structure.
➤ The two devices and showings used to give ought to be significant and gainful with less power usage.
➤ Complications diminishing of the G-IoT foundation.
➤ The varied between gainful stand-out range recognizing and skilled range of the directors.

➢ Cloud services are required to be efficient for minimum power usage.

➢ The security systems should be efficient like encryption and controlled route of transmission.

12.12   Future of Green IoT

The prospect of G-IoT will make our surroundings better and greener with high QoS, social and environmental sustainability, and more cost-efficient. Today, the main focus of the researchers are on greening things, for example, green connection and networking between the communicating devices, green plan and executions, G-IoT administrations and applications, power-efficient systems, incorporated RFIDs and sensor organizations, versatility, and organization of the board, the participation of similar and miscellaneous networks, smart things, and green confinement. The subsequent examination areas are required to be examined to establish an excellent and adequate solution for greening IoT:

1. UAVs are required to take over a huge sum of IoT gadgets particularly in areas like farming, traffic, and observation that will benefit in decreasing power usage and contamination. UAV is an auspicious innovation that will help in greening IoT and is outlay-efficient and also has a high-efficiency rate.

2. Transmitted information coming out of sensors to the mobile cloud will be extra valuable. Sensor-cloud is combining the Wi-Fi sensor network and portable cloud. It is the most efficient and guaranteed solution for greening IoT. A green Social Network as a Service (SNaaS) may examine the need for power competence of the framework, utility, WSN, and cloud administrations.

3. M2M connection performs an important role in decreasing power usage and contamination. Intelligent Machine needs to be more advance to prepare computerized systems. Machine computerization prolong should be diminished in event of traffic and necessary and urgent response should be taken.

4. High QoS and excellent performance design G-IoT should be introduced. To make G-IoT much efficient and effective,

certain techniques are required to improve the restrictions of QoS such as bandwidth and prolong.

5. Progressing with greening IoT, less energy, searching for new assets, declining the adverse impact of IoT's on the well-being of humans, and contaminating the environment will be required. At that point, G-IoT can contribute toward making the environment green and sustainably smart.

6. In a request to accomplish power-stabilizing for upholding the green connection between different IoT gadgets, the radio recurrence power gathered needs to be addressed.

7. Further examination is anticipated to develop the plan of IoT devices that assists with lessening CO_2 emanation and energy consumption. The very basic responsibility for smart and green natural life is conserving power and declining CO_2 emissions.

12.13   Conclusion

G-IoT technologies had been deliberated in the study. The main motivation behind the study is the challenges and benefits of G-IoT. To accomplish a G-IoT procedure, all the required technologies and the G-IoT life cycle are also examined in this study. The use of developing the smart city and 5G technology is also discussed. Besides, all the challenges and future research direction are also presented. It has certainly shown task about motivations toward enabling G-IoT and more studies are progressing headways about sensor-cloud and anticipating the prospect sensor-cloud, and also this study has been shown a couple of employments of G-IoT with perfect and viable responses for greening IoT. G-IoT research applications have also been discussed which includes applications like smart homes, modern automation, smart healthcare, smart grid, and energy-efficient architecture that are reviewed in cloud servers. Plus green cloud technology is reviewed.

References

1. Abdmeziem, M., Tandjaoui, D., Romdhani, I., Architecting the Internet of Things: State of the Art, *Robots and Sensor Clouds*, 55–75, 2015, https://link. springer.com/chapter/10.1007/978-3-319-22168-7_3

2. Agarwal, N. and Agarwal, G., Role of Cloud Computing in Development of Smart City. *IJSTE || National Conference on Road Map for Smart Cities*

of Rajasthan (NC-RMSCR), 2349-784X, 2017, https://ijste.org/C_Article. php?manuscript=RMSCRP047

3. Ahlgren, B., Hidell, M., Ngai, E.C.-H., Internet of things for smart cities: Interoperability and open data. *IEEE Internet Comput.*, 20, 6, 52–56, 2016.

4. Albreem, M.A.M., 5G wireless communication systems: Vision and challenges. *2015 International Conference on Computer, Communications, and Control Technology (I4CT)*, IEEE, 2015.

5. Al-Turjman, F. *et al.*, The Green Internet of Things (G-IoT). *Wireless Communications and Mobile Computing 2019*, 2019.

6. Ashton, K., That 'internet of things' thing. *RFID J.*, 22, 7, 97–114, 2009.

7. Dey, N. (Ed.), *Internet of things and big data analytics toward next-generation intelligence*, Springer, Berlin, 2018.

8. Ejaz, W. *et al.*, Internet of Things (IoT) in 5G wireless communications. *IEEE Access*, 4, 10310–103145, 2016.

9. Elkhodr, M., Seyed, S., Hon, C., The internet of things: Vision & challenges. *IEEE 2013 Tencon-Spring*, IEEE, 2013.

10. Fehske, A. *et al.*, The global footprint of mobile communications: The ecological and economic perspective. *IEEE Commun. Mag.*, 49, 8, 55–62, 2011.

11. Gaur, A., Scotney, B.W., Parr, G.P., McClean, S.I., Smart City Architecture and its Applications Based on IoT. *ANT/SEIT*, 1089–1094, 2015, https://dblp. uni-trier.de/rec/conf/ant/GaurSPM15.html.

12. Green Power for Mobile, The Global Telecom Tower ESCO Market, Technical Report, 2015.

13. Ijaz, A. *et al.*, Enabling massive IoT in 5G and beyond systems: PHY radio frame design considerations. *IEEE Access*, 4, 3322–33395, 2016.

14. *IMT Vision-Framework and Overall Objectives of the Future Development of IMT for 2020 and Beyond*, 2015, document Rec. ITU-R M.2083- 0.

15. Kaur, G., Tomar, P., Singh, P., Design of Cloud-Based Green IoT Architecture for Smart Cities, *IEEE Trans. Broadcast.*, 60, 3, 2014, https://ieeexplore.ieee. org/stamp/stamp.jsp?arnumber=6874529.

16. Koutitas, G., Green network planning of single frequency networks. *IEEE Trans. Broadcast.*, 56, 4, 541–550, 2010. https://ieeexplore.ieee.org/stamp/ stamp.jsp?arnumber=6874529

17. Mahalank, S.N., Malagund, K.B., Banakar, R.M., Device to device interaction analysis in IoT based Smart Traffic Management System: An experimental approach. *2016 Symposium on Colossal Data Analysis and Networking (CDAN)*, IEEE, 2016.

18. Meghashree, N., Girija, R., Sumathi, D., Understanding Green IoT: Research Applications and Future Directions. *2019 JETIR*, 6, 6, June 2019, https:// www.jetir.org/papers/JETIR1906180.pdf.

19. Montgomery, B., Future Shock: IoT benefits beyond traffic and lighting energy optimization. *IEEE Consum. Electron. Mag.*, 4, 4, 98–100, 2015.

20. Murugesan, S., Harnessing green IT: Principles and practices. *IT Prof.*, 10, 1, 24–33, 2008.

21. Palattella, M.R. *et al.*, Internet of things in the 5G era: Enablers, architecture, and business models. *IEEE J. Sel. Areas Commun.*, 34, 3, 510–527, 2016.
22. Poongodi, T. *et al.*, Application of IoT in green computing, in: *Advances in Greener Energy Technologies*, pp. 295–323, Springer, Singapore, 2020.
23. Gadre, M. and Gadre, C., Green Internet of Things (IoT): Go Green with IoT. *Int. J. Eng. Res. Technol. (IJERT) - 2016 Conf. Proc.*, 4, 29, 1–6, 2016.
24. Ramaswamy, P., IoT smart parking system for reducing green house gas emission. *2016 International Conference on Recent Trends in Information Technology (ICRTIT)*, IEEE, 2016.
25. Rysavy, P., IoT & 5G: Wait Or Move?, *Cahnnel Partners*, 2016.
26. Samih, H., Smart cities and internet of things. *J. Inf. Technol. Case Appl. Res.*, 21, 1, 3–12, 2019.
27. Shuja, J. *et al.*, Greening emerging IT technologies: techniques and practices. *J. Internet Serv. Appl.*, 8, 1, 9, 2017.
28. Shyam, G.K., Manvi, S.S., Bharti, P., Smart waste management using Internet-of-Things (IoT). *2017 2nd international conference on computing and communications technologies (ICCCT)*, IEEE, 2017.
29. Strategy, Accenture, *SMARTer2030: ICT solutions for 21st century challenges*, The Global eSustainability Initiative (GeSI), Brussels, Brussels-Capital Region, Belgium, Tech. Rep, 2015.
30. Suh, Y. *et al.*, A study on energy savings potential of data network equipment for a green Internet. *16th International Conference on Advanced Communication Technology*, IEEE, 2014.
31. Shukla, V.K. and Singh, B., Conceptual Framework of Smart Device for Smart Home Management Based on RFID and IoT. *2019 Amity International Conference on Artificial Intelligence (AICAI)*, pp. 787–791, Dubai, United Arab Emirates, 2019.
32. Zhou, J. *et al.*, Cloudthings: A common architecture for integrating the internet of things with cloud computing. *Proceedings of the 2013 IEEE 17th International Conference on Computer Supported Cooperative Work in Design (CSCWD)*, IEEE, 2013.
33. Chandrashekhar, D., ReadWrite, What are the 4 layers of data "architecture" needed for smart cities?, [Online] https://readwrite.com/author/chandra/ Accessed on Feb 2021. https://readwrite.com/2016/12/19/architecture-smart-cities-cl1/
34. Wetherill, J., What Does it Mean to be "On" The Internet of Things?, [Online] https://thenewstack.io/what-does-it-mean-to-be-on-the-internet-of-things/, Accessed on Oct 2021.
35. Postscapes, IoT Sensors and Actuators, [Online] https://www.postscapes.com/iot-sensors-actuators/, Accessed on: Feb 2021.
36. RF Wireless World, Advantages of Green Technology | Disadvantages of Green Technology, [Online] https://www.rfwireless-world.com/Terminology/Advantages-and-Disadvantages-of-Green-Technology.html, Accessed on: Feb 2021. https://www.rfwireless-world.com/Terminology/

37. Mahmoud A.M. Albreem, Ayman A. El-Saleh, Muzamir Isa, Wael Salah, M. Jusoh, M.M., Azizan, A. Ali, *2017 4th International Conference on Smart Instrumentation, Measurement and Application (ICSIMA)* pp. 1–6, IEEE, 2017 https://ieeexplore.ieee.org/document/8312021/figures

Index

Printed and bound by CPI Group (UK) Ltd, Croydon, CR0 4YY